The Irish tower house

Manchester University Press

Social Archaeology and Material Worlds

Series editors
Joshua Pollard and Duncan Sayer

Social Archaeology and Material Worlds aims to forefront dynamic and cutting-edge social approaches to archaeology. It brings together volumes about past people, social and material relations and landscape as explored through an archaeological lens. Topics covered may include memory, performance, identity, gender, life course, communities, materiality, landscape and archaeological politics and ethnography. The temporal scope runs from prehistory to the recent past, while the series' geographical scope is global. Books in this series bring innovative, interpretive approaches to important social questions within archaeology. Interdisciplinary methods which use up-to-date science, history or both, in combination with good theoretical insight, are encouraged. The series aims to publish research monographs and well-focused edited volumes that explore dynamic and complex questions, the why, how and who of archaeological research.

Previously published

Neolithic cave burials: Agency, structure and environment
Rick Peterson

Forthcoming

An archaeology of lunacy: Managing madness in early nineteenth-century asylums
Katherine Fennelly

Images in the making: Art, process, archaeology
Ing-Marie Back Danielsson and Andrew Meirion Jones (eds)

Communities and knowledge production in archaeology
Julia Roberts, Kathleen Sheppard, Jonathan Trigg and Ulf Hansson (eds)

Early Anglo-Saxon cemeteries: Kinship, Community and Mortuary Space
Duncan Sayer

Urban Zooarchaeology
James Morris

An archaeology of innovation: Approaching social and technological change in human society
Catherine J. Frieman

Time for healing: Cultural heritage in post-conflict Syria and Iraq
Zena Kamash

The Irish tower house

Society, economy and environment,
c. 1300–1650

Victoria L. McAlister

Manchester University Press

Copyright © Victoria L. McAlister 2019

The right of Victoria L. McAlister to be identified as the author of this work has been asserted by her in accordance with the Copyright, Designs and Patents Act 1988.

Published by Manchester University Press
Altrincham Street, Manchester M1 7JA, UK
www.manchesteruniversitypress.co.uk

British Library Cataloguing-in-Publication Data is available

ISBN 978 1 5261 2123 3 hardback
ISBN 978 1 5261 5593 1 paperback

First published by Manchester University Press in hardback 2019

This edition published 2021

The publisher has no responsibility for the persistence or accuracy of URLs for any external or third-party internet websites referred to in this book, and does not guarantee that any content on such websites is, or will remain, accurate or appropriate.

Typeset by Toppan Best-set Premedia Limited

Contents

List of figures		*page* vi
Acknowledgements		viii
Introduction		1
1	Around the castle wall: The tower house complex and rural settlement	26
2	The medieval agrarian economy: Lifeblood of the tower house	65
3	Rivers in pre-modern Ireland: Environment and economy	90
4	Movement, transport and communication: Tower houses and waterways	124
5	'Urban' tower houses	160
6	Tower houses, late medieval Ireland and the connection with the wider world	192
Conclusion: The social, economic and environmental contexts of the Irish tower house		231
Appendix: Sites referred to in text		245
References		250
Index		272

Figures

All figures are the author's own unless otherwise stated.

I.1	Map of tower house distribution.	13
I.2	Donore Castle.	16
1.1	Ardmayle Castle.	30
1.2	Ardmayle digital elevation model.	32
1.3	Ballynahinch Castle.	33
1.4	Ballynahinch digital elevation model.	34
1.5	Aughnanure Castle.	37
1.6	Rathmore Castle.	38
1.7	*Down Survey* depiction of Knockainy, © The Board of Trinity College Dublin.	53
1.8	Glenogra Castle.	55
1.9	Bourchier's Castle.	57
1.10	Cashlaundarragh Castle.	59
1.11	Derrymaclaughna Castle.	60
2.1	Lisfinny Castle.	74
2.2	Ballynacarriga Castle.	82
2.3	Newhaggard Castle.	84
3.1	Kilteel Castle.	93
3.2	Dunmoe Castle.	106
3.3	Depiction of Dunmoe Castle by Du Noyer, © Royal Society of Antiquaries of Ireland.	107
3.4	Kilcrea Castle.	108
3.5	Dunmanus Castle.	116
3.6	Muckinish Castle.	117
3.7	Ballyhack Castle.	120
4.1	Minard's Castle.	128
4.2	Coolhill Castle.	133
4.3	Fiddaun Castle.	135

4.4	Kilclief Castle.	139
4.5	Cowd Castle.	141
4.6	Ferrycarrig Castle.	143
4.7	Leighlinbridge Castle.	153
5.1	Kilmallock Castle.	169
5.2	Cashelboy Castle and church.	179
5.3	Youghal as depicted on *Pacata Hibernia*, © Royal Irish Academy.	184
6.1	Lynch's Castle.	213
6.2	Mahee Castle.	221
C.1	Leamaneh Castle.	239

Acknowledgements

A very many people helped make this book a reality; therefore I beg forgiveness at the outset for those I have inadvertently overlooked here. Terry Barry is the person I have to thank for setting me on a path to tower house obsession. Once upon a time I was an undergraduate taking his castles class because it sounded cool, and the rest, as they say, is history. Since then he has been my mentor, advisor and supporter. 'Thank you' seems a bit paltry in that context.

Behind the pretty photographs and site descriptions is an unflagging and enthusiastic small army. Capable fieldwork assistance has been provided by Emma Arbuthnot, Samantha Brown, Laura Magnier and Linda Shine. In exchange for some chips in a country pub they navigated me to hundreds of obscure tower house ruins and chatted to countless farmers. This fieldwork would never have been possible without financial support from both the American Philosophical Society and Southeast Missouri State University. In particular, funds were awarded by the Franklin Research Grant programme and from the Grants and Research Funding Committee and the Office of the Provost. Thank you to all the people behind these, who made this research as straightforward and pleasant as possible.

I must express huge appreciation for the red pens of Jennifer Immich, Laura Magnier and Lily Santoro, who so quickly helped me whip the book into shape. Any word repetition still remaining is definitely my fault and not theirs! Brianna De Witt provided research assistance, for which thanks are also owing to Wayne Bowen and the Department of History for funding this. Jennifer Immich was such a help with geographic information systems, digital elevation models and mapping, while Paul Naessens of Western Aerial Survey provided the data used here from drone-based surveys. Academic assistance and access to materials were given by many, including Brian Donovan, Fiona Fitzsimons, Mark Gardiner, Rory Sherlock, Linda Shine and Meg Smith.

Acknowledgements

Many thanks go to the landowners who graciously granted access to their fields, farmyards and homes, even if it got in the way of their busy farm, their work or their tourist visitors. It has been an enormously heartening experience to have encountered so many landowners with a keen interest in the history of the archaeological sites on their land. Research was undertaken at a number of archives and repositories in Ireland and the United Kingdom; my heartiest thanks go to the professionals of the Kent Library at Southeast Missouri State University (especially Susan Welker in Interlibrary Loan), the National Archives of Ireland, the National Archives at Kew, the National Library of Ireland, the National Monuments Service Archive, the Office of Public Works, the Public Record Office of Northern Ireland and Trinity College Library. For permitting me use of illustrations I would like to express gratitude to the Royal Irish Academy, the Royal Society of Antiquaries of Ireland and Trinity College Library. I am grateful to my editor at Manchester University Press, Meredith Carroll, Assistant Editor Alun Richards and the anonymous reviewers whose suggestions have greatly strengthened this work.

So many colleagues have kept me (comparatively) sane during this process: my fellow postgraduate students at Trinity College Dublin and the University of Cambridge when I started the tower house research, followed by my faculty colleagues in the history department at Southeast Missouri State University. Thank you to Wayne Bowen, Eric Clements, Rusty Curtis and Steve Hoffman for their mentorship and guidance as I navigated the tenure track and the intricacies of publishing. I have been very fortunate to enter a world of extremely supportive and enthusiastic medieval scholars here in the United States. Pretty much the entirety of the American Society of Irish Medieval Studies and the Southeastern Medieval Association deserve all thanks, but Lindy Brady, Melissa Ridley Elmes, Benjamin Hudson, Bridgette Slavin, Joshua Byron Smith, Kat Tracy, Mary Valante and Patrick Wadden warrant particular mention. A big shout out to my students, especially those in my Castles in Context classes, who helped me see my research in new ways and provided new perspectives and food for thought. Of course, I could not have done this without all my friends, both within academia and far away from it, who helped me escape from the minutiae.

This book is dedicated to all the inspirational women in my life and to the memory of Varian Jones McAlister, Celia Bennett, John Jones, Sally Jones and Jenny McAlister, without whom this work would never have existed.

Introduction

Medieval Ireland is increasingly viewed within its wider social context, including its experiences framed as a pan-European phenomenon, or even in the context of a globalised Middle Ages. This book seeks to push such developments even further, to argue that tower houses are a remarkably effective means of understanding the socio-economic actions of the majority of people within late medieval Ireland. In part, this is due to who built tower houses – a type of castle dating from the later Middle Ages and opening decades of the early modern period. The small size of tower houses meant their construction was within the financial reach of many, including lords, ecclesiastics and merchants. They were also popular with the emerging gentry class. As prominent features of both rural and urban Ireland, they can be used to understand not only the people who lived inside them, but also the individuals who lived and worked around them. Few studies have looked at Gaelic-Irish, Anglo-Irish and early modern building forms as a unified whole. Fewer still have sought to locate tower houses within a wider tradition. Ó Danachair suggested several decades ago that the tower house originated with a continental influence, and this, alongside other interpretations of their origins, has been fought over by archaeologists (1977–79). Turning inwards to debate the structure's origins may be another manifestation of Celtic exceptionalism, possibly encouraged by the fact that some of the most visually arresting examples of tower houses were constructed by the Gaelic-Irish. It also might explain why most studies stop abruptly at the end of the Middle Ages, even though tower houses were being constructed until the middle of the seventeenth century, well within the early modern period. Inserting such temporal boundaries into research ignores the lived experience (McAlister, 2015).

The sheer number of tower houses means they can assist us in being better students of history by bringing us closer to this lived experience. Those living in and around tower houses viewed themselves as having a place within the wider medieval and early modern worlds, and used their built environment to maintain their identities. Ireland over the time period of tower house construction shifted from being on the medieval periphery to being a secondary, but still important, element within the Atlantic World. Throughout, we see that people wished to profit from their place in the world and used tower houses in an often unique manner to accomplish this. Far from suffering from isolation and neglect from the English government, Irish tower house builders turned the political reality to their advantage to create a dynamic and increasingly modern society.

Another unusual facet of this volume is that it examines the entirety of Ireland, with case studies and supporting examples from across the country. Until now, the majority of publications about tower houses have had a regional focus, including this author's own work. In large part, the reluctance to write a book on the tower houses of Ireland is due simply to the thousands of standing remains associated with the monument type, which has discouraged an inclusive approach, since a life's work would not even allow visiting every site recognised in the *Archaeological Survey of Ireland* (ASI) of the National Monuments Service and the *Northern Ireland Sites and Monuments Record*. It is thanks to generous research funding from the American Philosophical Society and Southeast Missouri State University, alongside the groundwork prepared during doctoral study at Trinity College Dublin, that enabled the scope necessary for this work.

A new approach to tower studies

This is not a simple overview of tower house chronology and architecture; rather, it demonstrates how tower houses, and material culture more generally, can be used in under-documented societies like late medieval Ireland to expose historical processes. The people living around tower houses were not the elites of political and religious life who dominate the surviving documentation, so this research provides new insights. There are many limitations to both the archaeological and historical records when examining the social experience of late medieval and early modern Ireland. A multidisciplinary methodology at times provides contrasting evidence that needs to be reconciled, but also compensates for each discipline's limitations. Tower houses provide a unique and appropriate focal point for such methodological efforts.

Tower houses also provide a way of synthesising distinct fields within historical study, hence the sub-title of this volume: 'society, economy and environment'. A book could easily be written on each of these themes with regard to later medieval Ireland, but the tower house provides a discrete means to compare and contrast these differing topics. Tower houses were built by the wealthy (or, at least, the increasingly wealthy) from both lay and religious backgrounds, while people from other social backgrounds, both rural and urban, lived around them. Few other monument types are this numerous while being a part of everyday life for so many people. Perhaps the only potential parallel is parish churches, but their survival is less evenly spread than the tower house and they tell us only of religious life. As tower houses were occupied by merchants, we could perceive them as having some overlap with vernacular architecture. In Ireland, we have no upstanding medieval vernacular buildings surviving; our knowledge of them instead comes from excavation and analogy. Tower houses also come from both urban and rural contexts. In short, if we are looking for an example of medieval material culture that transcends divides, then the tower house is the best option.

This volume examines the multitude of contexts present at tower house sites, and uses the tower house as a methodological tool through which to examine these contexts. A number of arguments unite the book, some of which implicitly challenge the historiography of tower houses. Foremost is tower house function. This has long been of interest to those studying tower houses, but has proved a struggle to securely determine. Different means have been utilised to determine the functions of spaces within the tower house, with most attention focussed on the hall, the central room of elite medieval society. While it is important to examine the tower house's interior, few have looked at what went on around the tower house. This book does precisely that, progressively widening the scope to the point where we reach international networks.

The traditional explanation for the existence of tower houses looks inwards and not outside to the wider world. This arguably reduces their inhabitants to passivity; by interpreting the tower house as a built response to threat and instability, its occupants are reduced to pawns sequestering themselves inside. People living inside tower houses instead used them to engage with the outside world – and not solely as a means of exploiting their landed estates for personal profit, but in many cases enabling them to act on a regional, national or international stage. Therefore, it cannot be stated that tower houses are defensive; rather, they are offensive – but not with a military function. These buildings served an active offensive role in social advancement, and reflect the ambitions of individuals who saw them as investments to secure their place in society and improve their economic fortune. As such, we can read them, and thereby understand something of the people who commissioned them. In the unstable political environment of the tower house centuries, ordinary people capitalised on unsettled conditions to carve out a new path for themselves as their usual social restrictions were removed.

Another issue is that the existing body of literature tends to focus on rural tower houses. However, there has generally been more willingness to recognise a diversity of purpose in the urban examples than has been granted to the rural. This has accompanied recognition that urban sites were occupied by merchants and wealthy town dwellers, whereas the rural ones are almost exclusively seen as the homes of local lords. It is increasingly appreciated by scholars that town and country were mutually dependent, particularly from an economic standpoint. This volume argues that there are often similarities between rural and urban tower houses when we approach them from a social perspective.

Some scholars have attempted to create a typology of tower houses based on architectural features, such as vaults and entrance ways. Overall, these have had minimal success and tell us little about the motivations behind the building. These classifications reduce the buildings to the sum of their parts, and drastically oversimplify complex social patterns that existed in the background. Even the most innocuous of these generalisations can obscure our understanding of the past. For example, it has often been remarked that western tower houses, especially those in Munster, were usually larger and more elaborate than eastern examples, particularly those located within the Pale (the counties surrounding the capital city of Dublin that by the late Middle Ages were the realised and cultural remnants of the Anglo-Irish colony) (McNeill, 1997; O'Keeffe, 2015; Sweetman, 2000). But to categorise them into simple dichotomy ignores the processes acting behind them.

The years following the catastrophic mid-fourteenth-century Black Death led to social transformations across Europe and Asia. Ireland was no exception. Coupled with political instability, Ireland's changes manifested in one form as the tower house. Thousands of tower houses were built, and although they were not particularly expensive to build, nor were they cheap and quick to construct. While some scholars have wondered how much of a meaningful impact a £10 government subsidy created in the mid-fifteenth century really had on encouraging construction, others have commented how unlikely it seems that there was sufficient wealth in small inland Irish towns to warrant as many tower houses as there were (McNeill, 1997). Wealth and an upwardly mobile society overlapped in the form of the tower house. The tower house may even reflect the growth of capitalistic elements during a commercialising economy. As Pirenne commented in his seminal work, 'that famous "capitalistic spirit" (*spiritus capitalisticus*) which some would have us believe dates only from the Renaissance ... It is not employing too modern an expression to say that the profits [people] realized were put to work as fast as possible to augment [their] revolving capital' (Pirenne, 1925: 118). While Ireland after the Black Death was not a capitalist economy, certainly elements of capitalism existed, with the tower house used as a means of advancement. In particular, it is reflective of consumption and was used as both an investment and a statement.

The use of the tower house as a declaration of social advancement was nothing new: material culture and the built environment have been used throughout time and space to make a visual statement of being in the world. This practice continued in the twentieth century in the form of aspirational country house purchasing, or what Evelyn Waugh called the 'cult' of the country house. In the twenty-first century, it is the upper middle classes striving to buy a second home in the country, reflecting 'a distinct bourgeois culture' (Ganesh, 2017). This can be paralleled with tower house builders striving to improve their position.

It is also a trend seen in many other medieval contexts. Landlords in medieval London with sufficient assets maintained sometimes extensive country estates. These assisted in connecting town and country, and sustained London's hinterland. At the most basic level, they used their country estate to supply their town home (Rees Jones, 2008). This process has been termed the 'urban manor' (*ibid.*: 91). Merchants were particularly involved in purchasing land outside cities from the fifteenth century. They either occupied these estates themselves or leased them to others as a 'commercial venture'. Therefore, in the later Middle Ages, rural mercantile enterprise was not unheard of; though it is very difficult to isolate exactly what impacts this had on the agricultural economy (Britnell, 1996). In Flanders this trend became particularly apparent after 1250 (Nicholas, 1976).

There are a few references to this occurring in Ireland, especially after the Dissolution of the Monasteries and in the seventeenth century when landholding was more in flux. But it can be argued that it was present earlier and instead went undocumented, like so many other social processes of the day. In the late sixteenth century, the traditional Gaelic-Irish property tenures began to cease, and in areas near major port towns this enabled merchants to become landholders. In feudal society landholding was a mark of social ascent, and even if facets of feudalism were decreasing, the cachet of possessing land remained. Possibly other manorial assets were likewise in demand; hence the merchant of Galway who was given the right to erect water mills (*Irish fiants*, vol. 3). That such actions changed the lifestyle of Ireland's merchant classes is reflected in statements like that made in 1586 that many Galway merchants had 'relinquished their mansions in towns and keep themselves in the country' (Gillespie, 1991: 21). A complaint from 1622 states that once merchants had accumulated wealth they moved into the country to farm and consequently neglected their trade, which presumably had negative impacts on the towns they left behind (*ibid.*). Comments like these might suggest trade was part time for many. This could also be applied to those dwelling in the countryside, who generated part-time income from dabbling in trade. This shows that merchants were not solely resident in Ireland's towns. Others leased tower houses in rural areas, as indicated by an entry in the *Annals of the four masters* (hereafter AFM) that 'Teige took Dunbeg, one of his own castles, from a Limerick merchant, who had it in his possession, in lieu of debt' (AFM, 1598, vol. 6). Grants of land included in the Tudor Fiants include a 1541 grant of 'Anee' in County Limerick to merchants from Kilmallock (*Irish fiants*, vol. 1). Aney, nowadays known as Knockainy, was the site of two tower houses only two hundred metres apart.

The Gaelic-Irish particularly experienced this pressure from predominantly Anglo-Irish merchants (Galloway, 2011; Naessens, 2009), although mercantile land expansion was also known within the Anglo-Irish-dominated Pale. The best known case is the Dowdall family, whose members included many merchants whose deeds for land in counties Louth and Meath survive (*Dowdall deeds*). The earls of Ormond assisted Waterford merchants in 'colonising' the lands north of the River Suir in County Kilkenny. In comparison with medieval London, we can state that this will have assisted in integrating that area into the city's hinterland. Some merchant families purchased land, while others leased it from the earl. This also increased the earls' control over the port and assured loyalty from the mercantile class (Galloway, 2011). Tower houses associated with this process might include Ballinlaw Castle, County Kilkenny, which is a tower house with attached early modern house, having a visual command over the salmon weirs on the River Suir.

This was not simple social emulation by the new social classes created by economic opportunity, but rather a more complex phenomenon. Several scholars have argued against a theory of social emulation in the Middle Ages, among them Gardiner (Gardiner, 2000; Rees Jones, 2008). Regarding England, Gardiner states against the theory of social emulation that:

> Pearson has noted that in Kent the wealthy yeomen were in the vanguard of innovation in the early 16th century. They were able to be more innovative in building design because they did not need the open hall for ceremonial purposes, and were able to experiment with fully two-storied buildings. Traditional plans might therefore persist amongst the gentry and nobility for reasons of social space or a desire to adhere to the symbolism of earlier forms, at a time when they were being abandoned by other classes. (Gardiner, 2000: 160)

That the merchant class had their own, extremely culturally influential, material culture has been explored by Gaimster in his studies of the

Hanseatic League. The Hanse, resident in port towns and outside of the local population, formed a mercantile diaspora. They displayed their separateness through both their built environment and their domestic goods (Gaimster, 2005, 2014). Their settlement and material culture forms especially 'allude to the shared religious and social values of the urban bourgeois elite' (Gaimster, 2007: 34). Following this, I tentatively propose that Irish medieval urbanites created a material culture that was then copied.

Tower houses represent the actions and perceptions of individuals. However, we need to remember that agency always has restraints. One of these was the technological abilities of the builders and workmen. This might in part explain the regional schools of tower house building noted in places like County Down, and the 'sectionally constructed' tower houses of the west, if the patrons were limited by what their architects could do (Donnelly, 1998; Eadie, 2015; O'Keeffe, 2015). Tower house construction needed some level of specialised skills. For example, in 1409, those building Mountgarrett Castle in County Wexford, outside the port town of New Ross, came from the counties of Kilkenny, Waterford and Wexford, indicating that it could not be built by local craftsmen alone (Colfer, 2013). Another possible limitation was the cost of builders' wages. Although in post-plague England, the wages of skilled workers, like masons, did not increase relative to those of agricultural workers, which ensured a relative reduction in building costs there. Increased pastoralism could reflect the applicability of this conclusion from post-plague England to Ireland. We also are uncertain of the cost of building materials, including stone, timber and tiles. The cost of tiles may have fallen (Gardiner, 2014), but the availability of building-quality timber in Ireland at that time is uncertain.

Regardless, the proliferation of tower houses after 1400 indicates a healthy economy, and that the cost limitations were mainly outweighed by the benefits. In the early 1600s Matthew de Renzy wrote that it cost £600–£700 to build the 'meanest' castle in County Offaly. Some think this cost exaggerated, as twenty-five years earlier it had cost £300–£400 in County Down. Indeed, a £10 government subsidy would be more impactful in the latter scenario than the former (Colfer, 2013; O'Keeffe, 2015). Tower house owners could further save significant costs by billeting their builders and workmen on their tenants (Colfer, 2013; O'Keeffe, 2015). Castles could be constructed expediently when it mattered, too, as the *Annals of Ulster* (AU) record Maghnus O'Domnaill building a castle of wood and stone at 'Port-na-tri-namat' (unidentified) over the course of the summer in 1527. That this was an unusual procedure is implied by the inclusion of the statement that it was 'finished in a short space' (AU, 1527, p. 567).

Overall then, personal agency outweighed the restrictions on building, but what features can we consult to gain the best insight into the former? Some have argued that there were a growing number of tower house contractors who could build based on lordly specifications. The evidence is not terribly detailed though. The planned construction of a castle in Enniscorthy, County Wexford, in 1582 is one such example, although it was never actually built. The owner here specified the dimensions, as well as that he wanted ogee-headed windows and murder holes and that he wanted it completed within the year. This indicates that the finer features on tower houses might be taken as reliable reflections of lordly demands, and so can be used as an insight into their perspective (Colfer, 2013).

Another example of a lord requesting specific design comes from 1547, when Richard Butler gave instructions to his construction supervisor, Derby Ryan, regarding dimensions. He also wanted a slate roof, two chimneys, a yett (an iron gate or grill that closed over the doorway to a tower house) over the door, a bawn (courtyard), and doors and windows. Unfortunately, no more precision is given regarding the doors and windows, and it was stated that the rest of the building details were to be resolved on site (McNeill, 1997). This unidentified castle of 'Bretasse' is at one point in the document likened to Poulakerry Castle, County Tipperary, especially that the barbican be modelled after it (*Calendar of Ormond deeds*, 1547–84, vol. 5). Presumably it was intended to appear broadly similar to this extant (and restored) tower house.

This second document, in contrast to the first, gives the impression that the owner did not dictate many of the more ornamental features, and indeed may not have been present for these decisions if they were determined on site. McNeill concludes that size and plan would definitely have been the remit of owners, as they were the ones who needed to identify function and how much they had to spend. However, he believes that decoration was also the owner's responsibility and that this could vary based on regional taste (McNeill, 1997). This leaves a great deal to the owner rather than the architect or builder; instead, technicalities (especially timberwork and flooring arrangements) may have been the latter's business (*ibid.*).

These same patterns of aspirational building are witnessed outside Ireland, even in terms of a shared chronology. In Dyer's study of cruck building in the Midlands of England (2013b), a peak construction period of the 1430s to 1470s was noted, echoing Pearson's finding for the entirety of England and Wales, which concluded that there was a building boom before the end of the fifteenth century. In both of these studies, solidly constructed buildings were over-represented, and this is again similar to the tower house's position in Ireland. The late medieval English building boom reflects higher incomes – when coupled with declining food costs, regardless of other problems in the agricultural economy, periods of increased building activity ensued (Gardiner, 2014).

Residents of Ireland also had increased political freedom, stemming from decentralisation, that enabled them to build fortifications. The Irish late medieval building boom went unchecked except by the market (represented by availability and cost of building materials and expertise). In fact, such building was explicitly encouraged, since the Dublin government provided a financial incentive in the form of the £10 subsidy to builders within the Pale.

The 'castle-building craze' arrived in Ireland with the advent of the tower house, reflecting a new class consciousness among the freeholders that accompanied new-found prosperity (Empey, 1981). This meant that the right, 'or more accurately perhaps, the capacity', to possess a castle 'trickled lower down the social hierarchy in English parts of Ireland than it had previously: people whom we do not "see" in the archaeological record prior to the fifteenth century announce themselves to us through their possession of castles, mainly tower-houses, in the late Middle ages' (O'Keeffe, 2015: 255). The widespread construction of tower houses was likewise the first stone-built-monument boom that the Gaelic-Irish enthusiastically contributed to (Breen, 2005).

In many settings the tower house was used in an outright attempt to control the landscape, often for personal or financial profit. Placement of the more visually ornate architectural features of tower houses (machicolations, larger moulded window headings, etc.) reflects the builders' priorities, and can be used to assess their intent regarding landscape command. We might observe that a greater number of more expensive building features are oriented towards a bridge, or a river route or a valley pass. A lack of building investment in the tower house faces that overlook rising land or less productive farmland has also been observed during the course of fieldwork. Such decisions decidedly reflect priorities, such as not to spend money on expensive architecture that nobody will appreciate. This also ties into themes of 'conspicuous consumption'. Assessing the exterior ornamentation of castles can therefore assist us in determining the worldview of their occupants.

This interpretation has a longer application in studies of internal arrangements. McNeill (cited in Creighton, 2010) has illustrated how access to the rooftops could be tightly controlled by spatial planning. Sherlock (2015) has also demonstrated access to halls vis-à-vis private space, and proposed methods for identifying the hall within towers. Creighton has described the use of large windows in such high-status rooms as the tower house internal hall to provide an 'artificially elevated gaze over the landscape', which 'was something special and unusual, to be experienced by a privileged minority'. He especially emphasised the use of window seats in enabling this, since it allowed command from a place of comfort, and therefore may also have been a female space, which are usually difficult to identify (Creighton, 2010: 38). Observed throughout fieldwork has been the architectural placement of the largest and most ornate windows to face out over a river or other communication route. This indicates that the biggest building investment was reserved for where the most people might have seen it, as well as for the most picturesque view for those inside.

At Creighton's example, Stokesay Castle in Shropshire, the view from the rooftop included 'all the symbols of rural lordship': mill, dovecote and parish church (*ibid*.: 40). Yet the castle was built by an urbanite merchant. This scenario can be paralleled with the tower house. Aspects of the landscape emphasised by castle views are parkland and water, as well as historic sites that might have had symbolic connotations. To take another perspective, the castle itself is visible from these locations. Creighton further argues that 'the availability of elevated views could influence the organisation of the tract of landscape immediately surrounding the castle' (*ibid*.: 45).

It was not a one-way process; a simple display of wealth was not the sole benefit tower house patrons received from their expenditure. Instead, tower houses offered a significant return on investment, and this also explains enthusiasm for them. Tower houses were an upfront outlay, but with the ultimate goal of creating more income. The tower house made a strong visual statement as to the occupier's wealth and ability; they exercised command both symbolically and practically, and used this command for wealth generation.

Many benefits came from a lack of centralised government oversight, as well as downsides. Residents of late medieval Ireland had the ability to enact measures that were restricted elsewhere in Europe during the same period to ensure the government retained control of them. In the absence of strong government, responsibility was instead delegated to locals, who kept the income from tolls and taxes that was otherwise the remit of central government (discussed in chapter 3 in particular). In this way, there was localised control over communication routes and environmental resources. Such localised control could expand as far as international relations; the best examples of this are trading customs and dues. The 'glocal' is increasingly discussed in medieval studies, and the tower house is a perfect embodiment (McAlister, 2016).

All of this reeks of a new economic and social confidence not usually associated with the medieval period. Tower houses could consequently represent a transition from medieval to modern. They reflect new landholders, ranging from merchants and gentry to adventurers and colonists. They also indicate that the traditional separation of medieval society into those who work, those who fight and those who pray is a gross oversimplification. Instead, within the one structure of the tower house we can witness the interplay between all three of these positions to greater or lesser extent. Certainly we might argue that 'those who work' are well represented.

Not only do we see a transition, particularly visible with the appearance of early modern architectural features, but it is evident that much of what we have considered 'high medieval' in character continued in use well into the later Middle Ages. The most overt manifestation of this is in the use of an accepted vocabulary of castle architecture past the time when much of England had ceased castle building. This alone reflects a medieval outlook and view of oneself in the world. The agrarian economy of Ireland also remained distinctively medieval arguably until the second half of the seventeenth century (though it was transforming in certain places before that time). This includes the continued presence of manorial features at tower houses, particularly manifested in their collocation with water mills.

Defining the Irish tower house

The tower house is the defining monument of the Irish Middle Ages. This book examines the context of this remarkable building, a part of material culture through which we can examine much larger issues. This includes studying the actions of historical people, a difficult task, as anyone already familiar with the vagaries of research into medieval Ireland is well aware. This is therefore not just a castle book, nor is it solely descriptive, but it illustrates how hidden aspects of history can be exposed through new methodologies.

Thousands of tower houses were constructed across Ireland over a period roughly 1350–1640. While the final dates of their construction are documented – one of the last was Bangor, County Down, in 1637 – their origins are much more contested. Certainly we know they were numerous by the fifteenth century and were symptomatic of social and political changes following the Black Death of the mid-fourteenth century. This makes them a tantalising reflection of the tumultuous later Middle Ages.

Despite their historical appeal, at first glance they do not appear to have such potential. Ornamentation, both interior and exterior, is frequently minimal, often in contrast to the status of the occupant. This plainness unfortunately regularly prevents reliable dating based on architectural features. We do not know the exact number that appeared in the medieval landscape, nor how many were in use at any specific time – as this book will show, destruction rates could be extremely high. Barry has adapted Cairns's numbers from his case study in County Tipperary (410 stone castles, all tower houses save a dozen; Cairns, 1987) to the rest of the country, concluding that between three and seven thousand tower houses were constructed (Barry, 1996). This led him to state that Ireland was the most encastellated part of the British Isles by the later Middle Ages (Barry, 1987). Leask's estimate of three thousand is probably severely under-representative, as it is based on Ordnance Survey (hereafter OS) maps, which only record those still extant by the mid-nineteenth century.

Looking at a site distribution map (see figure I.1), it is immediately apparent that tower houses are not evenly spread across the country. Rather, densities occur along coasts and rivers, within southern counties where there was fertile agricultural land and in the great late medieval lordships. County Limerick is one of the counties with the densest distribution of tower houses, with '[0].380 towers per square mile, followed by Kilkenny with [0].245 and Tipperary with [0].154' (Mac Curtain, 1988: 440). There is a notable absence of tower houses in the north, particularly within the Gaelic-Irish O'Neill lordship.

Tower houses were constructed of stone, though it seems likely that timber versions were built that simply have not survived. They are usually rectangular in plan, with a lesser amount of square and circular examples, while others have side turrets that project. The entrance was usually on the ground floor, but there are some interesting exceptions to this rule. They were several storeys in height with a vault, usually barrel shaped, over at least one floor – which floor seems to be dependent on regional and county-level building styles. Therefore their overall appearance is vertical. Upper floors tended to have better windows, fireplaces and other features indicative of comfort. The internal layout may have a single chamber at each level or have ancillary rooms to the main chamber. While tower houses today tend to have exposed stonework, contemporary references indicate that they were once limewashed or harled, so they would have been white coloured (there are several references to 'white castles' and 'white-washed edifices' – AFM, 1572, vol. 5; 1580, vol. 5; 1583, vol. 5 – and to castles being built of lime and stone – AFM, 1601, vol. 6).

The historiography has emphasised the tower house's proliferation as a direct consequence of the turbulent history of late medieval and early modern Ireland (McNeill, 1997). Politics of the period roughly 1300–1600 can be best described as decentralised, with periods of open warfare accompanying the Tudor Conquest and in response to rebellions against the authority of the English Crown. These years are popularly viewed as unsettled, lawless and violent. Taking this perspective, then,

Introduction

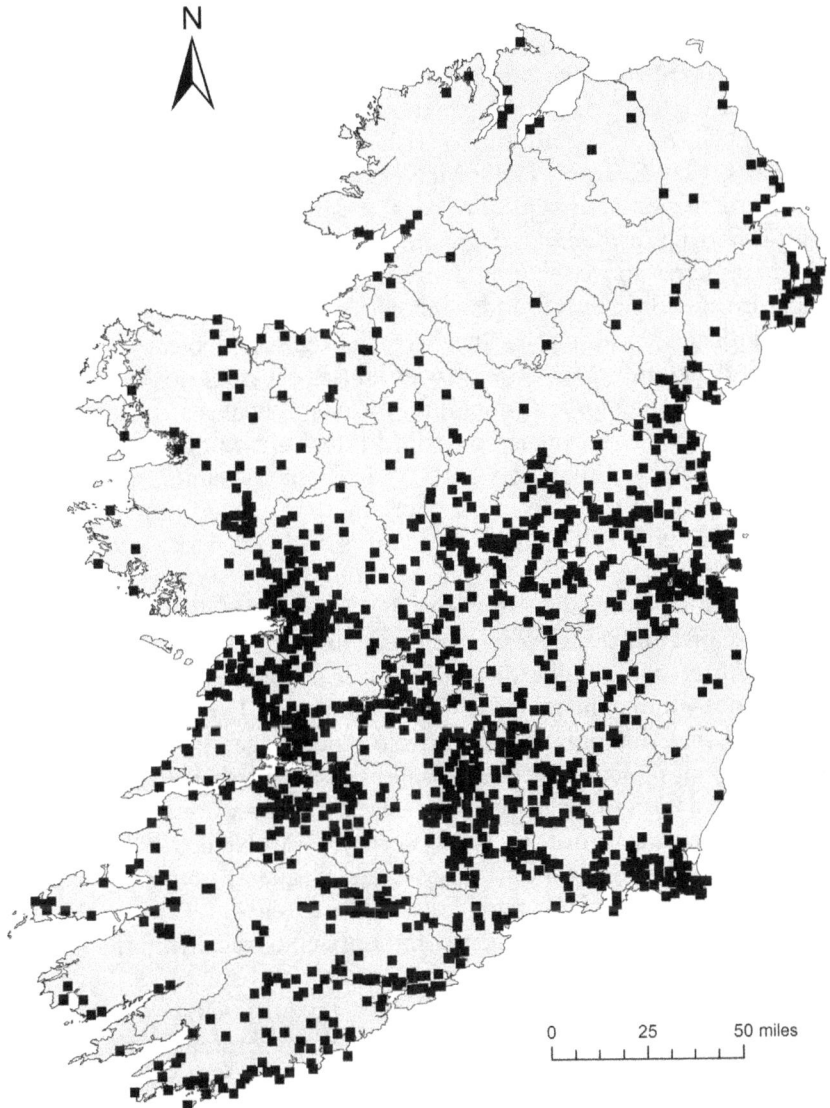

I.1 Distribution map of tower houses across Ireland based on site classification within the *Archaeological Survey of Ireland* and *Northern Ireland Sites and Monuments Record*.

the tower house becomes a constructed response to such conditions, offering defence to a lord, his family and their possessions. A common attribution for the proliferation of tower houses is the decline of central authority from Dublin, which allowed for local power bases (Barry,

1987, 1993a). But reducing the tower house to its essential political context ignores its many manifestations.

The aforementioned lordly 'possessions' are usually taken to mean cattle herds. The 'creaght', or cattle herd, conferred status and wealth on both Gaelic-Irish and Anglo-Irish lords, following Gaelic cultural practices (Mac Curtain, 1988; McNeill, 1997). Tower houses have also tended to be viewed as typical of rural Ireland, and many are associated with low-lying fertile land. They are virtually unknown more than five hundred metres above sea level (Donnelly, 2001; McAuliffe, 1991). These agriculturally productive lands tended to overlap with the centres of the great lordships, meaning that they were not the most violent and unstable parts of the country. However, tower houses are not known from all of the magnate lordships – as noted, they are largely absent from northern O'Neill territory for reasons we still do not fully understand.

In the late Middle Ages an advancement in tenant status led to increased prosperity, a factor contributing to the sheer number of tower houses (McNeill, 1997). Increased status and prosperity caused more tower houses to be built, while at the same time more tower houses led to a growth in status and prosperity, but it is impossible to know which was the causal factor. Several families could effectively live under one tower house roof, thanks to the Gaelic-Irish system that apportioned inheritance among heirs (Mac Curtain, 1988). Donnelly (2001) has suggested that this practice of partible inheritance also contributed to the density of tower houses. The buildings are further associated with the fragmentation of large lordly estates, with tower houses located in a situation convenient for their lordly occupant (McNeill, 1997; O'Keeffe, 2000a). In addition, tower houses were frequently built by wealthy town inhabitants (such as merchants) and ecclesiastics. Prior to the later Middle Ages, castles were most commonly constructed by the king or by great magnates and were therefore truly elite structures. But tower houses had popularity beyond this tiny and ultra-elite percentage of medieval people and, as will be shown, many ordinary people lived around them.

Tower houses and other residential towers physically resembling them are not exclusive to Ireland. The best studied contemporaries are the pele towers and bastles of the Scottish-English borders. These were located exclusively on good agricultural land, especially on coastal plains, with more in Scotland than England (Dixon, 1979). It has been suggested that the opportunity for tower house construction arose after the cessation of raiding across this border, which, combined with continued low rents, provided a significant increase in personal wealth (*ibid.*; Dixon, 1992). Medieval residential towers are also known beyond the British Isles, on the European continent, in diverse places from the Netherlands to Greece.

They are even known outside Europe, in Arabia, the Caucasus, Afghanistan and West Africa (Mac Curtain, 1988).

A much-debated theory is that tower houses originate in government incentive. Leask was the first proponent, identifying a statute from the eighth year of the reign of Henry VI (1429) which gave a building grant of £10 to residents of the Pale. The description accompanying the legislation evokes a tower house: embattled or fortified, at least six metres (twenty feet) by five metres (sixteen feet) in ground dimension, with a minimum height of about twelve metres (forty feet). This description fits one tower house in County Meath in particular – Donore Castle (see figure I.2). As the statute dates from 1429, it is probable that this grant did not create tower houses, but rather assists in explaining their popularity (Leask, 1944; Mac Curtain, 1988; Sweetman, 2000). However, it has also been argued that such a comparatively trivial sum was unlikely to have had much impact on either the development or cessation of tower house building (McNeill, 1997; O'Keeffe, 2015).

Both the terms 'tower house' and 'castle' are used within the text. Tower houses are usually viewed as a type of castle: one of the latter types within a chronology that commences with earthwork castles. Like other forms of castle, such as mottes and the great masonry castles, tower houses have the same three intrinsic functions: residence, defence and administration. These were present to greater or lesser extents at different sites. In the case of the tower house, defence is probably the most debated function, despite a pervasive argument that it is this defensive appearance that explains their acceptance as a form of castle (McNeill, 1997). The inclusion of the term 'residence' indicates that castles are definitively private constructions, not communal or public fortifications like citadels or encampments. 'Castle' can therefore be understood as a more inclusive word to describe the whole range of medieval fortified architecture, whereas 'tower house' refers to the specific monument type.

The term 'tower house' was not coined until the mid-nineteenth century; however, it is an apt phrase in terms of the castle form it describes (*ibid.*). In documentation contemporary to their construction we find them described as castles; most often '*castellum*', '*cúirt*' and '*fortalicium*', the latter sometimes written as '*fortalice*'. Consequently, despite their small size, it is apparent that late medieval society viewed them as a continuation of the castle-building tradition – one reason why they are addressed in castle studies (*ibid.*; O'Keeffe, 2015).

Because of the number and distribution of tower houses, even with financial support a sampling strategy had to be adopted. This focussed on tower houses with significant standing remains – those with just foundations or fewer remains were not studied, except in the rare

I.2 Donore Castle, County Meath, is the tower house that aligns most closely with the description given in the £10 subsidy for builders in the Pale. It is located above the River Boyne and is architecturally very plain, its only notable feature being the one circular corner turret.

circumstance that they were well documented. The reason for this limitation was to provide a precise location within the landscape: most documented tower house sites with no archaeological remains do not have a specific location beyond the townland (Ireland's historical smallest land unit). Aspects of this study required exact locations to draw convincing conclusions; and although not an architectural history it also needed some building fabric to interpret. In this way, remains can be used to determine orientation, outlook and function.

Within this basic criterion we are still left with ample prospects. Due to the research questions at the heart of this project, most of which concentrate on the tower house's role within the larger landscape, those sites located in proximity to other medieval or natural features of interest were prioritised. For example, in sections analysing maritime and riverine tower house distributions, sites within half a kilometre of a major river or coast were identified using a Euclidian distance buffer within geographic information systems (GIS). Tower houses that were within half a kilometre of a medieval parish church, earlier castle site, deserted or current settlement, historical field system, or bridge were also prioritised. This produced a list of over two hundred sites from across the country – an achievable if large number. The sample size means that conclusions have been developed with a range of experiences and landscapes in mind. At each site the tower house itself was surveyed and recorded. Fieldwalking in the vicinity of the tower house was undertaken, and investigation of any associated archaeological or natural features (whether previously identified or observed on the ground). Each site was extensively photographed and measured.

This sampling methodology ensured that detailed records from a range of tower house contexts were studied and included. However, there are some limitations. One of these is a geographical bias, since the primary factor when selecting sites was standing remains. Unfortunately, urban tower houses are the least likely to have survived, as it is Ireland's cities that have undergone the greatest transformation since the Middle Ages. This does not apply equally to all towns in Ireland, but a notable example is Dublin city. There is no surviving tower house standing in this city today, though some extant suburban examples have been included. Instead, generalisations based on the historical record tend to dominate for Ireland's major cities. The comparative documentation surviving for Ireland's cities contrasts with under-documentation for its medieval countryside, meaning that it is tempting to accord the cities a significance not necessarily warranted.

This study rests on both the archaeological and historical records; again, a goal from the outset despite the difficulty of reconciling this sometimes contrasting evidence. As well as working with a very large archaeological corpus in the form of thousands of monument examples, it would be easy to get lost in the written documentation for these thousands of sites, searching for the proverbial needles in haystacks. Again, this is the enormous benefit in identifying just two hundred sites upon which to focus analysis. Hopefully this book will act as a call to arms to encourage historical archaeologists to be ambitious in their goals, and over time new evidence will prove (or disprove!) many of the arguments presented here.

A significant limitation on documentary research is the poor survival rate of official written records from the Middle Ages in Ireland. This unavoidable bias favours the major landholding families of Ireland, whose estate records have survived to the present day, mainly because they managed to retain at least some of their original lands into the modern era. The Ormond family papers in the National Library of Ireland (NLI) in Dublin and the Lismore Castle papers from the earl of Cork's estate have proved particularly valuable. The surviving records also prioritise the later period of tower house construction, since there is a notable uptick in surviving government-produced documentation following Tudor interest in the country. Fortunately, scholars conclude that we can usually extrapolate later records regarding the Irish landscape to earlier centuries, with some restrictions and awareness.

The events that have destroyed much of the documentary record are too numerous to detail here, but the most famous episode is the Four Courts fire of 1922. This catastrophic fire burned almost all the medieval documents housed in the Irish Public Records Office, creating a huge break in the material available to modern-day historians. Even before this fire, there were impactful losses of medieval records. Herbert Wood, who authored his guide to the Irish Public Records Office in 1919, noted the poor condition of documents, and their inadequate storage facilities before his time. Many government documents by the eighteenth century were stored at Dublin Castle, where exposure to rain and fire damage led to dreadful preservation conditions. Records were also lost, a significant cause being the tradition of the Lords Lieutenant of Ireland taking their official governmental materials with them when they left the country. Wood's guide gives an overview of the records that existed shortly before 1922. Through this publication we know that Chancery and Exchequer records; wills; parliament records; and plea, pipe and other rolls, among many other records, were destroyed in the fire (Wood, 1919). The Four Courts fire was not the only one of the 1920s affecting medieval documents, as the Custom House was also set alight, as were many Anglo-Irish Protestant country houses. The immolation of the latter meant the loss of private records as well as public ones.

Investigating tower houses is especially problematic given that this research relies on specific places being mentioned in the historical records. It also presumes that documentation was originally created. For instance, as can be seen in the *Kildare rental*, even as late as the sixteenth century customs collection in the port towns was leased out to individuals, who did not report their numbers to a central authority. Although interest from the English Crown affects the volume and nature of the written records, there are still serious problems with what was documented in the first place. In particular, records are primarily concerned with the Irish counties that underwent Plantation and political events. For example, much of the sixteenth-century government records regarding land concern the Dissolution of the Monasteries (Crooks, n.d.; Dryburgh and Smith, 2004; Edwards and Donovan, 1997; Mac Niocaill, 1992).

The history of tower house studies

Recent years have witnessed a reassessment of the role of castles within medieval society, and this change in the theoretical framework has affected tower house studies no less than other topics. Much of this reinterpretation has moved away from a military emphasis and instead is more landscape based, recognising that castles were raised for a variety of social and economic reasons rather than as a response to a singular threat with 'the castle site represent[ing] some level of compromise between the needs to protect property, administer estates and generate revenue' (Liddiard, 2005: 24). Defensive architecture has been argued to represent lordly symbolic power more than real offensive military might, though in more recent years this pendulum is swinging back (Coulson, 2003; Johnson, 2002). Much of this work has concentrated on English elite sites (often royal), and subsequently been applied elsewhere, including to Ireland. The analysis of castle distribution as part of this trend led to the proposition that the true motivation behind castle location was the control and ownership of territory. A common conclusion was that topography was specifically selected in order to make the castle more prominent and thus emphasise it as a symbol of power, or provide proximity to communication routes (Creighton, 2002). Where there were large numbers of freeholding tenants, that would probably have been a deterrent to the construction of castles, as would large and influential ecclesiastical estates (*ibid.*; Liddiard, 2005). We have already seen that the presence of large numbers of wealthy tenants encouraged tower house building in Ireland, which reminds us to be cautious when applying conclusions derived from other countries.

A tower has been interpreted as presenting a certain kind of lordship concurrent with an accepted symbolic vocabulary of the Middle Ages

(Johnson, 2002; O'Keeffe, 2000a). As a highly visible manifestation of authority, the tower made an impact on, and perhaps reshaped, the surrounding landscape (Creighton, 2002; O'Keeffe, 2000a). In the Middle Ages, the resources required to support a lord and his castle came ultimately from his landed wealth, thus the immediate landscape reflected the elite pursuit of maintaining or advancing social rank (Liddiard, 2005). As a result, castles were often constructed at interfaces between different productive landscapes so as to maximise available profits. As with the Irish tower house, however, there tends to be little correlation between castle density and pastoral land (Aalen, 1978; Creighton, 2002). Certain features are frequently associated with castle sites to assist with exploitation, including mills, parish churches, villages and deer parks. These receive special attention in this volume as unique manifestations of the relationship between the tower house lord and his world.

Many of these broad ideas about castle use have been applied to Ireland and tower houses. However, there are some notable differences. One is that tower houses are usually not viewed as symbolising invasion or the subjugation of the native population, unlike Anglo-Norman earth-and-timber castles. The Anglo-Normans are often credited with a surge in castle building in the wake of their late twelfth-century invasion of Ireland. Their castles mark administrative centres, although they may not have been centres of population or agricultural production, as this depended on the success of each lordly conquest (O'Conor, 1998). Accompanying the arrival of the Anglo-Normans was the emergence of a number of dominant noble families as a consequence of their feudal society, which followed them across the Irish Sea (Mallory and McNeill, 1991).

This is intended as an extremely brief overview of Irish history as it directly affected tower house construction, and is a vast oversimplification of the social processes governing the daily lives of tower house builders and occupants. It removes their agency entirely, leaving them no more than pawns passive to outside events, when, as shown here, these people were in fact seeking to improve their socio-economic status, their social connections and much more. Their lives were not ruled by forces beyond their control.

The socio-political backdrop created following the Anglo-Norman Invasion was changing by the era of the tower house. The lands held by the descendants of the Anglo-Normans progressively shrank in area until their main area of influence became the Pale. This was the real and imagined region of control of the Anglo-Irish (as the Anglo-Norman descendants came to be known, as their connections with their original homelands weakened over time), centred on Ireland's main city, Dublin. The area within the Pale continued to decrease over the later Middle Ages, so that parts of counties Dublin, Meath and Kildare were effectively all that remained by the end of the period. There were other isolated pockets of Anglo-Irish control outside the Pale, including eastern County Down in the northeast and parts of Munster in south Ireland. Accompanying this process, the influence of royal government from Dublin waned, particularly from the fourteenth century. Edward Bruce landed at Larne in the south of County Antrim in 1315, and the ensuing Bruce Wars lasted until his death in 1318; the Black Death killed at least one-third of the population, if not more, causing further untold numbers to relocate to better social and agricultural conditions elsewhere in Ireland (Gwynn, 1935). Outside of the Anglo-Irish centres, Ireland was dominated by Gaelic-Irish culture – that is, the native Irish population. Many of the Anglo-Irish came to adopt Gaelic-Irish customs and habits, in a process termed 'degeneracy', also referred to as Gaelicisation. This advance of Gaelic-Irish culture is often referred to as the Gaelic Resurgence. Throughout this text, the terms Anglo-Irish and Gaelic-Irish are preferred to refer to these two cultural groups. 'English' and 'Scottish' designate people who came from those countries during their lifetimes, therefore they tend to be most frequently encountered in the early modern period.

Conditions were ripe for these socio-political processes, largely owing to the declining effectiveness of government imposed from England. Faced with internal problems between the fourteenth century and the Tudor Conquest, the English Crown paid only sporadic attention to Ireland. Traditionally, the explanation for the existence of the tower house in Irish society has been that it was a material-culture response to this climate. Within this intellectual framework, tower houses were private defensive responses to political insecurity and the ever-present threat of violence, especially at a local level. In the power vacuum that formed from the decline of Crown authority, great magnate lordships coalesced. This enabled certain lords, both Anglo-Irish and Gaelic-Irish, to act effectively as petty kings over their areas of jurisdiction. These included the Anglo-Irish Geraldine lordships of the earls of Kildare in the east and of Desmond in the southwest, as well as the Butler lordship of the earldom of Ormond in the centre of the country. The largest of the Gaelic-Irish lordships in the later Middle Ages was the O'Neill territory, comprising a large chunk of the north, especially around modern County Tyrone. Numerous prominent families controlled other parts of the country and they are discussed throughout this text in their capacity as tower house builders.

Despite historians claiming this to have been a period of unrest, there were few pitched battles or extensive periods of open warfare. Instead, cattle raiding is the most frequently documented martial activity.

A frequent assumption is that tower houses were ideally suited to defence against raiding, since they could provide protection for a lord and his family against a small badly equipped group seeking a speedy attack. In this interpretation of tower house function, the bawn was important, since it could act as a corral for animals. However, the number of extant or documented bawns is quite low, with potentially only twenty per cent of tower houses having them (Barry, 2006; McNeill, 1997). Their scarcity might be explained by the disassembly and removal of bawn walls for their good building stone (Leask, 1944).

Large-scale and bloody warfare was, however, a feature of the Tudor Conquest of Ireland. This was a lengthy war, intermittently raging during the sixteenth century. It included the pivotal events of the Desmond Rebellion, which transformed the political landscape of Munster in 1569–73 and 1579–83, and the Nine Years' War of 1593–1603, which was particularly focussed on Gaelic-Irish Ulster. Conquest was followed by Plantation (both official and informal) in certain Irish counties. The effectiveness of this process, whereby confiscated land was granted to English and Scots settlers loyal to the Crown, varied across the country. The process demarcates a cultural sea change affecting the landholding classes and thus, by extension, the social groups responsible for tower house construction. The attractiveness of Ireland to these colonists was socio-economic – ambitious men were actively seeking new places to gain land and to trade with (Gillespie, 1985).

Tower house construction was minimal during the most intense periods of the Tudor Conquest, which has sometimes been used as evidence that low-level endemic violence motivated tower house creation. A secondary tower house building boom occurred in the financially more successful opening decades of the seventeenth century, and economic crises in the 1630s are mirrored in tower house construction patterns. Repeated harvest failures and attempts at increased control by the Crown served to increase tensions (Gillespie, 1985; McAlister, 2015), and in 1641 rebellion broke out, rapidly becoming a series of massacres and attacks on settlers. In the aftermath of the 1641 Rebellion and the Confederate Wars, Irish society was rather different. A wave of new colonists had arrived by the 1660s and local government was overhauled by the Cromwellian administration. Increased taxes put many landlords in a weakened financial position, causing many to sell their Irish lands. By the middle of the seventeenth century, the period of tower house construction was over.

The published literature on tower houses has emphasised their chronology and architecture. This book steps away from both issues, which might seem unusual in the first ever book dedicated to tower houses. By doing so, the findings will resonate in geographic and temporal zones beyond late medieval Ireland. This is despite a not uncommon scholarly belief that tower houses do not resemble their contemporary buildings in England, and that they do not form part of the European Gothic architectural narrative (Breen, 2005; McNeill, 1997; Ronnes, 2007).[1] This study instead shows that when we use tower houses as a mirror to their world, they reflect a great deal.

The work of Sherlock and Eadie, among others, has done much to increase our knowledge of the interior uses of tower houses, and enables this project to turn its attention to beyond the building proper. Thanks to these authors we have a clearer understanding of the use of space and function of features inside the tower house (see, for example, Eadie, 2009, 2015; Sherlock, 2006, 2010). They have also utilised comparisons between different counties in Ireland, encompassing sites held by both Anglo-Irish and Gaelic-Irish from east and west alike. This makes their work particularly valuable, since most publications on tower houses have been regional case studies, owing partly to the intimidating number of extant tower houses in the landscape today. Possibly as a consequence of sample size limitations, many previous tower house studies have been reluctant to draw larger conclusions about the landscape.

Ní Loingsigh's study of County Donegal tower houses was one of the first to make extensive remarks upon the non-military aspects of the tower house. Her study aimed to explain their concentration in relation to landowning. The conclusion was that landscape had a major influence on tower house distribution, with an 'overwhelming incidence of siting with access to the sea or to a navigable river' (1994: 148). Economics in the form of trade, rather than politics, was determined as the motivating factor behind tower house siting (*ibid.*). Naessens's studies of the coastal tower houses of south Connemara continued the scholarly emphasis on the maritime landscape. He identified a strong link between the building of tower houses and an increase in trade (2007). He observed a desire to control fishing grounds, in addition to a number of other social functions of the tower house, such as acting as a status symbol (*ibid.*; Naessens, 2009). The relationship of tower houses to other settlement forms of the Middle Ages has also been recognised. Literary and historical examination has shown them to be 'anything but isolated strongholds. In fact they were the focal point of their respective communities' (Barry, 2006; Budd, 2004: 278).

Summary

The layout of this book has been deliberately structured to mirror the different extents of the tower house's influence. It commences at the most local level and culminates with a discussion of their use in maintaining contact with the wider world. In this way it also echoes the environmental goods that were the backbone of Ireland's economy. Though this approach oversimplifies what was in reality a complex web of networks, it reminds us that tower houses and by extension medieval society did not stand isolated in any of their landscapes. Furthermore, there are two interconnecting themes running throughout that can be summarised under the headings of 'land' and 'water'.

Chapter 1 examines what was around the castle walls. It has long been believed that tower houses were not solitary masonry towers, as they appear to us today, but rather were the focal point of more diverse arrangements. But concrete evidence for this has been minimal to date. The book opens with a discussion of what we could expect to find by the tower house, often within the bawn (the enclosing courtyard). Tower house dwellers needed people to work the surrounding land as well as to service the castle itself. It is possible to calculate where these people lived in relation to the tower house, as often it was the centre of rural settlement, especially rural nucleated settlement. Broadening the scope further, chapter 2 then discusses what agriculture was being practised in the vicinity of the tower house. In short, it discusses the economy that supported the tower house at a grassroots level.

Mills bridge the gap between landed interests and the use of water. The evidence presented in chapter 3 is for a strong association between tower houses and mills, which challenges previous views of the Irish economy becoming increasingly pastoral in the wake of the Black Death. Many tower houses are located close to Ireland's major rivers. These same rivers were frequently used as boundaries and borders, which obscures tower house distribution patterns and functionality. By viewing rivers as purely political we overemphasise the defensive role of castles. Instead, rivers were economically productive and valuable. This is particularly true because of their fish, which were elite icons; rivers both provided income and reinforced status. This role was often fulfilled by fishponds elsewhere in Europe, but in Ireland efforts instead concentrated on exploitation of rivers. Marine fishing was also a major source of income, albeit without the status connotations. Several other scholars have previously noted the relationship between tower houses and Ireland's coastlines, but control of maritime resources was even more widespread than heretofore believed.

Water was also the basis of networks. Tower houses that controlled water therefore controlled these networks. Tower houses seized the nodal points within these networks, and operated as navigational aids, supervised ferries and restricted access to bridges and fords. Their control included both water-based and terrestrial communication and transportation routes. These routes bring us to the urban tower houses of chapter 4.

Tower houses had a role as the interface between the rural and the urban. At the same time, many urban tower houses were different to their rural counterparts. In medieval towns, the lines between tower houses and other types of fortification blur – here they were not only lordly residences but the homes and businesses of merchants. They also were not wholly private structures, but had a valuable role within the urban community.

Finally, it is from these port towns that most of Ireland's connections with the wider world were made, particularly in the form of international trade. The historical and archaeological records are limited here, but they hint at a fascinating web that tied Ireland to the rest of the British Isles and beyond, to the European continent. This network was potentially more elaborate than has previously been recognised, and it is argued that connections were sustained by the presence of the tower house.

Note

1 Although McNeill likens tower house design to the late Gothic styles of Irish friaries, and from this derives an earliest-origin date for tower houses in the early fourteenth century (1997).

1

Around the castle wall: The tower house complex and rural settlement

The 'revisionist' approach to castles, starting in the 1970s, has sought to place them within their managed environment. In this way, features such as formal gardens have been identified, and the symbolism of deer parks in particular, but dovecotes, rabbit warrens and artificial fishponds have also been discussed. The relationship of the castle to that other local landscape feature, the dependent settlement, has similarly been of interest (Creighton and Barry, 2012; Murphy and O'Conor, 2006). Arguably, this tradition of an integrated landscape study has a longer history in England than in Ireland. This is in no small part because extensive investigation of the immediate landscape context of tower houses has been hampered by a lack of material evidence. However, there is a significant body of work on different facets of Ireland's rural landscape, including study of medieval rural settlement. O'Conor (1998) has noted that since we see castles today as isolated in the landscape, we tend to lack the imagination to envisage how this was not always the case. Tower houses, too, have a tendency to be regarded as solitary within the landscape, a view assisted by the disappearance of the buildings that undoubtedly stood around many of them. Oram (2010) has gone so far as to say that castle scholars have misconceived these associated buildings as later additions, thus further obscuring the real picture.

Likewise, there is a long history in Ireland of investigation of deserted medieval, or post-medieval, settlements, commonly referred to as 'deserted medieval villages' (DMVs).[1] Newtown Jerpoint, County Kilkenny, is probably the most famous and intensively studied DMV, but notable attention has also been paid to Piperstown in County Louth, Newcastle Lyons in County Dublin and to Rindoon in County Roscommon. An added complexity to the study of rural settlement in Ireland is that we cannot presume that all of it was nucleated. In fact, it is very likely that a significant proportion of the population of medieval Ireland, especially in Gaelic-Irish areas, lived in dispersed settlement. Even in the old Anglo-Norman areas there have been suggestions that Gaelic-Irish tenants lived separately from the main manorial settlement, in so-called betagh settlements on the outskirts of town lands, or in more isolated farmhouses.

Evidence is for a diversity of rural settlement forms neighbouring tower houses. The argument for a nucleating effect of tower houses, even in more sparsely populated Gaelic-Irish areas, is particularly convincing. In fact, the social differences between the Anglo-Irish and the Gaelic-Irish may be overstressed (O'Conor, 1998). That tower houses were constructed and occupied by both ethnicities with minimal (if any) architectural distinctiveness is testament to the tower house's unique role as a settlement form transcending common medieval social signifiers. It also suggests a shared material culture. Here, the tower house parallels the parish church, which is commonly studied in other European and British contexts as a built form transcending other divides (*ibid.*).

We need to view the castle and the landscape and settlement features in its vicinity as interconnected, and that is the approach of this chapter in examining the rural landscape elements surrounding the tower house. It broadens this territorial scope in stages, starting with the buildings we might find next to the tower itself, as components of a larger complex. Each tower house will have drawn from a personal hinterland; and in rural Ireland most likely from peasants or farmers toiling the land for their lord. Therefore, we can use the tower house as a starting point for uncovering ordinary people, and to study the socio-economics that nurtured it.

No solitary tower: The immediate castle complex

The small size of many tower houses combined with the varied social status of their inhabitants has led to the suggestion that the stone tower was merely the centre of a much larger complex, with not all functions housed within the tower (Creighton and Barry, 2012; O'Conor, 1998; Oram, 2010; Tabraham, 1997). The cabins recorded in such sources as the *Civil survey* probably resembled the small, rounded and windowless structures depicted by Richard Bartlett in *Bird's-eye view of Armagh city*; *Map of the fort at Mountnorris*, between Armagh and Newry; and the *Rath at Tullaghoge with the nearby stone inaugural chair of the O'Neills* (NLI, MS 2656). Some evidence for buildings has come from excavation, and new non-invasive techniques are revolutionising our comprehension of what lay around the castle. Two case studies illustrating some of the methodology are employed: Ardmayle and Ballynahinch, both in County Tipperary. Combining this information with historical sources, we can achieve greater knowledge of the activities taking place in proximity to tower houses.

Preservation is a major problem though, as ancillary buildings were often constructed of impermanent materials. Based on his study of tower house halls, Sherlock comments that 'the free-standing hall was a "soft building", in the sense that it was constructed of materials other than stone and slate and it is important to acknowledge that physical evidence for such structures may be found only, if at all, through excavation' (Sherlock, 2015: 105). Constructions made of impermanent and organic materials – such as peasant housing or buildings of secondary importance to the masonry tower house – frequently do not survive in the archaeological record. The contemporary historical and cartographical record for Ireland is similarly lacking in precise details. In terms of documentary evidence, aside from a few notable writers, such as Luke Gernon, Richard Stanihurst and the Gaelic bardic poets, the appearance of castles and the impression they made on those who saw them are little discussed (Barry, 2006). As a useful visual source concerning dependent settlement at castles, however, we have early modern campaign maps from English military actions in Ireland, the best known and most useful of these drawn by Bartlett.

Evidence provided by excavation is often lacking. Barryscourt Castle in County Cork is one of the very few tower houses that has had the area within its bawn excavated. The results suggested that the tower house and an associated kitchen building were constructed at the same time. A further building located against the bawn wall was interpreted as a gallery or hall, and there may have been an enclosed garden. The excavation did not seek to uncover the whole bawn area, so the finds are incomplete. Of interest, however, is the presumption by the excavators that most of the enclosure was occupied by farm buildings (Pollock, 2004). Excavations at Kilcolman Castle, County Cork, again targeted a limited area of the bawn, but tentative conclusions were drawn about its use, including that it had housed cattle (Klingelhofer, 2010). Buildings in the southern part of the bawn were identified, suggested to be a great hall, parlour, kitchen and other service buildings (*ibid.*). Comparative evidence from tower house excavations in Scotland does not provide much additional data. For example, excavations at Threave Castle in southwest Scotland only uncovered two additional buildings. One of these was interpreted as a hall, while the other structure as providing additional lodging and a chapel. As at Barryscourt, there were probably other ancillary buildings not exposed (Tabraham, 1997, 1998). Halls, kitchen blocks with service roles (for example, bakehouses and brewhouses) and chapels are the buildings most commonly found in association with tower houses in Scotland (Oram, 2011). As in Ireland, the limits of excavation mean these results are tentative, necessitating scholars of Scottish settlement to use interdisciplinary methods to recreate what once stood at the isolated towers (Oram, 2010). Another restriction is that determining function based solely on building foundations is very problematic, as use is often ascribed based on only scale, dimension and orientation (Oram, 2011; Tabraham, 1998).

Identification has furthermore been hampered by the low resolution of aerial imaging at many tower house sites, while lidar and three-dimensional imaging remain prohibitively expensive. An alternative is the digital elevation models (DEMs) that can be generated from drone-based survey. Two sites surveyed have returned potentially exciting results. Drone surveys were completed in winter 2017 at Ballynahinch and Ardmayle. Both sites have historical documentation attesting to the existence of burgesses in the same townland as the tower house. Ardmayle (figure 1.1) is described by Glasscock in his gazetteer of deserted Anglo-Norman settlement sites as being a small settlement outside Cashel on the east side of the Suir River, with the remains of a motte and medieval church. He even went so far as to describe it as the 'perfect river-side site for Norman burgage settlement' (Glasscock, 1971: 295). Ardmayle motte is located around two hundred metres north of the tower house, with a medieval parish church across the modern road from the tower house. In 1212 it was documented as having a recently constructed mill, granary, ditches and bridge (Davies and Quinn, 1941; Hennessy, 1996).

In 1305, probably before the tower house was built, Ardmayle was valued at over £34, making it at a minimum an important manor and borough (Hennessy, 1988, 1996). This 1305 extent, enumerating the assets of the landholding, states that there were burgesses who paid £17 3s. 3d. for their land, as well as two mills with fishing weir (*gurgitibus*), a town oven and a warren (*Red book of Ormond*). The surviving extent for Ardmayle records that the motte castle was located beside the 'curia', or the buildings comprising the manorial centre, the buildings serving partly residential and partly agricultural purposes (Murphy, 2015). Next to the curia was the garden, which may have been more akin to an orchard as the terms were used interchangeably (*ibid.*). An inquisition taken in 1338 states that there were no buildings in the manor and only a handful of free tenants and burgesses. The only features generating any revenue were a dovecote, a rabbit warren and a leased-out fish weir, as two water mills with fisheries were in disrepair (*Inquisitions and extents*). In total, the manor was valued at £20 15s. 3d., showing that it had declined considerably over the opening decades of the fourteenth century. That the tower house was later constructed suggests that some prosperity returned after the difficulties of that century, as by the time

1.1 Ardmayle Castle, County Tipperary, is located in a shrunken settlement complex, along with a medieval parish church and motte castle. It has been the subject of drone-based investigations.

of the *Civil survey* it is recorded as a 'good' castle with several other small cabins (*Civil survey*: vol. 1).

The agricultural area by the castle was often referred to as a 'haggard', and could have been used for grain storage in lieu of a granary building. Many haggards were surrounded by ditches or walls and could be sizeable areas, potentially even larger than the rest of the curia (Murphy, 2015). Based on such documentary references, such an enclosure could, from an archaeological perspective, physically resemble a bailey, bawn or moated site, which complicates the identification of features based on fieldwork. One is described at Caherconlish in County Limerick, where houses were located on both sides of the enclosing ditches (*ibid.*).

If we compare the DEM-identified patterns at Ardmayle (see figure 1.2) to Lisronagh in County Tipperary, then some conclusions might be drawn. At Lisronagh there is also a medieval parish church around one hundred metres to the north of a ringwork, and there is a tower house of presumably later date in the settlement. It is a small crossroads settlement (Glasscock, 1971). Lisronagh resembles Ardmayle in that earthworks potentially reflecting a DMV have been recorded adjacent to the tower house. In 1333 around forty-eight burgesses lived across six settlements within about a mile of the castle (Frame, 2012; Glasscock, 1971). Together, these may indicate that agricultural and other manorial buildings were located within the earlier castle complex, and peasant settlement is instead more associated with the later tower houses. Whether the tower house acted as a nucleating impetus or was deliberately constructed close to continued peasant settlement is moot. At Lisronagh, as at Ardmayle, we have written record of a haggard with stone-walled grange (*grangia*), a garden, a 'Park' and rabbit warrens (Curtis, 1935–37).

A manorial function might be tentatively assigned to the 'enclosure' listed in the ASI at Ardmayle. This archaeological feature is a raised circular area with enclosing bank, roughly 330 metres to the southwest of the motte and 225 metres to the northwest of the tower house. Although it is today tree covered, it appears to be mostly flat in the interior. As it is covered in vegetation, it was not surveyed by drone, but we can see in figure 1.2 that the area surrounding it (in the top-left corner) has less evidence for manmade alteration compared with the vicinity of the tower house. Manorial buildings therefore may have been located within the enclosure, rather than around it, as evidenced by the written documentation.

The tower house at Ballynahinch (see figure 1.3) is also listed with its isolated medieval church, and has earthworks around it shown in some detail in the first-edition OS mapping from 1840–41. These earthworks can be confirmed by aerial photographs (see Cambridge University Collection of Aerial Photography (hereafter CUCAP)), and

1.2 DEM of Ardmayle, depicting the features identified through drone-based aerial imaging. The tower house is the small raised square to the centre right, the church and graveyard are the raised area and geometric shape in the centre. The semicircular raised area at the top-left corner is the enclosure.

1.3 Ballynahinch Castle, County Tipperary, is a tower house with bawn, located on the River Suir. Like Ardmayle Castle, it was the subject of drone-based aerial analysis.

Glasscock has interpreted them as a 'complex of massive stone-cored banks and structures especially south and east of the castle' (1971: 296). One of the aerial photographs shows three regularly spaced plots adjacent to the castle (CUCAP, APD025). The regularity is suggestive of burgess plots, although it might also reflect a designed feature like an orchard owing to the overlap with the castle bawn. Ballynahinch therefore contains earthwork remains adjacent to the tower house, whereas Ardmayle shows no above-ground remnants, such remains as there are only visible after DEM analysis (see figures 1.2 and 1.4). However, Ardmayle is better documented, enabling comparison of the historical and archaeological records. If we can apply the historical record to state that the activity by the tower house is potentially not from agricultural structures, then this may be the site of peasant housing.

It is probable that the traces we can see above ground today (such as at Ballynahinch Castle in County Tipperary) are stone foundations. However, timber was used extensively as a building material in the Middle Ages. This included in high status buildings. Modern scholars perhaps have not been accepting of the possibility that high-status structures could have been constructed of organic materials. This perception probably originates in the early-modern-period English commentators

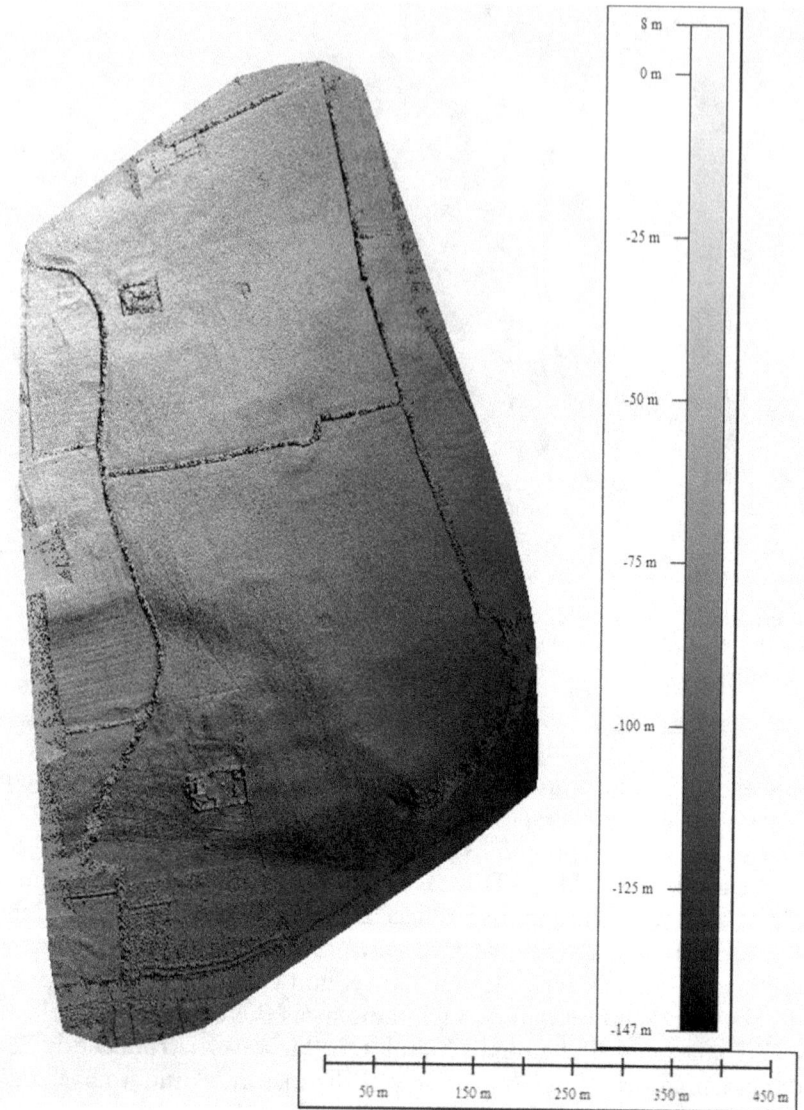

1.4 The DEM for Ballynahinch Castle depicts the tower house and bawn, alongside other features discussed in the text. The tower house is on the left-hand side of the rectangular bawn, towards the bottom of the image. Other buildings are visible within the bawn. The River Suir lies at the very bottom of the image, with a visible bank. The medieval parish church and graveyard are visible as a rectangle towards the top of the image.

whose writings dominate the surviving written material, and who often viewed Irish building techniques as barbarous. Not only could castles be constructed of timber (hence mottes and ringworks), but timber could also make up significant parts of masonry castles and entire high-status residences could be constructed of it (Oram, 2010). Nevertheless, stone footings might be used in mud buildings such as the thirteenth-century houses at Jerpointchurch in County Kilkenny (about three hundred metres distant from the DMV of Newtown Jerpoint). All of this could explain why some features show up on DEM while others do not (Foley, 1989).

One of the few features still surviving in the modern landscape that undoubtedly formed a part of the castle complex is the bawn wall. Ballynahinch has a masonry bawn with circular corner turret standing (see figure 1.3), but there is no evidence for one at Ardmayle tower house. This reflects the likelihood that more bawns existed historically than stand today. But McNeill has estimated that only around twenty per cent of tower houses had a bawn, a figure that Barry's study of Limerick tower houses has supported (Barry, 2006; McNeill, 1997). A further complication is that a bawn wall need not have been built out of stone. Seventeenth-century references by Nicholas Pynnar are to bawns made out of sods (Ó Danachair, 1969). In this instance, we are unlikely to find any archaeological remnants of this construction material, even less than we are ditches, cruck construction or ground-set timber. Bawns that are now no longer standing are sometimes identifiable from aerial photography. A good example of this comes from Anbally Castle in County Galway. This tower house looks to have remains of large bawn-type enclosures: as well as a smaller stone-walled bawn, oblique photographs show two other enclosures, one of which is surrounded by a prominent fosse and bank (CUCAP, ATF013).

Probably the building most discussed in tandem with tower houses is the external hall. Leaving aside the debate of internal versus external hall and whether the two could co-exist, there is much evidence for halls close to, but still external to, the castle. The list of tower houses with documented references to these halls is comparatively extensive. O'Keeffe (2015) notes that there was a hall in 1568 at Dysert O'Dea Castle in County Clare for which there is no visible evidence above ground today. This hall building may not have housed solely the hall: Desmond Castle in Castleisland, County Kerry, had a hall with adjoining parlour, with two chambers above it and a dining chamber. In addition, this site had a chapel with attached tower and other lodgings. Both it and Mallow Castle in County Cork had vaults used for storage of food and other items. In the case of Mallow these vaults connected the external hall to the tower house (*ibid.*). The Anglo-Norman Trim Castle, County

Meath, has a later two-storey hall with a basement at river level to assist with food supply and storage.

While we do not have physical remains standing to full height, we do have some contemporary descriptions of the appearance of such halls. The best-known description is by writer Richard Stanihurst, who described a hall constructed of 'white clay and mud' where banquets would be held, from where the tower house owners would retire to their tower to sleep. In contrast, Ludolf von Munchhausen describes people sleeping in the hall and using the tower for refuge, while Luke Gernon also wrote that people slept in the hall. William Camden notes the halls he saw as being made of turf with thatched roofs (O'Keeffe, 2000a, 2015). Although the minutiae differ in these late-sixteenth- and early-seventeenth-century accounts, it is clear that the external hall served a communal function particularly surrounding hospitality and eating, whereas the tower proper was a more private space. Such halls could also serve an administrative function (O'Conor, 1998), as suggested by the documentary references to court barons and court leets, and by the need for tenants to pay rents to their lord.

The contemporary descriptions also remind us that while these buildings were obviously integral to the successful functioning of the tower house in its contemporary use, they did not have to be built of stone as the tower was. We therefore return to the problem elaborated above – identifying organic building materials. Some scholars have stated that while we have the most frequent documentary references to external halls, there probably were many other such timber or clay-walled buildings serving other functions clustered around castles (*ibid.*). External stone buildings in fact only exist in a very small number of cases, such as Audley's Castle in County Down, Taaffe's Castle in County Louth and Aughnanure in County Galway (see figure 1.5). In the case of the former two, this author has argued for them as warehouses. Since the rectangular building at Audley's Castle does not survive above ground level, we lack dateable features. Consequently it is possible that the building was a later construction. Fraine, County Meath, is located outside the market town of Athboy near the Westmeath county border. As well as a ruined tower house, there are the clear foundations of a rectangular structure – the outline of a building (with external dimensions of 21.8 by 9.5 metres) – visible through fieldwalking and aerial imaging. A bawn is indicated by remnants of a bank and ditch. This hall is sizeable when compared with the small tower house, and is only around 9 metres from the upstanding tower house walls, suggesting they had a close relationship. Fraine was located within the Pale border area, and therefore shows that non-military concerns were as important to people living in contested areas as they were to those in more stable regions.

1.5 Aughnanure Castle, County Galway, has a partially standing external masonry hall. This is located to the rear centre and left of the photograph. It has highly decorative window inlays on the inside, and the double-headed ogee of the external face of one window is visible. The small circular building to the centre front of the photograph is a dovecote, converted from a bawn corner turret.

An interesting example of a stand-alone hall associated with a tower house comes from Rathmore, County Meath (see figure 1.6). The tower house here was built into to an earlier motte castle. The tower house builder then had the motte reshaped into a quadrilateral. This provided a raised platform for a rectangular building. Presumably, considering its proximity to the tower, this created a raised hall. Not only would this have given impressive views towards the medieval parish church around three hundred metres to the southwest, but it also would have made a social statement in its reuse of an Anglo-Norman castle. It is unfortunate that we cannot identify the tower house builder to uncover more of this story.

A partially upstanding hall survives at Aughnanure in County Galway (see figure 1.5), sited overlooking the river – as does the one at Trim Castle – which would have provided bucolic views and assisted with access and provisioning. Unfortunately the river undermined the building, leading to its partial collapse. The windows on two levels in the hall indicate there was a hall and service area at ground level and a chamber or gallery above, as in the tripartite plans of English halls (Sherlock, 2015). Fine windows survive in the upstanding wall, which look into the bawn, suggesting that they mirrored possibly even finer ones on the river side. The hall is close to the tower house, located between the

1.6 Rathmore Castle, County Meath, is a ruined tower house built into an earlier motte castle. Fieldwork has indicated that the motte was reshaped to provide a solid foundation for an external hall, which may have been accessible directly from the tower house through connecting doorways.

earlier inner bawn and the outer one. A dovecote stands within this bawn, adapted from what was originally a corner tower in the first incarnation of the bawn (Naessens, 2015). This would have added extra symbolic weight, visually reinforcing lordly identity, to the eyes of anyone proceeding between the tower house and the stand-alone hall.

We might also expect to find accommodation for servants and soldiers at, or very close to, a tower house. Logically, these were the people required for the day-to-day running of the place, and it is unlikely that they were housed inside a high-status tower. It is possible that lords billeted builders and soldiers on their tenants to cut down on their personal expenses, and this could explain a dearth of barrack-like accommodation within castle complexes (O'Keeffe, 2015).

A further, yet fascinating, complication arises once we start to ponder who lived in the bawn. We might immediately guess at a castle guard, but Nicholls has consulted legal documents that indicate another scenario. He cites a law case from Ballycapple in County Tipperary from 1584, where it was decided that the richest of the sept should have sole use of the castle 'and the little bawn and the use of the great bawn as well, which however he must share with any other coheir who might wish to occupy his proportionate share of it and erect buildings on it; if he did not build, the share was left at the disposal of the senior. Every person so building must pay the senior a goat and half a sheep yearly', alongside a day's work from each householder residing in this bawn. A clause was included which gave the senior (which Nicholls equates to richest) the most grazing nearest to the castle (Nicholls, 1985: 95).

This legal action may be unusual, but if it actually reflects Irish society and the use of castle complexes then this adds a further dynamic to our search for associated buildings. It also indicates that we might need to be aware of other higher-status people around the castle walls, who may have had agency when it came to landscape considerations. We cannot presume that those resident in the environs of tower houses were automatically lower-status dependents. We may have to seek subtle signs of such higher-status occupation in the castle complex. For instance, Baker's excavations of Killeen Castle in County Meath found a silver penny from the York episcopal mint and a door key in earth-cut structures located near the tower house. The presence of local pottery led her to conclude that this structure was agricultural in nature, for crop processing or animal corralling, but the wealth indicated by the two metal finds does serve as a warning when ascribing status to uncovered structures (Baker, 2009).

The historical documentation can be more insightful than the archaeological evidence, though it varies hugely depending on the manuscript collection. For example, the Ormond papers contain estate documents, but only some of these mention what buildings were present on their lands, including at castle complexes, depending on whether they would have affected their value. An account of Rathvilly, County Carlow, lists a hall, kitchen, orchard and haggard at the castle, with a village in the demesne (NLI, MS 11,053/2A). Rathvilly is listed in the ASI as an unclassified castle, but its documented occupation into the early modern period implies a tower house once stood on the site. Unfortunately referring to an Anglo-Norman masonry castle and not a tower house, a 1566 survey of Dungarvan, County Waterford, details a curia by the castle where there were a large hall, four rooms (*camerae*), three cellars, and near the castle other houses as well as what might be a large stable (NLI, MS 43,308/1, 'Mr Michaell fitz Williams the generall surveyhor of Ireland his surveye of the mannor of Dongarban in 1566').

Less detail on surrounding buildings comes from the Lismore Castle papers and the Leinster manuscripts, which instead focus on land use and natural resources. Probably the most useful information therefore comes from the manorial extents. These extents tend to date from the period preceding the tower house, but several of the sites with manorial buildings discussed by Murphy continued in use into the later medieval period, as attested to by the presence of tower houses. Overall, ninety-eight places are mentioned within the manorial accounts in conjunction with buildings (Murphy, 2015). Unfortunately the geographic distribution of these places is clustered in certain parts of the country, particularly counties Dublin, Kildare, Carlow, Kilkenny, Tipperary and Limerick (*ibid.*). The external hall is often the first building to be elucidated and is mentioned in thirty-seven of seventy-eight extents. A slight majority of the halls were masonry, but there were still a significant number of timber ones, with the description of the hall at Castleisland in County Kerry indicating cruck construction. Other common structures include kitchens, bakehouses and larders. Computing the instances involved, Murphy concluded that halls, chambers and kitchens were 'basic features' (*ibid.*).

While we hunt for associated buildings in the immediate surrounds of tower houses, we need to remember that other structures could also be located by them. Gardens were both visually appealing and practical (Oram, 2010). In Lyttleton's and Herron's reconstructions of Kilcolman Castle, the tower house occupied by the poet Edmund Spenser, they have included pleasure and herb/kitchen gardens, suggested by excavation as being located in the northern section of the bawn (*Centering Spenser*; Klingelhofer, 2010).[2] Perhaps the best solution in the long term for secure identification of gardens at castle sites is through pollen analysis as part of excavation.

Gardens and orchards are recorded numerously in a range of sources, including the *Desmond survey* and the *Civil survey*. Orchards are among the most numerous features recorded in proximity to tower houses in the *Civil survey* – for instance, ten out of thirty-eight conclusively identified tower houses in County Limerick record orchards. Dovecotes were sometimes within this area, too, as at Dowth in County Meath, which had a garden and dovecote and became the site of a tower house and medieval parish church (Murphy, 2009, 2015). Aughnanure Castle has a well-preserved stone dovecote within the bawn. Despite the fact that grain could be contained within a bawn, there is a much higher recorded instance of grain-storage buildings compared with English manorial extents.[3] Hay and wool were apparently stored in 'granges' as well (Murphy, 2015). However, tower houses may not have needed these since their ground floors could be used for grain storage if we compare tower house dimensions to grange and *hospitia* space (*ibid.*).

Perhaps one significant reason for the quietness of the digital models produced is the ephemeral appearance of many of these manorial buildings. The documents Murphy consulted refer to the need for maintenance, and rapid deterioration if this was lacking. Despite these references, the accounts also signify that cruck construction methods may have been employed, and that the buildings could have been sizeable – ranging from 32 by 4.6 metres to 41.1 by 4.6 metres – and were used chronologically much later than their English counterparts (*ibid.*). Recent evidence from English studies demonstrates that cruck buildings were much sturdier and had greater longevity than first thought (Gardiner, 2000, 2014). Ground-set timber buildings (where timbers were placed directly on the ground) became popular since their positioning completely above the ground ensured that decay could be easily treated (Gardiner, 2014). The latter will not be identified using remote survey methods.

In addition to archaeological, technological and written documentary sources for the rural features surrounding tower houses and castles, we have visual sources. In particular, the cartography of Richard Bartlett, created during the early modern Elizabethan wars, depicts buildings around tower houses. Most of these buildings are small in size compared with the tower house, meaning that they could have been the homes of the peasantry (Ó Danachair, 1969). A number of these have chimneys depicted, a sign of residential function, but those lacking a chimney could equally have been agricultural buildings like those described in the manorial accounts. Other houses Bartlett draws are larger in size, and sometimes of two storeys' height, which might indicate the homes of more important tenants or minor gentry, or they could have been barracks (*ibid.*). That the more junior members of the extended family could be the ones occupying larger houses within the bawn is suggested by the legal case cited by Nicholls. Again, the presence of chimneys may or may not rule out the use of the larger buildings, such as three shown at Augher fort in County Tyrone, as external halls. Chimneys might have been needed if cooking or food preparation were undertaken within the hall in an era when open hearths had gone out of use. In all Bartlett's depictions, these buildings located by the tower house are made of organic materials. They look as though they might have been constructed of wattle and daub, and have thatched roofs.

Other accounts of buildings around castles record more diverse examples in or near the castle complex. Although earlier in date and therefore not at a tower house, the *Red book of Ormond* lists a wooden chapel, kitchen, fish house, stables and malt kiln in 1303 at Inch, County Tipperary (O'Conor, 1998, 2004). Other features such as mills, rabbit warrens and gardens are listed in the *Red book of Ormond*, though they may have been located slightly further away from the castle than these agricultural buildings (O'Conor, 1998). The documentary sources imply that buildings located within a castle complex tended to be manorial buildings. However, more intensive use is potentially reflected through the archaeology. It is possible that tower houses were more associated with peasant rural settlement than agricultural buildings.

Settlement nucleation and the rural borough debate

Identifying buildings outside of the bawn, including associated rural settlement, has proved even more difficult. In contrast to the English evidence, often few earthworks survive above ground in the modern Irish landscape that would assist with rural settlement identification, although technologies such as lidar will hopefully advance our knowledge of what lies below ground in the coming years (O'Conor, 2004). Comparison of settlement evidence for Irish vernacular building practices suggests that it may not be possible to identify these buildings through excavation (O'Conor, 1998). Some native Irish buildings were constructed of wood and mud, with the construction technology often using interwoven branches to make buildings with a rounded appearance (Barry, 2006), as depicted in Bartlett's maps (NLI, MS 2656); a useful and brief summary of the building evidence of Irish vernacular housing from excavation has been provided by Horning (Horning, 2001). While these huts could be built in a matter of hours, the precise techniques are uncertain; but the likelihood is that neither postholes nor beamholes were necessary for support and so little evidence will survive below ground (O'Conor, 2001). This conclusion stands in contrast to results reached in studies of English peasant housing, which have found that buildings previously considered to be impermanent and unsubstantial could, in fact, be maintained over long periods of time (Dyer, 2000; Dyer and Everson, 2012; Grenville, 1997). Although Bartlett was depicting the province of Ulster in the early seventeenth century, O'Conor (2001) argues that there is evidence for the building form centuries earlier than this and from across the country.

We find more evidence for such structures in later documentary sources, such as the *Civil survey*, than we do through excavation. Luke Gernon describes such buildings as follows: 'The baser cottages are built of underwood, called wattle, and covered some with thatch and some with green sedge, of a round forme and without chimneys, and to my imagination resemble so many hives of bees, about a country farme' (Gernon: 355). The *Civil survey*, an inquisition into mid-seventeenth-century landholdings, originally covered most of the country, but today the records for only some counties survive, as the originals were destroyed by fire in 1711. As it forms the earliest settlement survey for much of Ireland, it is the source most often used to identify settlement, and it probably does reflect continuity from the Middle Ages (Barry, 2006; Murphy, 2009). For each local land area, the survey records features such as castles and other buildings, as well as land use. The survey therefore lists buildings associated with tower houses, including dining halls, kitchens, granaries, storehouses, brewhouses, stables and guard accommodation (as suggested by examination of the County Meath survey; vol. 5). The *Civil survey* also often notes if there were cottages and houses associated with castles. It is quite unusual among sources in offering this level of detail: by contrast, for example, the sixteenth-century rentals of the Ormond estates in southeast Ireland list the names of lands and their value, but only very occasionally is any more specific feature mentioned (NLI, MSS 2506–10). The feature most frequently encountered in the Ormond Rentals is a water mill.

The tower house occupants needed people to work their agricultural lands, so at a minimum we might expect to find the 'famuli', or the core group of essential farm workers, living somewhere near the lands they toiled and, by extension, near the tower house. These numbered ten individuals on average, though more and fewer have been recorded, and they received wages and maintenance for their work (Down, 1987). Luckily, the issue of rural settlement is a well-trodden one. Two of the central debates have been the differences in rural settlement patterns between Anglo-Irish/Anglo-Norman and Gaelic-Irish regions of Ireland, and the extent to which nucleated rural settlement, provoked by manorialism, existed on the ground.

One of the most evocative images of medieval rural settlement is that of the DMV. When searching the ASI database, the category of 'Settlement deserted – medieval' returns 327 results, but the evidence accumulated through this study shows that this figure can be revised much higher. It excludes sites like Ardmayle, where there are few earthwork remnants of settlement but where more intensive imaging and documentary investigation reflects historical activity at the site. The paucity of surviving written evidence, combined with a general lack of above-ground earthwork remnants (which might be the consequence of shorter-term occupation), has long meant that DMVs in Ireland are difficult to identify. A further constraint is the level of settlement dispersion in Ireland, as dispersed settlement is even more elusive. For more-nucleated medieval settlement, examining the proximity of medieval parish churches to tower houses can give us a good indication of rural settlement patterns.

Tower houses acted as rural settlement nucleation points. This function has been noted from a range of contexts, including in the marches/frontier between the Gaelic-Irish and the Anglo-Irish (Ellis, 2015), where tower houses might have offered protection, an attractive feature in times of instability (Graham, 1975), as well as in areas of the Pale that experienced Anglo-Norman colonisation. Based on analysis of Gaelic-Irish bardic poetry, Budd concluded that tower houses were the focal point of their communities; however, this means as a social focus rather than a physical community centre (Barry, 2006; Budd, 2004). The role of the manor has long been associated with rural settlement, although the exact appearance of such settlement is debated. The legacy of the manor was the possession of a borough, with the larger lands tending to be associated with a town (Empey, 1985). These manors usually overlapped with the medieval parish, hence the frequent association with churches, and were mainly adaptations from earlier native Irish boundaries and settlements (Otway-Ruthven, 1965; Simms, 1988a). Tower houses in many cases represent continuity of earlier manorial settlement functions. While manors are best associated with the Anglo-Normans, who from the late twelfth century brought the manorial system to Ireland, the system was also used by other groups. Indeed, manors served as useful colonisation tools for the English and Scottish coming to Ireland during the sixteenth and seventeenth centuries (Shanahan, 2005).

One of the defining aspects of medieval Irish rural settlement is the rural borough. Rural boroughs were akin to English medieval villages, but unlike the English villagers the inhabitants of Irish rural boroughs had the increased legal rights of burgesses, usually reserved for freeholding urbanites. The reasoning behind this special legal status was to attract English settlers to Ireland to new estates, the incentive being social advancement (Barry, 1996; Graham, 1975; Otway-Ruthven, 1965). Despite the legal standing of the residents, it is likely that most of these places never became truly urban (towns), instead they were probably mainly agricultural in outlook. In places like Meath, we can see from the *Civil survey* that overall settlement remained nucleated in pattern by the early modern period (Graham, 1975). The burgesses, although holding service and craft occupations in a European context, may have been solely or mainly cultivators in Ireland, or worked in related areas like milling or brewing (Graham, 1988a, b).

As there is documentary reference to burgesses it is presumed that the rural boroughs were nucleated settlements in most instances, especially in scenarios where the castle and church stand close together. This has led several scholars to propose that where castle and church stand together in isolation, this probably represents deserted manorial settlements for which we have no documentation. This would have the effect of increasing the recognised number of deserted settlements from the Middle Ages, although it should be borne in mind that a significant proportion of the medieval churches may well have originally stood in isolation (Glasscock, 1970; Graham, 1975, 1993). In addition to these sites where only those two buildings remain, there are what have been termed 'shrunken rural boroughs', where a few houses still stand today in the vicinity of castles and/or churches (Glasscock, 1970). Many tower houses fall into this latter category, suggesting that the number of rural settlements at tower houses is far higher than we have documentary evidence for. Indeed, using the presence of church and castle as an indicator of past rural settlement is very likely still underestimating the number of nucleated-type settlements from medieval Ireland. On the other hand, even in agriculturally fertile parts of the country where we might expect a higher population, there is often not a church in tandem with a castle. This scenario applies to much of the western half of the country, where there are much lower incidences of a medieval castle and church together. It is highly unlikely that religious adherence was any less in the west of the country; instead there must have been different settlement patterns at play.

The castle played a strong role in organising settlement nucleation in Ireland. Several scholars have attempted to provide numbers for this trend, such as Graham's finding (1993) that almost seventy per cent of the borough sites he considered had developed around a castellated core. At the urbanised end of the scale, almost all the Anglo-Norman towns originated as seigneurial centres with castles at their core (Bradley, 1995). This correlation is also strong with rural boroughs, which Graham describes as 'rural-castle-boroughs' (1988a: 28). Smyth (1985) takes this correlation even further, arguing that castles had a major impact on settlement concentration, especially when acting in conjunction with a parish centre (identified as a church, graveyard and glebeland), but also with a mill. His analysis echoes Graham's findings, stating that almost half of the settlements in County Tipperary 'pivoted' around a tower house and, in many cases, a mill was also present. He termed the settlements around these tower houses 'castle villages' with populations of around one hundred people. Although small, these may not have been just agricultural agglomerations, as a sizeable minority of around a third of the total sites had a population engaged in artisanal activities (*ibid.*). Peasants who lived in rural boroughs had some connection to a cash economy, which marked them out from those living more dispersed lifestyles with limited contacts for goods exchange (Graham, 1993). The tower house was therefore more encouraging of settlement nucleation than a church centre, but weaker than a manorial parish centre (the combined setup of castle, church and mill) (Smyth, 1985).

Within the *Civil survey*, the feature most commonly recorded alongside a tower house is a small settlement of some description. For example, nineteen out of twenty-nine conclusively identified tower houses within the western and northern baronies of County Tipperary had this association (*Civil survey*, vol. 2). In contrast, only two of these tower houses were located by a church and only three by a mill; instead, orchards or gardens were the second most frequent feature, with five recorded. Almost the same patterns can be identified in County Limerick:

settlement (taken as more than two residential-type buildings separate from the tower house) was the most commonly encountered feature recorded near tower houses, with sixteen references out of thirty-eight conclusively identified tower houses (*Civil survey*, vol. 4). In County Limerick, mills are often found in the same townland as a tower house. This led O'Connor to argue that tower houses were not independently capable of acting as nucleation points, but did so in conjunction with other features, especially mills and rivers (cited in MacCurtain, 1988). The building of mills was apparently a priority, to solidify arable cultivation and thus increase land income (Hennessy, 1996).

The urban–rural divide is important to bear in mind, as not all boroughs ever became towns; in fact, most of them stayed inherently rural in nature. It has been estimated that of around three hundred boroughs established in Ireland, only sixty or so developed into towns proper (Bradley, 1999). In this, a part was probably played by their origins: royal permission was not needed to create a borough in Ireland until the fifteenth century, and this meant that even minor landlords created them in the hopes of attracting tenants (Graham, 1975; Otway-Ruthven, 1965). On the other hand, in the Middle Ages urban areas bore more resemblance to the countryside than they do today. Even in a significant medieval town like Kilkenny city there was agriculture on a small scale, and we have evidence for fishermen living within the town confines. The difference may be in the extent – the fishermen also traded in the town, and there was probably a wider craft base than in the rural boroughs (Bradley, 1999).

Settlement dispersion, or, where were medieval people living?

Who lived in these rural settlements is another issue. Fourteenth-century manorial extents indicate that the social hierarchy descended from freeholders, free tenants or socage (a free but non-military tenure) holders, to farmers or customary tenants, to cottiers or poor tenants, who were the ones owing labour services (Murphy and Potterton, 2010; Simms, 1983). There was also the peculiarly Irish class of gaviller – akin to tenants at will of the lord, though they were personally free and their lands in reality were hereditary (Otway-Ruthven, 1951). Being free tenants meant they could appeal to the royal court over their lord's authority to assert their rights (Hennessy, 1996). There was also the native Irish betagh, who held land in common and also owed the lord labour services (Simms, 1983). Although lowly in status, they need not have been at the very bottom of the social scale as their landholdings could be quite extensive (Murphy and Potterton, 2010). Below the betagh was the cottar or cottager, who was free but had very small landholdings (*ibid.*). Lordly demesnes were cultivated by such unfree tenants as well as hired workers, as immigration from England will have been in comparatively small numbers, thus necessitating Irish tenants to remain on the land (Empey, 1981). Overall, labour duties remained lighter than what was owed in England, another incentive to move to Ireland. Burgesses sometimes rendered services, but monetary payment became increasingly common (Down, 1987).

Those living at the manor or borough had their open fields and grazing beyond the settlement (O'Conor, 1998). The free tenants, the most senior on this scale, may not have lived at the manorial centre, but rather in townlands near to the larger units of their landholding. Fascinating for this study is Simms's suggestion that this explains the location of some castles (Simms, 1983, 1988b), and certainly tower houses were within the financial reach of these wealthier free tenants. Within the Dublin region, free tenants' holdings could be up to around five hundred acres (Murphy and Potterton, 2010). This might explain the startlingly high density of tower houses in places like County Kildare, where there are multiple examples in each parish by the time of the *Civil survey*. Murphy writes about social emulation by free tenants of their lords (Murphy, 2015), and it is very possible that this included building styles as well as smaller goods consumption.

Smyth argues for a redistribution of the population in the later Middle Ages and early years of the early modern period, describing people moving from dispersed settlement to nucleated settlement around a tower house as 'refugees' (1985: 126). Presumably, the comparative security of the tower house was an attractive prospect and would explain the continuation of nucleated settlement after the demographic collapse of the Black Death, if the people previously living in dispersed patterns migrated. In conclusion, this may represent nucleated settlement even in a period of low population levels.

The dispersed settlement of free tenants could be part of the reorganisation of populations following the Black Death. The lower-status tenants would meanwhile have lived in nucleated settlement at the manor centre (Murphy, 2009). Others have found free tenants of English descent closer to the castle, and instead state that the betaghs were living in other townlands away from the centre. Betaghs farmed in common using an infield-outfield system rather than the typical manorial practice of three-field crop rotation, and travelled to the lord to perform labour services (Curtis, 1935–37; O'Conor, 1998). The mid-fourteenth-century documents for the manor of Nenagh, County Tipperary, indicate that the native Irish tenants held the lands closest to the manor centre (Gleeson and Leask, 1936). This potentially contradictory information suggests that there was diversity in the make-up of individual rural settlements.

While manorial settlement has been discussed thus far, it is important to remember that this was an imported system, imposed upon pre-existing land tenure. To some degree, in most regions of Ireland, a melding between the Anglo-Norman and Irish systems occurred. Simms has taken this to mean that the native tenure prevented centralised settlements from forming at manors, and so the 'manorial villages' described above were more like administrative centres (Simms, 1983). There is still an association between such manorial villages and tower houses (Graham, 1974). Connacht is usually cited as the best example of this, where castles represent a class of people who merely 'inserted' themselves above the native population and had this population work for them (Frame, 2012). The upshot of this merging is that manorial villages could have existed at the same time as dispersed rural settlement, the village just being much smaller in size than its British and continental equivalents.

An excellent example testifying to the continued usefulness of excavation comes from Mullamast in County Kildare, where a large late medieval deserted village was uncovered only during road construction. Even with excavation, the 'castle' mentioned in the seventeenth century as being there has still not been located (Rubicon Heritage, 2011).

A lack of earthwork remains above ground might be indicative of widespread settlement shrinkage following the Black Death. Elsewhere in Europe, most settlement desertion appears to have taken place after the demographic collapse of the Black Death, yet it has frequently been convincingly argued that this theory cannot be applied to Ireland. Instead, the building boom characterised by the tower house is indicative of adaptation rather than true decline (Barry, 1988). This trend might apply to certain areas of the country more than others, particularly the more prosperous parts such as the river basins of the Three Sisters rivers in the southeast of the country (*ibid.*). This region corresponds with a high tower house density which acted in tandem with the migratory trend observed by Smyth in County Tipperary. Others have argued that certain regions like the Pale had more population stability, with settlements merely weakened after the Black Death and desertion occurring after the time of the *Civil survey* (Graham, 1975). Ardmayle may have fallen into this pattern, as by the 1641 Rebellion 'there were only seven or eight inhabitants left of a probable burgess household population size of at least 1,715 in 1305' (Barry, 1988: 354).

The major justification for this theory comes from excavation of Piperstown, County Louth. Although not the site of a tower house, like many tower house sites Piperstown has no associated church or graveyard, which led to a delay in its identification as a deserted settlement. Excavation indicates that settlement desertion was mainly linked to the turbulent social, political and economic effects of the Cromwellian Wars, a finding that is paralleled by this author's observations as to the decline of the tower house building form (Barry, 2000a, b; McAlister, 2015).

In some parts of the country, settlement desertion may have been associated with earlier political events, but still not with the Black Death. In County Limerick, for example, O'Connor found that most of the deserted settlements dated from the time period between the *Desmond surveys* (starting 1584) and the mid-seventeenth-century *Civil survey* (cited in Mac Curtain, 1988). This is earlier than described by Barry, but notably outside of the patterns observed in England and on the continent.

Several scholars have suggested something that sounds a bit more like mixed nucleated-dispersed settlement as being prevalent in Ireland in the later Middle Ages. O'Keeffe (2000b) in particular is a proponent of this conclusion, stating that we should be thinking within the framework of a scale from 'nucleated' to 'not nucleated', rather than the traditional nucleated to dispersed, especially within the complex legal frameworks granted to settlements in medieval Ireland. This is persuasive in the context of tower houses in an increasingly pastoral economy, and has led to a reluctance to identify nucleated settlement in the more strongly Gaelic-Irish areas, like Connacht (Nicholls, 1972).

In the later Middle Ages, the system of tenancy outlined above – whereby free tenants paid a fixed rent and only those on the lower rungs owed service obligations – changed to metayage. Metayage was a system whereby the crop yield was divided between lord and tenant in exchange for the lord providing a share of the seed for planting. This method was also closer to the practices of the native Irish (*ibid.*). These tenants 'would have been persons of some standing, possessing their own stock and so able to contract with their landlord on equal terms, and often his equals in wealth and position' (*ibid.*: 116). It is very possible that those under metayage were free tenants of status and wealth sufficient to construct tower houses.

McNeill (1980) has argued that manorial centres were almost purely administrative in function and so do not reflect habitation clusters, at least in his study of Anglo-Norman Ulster. The remnants of this administrative centre in the modern landscape would be remarkably similar to those villages – a castle, church and mill – adding further complications for the modern scholar. This scenario was not limited to Ulster, but may have existed elsewhere, such as in County Wicklow. There are few tower houses recorded in that county, but there may be little evidence for more than service settlement at the manorial centres, with most tenants living away in their own townlands (Shanahan, 2005).

This concept, however, does not exclude the possibility of two settlement centres – one the manorial centre and the other the tenant's centre, so long as the tenant were wealthy enough. Within the system they had established, the first Anglo-Norman magnates created a manorial centre for themselves, then gave their followers chunks of land called 'vills' that were dependent on the manorial caput. The term 'baronial manor' was coined by Empey (1981) to describe this manorial caput lording over the sub-manors, and he equated it to a cantred-sized area. Although describing the high Middle Ages, the legacy of this might be represented in higher concentrations of tower houses in certain counties.

Phosphate analysis has been used in a handful of instances to identify the location of settlements, including at Oughterard in County Kildare and Newcastle Lyons in County Dublin. These investigations highlight that there need be no above-ground features for peasant housing to have once existed on the site (O'Conor, 1998). This scientific method has not been extensively used in more recent years, but its application at Newcastle Lyons again supports the idea of mixed settlement at tower houses, and this time from within the Pale, a very different social context to the earldom of Ulster. Newcastle Lyons had a motte castle, church and tower house clustered together. Around three hundred metres to the south-southwest are the remnants of a further two tower houses. Village houses were apparently located in the field across the road from the church (Edwards *et al.*, 1983). The tower houses were specifically taken as being 'a late component of the manorial system in Ireland', and the chief tenants were associated with these buildings (*ibid.*: 363). Presumably this explains the two proximal tower houses, with the tower house in the village coming to replace the earlier motte castle.

The settlement arrangement was interpreted as reflecting that some of the tenants lived in a village-type environment near the church, while others lived away in townlands of their own – especially the native Irish betaghs, who may have lived in the neighbouring townland. The mix of settlement, reflective of McNeill's descriptions, Edwards and colleagues interpret as being a consequence of the stronghold of the native Irish system of townlands, which prevented large common field holdings and the nucleation of sizeable villages. As at the English manors the lords sought to emulate, though, agriculture was mixed (*ibid.*).

Using phosphate analysis, clusters of activity were found along the modern road (presumably a continuation of the medieval road) and to the south of the southernmost tower house. Two of the three settlement clusters identified are by tower houses (*ibid.*). This is very similar to what was picked up in DEMs at Ardmayle and Ballynahinch, even though

County Tipperary is geographically distant, implying that tower houses were commonly sited at settlement clusters, even in different regions.

It also suggests that a continuation of manorial activity and settlement was located by the tower house. This migratory pattern of manorial centre and adjoining village from earlier to later castle site has been observed by other scholars (Gardiner and O'Conor, 2017). By extension, we can tentatively claim that tower houses could often be taken as signs of now-disappeared rural settlement.

Dispersed settlement could include tower houses and their complexes standing in isolation, with no associated settlement. This was most pronounced in areas with less manorial entrenchment, such as County Galway, where pastoral agriculture dominated, the workforce was smaller and Gaelic-Irish traditions endured (Simms, 1988a). Some scholars go so far as to say that in Gaelic Ireland, 'agglomerations of dwellings were rare and for the most part confined to ecclesiastical centres' by the late Middle Ages (Nicholls, 1987: 399). Tower houses can be taken as underlining the importance of dispersed settlement across Ireland and across cultural contexts (Barry, 1996). This would mean that settlements even in Anglo-Irish areas looked more like the Gaelic-Irish form than perhaps they did the English (Barry, 1988, 1996). One possibility is that free tenants lived in something resembling clachans: small hamlets where all the buildings were residences or out-buildings, and the occupants farmed the land in partnership. Although these are not really known in Ireland from before the seventeenth century, they have been described as having a 'remarkably medieval' appearance, meaning they could be later manifestations of a settlement type known from the Middle Ages (Glasscock, 1971). Members of a common family may have resided in these hamlet-like settlements, referred to as 'kin clusters'. Kin clusters are known from across Gaelic-Irish areas, including those that were under Anglo-Norman control and became Gaelicised over the late Middle Ages (Barry, 1993b). Clachan-type settlements in Anglo-Irish areas like County Meath have been interpreted as the settlements of betagh tenants (Graham, 1975).

Dispersed settlement is therefore particularly associated with the Gaelic-Irish, although when it is identified it is often impossible to ascribe ethnicity (O'Conor, 1998). The contemporary pictorial evidence, such as by Bartlett, depicts Gaelic-Irish huts called 'creats' beside tower houses in Gaelic-Irish areas, and these might represent small service settlements (Barry, 1988; O'Conor, 1998, 2001). Despite their flimsy appearance, their depiction by tower houses and on the outskirts of larger settlements indicates that they had a permanent residential function (O'Conor, 2001). As Gaelic culture spread across the country in the later Middle Ages as part of the Gaelic Resurgence, this type of dispersed settlement might have become much more uniform in the tower house era.

Archaeological studies have been made of the temporary building forms constructed by the Gaelic-Irish, including creats/creaghts and booley huts. A creaght was a social and farming unit, defined by Simms as a 'massed herd of livestock representing the individual holdings of a number of people grouped under a single leader, or ruling family, who were grazing land that did not belong to them, either as temporary tenants paying rent or military service, or as trespassers hoping to establish a more enduring claim to possession' (Simms, 2015: 115). Transhumance associated with booleying, the seasonal movement of cattle between winter and summer grazing lands, has been a fruitful area of study, in particular in the 2010s. Aside from the wattle huts described above (e.g., O'Conor, 2001) others may have been made of sods and turf; they could then be disassembled, rolled up and then carried to the new grazing lands on a pole. The turf would have been constructed around internal wooden posts that probably rested on the ground, so that height could be easily adjusted; it is not at all surprising therefore that no physical traces were left behind. Cruck construction techniques may have been adapted, since the roof timbers could be taken down and removed (Estyn Evans, 1969; Horning, 2013; O'Conor, 2001). These moveable houses could also have been made out of wattle that was plastered and whitewashed; these are more like the structures drawn by Bartlett. They may have had annexes, which presumably could have sheltered the cattle, or dairy products. Houses were clustered together in groups of two to twelve (Costello, 2016b; Horning, 2013), and the number depended on the extent and quality of the nearby grazing, the site altitude and accessibility from the permanent settlement (Gardiner, 2012). Stone booley houses may have been built, though known instances from western Ireland date from the modern period (Costello, 2016a; McDonald, 2016). Sod-built examples were small, circular types with annexes, appearing similar to those depicted on early-modern-period maps. A rectangular version could have multiple rooms, and this type has been suggested to be more recent, from a time when there was less intense use of the upland grazing areas (Gardiner, 2012).

Settlement desertion: Obscuring the relationship of the tower house with peasant settlement

Many tower houses today stand in isolated locations in rural areas. While it is possible that the tower house and its immediate complex and associated church always stood in isolation, the evidence presented here convincingly shows that either medieval or post-medieval settlement desertion has occurred, so obscuring medieval rural settlement patterns.

By examining the different theories surrounding rural settlement we can see that tower houses were compatible with a multitude of manifestations. The *Civil survey*, even within one county (Tipperary), shows that a variety of settlement forms existed at tower houses, ranging from dispersed settlement to urban areas, to clusters inhabited by extended kin (Smyth, 1985). A classic layout of medieval nucleated settlement was linear, with the houses located along the street and the burgage plots laid out behind. A marketplace could be on either the main street or a triangular area at one end of this street. Castles tended to be either on the edge of or just outside the settlement. This description would support the layout noted at Ardmayle, with peasant housing (the area showing densest usage) near the tower house (see figure 1.2). It also is well suited to Knockainy (figure 1.7).

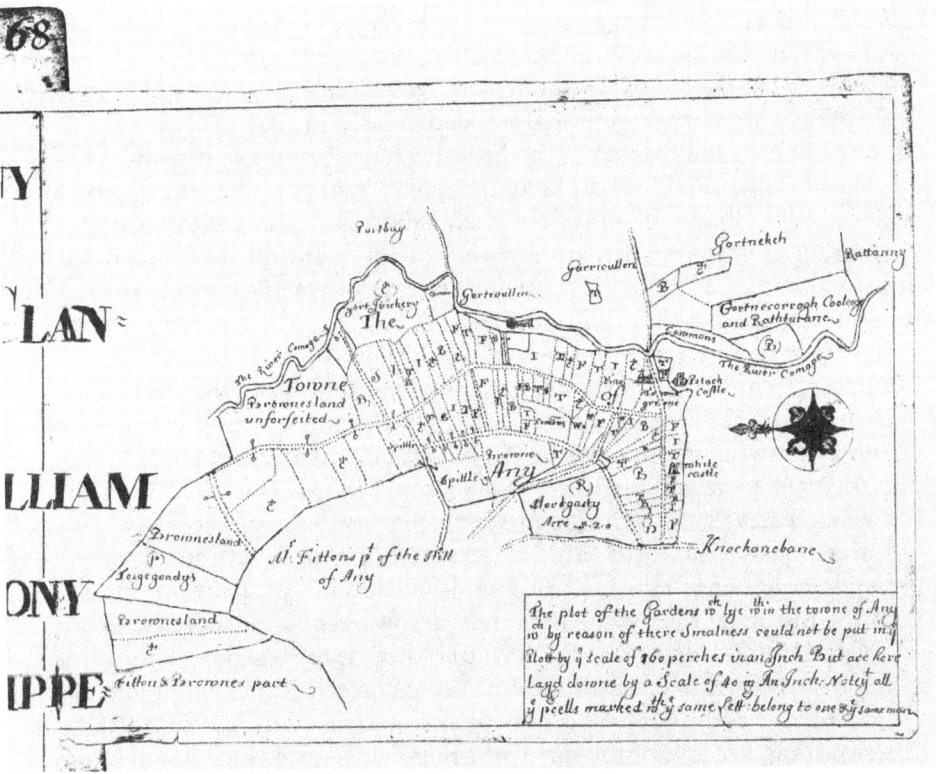

1.7 This extract from the *Down Survey* of the Barony of Small County, County Limerick (B68), depicts the now shrunken settlement of Knockainy. Comparison of this mid-seventeenth-century map with the standing archaeological remains has allowed identification of features.

Knockainy, or Aney, in County Limerick has one upstanding tower house and another documented, on either side of a crossroads and church, two hundred metres apart. There are some modern houses, but the documentary evidence indicates substantial settlement shrinkage. The first detailed references to the settlement occur in a 1321 inquisition. It appears one of the tower houses may have been preceded by 'a stone hall with a new chamber constructed mostly of timber', and there was a stone-built granary in the haggard. In the surrounding lands were eighty oak trees, warrens, two water mills with fishery, a lake generating income and a dovecote. The market was already established by this point (*Inquisitions and extents*). Knockainy is described in the *Desmond survey* as being 'burgesses lands' and there was a substantial twice-yearly fair held there. Around the same time as this survey the water mills were referenced, so we know they continued in use throughout the period under investigation (NLI, MS 43,308/1). Knockainy is represented on the *Down survey* maps at both parish and barony levels. Here is it described as 'Any town', with the 'Black Castle' and the 'White Castle' shown on land plots on one side of a road (see figure 1.7). The Black Castle is marked next to the town green and is upstream of a mill. Another curved road running perpendicularly to that upon which the tower houses are located is the location for most of the historical settlement, with what look to be burgess plots marked. Overall, the town lies in a 'T' shape. In addition, several shorter streets are marked, one running almost parallel to the curve of the main north–south route. Development of the town on the other side of the river seems to have been restricted by the mill and river. While the *Civil survey* records only nine cabins and a mill seat (*Civil survey*: vol. 4), the *Down survey* shows upwards of thirty long, narrow plots, suggesting that settlement shrinkage was underway by the mid-seventeenth century. The *Down survey* drawing of the town on the parish maps does reflect the modern settlement plan, although it is not oriented north. Comparison of the two indicates that it is the White Castle that still stands – an ivy-covered tower house reduced to three storeys in height and with much of the window dressings removed. The modern church is probably on the site of the historical one, while the modern houses echo the more extensive seventeenth-century plots. This would also mean that the locations of the historic towns given in the ASI are incorrect. Knockainy therefore might be a fruitful place to conduct more investigations, such as through test pitting, because of the rarity of being able to piece together multiple sources clearly and easily.

The standing remains at Glenogra Castle in County Limerick are a large bawn with partial remains of a tower house (see figure 1.8). The site is situated 260 metres southwest of a medieval parish church dedicated

1.8 Glenogra Castle, County Limerick, is a much-ruined tower house situated in the corner of a large bawn. Documentary evidence indicates that it was located by a DMV, but no evidence for this exists in the modern landscape, beyond a medieval parish church.

to St. Nicholas, and a bridge crossing over the River Camoge is around 500 metres to the north. In 1298 it was documented as having around 120 burgesses resident, and a fair green is shown on the first-edition OS maps. Ground survey shows some indication of earthworks in the fields south of the church (Glasscock, 1970, 1971; Otway-Ruthven, 1965). There is no above-ground trace of these burgesses' homes today, including in aerial photographs, leading to conclusions that Glenogra never had much of an urban character (Empey, 1988; Otway-Ruthven, 1965). The *Desmond survey* supports this theory – it documents that by the sixteenth century both the castle and bawn were decayed and indefensible, with only one house located nearby and this uninhabitable save for one floor. Similarly, the water mill was decayed and unused. The survey does indicate that Glenogra was until then a vibrant local centre and had the potential to be so again. It states several times that the quality of the land around was excellent and included underwood, and that the vill called 'Creans' by Glenogra had buildings prior to the Desmond Rebellion. This village may have been located around the medieval parish church, 260 metres to the northeast, it too described as a shell. Its rent was stated as comprising money, cattle and grains, implying a mixed agricultural economy in the area (*Desmond survey*).

At Bourchier's Castle on Lough Gur in County Limerick, excavations showed that a village had been clustered around, and pre-dated, the tower house (see figure 1.9). One of the houses was occupied until the early fourteenth century and may have had an attached barn. The coins found on site provide evidence for something of a market economy

(O'Conor, 1998). Settlement transition might explain why we sometimes find tower houses near to evidence of abandoned and/or earlier settlement remains. The tower house here might have succeeded an earlier castle in providing a centre to rural nucleated settlement (Barry, 1988). While Lough Gur is an active archaeological area, the majority of the sites date from the prehistoric period. Today the tower house stands isolated in a modern farmyard, and there is no above-ground evidence of other medieval buildings or a church. The *Desmond survey* provides unusual levels of detail on this site. The tower house itself is described as having an iron door (likely a yett), and within were nine sleeping rooms ('cubicul') and two reception rooms ('loci easeament'). It had two separated entrances: one approached via a narrow causeway with two gates and the other through a 'small castle or peel' with drawbridge. Outside the castle proper it apparently held an orchard and garden on its north side, as well as there being many other buildings and cottages. In these it is specifically said 'dwell divers tenants' (*Desmond survey*: pp. 151–2, entry 388, MS f. 5, 682). The buildings around, but pre-dating, Bourchier's Castle at Lough Gur, County Limerick, excavated by Clery, have been interpreted as the homes of servants, estate workers and other such dependents. These were clustered around the earlier castle, now underneath the tower house, reflecting the continued settlement focal point of the later building (Barry, 2006).

Fieldwalking may in rare instances be another method of identifying now-abandoned rural settlement at tower houses. The approaches to Audley's and Ardkeen castles from the shoreline are not direct, but turn through ninety-degree angles. This raises the possibility that they were once routeways passing through (now vanished) settlement. Unlike at other tower house sites discussed here, there are no high-status manorial features near these sites. A medieval church is located opposite the routeway at Ardkeen, while fieldwalking has identified roof tiles of post-medieval date that had been thrown up by ploughing. Ardkeen was the caput of a mensal manor of the earls of Ulster; therefore, it was a manorial centre from at least the high medieval period (McErlean *et al.*, 2002). Ardkeen was excluded from the seventeenth-century *Down survey* mapping since it was land held by Protestants, whereas the survey was concerned with enumerating Roman Catholic land assets. Other maps of the early modern period are frequently too small in scale to include details of vernacular rural settlement. Knockainy in County Limerick is a rare and notable exception.

In County Meath, we have evidence for continued manorial village use on into the later Middle Ages at both Ardmulchan and Dunmoe, two townlands located on opposite banks of the River Boyne (Graham, 1974; Lewis *et al.*, 2008). Dunmoe is the site of a tower house, whereas

1.9 Bourchier's Castle at Lough Gur in County Limerick is a rare example of a tower house where the surrounding site has been excavated. This excavation found evidence for earlier vernacular housing, suggesting that Bourchier's Castle supplanted an earlier castle site. No evidence of this is visible above ground today.

Ardmulchan has a motte. These monument types would reflect a shift of castle type from high to late medieval. Downstream along the River Boyne, a similar pattern emerges at Slane. Slane, now a village, might have been a settlement gathered around a road (Seaver, 2005). It was more than just an agricultural settlement – it also had a market and a fair, these documented as granted in 1412 to encourage the inhabitants to remain, following raids by native Irish. There are several tower houses in the townlands outside Slane village, though Seaver thought it unlikely the burgesses would have had the funds to build a tower house. Instead, he proposed that Carrickdexter, now listed in the ASI as Slanecastle Demesne, was probably on a townland granted to one of the free tenants who built the tower house there. The chief agent of the Fleming family, lords of Slane, seems to have built the tower house at Newstone to the north at Drumcondra, while the parish priest apparently lived in a tower house, at least from the sixteenth century (*ibid.*).

Other sites, like Rathcannon in County Limerick, have significant earthwork remains that can be seen in the field, with more showing up through aerial photography. The aerial base maps available online via the ASI show intensive activity at the base of the rocky outcrop upon which this site is located. Around the tower house several larger bawn-like enclosures have been recorded, and to the north and east there are irregular enclosures and what look like field-system remnants. Smaller enclosures closer to the outcrop base may be building foundations. Rathcannon would be a worthwhile case study for a future project using remote-sensing methods. Unfortunately, few written references were identified during this study to direct investigations. Dunnaman in County Limerick has the opposite problem – it is better documented but with no earthwork remnants visible above ground. It may be best known for its impressive Sheela-na-gig, but there is also a church with graveyard located four hundred metres to the northeast. In 1587 a grant was given to erect houses for twelve families at the site (*Irish fiants*: vol. 3). While none of these homes survive to the naked eye, inhabitation around the tower house was recollected by the landowner as local lore. This again reinforces the notion that much of the medieval settlement that once existed in the vicinity of tower houses has vanished, with no traces visible today.

However, there may have been manorial activity in the high medieval period without an earlier castle site to indicate it, as the historical documentation shows that most manors were built without defensive considerations until the tower house era (Empey, 1981). Keegan (2005) observed that these sites do not have an association with designated rural boroughs. The discussion surrounding rural boroughs implies that nucleated settlements existed only where this special status was granted: 'There is,

1.10 Cashlaundarragh Castle, County Galway, appears as a plain ruined tower house in the landscape today. However, it was the focal point of a DMV that partially consisted of stone houses. The field surrounding the tower house is rocky, unlike the farmland in the vicinity. What may be the remains of an entrance to a stone bawn is visible to the right of the image.

however, some evidence to indicate that nucleated settlement may have occurred at a number of manorial centres without the endowment of borough status' (*ibid.*: 33). Bourchier's Castle was cited as an example here, as there is no documentation of burgesses despite the archaeological evidence.

DMVs at tower houses are most associated with Anglo-Irish controlled areas. However, this was not an exclusive relationship, but instead probably reflects the bias inherent within the scholarship. Cashlaundarragh Castle in County Galway has an associated DMV listed within the ASI (see figure 1.10). The ASI describes this as the foundations of at least eleven stone-built rectangular houses, along with an irregular field system. A possible roadway is also present. It is not possible to discern these features at Cashlaundarragh through aerial imaging, and the precise shapes were difficult to identify even on the ground through fieldwalking. The one feature that remains quite clear in the modern landscape is a possible bawn surrounding the tower house. Irregularities in the area enclosed by the bawn might indicate stone buildings. The ground in the vicinity of the site is stony, which makes identifying features difficult, although there is good, low-lying farmland around.

The number of DMVs identified in Ireland remains low. It has been suggested that examining the proximity of medieval parish churches to tower houses may give us a good indication of rural settlement patterns, since peasant settlement of short duration might not leave the extensive earthwork remains so frequently seen in English contexts, and that the paucity of Irish earthwork remains might be because short-duration peasant settlement was a feature of medieval Ireland. Geophysical survey of Castleboy, County Down, has suggested that metalworking activity was taking place in the area between the tower house and the (now ruined) church. The report also proposed that what were found might actually be the remains of rectangular buildings. Considering the findings from elsewhere in the country, this is more probable. A water source would have been required for the scale of metalworking indicated by the geophysical results, and there is no source of running water in the immediate vicinity of the site (the nearest stream is about four hundred metres away). The orientation of the tower house, about a hundred metres south-southeast of the church, would imply that these buildings were either ancillary buildings of the tower house, or are the remnants of a small settlement that potentially ran perpendicularly to a track between the tower house and church.

A different version of this layout is apparent at Derrymaclaughna Castle, County Galway (see figure 1.11). The tower is house is about

1.11 Derrymaclaughna Castle in County Galway is associated with a medieval parish church. However, unlike other castle–church settlement centres, there is a natural depression separating the two that would have had an impact on the clustering of peasant settlement. This image shows the rear of the tower house, looking over to the parish church across the depression.

125 metres to the northeast of a medieval parish church, which might imply that there was rural settlement clustered around the two sites. However, the large depression running perpendicularly between them would have prevented many buildings from being constructed between the two, so if there was peasant settlement present it presumably clustered around one or the other, or both.

Shine (2005) has suggested that the proximity of the tower house at Earlstown, County Kilkenny, to the church might indicate that its occupant was the parish priest. Seaver, in the same essay collection (2005), argues that aside from lords the only social group with wealth enough to build tower houses in his study area were churchmen. This is an interesting idea. However, physical closeness cannot be taken as the sole indicator of occupation. A significant number of tower houses are located close to the medieval parish church and away from the earlier castle site, and therefore we cannot always equate the two. Residential towers associated with religious sites are more secure in their identification as such at a few places observed during fieldwork, including Cashelboy in County Sligo, where the tower house is only five metres from the church. Cross East in County Mayo has been listed in the ASI as a tower house, but is undoubtedly a residential church tower at one end of the church building.

Much of the published material has focussed on Anglo-Norman manorial settlement, and on Gaelic-Irish dispersed settlement in tandem with pastoralism. This framework neglects one potentially sizeable settlement group that transcended ethnicity – settlements clustered because of fishing. These have been described in an English context as 'cellar settlements': a small collection of huts at a good landing place that acted as a base for treating catches of fish (Fox, 2001). This author has argued (McAlister, 2016) that the tower house formed a focal point of such 'cellar settlement', with fishermen clustered in settlements with proximity to shoals, weirs and traps. Many of these fishermen were possibly only part time in that role, and the rest of their employment was spent in agriculture. Proximity to fish resources and the manpower needed for fishing would have encouraged clustered habitation, even though fishing was comparatively less intensive than arable agriculture. O'Sullivan noted in his study of the fisheries of the Shannon estuary that tidal fish traps needed to be emptied twice a day and frequently repaired, necessitating those in charge of them to be based close by (O'Sullivan 2001, 2003). As will be discussed in chapter 3, there is a strong correlation between tower houses and estuarial and freshwater-fish exploitation.

Not only would settlements have developed based on the fishing activities of residents, but the fishing industry encouraged the migration of foreign fishermen, too. To some degree fishing-oriented settlement will have varied in terms of numbers of residents depending on the season, with some settlements probably temporarily abandoned out of season. It is difficult to elucidate these numbers, but there were certainly hundreds if not thousands of foreign fishermen at large ports, as well as small coastal places near fishing sites. One identified example of a small coastal fishing settlement was at Ballynacallagh on Dursey Island, County Cork, which had seven houses sited close to a landing place adjacent to the fishing grounds off Bantry Bay. That this was a seasonal fishing settlement cluster occupied by Spanish fishermen is supported by the material culture uncovered during excavation: Spanish roof tiles and Spanish ceramics similar to Cotrel or Seville coarse wares (Breen, 2016). An unclassified castle is listed in the ASI for Ballynacallagh and there are no standing remains of this site, just a historical reference to its garrisoning. This is a unique and fascinating discovery that suggests other insightful features might be uncovered during future excavation of coastal settlement sites.

One potential avenue for future research might be through the already comparatively understudied topic of fishing settlement. This has been more extensively discussed in Scandinavia, where it has been shown that fishing settlements tended to last through the population crisis following the Black Death, and indeed that new fishing villages were founded in the later Middle Ages. Instead, as potentially in Ireland, these villages were deserted in the seventeenth century owing to economic problems and a market collapse for fish (Barrett, 2016).

Conclusion: Tower houses as centres of rural landscapes

While it is somewhat easier to describe the kinds of buildings that might have been located next to the tower house, a range of convincing theories have been proposed by several eminent scholars as to what form the associated rural settlement took. The findings from field study of tower houses across Ireland suggest that the reality was somewhere in the middle of these suggested patterns and depended on local circumstances. Tower houses represent a continuation of rural settlement from earlier in the Middle Ages, or if they were on 'new' sites they could have acted as magnets for people living in the surrounds. The popularity of tower houses does indicate that after the demographic collapse of the Black Death a number of clustered settlements persevered, and that we are dealing more with DPMVs (deserted *post*-medieval villages) than DMVs in Ireland.

This chapter has attempted to identify the rural surrounds of tower houses. Unfortunately, at its conclusion our answer to this is still 'it depends'. This is because tower houses were well suited to all rural settlement contexts. Barry (1996) has argued that the differences in settlement types between Gaelic-Irish and Anglo-Irish were not that profound, with the environment acting as the great leveller. This concept is supported by most of the evidence presented here, and certainly by tower houses themselves, which were constructed by both ethnicities with no differences in building form discerned to date.

Tower houses also existed in areas of Ireland with differing economies. The context therefore seems to be as general as economically active enough to support tower house construction. This was the beauty of tower houses – their adaptability. It also probably explains in large part the sheer number of tower houses and the wide range of environmental contexts to their locations. Tower houses fit well even in places in both Anglo-Irish and Gaelic-Irish Ireland where there was no previous castle-building tradition. Indeed, Empey (1981: 333) has written that in County Tipperary the 'castle-building craze' did not start until the tower house. This craze he attributes to a new class consciousness among the freeholders that accompanied profound new prosperity. New-found wealth and a new intensity of resource exploitation are a perpetual theme in this volume. The extension is that the form of landholding or agriculture mattered little, so long as income was being generated from it.

Evidence has been consistently uncovered for the continued occupation of settlement associated with tower houses into the early modern period. This in turn lends support to the theory that the biggest rural changes in Ireland occurred following the Cromwellian Wars and not after the Black Death. This does not necessarily mean that the demographic impact of the Black Death was less extreme than previously thought. Indeed, it is likely that Ireland underwent severe population depletion, and probably especially in nucleated settlements whether urban (as discussed by the likes of Friar John Clyn for Kilkenny) or rural. Rather, it appears that the Irish population migrated locally following the Black Death. As fertile lands were vacated, people may have increasingly moved from more marginal lands to the fertile heartland, so repopulating manorial villages. In the same process, large swathes of unoccupied land opened up for pastoral cattle-based agriculture, especially the medieval socio-economic practices of booleying and creaghting. Combined, this might suggest that what we have taking place in late medieval Ireland is increasing polarisation between these two forms of settlement and associated agriculture: that more people moved to clustered settlement and more people adopted transhumance. These people came from the dispersed settlement forms associated with subsistence farming and low-status tenantry. This might explain the phasing out of betaghry noted by some scholars. The migration to clustered settlement in old manors might be most marked in the hinterlands of the great river systems, which would explain the instances of earthworks in counties Tipperary and Kilkenny. There is similarly strong correlation between tower houses and rivers.

Notes

1 The term is actually an oversimplification since 'village' implies nucleation and 'medieval' implies desertion in the Middle Ages, whereas ample evidence exists for abandonment after this date (Barry, 1996).
2 See especially http://core.ecu.edu/umc/Munster/objects/B_garden.html.
3 In this context, a grange (*grangia*) referred to a grain-storage building rather than the estate associated with a religious order.

2

The medieval agrarian economy: Lifeblood of the tower house

Having identified the types of buildings and settlement around the tower house walls, our attention now turns to the occupations of the individuals living in and around tower houses. Agriculture was the basis for all economic activity in Ireland during the tower house era. It produced food for consumption but also surplus, which readily found demand on both national and international markets. How these goods made it to sale, and the unique position of the tower house in facilitating this, is the subject of chapter 4. This chapter examines how people made a living in the Middle Ages.

Historians have stressed that the late Middle Ages in Ireland was a period of increased pastoral activity, also referred to as animal husbandry. Particular emphasis has been placed on the dominance of cattle within this economy, with some scholars going so far as to argue that this had an impact on overall settlement patterns. However, this semi-nomadic cattle herding, known as creaghting and booleying, initially appears essentially incompatible with tower house occupation, since the level of financial investment necessary for the stone structure implies inhabitation at least most of the time. As pastoralism increased, arable agriculture, or crop growing, has been said to have decreased, with only some regions of the Pale continuing with the farming practices developed by the Anglo-Normans in the high Middle Ages.

In contrast to these long-accepted conventions of late medieval Irish agriculture, there is strong documentary evidence for water mills located close to, and controlled from, tower houses. This demonstrates that grain was being grown in the vicinity. Surprisingly perhaps, such mills are recorded in fertile regions across the country, not solely within the bounds of the Pale. A mill was one of the key components of a manor; therefore, this chapter evaluates to what extent a manorial economy survived into late medieval and even early modern Ireland. The continued use of a mill is strongly suggestive of at least a partially grain-based economy. Mills likewise provided a neat linking point between land and water, and water will be the focus of the following chapters.

Agriculture in late medieval Ireland is a vast and almost inexhaustible subject that simply cannot be done justice in a work with a wider scope, such as this one. Instead, only a brief synthesis has been attempted, with the aim of keeping the focus firmly on the tower house and what agriculture was taking place in its immediate environs. At its most elemental, agriculture provided the backbone of the medieval Irish economy, as well as the basis for its trade goods and networks. Agriculture may also have directly influenced tower houses, and some have suggested a basic correlation between tower house size and land quality (Jordan, 1991; Samuel, 1998). This author has noted little correlation, however, especially since precise landholding patterns can usually not be determined, but are important to consider alongside soil quality. Furthermore, size might have been restricted by other factors, such as the burgage plots of urban or borough environments.

The later Middle Ages to the early modern period were centuries of transition. The *Civil survey* and the *Down survey* are invaluable materials for a researcher with an interest in late medieval settlement history, but these are mid-seventeenth-century records. It is unlikely that wholesale transformation of the Irish landscape had happened by the time of their creation, and instead these sources provide evidence for continued manorial practices long past the high Middle Ages. As Empey aptly describes it, the institution of the manor stood between the thirteenth and seventeenth centuries – it was the society around it that altered (Empey, 1981). Ireland underwent massive change accompanying the Dissolution of the Monasteries and Plantation. This affected different parts of the country at different times. For instance, the Lismore Castle papers regarding the earl of Cork's early- and mid-seventeenth-century estates constantly refer to landscape change and exploitation. In almost all his grants, the earl made it clear that he retained the rights and access to such activities as quarrying and mining. Terms of land leases often had conditions attached, including the often-encountered demand to build in the 'English style'; to have only Englishmen as tenants and not Irish, despite the ease of working with the latter; and installing orchards and gardens (NLI, MS 43,153). These clauses show concerted intent to utilise the Irish natural environment in a way that heretofore had not been seen. It might be safe to conclude, therefore, that the Civil and Down surveys for sizeable parts of County Cork do not reflect late medieval land activity. This conclusion may be tentatively applied to other regions with successful Crown-sponsored Plantation.

Agriculture can be described as either arable (crop growing) or pastoral (animal husbandry), or a mix of the two. Land suitable for arable agriculture encouraged Anglo-Norman colonisation (Graham, 1975). Soil type seems to have been of less concern than land altitude, with most high medieval settlement concentrated on lower-lying areas, a trend also echoed in tower house distribution (*ibid.*). Traditionally, the late medieval and the beginning of the early modern period in Ireland have been interpreted as becoming increasingly pastoral, with crop production decreasing (Down, 1987; O'Neill, 1987). This transition was apparently more pronounced in areas that previously had been dense areas of arable agriculture, such as counties Tipperary and Kilkenny (O'Neill, 1987). Historical documentation indicates that mixed agriculture persisted in some areas, certainly within the Pale in County Meath (Graham, 1975). This study finds more evidence for mixed agriculture; comments such as that made by the Irish parliament of 1409–10 that 'the husbandry and tillage of the land is on the point of being altogether destroyed and wasted' are hyperbolic (O'Neill, 1987: 20–1). Decline may have been concentrated in certain areas; certainly the Pale was still exporting grain to a variety of places like Ulster, Wales, England and the south of Ireland in the late fourteenth and early fifteenth centuries (*ibid.*). Colfer has identified a connection between the grain industry and tower house building in County Wexford, as with the collapse of arable agriculture and related grain shortages in late medieval Ireland good profits were assured for those able to continue with this manpower-intensive farming practice (Colfer, 2013). Nicholls concluded: 'There has certainly been a tendency to underestimate the importance of [arable] agriculture and correspondingly overestimate that of pastoralism in the Irish economy of the later Middle Ages; but this conclusion itself is probably derived from the conditions of the sixteenth century, when cultivation declined owing to the increasing violence and disturbance of the period' (1972: 114). Even at the same time as the Anglo-Normans were consolidating the manorial system, references to mills and grains in Gaelic-Irish areas show that this ethnic group did not solely practice pastoralism (McNeill, 1980).

Mixed agriculture was practised in many places in eastern Ireland in the tower house era, according to early-modern-period documentation. The surveys contained in the *Ancient Demesne of the Crown* from 1540 to 1541 note that there were both arable land and pastureland (*Crown surveys of lands*). Items derived from pastoral agriculture are listed in the early seventeenth-century Port books (Public Records Office of Northern Ireland, Belfast (hereafter PRONI), MIC 199/1). Grain deposits dating from both the later Middle Ages and early modern period have been recovered from excavation (Gardiner, 2005).

That is not to say that pastoralism did not increase relative to arable cultivation, even in areas of mixed agriculture. A number of reasons for this have been cited by historians. They include the impact of warfare as part of the Gaelic Resurgence (Empey, 1985), which may have encouraged some tenants to relocate to England where it was more politically stable and lands had reopened after the Black Death (O'Neill, 1987). Commentary from the time mentions lords living along the border of the Pale phasing out crop growing in favour of pastoralism, as this would free up more time among their military followers (Nicholls, 1972). Another trend of the later Middle Ages was the increased ability of betaghs and other tenants to accumulate larger landholdings, after land was left vacant by Anglo-Irish tenants or other betaghs (Down, 1987). The Dissolution of the Monasteries released monastic land for private ownership, although it has been argued that this event did not have a great impact on land-management practices, since the land continued to be rented to the same people as the monasteries had leased it to (Riordan, 2015).

Some scholars have attempted to define how much land in different parts of Ireland was under tillage. Ellis found that the subsidy extents show increasing cultivation over the course of the later fifteenth to the middle of the sixteenth century, which he interpreted as being an increased area rather than expansion of the existing framework.[1] In Meath the monastic extents show that arable land constituted between eighty-three and ninety per cent of total land, that statistic including all the land lying fallow. Arable land here was very valuable and equivalent to prime meadowland; it was cultivated using the open-field system, with wheat and oats dominating (Murphy, 2009). Jager (1983) has interpreted the Irish situation as unusually intense compared with European figures, and found much higher percentages of farmed land used for arable agriculture in the late medieval Pale, averaging seventy to seventy-five per cent.

Outside of the Pale, the territories of some of Ireland's greatest magnate lordships correspond with some of the densest concentrations of tower houses. Their estate accounts tend to be vague, listing land types associated with various townlands and their rents, but some conclusions can be drawn. The Leinster manuscripts tend to mention arable land, but other documents less so, suggesting that arable land had special significance, particularly perhaps for specific areas of the country. A County Limerick rent roll from the sixteenth century in the Leinster manuscripts is one example that emphasises arable land, with few other land types referenced (PRONI, D3078/2/1/4). At other times a formulaic description of meadow, turbary (land where peat is dug or cut), pasture, moor, wood, water and waterway is given, though with slight variations that might indicate accuracy. For many of the County Kildare lands this is expanded to include wood and underwood, for instance (PRONI, D3078/1/1/3). Within the Ormond papers land use is often not even given, with 'acr ter' (acres of land) the most commonly encountered description. Some estate summaries detail acreage and how the land could be used. Even then, arable and pastureland are usually lumped in together, as was the case for the 'Division of Templemore'. In this account, wood, moorish pasture, woody pasture, moor, red bog and turbary are the other designations (NLI, MS 11,053/2A, 'Division of Templemore Aghalebg Farendery and Shanclone'). Although this combined evidence is slight, it does somewhat indicate a recognition of the desirability of arable land.

Agriculture and the manorial economy

The manorial economy is associated with arable agriculture using three-field crop rotation, with pastoralism a less important component. Open fields prevailed in most parts of the country, with temporary fences made out of soft materials like wicker, which could then be reused as fuel over the winter (Nicholls, 1972). There was some ethnic divide in land practices, although both the Anglo-Irish and Gaelic-Irish used common field systems. The Gaelic-Irish used an infield-outfield system (also referred to as the rundale system) instead of three-field systems, which worked better alongside pastoralism (Glasscock, 1987).

Debate surrounds the issue of the lack of ploughing remnants in the landscape. Known as ridge and furrow, the distinctive profile from the Middle Ages can be seen even today in fields across Europe (O'Sullivan and Downey, 2007). Except in Ireland, that is, where remnants remain mystifyingly elusive. A rare example can be seen beside the Hill of Dowth, adjacent to Dowth tower house in CUCAP aerial photography, the distinctive headland banking providing identification (CUCAP, AJO103). One reason for this might be that flat ploughing was preferred, whereby a furrow was cut through the previous season's ridge (O'Conor, 1998). This would reduce the ridge-and-furrow profile, but still ensure the headlands, where the large plough team was turned around at the end of the field, accumulated. There are remains of this at Oughterard and Castlewarden in County Kildare, even though the Irish soil was not generally well suited to this ploughing technique (Hall et al., 1985; O'Keeffe, 2000a). Recent countrywide excavation in association with infrastructural development has found very little evidence for the practice, although it did provide limited examples of medieval field-enclosure practices (Gardiner and O'Conor, 2017).

Arable agriculture in the Pale was dominated by the cultivation of wheat (Barry, 1988). Wheat remains the most common grain in examined excavated contexts dating from the late Middle Ages, and was used in making bread (Dillon and Johnston, 2009; Lyons, 2016). Oats were also a popular crop since they would grow in a wider variety of conditions compared with wheat (Down, 1987). Wheat and oats were grown by both ethnic groups (Glasscock, 1987; Nicholls, 1972), though Nicholls thought that they were most intensively cultivated in the Pale and the southeast of Ireland. Rye and barley were not as extensively cultivated in Ireland – they were restricted to the Pale as the Gaelic-Irish could make ale from oat malt (Nicholls, 1972). The main fertiliser used was sand, brought upriver from tidal estuaries (Down, 1987). Unfortunately, we have no documentary references to this practice, which indicates that it probably did not occur for commercial gain but as part of labour obligations.

The late medieval contexts from Bective Abbey (a monastic site including a tower house) indicate barley then oats were the next most grown crops after wheat, but in much smaller proportion (Lyons, 2016). Peas and beans were also grown. Finding either historical or archaeological evidence for legumes (peas and beans) indicates crop-rotation practices and Anglo-Norman-style manorialism in particular (Dillon and Johnston, 2009). An interesting observation from Bective Abbey was that legume numbers (mainly the field pea) might be slightly increased in the late medieval contexts compared with earlier (Lyons, 2016). This could indicate a re-expansion of arable agriculture in the tower house period.

The Anglo-Norman manorial system was not involved solely in grain growing; sheep husbandry for wool production was also a dominant form of agriculture, and sheep manure was a good fertiliser for grain (O'Neill, 1987; Riordan, 2015). Sheep rearing is also associated with religious orders, especially the Cistercians who had been in Ireland since 1142. The mother houses of this order were located in England, and they sent much of the produce from their Irish lands there (O'Neill, 1987). Soil type mattered, and most Cistercian farms for sheep husbandry were located in limestone areas (*ibid.*). Faunal analysis from the Cistercian Bective Abbey in County Meath found that sheep and/or goats comprised the largest grouping from the monastic period, but that changed to cattle after the Dissolution of the Monasteries (cattle having been secondary in importance beforehand) (Beglane, 2016).

Combined with the large Anglo-Norman manors also practising sheep husbandry, this meant that southeastern Ireland was dominated by wool production (O'Neill, 1987). The location of Cistercian farms along major rivers was convenient for long-distance sea-borne trading. The rivers Suir, Nore and Barrow passed through the lands of ten major Cistercian abbeys. Evidence for wool production has been found through excavation outside of this area, including at Kilcolman Castle in County Cork (Klingelhofer, 2010). Smaller farmers also weighed in on this activity, it was not just the remit of the big estates. As foreign merchants were not allowed to buy directly from local farmers, their wool instead went to the nearest town for bulking (O'Neill, 1987).

The relative emphasis on the different forms of agriculture will have depended on local land quality. Documentary evidence for triennial crop rotation tends to be from before the Black Death and in areas with good soil (Down, 1987). Even in what we would consider more marginal land in Gaelic-Irish western counties, there were small pockets of arable agriculture according to the *Down survey* maps. As one example, the barony map for Corcomroe in County Clare shows small areas marked as arable near the tower houses at Doolin and Doonnagore (*Down survey*).[2] These arable areas were located near the bottom of river valleys, while the long, thin appearance of landholdings, running uphill, is suggestive of possible booleying. The small areas of arable land were comparatively scattered, which further indicates that three-field crop rotation would not be easy to practise; instead the infield-outfield, or rundale, system seems more probable.

Rabbit warrens are another feature that we often find in conjunction with castles and manors in English and continental contexts. Rabbits were an elite food and their husbandry associated with lordship. Despite this, evidence is low for rabbit farming in Ireland, and no pillow mounds (earthen warrens) have been identified. Rabbits alternatively might have been managed in fields with palisades or reused earlier earthwork fortifications (O'Conor, 1998, 2004). Several warrens have been identified through the written records in association with tower houses, including at Carrick-on-Suir and Ardmayle in County Tipperary and Knockainy in County Limerick. However, it is likely that these rabbit warrens were remnants of the high medieval Anglo-Norman manors that preceded the tower house, and continued in use, rather than being created at the time of the later castle. We see this earlier origin reflected in the location of the warrens on the periphery of the manor – for instance, the warren was on the County Waterford side of the River Suir at Carrick-on-Suir, the side opposite the castle and town (*Red book of Ormond*).

Many areas of Ireland brought under manorialism did not have land suitable for tillage, so forestry might have assumed more importance (Empey, 1985). Despite the ongoing need for wood and timber, by the sixteenth century much of Ireland was deforested and prevented from naturally regenerating by animal grazing (Nicholls, 1972). Deforestation was motivated by a huge demand for timber, especially high-quality oak for ship building. A new phase of woodland destruction in the early modern period reduced Ireland's once vast woodland to scrub (McCracken, 1971; Nicholls, 2001). There is little evidence of this woodland today. For instance, a gift of two hundred oaks was made from Cratloe forest,

County Clare, in the mid-thirteenth century, which it has been suggested were used in building nearby Bunratty Castle (Beglane, 2018; O'Conor, 2004). Rich woodland might explain the density of tower houses there, with Cratloemoyle and Cratloekeel only a few hundred metres from each other, and only a few kilometres from Bunratty Castle. Cratloe had been designated a legal forest, belonging to the king, meaning that in this instance 'forest' meant both the medieval legal entity and a wooded area (Beglane, 2018).

As well as the economic motivation for the destruction of ancient woodlands, there was no doubt a security concern at play. Woods had long been employed in Gaelic-Irish warfare, referred to as 'fastnesses'. Also, descriptions of 'passes' do not solely refer to mountain or bog passes, but were equally used to mean passes through woods. Generally, descriptions evoke the danger of passing through these woods, and so the Tudor government saw the removal of dense forest as a means of flushing out opposition. At least one scholar has interpreted early-modern-period woodland clearance as being in part a response to this situation, particularly in keeping existing passes clear, rather than representing wholescale colonial exploitation (Everett, 2014). Forests in Ireland also served a symbolic purpose, with timber – alongside venison from the deer living within the forest – serving as a highly meaningful gift item. Therefore, Irish forests may have served more social functions than did their English counterparts (Beglane, 2018).

Agricultural practices varied depending on soil and land conditions and the ethnicity of those doing the work. The upshot was that there were significant differences on as local a level as the individual manor (Barry, 1993b; Glasscock, 1987). Landholding patterns were not stable throughout the tower house period either. A good example of this, if perhaps extreme, is the acquisition of large tracts of land in counties Cork and Waterford by Richard Boyle, Earl of Cork, from the late sixteenth century. Students of the Irish landscape often estimate that we can make use of accounts dating up to the mid-seventeenth century in recreating earlier landscapes. For the areas under Boyle's authority this date needs to be moved earlier. The deeds contained in the Lismore Castle papers speak to a desire to 'improve' the land, particularly through creation of orchards, gardens and meadows. Boyle was careful to retain for personal use all wood and underwood beyond the minimum required for repairs and upkeep by the tenant for his personal use, but also allowed tenants' animals to graze in the woodlands in what sounds like the practice of agistment, animal grazing that could even include cattle (Beglane, 2018; and see e.g. NLI, MS 43,153/3, 1607; MS 43,153/4, 1627). He likewise reserved the right to cut down the woods held on his tenants' lands and to fence or enclose these woods to protect the young wood from his tenants' cattle when required (NLI, MS43,153/10, 1656). Such specifics indicate that woodlands were still extant by Boyle's arrival, and that they were managed.

The Lismore Castle papers are detailed in their descriptions of the land – more so than the ones of Ormond or Kildare, which are slightly earlier in date. This might be a consequence of Boyle's more commercialised mindset, as his leases tended to include provisions in case 'treasure trove mines mineral and quarries' were discovered on the landholding (e.g. NLI, MS 43,153/4, 1627). It may also reflect attitudes towards environmental resource exploitation. One manifestation of this was a search for minerals to mine, with copper, lead and silver sought. Mines in late medieval and early modern Ireland were small in number, but tally with a few tower house concentrations. With such a low number to work from we cannot conclusively state a connection between the two. Mines included lead at Ardglass, County Down; outside Leighlinbridge, County Carlow; Clonmines, County Wexford; and Kilmallock, County Limerick. Lead and copper were mined in the vicinity of Insitioge and Jerpoint in County Kilkenny (*Calendar of state papers relating to Ireland* (hereafter CSPI), vol. 11, *1601–03, reign Henry VII*, 'Addenda Dr Meredith Hanmer's collection of MS690', SP63/214, f. 24, 'List of mines in Ireland, 1497'). Boyle established an iron refinery for his nearby iron mines at Lisfinny in County Waterford in 1621, somewhere in the vicinity of the tower house (Rondelez, 2018; Rynne, 2018). Lisfinny tower house is a fine building standing to four storeys and, although it is set back from the River Bride by two hundred metres (likely to negate flooding as it is on rising ground) and from the modern bridge by seven hundred metres, it still has commanding views over both (see figure 2.1). The most impressive windows face out over this perspective. A wicker-centred barrel vault covered the ground floor and some ogee-headed windows remain, early architectural features that indicate its construction was prior to the earl of Cork's involvement in the metalworking enterprise, although a fireplace and chimney may be later insertions.

Pastoral agriculture and the tower house

Pastoralism remained popular throughout the Middle Ages in Gaelic-Irish areas, but it spread across Ireland and intensified after around 1300 (O'Keeffe, 2000a). Pastoralism in an Irish context tends to refer to cattle husbandry, although sheep and pigs were also kept, particularly in the south. Goats became more popular, though were still not widespread by the end of the medieval period, while horse breeding was a small but significant aspect of the Gaelic-Irish economy (Nicholls, 1972, 1987). That pastoralism could include more than just cattle is attested to by

2.1 Lisfinny Castle, County Waterford, is located on a natural rise above the River Bride. It had excellent visual command over the river and bridge downstream, and was also the site of an iron refinery established by the earl of Cork.

the *Rental Book* of Gerald, ninth earl of Kildare from 1518. This lists the duties the earl placed upon the Gaelic-Irish residing on his lands. From McMorrow's country,[3] he received a share of every herd of cattle, sheep and pigs, though cattle were the most numerous by head. The

MacGillpatricks likewise provided sheep, cattle and pigs, but the O'Mores owed sheep and swine. From O'Byrne he received cattle, sheep and pigs, as well as butter (twenty gallons is specifically mentioned) and a labour obligation for work to Cloghenogan Castle (unknown).[4] The O'Mayles of 'Cleancappe' were to deliver for every town a mutton, one pork and butter (PRONI, D3078/2/2/1).[5] The O'Mayle territory has been more difficult to securely identify – it could be connected to the O'Melaghlins of northern County Offaly rather than the O'Malleys of Mayo, considering the distribution of the other entries. Whether such duties were expected from his Anglo-Irish tenants is unfortunately not extemporised, only the duties from the Gaelic-Irish lords are documented. But the records indicate that pastoralism, even in Gaelic-Irish areas, was not focussed solely on cattle.

Pastoralism is often associated with dispersed settlement patterns, since cattle husbandry in Gaelic-Irish areas sometimes involved transhumance. It was easier for people to move with their herds to pastures than regularly travel distances to the changing grazing areas. This system was required in regions with low soil productivity, where grass for fodder did not grow so well. This transhumance, known as booleying, was not limited to uplands, but was also practised on unused or unoccupied lands (Nicholls, 1987), and involved the movement of livestock, along with their herders, from 'permanent settlements' in lowland areas to upland summer grazing (McDonald, 2016). It was well suited to the aftermath of the Black Death, as people vacated more marginal lands, and it still could be compatible with arable agriculture as it freed up more land for crops (Costello, 2016b, 2016–17). Consequently, it is often associated with the rundale system, with open-field arable farming taking place around the permanent settlement (McDonald, 2016). Booley sites so far identified have tended to be from upland areas (Horning, 2013). Localised investigations have found that booley settlements were associated with protected sites away from the highest mountain altitudes (Gardiner, 2012). The booley settlement might be two to eight kilometres away from the permanent settlement, and morphologically resembled a nucleated and unplanned settlement (McDonald, 2016). Not everyone accompanied the cattle during the summer. McDonald has argued that the wealthier people did, since they owned the cattle, whereas Costello thought that women and younger residents would have been dispatched (Costello, 2016a; McDonald, 2016). However, these conclusions were based on studies of more modern transhumant practices and so may not directly apply to the Middle Ages.

Another transhumant practice was creaghting. A factor in the spread of pastoralism was the decline of betagh status, which gave tenants a lot more mobility, lending itself to herding. Increasingly they were termed 'poor husbandmen' or 'tenants-at-will'. The social changes of the later Middle Ages are reflected, too, in that some of these creaghts were led by nobles of Anglo-Irish as well as Gaelic-Irish lineage (*ibid.*).

Hampering our understanding of transhumance is the pronounced bias within the contemporary evidence, authored by English observers who viewed the practice as reflective of innate barbarism (Gardiner, 2012). Regardless of such bias, scholars now confidently assert that pastoral agriculture was intrinsic to Gaelic-Irish culture. But it was not limited to Gaelic-Irish areas. Pastoralism increased following English colonisation in Munster in the later sixteenth century. Transhumance raises the question of whether it was worthwhile investing in large building projects in regions where it dominated (O'Conor, 1998). Not every person necessarily participated in transhumance, so tower house occupants may have stayed behind (Smyth, 1985). Cattle also played an important role in the agricultural economy of the Pale, as attested to by the large numbers listed in County Meath in the pipe rolls of John 14 (1211–12), although a significant number of these were oxen for plough teams (Davies and Quinn, 1941). A commitment to cattle husbandry is reflected in the export of hides from across the country and the efforts made by lords to control this, since high prices could be commanded in their sale (Simms, 2015). For instance, the O'Malley lord claimed the right to the hides of all the cattle slaughtered in his territory (Nicholls, 1972). Hide export worked in tandem with the fish trade to assist in the development of a consumer economy in the Gaelic-Irish west of Ireland, as analysed in chapter 6 (and see Simms, 2015).

This author wonders whether the ground floor space of the tower house could have been used as an animal byre, having often seen tower houses adapted to this same use in the present day during fieldwork. Often, no modifications have been made to the tower house entrance, so long as it proceeds directly into the ground floor room, possibly via an entrance lobby. We know already that the bawn was used for animal sheltering. As one example, a 1601 attack on an unnamed castle led to the attackers taking the animals from within the bawn, enumerated as cows, nine 'beaves' (beef cattle), sheep, and seven or eight harness horses (CSPI: vol. 11, SP63/209/1, f. 131, 1601). According to sixteenth-century descriptions, Irish cattle were small and hardy (McDonald, 2016). But ascertaining whether tower houses were in fact used in this way is another matter (identifying animals in buildings is discussed in Gardiner (2000)). Animals lived side by side with humans in lower-status medieval houses, like the earlier longhouse, and the Gaelic-Irish legal corpus indicates that some cattle could be worth significant sums of money. Drains might not have been necessary for occasional use, but maybe this is a feature future excavations should be mindful of. Modern farmers manage to remove animal effluent from the tower house interiors regularly enough without the need of drains to assist them. Docile animals (considering the level of interaction with humans implied by transhumance and the animals' value, it seems likely that they would be used to humans) would not need to be tethered if they were just being temporarily sheltered, so long as they could be prevented from roaming into other areas of the building.

Mixed agriculture at tower houses

Some academics propose that too much emphasis has been placed on the written record's account of pastoralism. They argue there is an archaeological bias against grain representation in excavated contexts. Grain remains are less likely to survive in acidic soils, meaning they might be unavoidably under-represented (Breen, 2007a). Oat cultivation in particular may have worked well alongside transhumance, as the oats could grow in the summer and autumn and then the fields could be used for cattle grazing over winter. This would also allow the land to be manured in time for the following year's planting, and avoid a fallow year (Watt, 1987).

Pollen analysis supports the contention that pastoralism was not exclusive. Analysis from east Galway found that cereal cultivation was at its highest levels in the period 1250–1500, which supports a lack of scholarly appreciation for late medieval arable agriculture. The use of the landscape for arable agriculture is described by palynologists as 'considerable'. Interestingly, there is a small dip in cereal-type pollen around the year 1350 in both Galway and another site in County Antrim, which then recovers and reaches a new maximum according to the plotted pollen curves. At Moneyveagh Bog, outside Athenry in County Galway, there is potentially a century-long break in cereal cultivation after the mid-fourteenth century (Hall, 2003). At Littleton Bog in County Tipperary (coincidentally, near to Lisronagh, the subject of Curtis's manorial study) after around 1200 cereals start to decline, followed by a decline of grasses after about 1350. Trees and bushes increase slightly in this period (before declining again in the Tudor era), suggesting that agricultural land as a whole decreased in this region (Mitchell, 1965). Overall, it looks as though we are witnessing a disruption in crop cultivation around the time of the Black Death, which would fit comfortably with the predicted impact of that event (Hall, 2000). This break is particularly associated with lowland areas of Ireland (Hall, 2003).

A decline in arable agriculture comes at a later date elsewhere. At Derryville Bog in County Tipperary, land was cleared for arable and pastoral agriculture after the mid-thirteenth century, and crop growing did not go into decline until the early sixteenth century (Hall, 2005). Before the sixteenth century, the amount of cereal cultivated has been described as significant. Arable agriculture also expanded in the later Middle Ages at Clonenagh in County Laois. This site provided evidence for flax cultivation, a very under-documented and elusive crop, possibly because it was viewed as being low status (*ibid.*).

Grass species increased in east Galway in the 1250–1500 time period, though not so profoundly as in the post-medieval period (Molloy and O'Connell, 2016). Outside Athenry, grasses indicative of pastoralism remained consistent across the time period, even as scrub woods were cleared in the mid-fourteenth and sixteenth centuries (Hall, 2003). In County Tyrone, heartland of the massive Gaelic-Irish O'Neill lordship, the pollen evidence indicates renewed pastoralism after the Black Death, with very little arable agriculture before the seventeenth century (Hall, 2000). This pastoral trend continues at Portmagee Bog in County Kerry and Gortahurk Bog in County Fermanagh, where it has dominated over the last thousand years (Hall, 2003).

Overall, the conclusions that can be reached from consulting the pollen record are that there was huge regional and local variation in agriculture (*ibid.*). Therefore, to state that Gaelic Ireland had a predominantly pastoral agricultural system and Anglo-Irish areas had mixed manorial agriculture is a gross oversimplification. The form that agriculture took instead might depend on local topography and growing conditions more than ethnicity. The decline in cereal production after the mid-fourteenth century, which in many cases recovered a couple of generations later, is also interesting in the context of tower houses. The resurgence aligns with the boom in tower house construction, supporting the theories of increased prosperity and settlement shifts, since the economy was evidently able to recover.

Water mills: Tower house control of land and water

Mills are by far the most common economic feature documented on tower house lands. They were a crossover point between terrestrial and aquatic resource exploitation. They were costly to establish, but the return on investment could be encouraging. Tenants could be obliged to assist in the repair of ponds and watercourses, but the owner held the mill suit, or a monopoly on grinding. This charge was in kind, reflected in the inventory for the King's Mills in Ardee, County Louth (site of several urban tower houses), where the 'enee', or copper vessel used to determine the toll, is listed. In Gaelic-Irish areas, this system of suit was less often encountered, and mills tended to be private enterprises rather than lordly manifestations (Rynne, 2003). The profit to the mill owner came either from the sale of this grain collected as a toll, or by leasing out the mill and collecting rent (Brady, 2006).

The presence of grain mills indicates crop cultivation. References to tuck and fulling mills – mills for the fulling of cloth – meanwhile, show engagement with sheep rearing. The incidence of mills in association with tower houses strongly suggests two things. First, that the changeover to pastoralism in the wake of the Black Death was not as extreme and universal as historians have proposed. Second, that elements of the manorial economy continued into the early modern period, even if the whole system was not retained.

Scholars working on the role of mills in later medieval England are fortunate that manorial records are well preserved. In Ireland, we know most about mills in the early and high medieval periods, and tide mills,[6] where the waterwheel was driven by the tide. Less research has been conducted into mills in later medieval Ireland, despite the increase in documentary references. Very few have been archaeologically identified and none survive as standing remains. The contemporary documentation is not terribly useful either, using vague and non-descriptive terms. 'Tuck mill', 'fulling mill', 'corn mill' and 'water mill' are sometimes encountered, though simply 'mill' is by far the most common description. These probably describe water mills, as there are only a handful of references to windmills, and it is probable that they were both of horizontal and vertical varieties (Brady, 2006).

A small number of mills are specified as tuck, or fulling, mills, which reflects manufacture of cloth (Langdon, 2004). In contemporary trade records we have references to Irish woollen cloth, and the Irish-made mantle (a fringed woollen cloak) was well known across Europe. Raw wool was transported to tuck mills for production and then moved along to a port town for export. In England, the number of tuck mills rose in the period following the Black Death (*ibid.*; Lucas, 2014), reflecting a general shift to pastoralism, as this increase in number was observed in rural areas where they could be repurposed from corn mills (Langdon, 2004). In Ireland, sheep farming was most associated with eastern parts of the country. With only two mills being noted in the *Civil survey* as 'tuck mills' in County Meath, at the heart of the Pale, we cannot determine the patterns and transitions between mill types in Ireland.

Comparative evidence from later medieval England indicates that mill use echoed periods of economic growth. That they are referred to in records dating from across the tower house era indicates solid periods of economic stability, possibly interrupted only by Elizabethan scorched-earth warfare. Mills located by tower houses were centrally placed within the wider estate, since the tower house served as an administrative and agricultural centre. The location of a mill by a tower house had the added benefit that the former could easily be closely monitored, with direct supervision of income. A mill served to reinforce the social status of the tower house and its occupants, if they held the rights to it (Buchanan, 2014), and could also be part of an overall elite landscape, serving as visual reinforcement of a castle (Hansson, 2014). No wonder, then, that it has been estimated that sixty-eight per cent of manors held at least one water mill. The mill could also be located some distance from the rest of the manorial appurtenances, complicating identification (Murphy, 2015).

Mills are one of the most common features to be referenced at tower houses in surveys such as the *Civil survey*. Castles and mills are the only specific buildings frequently observed in family estate accounts, such as the Ormond papers and the *Kildare rental*. Mills are often mentioned alongside weirs, and more generally have a correlation with settlement. Medieval nucleated settlement, if not located on navigable stretches of major rivers as many were, tended to be at least on smaller rivers. These could provide power for mills (Glasscock, 1987).

Both vertical- and horizontal-wheeled mills were used: the Anglo-Normans and the Cistercians used the former on their manors, while smaller horizontal-wheeled mills were known in the west of Ireland even until the mid-nineteenth century (Rynne, 2000, 2011). The type of mill used may have been divided along ethnic lines, based on a seventeenth-century reference in the Harleian collection in the British Museum to 'English' and 'Irish' mills in Sligo (Rynne, 2011). In County Down, some mills are described as 'Scottish', and an eighteenth-century reference to horizontal mills indicates that the Scottish type may have resembled the Irish (*ibid.*). Until the second half of the eighteenth century, mills in Ireland were constructed entirely from wood, although the nails and bearings were made of metal (Rynne, 2003, 2006). This accounts for much of the difficulty in establishing the precise location of the mills mentioned alongside tower houses. Very few have been archaeologically identified, implying that many sites were reused, while others have simply yet to be found (Rynne, 2003, 2009).

Mills could be located in medieval towns, while in rural areas they were particularly associated with river tributaries on higher ground that connected with the main river's tidal estuary (Brady, 2006; Rynne, 2000, 2003). We can sometimes see this distribution echoed in the *Down survey*: there is a corn mill depicted outside Navan, and two mills right outside the walls of Kilkenny city.

Water mills could be powered using several different methods. A leat, or channel, could run between a river and a mill, with the river higher in altitude than the mill. Alternatively, a weir-and-leat system allowed for a shorter leat, as the weir built up the head of water otherwise

The medieval agrarian economy

provided by the distance (Langdon, 2004). In most cases the mill was powered by a small, fast-flowing stream. This stream was obstructed by a dam to create a reservoir, or millpond. From this, a channel, or mill race, ran to the mill building itself (Rynne, 2003). The benefit of a race over a natural stream was that the water supply could be better managed to prevent flood damage (Lucas, 1953).

A millpond, sometimes referred to as a *stagnum*, was an attractive option because it had the side effect of functioning as a fishery. The millpond was the most popular way of powering water mills in later medieval England, with weirs and leats found at more sizeable operations (Langdon, 2004). This may explain the distribution of mills near to castle sites, as it gave the lord the benefit of the status implicit in a fishpond. We have extensive evidence for weirs. This could imply that Irish mills were powered by a weir and leat or, considering the country's topography, a simple leat, since an altitudinal drop would have been possible over very short distances. Powering by the leat system is reflected in the documentation when a *cursus acquae* is mentioned: a water channel that connected with a mill rather than the literal watercourse (*ibid.*). Mill weirs could be used to catch fish, particularly eels; therefore, it is very possible that there was an overlap in weir function, with a number of later medieval mills being powered by weirs. However, Arthur Went, author of a significant series of histories of Ireland's river fisheries, stated that this was very rare in Ireland until the last century (Went, 1955).

Occasionally, identification of a millpond in the modern landscape is possible during fieldwork, such as at Ballynacarriga in County Cork (see figure 2.2). The modern landscape has a stream running along the base of the tower house on the western side, which makes a loop around a small car-parking area for those seeking to use nearby Ballynacarriga Lough recreationally. The still waters and infill shape are reminiscent of a pond. Indeed, a millpond is marked in this location, about thirty metres to the southwest of the tower house, on first-edition OS six-inch maps, though not on those subsequent. The outline of this millpond is visible on some aerial photographs (CUCAP: APB092). This millpond appears to have been manmade, formed by slightly straightening the natural stream as it ran into the lough, to better control the water flow and thus mill power. On the OS map, the mill (appropriately named 'Rock Castle Mill') is around a hundred metres to the north of the millpond. As the tower house is located on a rocky outcrop, the occupants would have had a fine commanding view over the mill and pond – an assertion of lordly income and authority – but the millpond probably also provided a scenic backdrop for this tower house, most commonly studied for its decorative masonry date stone (O'Keeffe, 2015; Ronnes, 2007).

2.2 Ballynacarriga Castle, County Cork, is located atop a rocky outcrop. The entrance to the tower house is pictured, but to the rear was a water channel that fieldwork and map investigation indicated was the site of a mill and millpond. The height of the tower house would have given a commanding perspective over this manorial feature.

Significant works could, on occasion, be undertaken to facilitate milling. At Athassel Abbey in County Tipperary, the mill race was cut across a mile-wide meander in the River Suir. The channel thus created was over two thousand feet long and needed a forty-foot bridge to be able to cross it (Rynne, 2003). This scenario was a rarity promoted by the extensive landholdings of the religious house. Lay landlords seeking to cut a waterway to their mill either needed to keep it entirely on their own land, or negotiate an agreement with the neighbour whose land it bisected. In the case of the latter, the compensation required could have seriously reduced the financial profitability of the mill (Brady, 2006). A moat could be adapted to function as a mill race, although again it is difficult to discern this usage based on modern mapping (Armstrong-Anthony, 2005).

We know that 'a third part of a watermill, weir, fishery and waters' was assigned as dower at Dunmoe Castle, County Meath, in 1415 (*Inquisitions and extents*: p. 208, 348, C138/17, 72). There are the ruins of a couple of stone mill buildings at the base of the outcrop upon which the castle stands. These are today well covered by thick vegetation, but their appearance is preserved in early nineteenth-century drawings of the disused mill by George Victor Du Noyer (Du Noyer, *c.* 1815?). These show that the river was banked and diverted to create a short leat. The likelihood is that the fifteenth-century mill was under the later building depicted.

Likewise, at Newhaggard Castle in County Meath, located upstream of Dunmoe past Trim, the tower house is sited within a couple of hundred metres of a modern mill structure (see figure 2.3). A mill is marked in precisely the same location as the modern structure on the *Down survey* mapping. This historic mill is detailed in Tudor-era fiants, including one to Lord Deputy Saintleger in 1543–44, and so was evidently a profitable site even in its proximity to the Pale boundary. Doubly attractive was the fishing in this stretch of the River Boyne (*Irish fiants*: vol. 1). At Dardistown in County Westmeath, there appears to be manorial-centre continuity from the high Middle Ages into the later Middle Ages. The tower house was located by a motte and modern mill buildings now stand nearby. A stream that could have powered the mill is also present, presumably manually diverted from the nearby River Deel, and a historical bridge crosses the stream at this point.

The overwhelming majority of riverine sites, like water mills and fish weirs, have not survived into the modern-day landscape; consequently, it can be difficult to gauge with accuracy how close a tower house was to such features unless they are marked on the *Down survey* mapping. Most of the mills mentioned in the Leinster and Ormond estate documentation are only listed in conjunction with a townland name. Presumably

2.3 Newhaggard Castle in County Meath has been much altered from its medieval state, including adaptation to a gatehouse and pigeon house. It is located atop a slight rise above the River Boyne, possibly at a crossing point, while the *Down Survey* maps indicate that a road ran past it. This image also shows the modern mills to the left, which appear to be on the same site as a documented late medieval and early modern water mill.

the documents were drawn up by people familiar with their locations. Comparing the mentions in the Ormond papers with the *Civil survey*, we can see more mills marked in the latter. This might imply post-medieval construction, or simply that some mills were omitted from the estate records, potentially because they were not turning a sizeable profit, or perhaps because they were not rented out but controlled directly by the estate.

Archaeology is therefore crucial to our understanding of historical milling. However, as noted above, incidences of later mill sites are fewer, and often we need to be content with excavation summaries. Many of the archaeological findings for mills and weirs come from County Kilkenny, because of the River Nore Drainage Scheme (also known as the Kilkenny Flood Relief Scheme). There is also a bias towards urban areas, owing to these being rescue excavations and not for research. While we know of tower houses in these urban areas, their association with a nearby mill is not as precise a conclusion as if the mill and weir were at an isolated rural tower house, as at Newhaggard.

This is precisely the case with Kilkenny city, an important medieval town. Excavation focussed on the Bishop's Mills, Ormond Mills and Archer's Mills complexes. The earliest written references to these sites date from the end of the fourteenth century. Bishop's Mills was a complex that included a mill race of 2.2 kilometres and a mill building constructed at least partly of stone (*Database of Irish excavation reports*: 2001:708, NOR-2, Mill Island and Green's Bridge Weir, Kilkenny). Archer's Mills were also stone built, and had roofs of thatch or part slate. By the mid-seventeenth century they were two corn mills and a ruined tuck mill for cloth finishing, indicating an earlier cloth industry in the vicinity of Kilkenny (*ibid*.: 2002:1008, NOR-17, The 'tuck mill'/'archer's Mills', Dukesmeadows, Kilkenny). More conclusive are the findings at the White Castle in Athy County Kildare, site of an important bridge. A mill race was uncovered, and a patio 'immediately surrounding the castle' possibly overlies the mill buildings (*ibid*.: 2006:928, The White Castle, Athy, Kildare).

On the manor of Strancally Castle, County Waterford, the tenants had to take their corn and grain to the lord's mill, while the miller got a cut of a sixteenth part as toll payment (NLI, MS 43,153/5). Unfortunately, no mention is made of the profits ensured by the lord. A 1473 indenture for a mill in Thomastown, County Kilkenny, alongside a castle, two gardens, meadows and a pond, stipulates that tenants had to grind their corn at this mill (*Calendar of Ormond deeds*: 1413–1509, vol. 3). The features that could be associated with a mill are seen at Mogeely Castle in County Cork. In early seventeenth-century deeds and leases, millponds, heads of ponds, watercourses and fishings are all mentioned as being 'under' the castle. A weir mentioned on the River Bride might have been a fishing weir, as indicated by the 'fishings' reference (NLI, MS 43,142/3). Two water mills at Killmafont Castle in County Waterford were for grain and corn grinding, and a grant specifically mentions 'all paths, ways, waters, streams, sluices, gates, milldams, ponds, tolls of corn and grain, together with pasture and meadow for the maintenance of two horses or geldings (to be employed for loads), two loads of hay for maintenance'. The grant also included a millhouse, presumably a residence for the miller, where he could fish from 'the lower room … from time to time' (*ibid*.).

Fewer in number, though fairly detailed, are the handful of references within the *Ormond deeds*. A 'mill place' was located at Mountgarrett, County Wexford, in 1504, site of a tower house (*Calendar of Ormond deeds*: 1413–1509, vol. 3, p. 306, entry 314). One Agnes Hervy was responsible for the building of a mill near the castle in Carrick-on-Suir, County Tipperary, in 1427, and a bridge was also located at this site by around 1470 (*ibid*.).

The *Civil survey* shows regional variation in what tower houses were associated with; however, caution must prevail as the individual volumes are not consistent in what features they record. Also, they do not cover the whole of the country, so generalisations about east versus west or north versus south cannot be made. In County Meath, where we have one of the more detailed surveys, and comparing with the tower house classification in the ASI, twenty tower houses have a mill listed in the same townland. A total of twenty-seven out of fifty-nine tower houses in this county were within half a kilometre of a river. It is common to see two mills listed. Most are simply listed as a 'mill' (that is, twenty-two in total) while only five are listed as 'corn mill', two as 'tuck mill' and two as 'water mill'.

The association of tower houses with mills cannot be determined across the country. It is rare to encounter mention of a mill in historical documentation in border areas such as County Down, which despite this seems to have practised mixed agriculture, as testified to by the grains found during excavation at Jordan's Castle in Ardglass by Gardiner. Much of western and southern Ireland includes fertile land, so we should not be surprised to find documentary references to water mills there, such as those in County Limerick. Glenogra was the site of a tower house, medieval parish church and DMV (*Irish fiants*: vol. 3). Ballingarry, still a town today, has a tower house that once commanded a garden or orchard, while a mill 'belonging' to the tower house was located on another land parcel (*Desmond survey*: MS f. 62). Mills were often located close to, but outside of, larger settlement centres, as at Kilmallock. The castle and land of Courtruddery (not extant but probably a tower house) are described as close to the town walls and controlled three different water mills – one of these is recorded as 'adjacent' to the castle, while another 'belonged' to it (*ibid.*).

England is often employed as a point of comparison because of geographic proximity and the importation of the manorial system in the high Middle Ages from there. However, we must not lose sight of disparities that can be significant, of which milling may be one. The values for mills tend to reflect size and capacity, and these values are significantly higher for Ireland than England. Historians are unsure specifically why, but the size of the manorial landholdings, competition (or lack thereof) and the controlling abilities of Irish lords probably each play their part (Murphy, 2015). Mills also provide further evidence for the continuity of some manorial practices. In tandem with the evidence for fish weirs, the presence of mills might indicate that lords in medieval Ireland were picking and choosing what aspects of this economy best suited them. Excavation, as well as sites like Newhaggard in County Meath, provides solid evidence for site continuity. It may be that later mill complexes reused medieval mills. That late medieval mills were constructed of timber would account for their extremely low rate of survival into the modern landscape.

Conclusion: Tower houses as agricultural and administrative centres

A significant conclusion from this chapter is that we have more evidence for the continued practice of mixed agriculture than has usually been recognised. In the more fertile parts of the country, economic activity even after the Black Death was still quite diverse. It should be restated, however, that this situation was present at tower house sites, and may not apply outside of the tower house's local influence reach. In large part, this association between tower houses and mixed agriculture appears to be due to the influence of manorialism. Usually viewed as a high medieval socio-economic system employed by the Anglo-Normans, research shows that aspects of it survived long into the later Middle Ages and outside of the Pale. In essence, the tower house operated as the manorial centre, in much the same way as the manor house or earth-and-timber castle did in the high Middle Ages. As was explored in chapter 1, the significant change between tower houses and other earlier castle forms may be that the former were located in closer proximity to nucleated peasant settlement, at least in some identified locations. This might represent restriction of agricultural activity alongside settlement restructuring after the crises of the mid-fourteenth century, most critically the ensuing demographic decline.

Pastoralism was, of course, still of enormous significance to the economy. A major benefit of pastoral agriculture was that it required less manpower than did arable. It was also well suited to more marginal topographies and soil fertilities. While tower houses are not known in uplands, booleying could still have been practised by communities associated with one. Not every person resident in a pastoral farming environment would have directly engaged in removal to uplands in summer. McDonald has suggested that the wealthier, cattle-owning population did, which could have an impact on tower house distribution (McDonald, 2016). In contrast, Costello (2016a) proposed that women and younger people would have been delegated the task, which, if widespread, would have a negligible effect on tower house distribution. We know, too, that the tower house builder need not live in the tower house constantly, for we have references to tower house lords vacating the tower during wartime to shelter in fastnesses. Throughout the year, tower houses could play a direct role in serving cattle herds, especially through providing shelter in their bawns. In England following the Black Death, wages of skilled workers did not increase in comparison to the income of agricultural workers. This ensured a relative reduction in building costs, which may have been paralleled in Ireland. Increased pastoralism would amplify this pattern further and so encourage building.

Perhaps a major theme of this chapter is to highlight the contribution environmental archaeology can make to our understanding of late medieval agricultural activity. Palynology has proved illuminating as regards the extent of mixed agricultural practices, even from a limited number and range of samples. It has shown that manorialism or mixed agriculture continued past the Anglo-Norman period. This includes for Gaelic-Irish areas of Ireland, and increasingly Gaelicised areas as suggested by the pollen record for east Galway.

Most of our archaeological knowledge of water mills is focussed on the predominantly early medieval horizontal mill. This stands in contrast to the general pattern of medieval material culture, whereby we tend to have more and therefore know more about later periods associated with increased consumption and materiality. Instead, our primary means of identifying mills in late medieval Ireland is through historical documentation, which has several profound limitations. One of these is ambiguity – these records tend only to mention the existence of a mill and perhaps how much income it generated, not details of appearance or social role. From this limited information we can assert that water mills were vulnerable buildings, in that they are often referenced as being 'waste' due to localised violence. Presumably they required a certain level of cereal cultivation to make their operation viable. However, they also appear to have been comparatively straightforward to repair and thus make productive again, since in some cases we find multiple references to the same mill site – both where several references over time indicate continued use and where a mill described as disused is later referred to as functional. In a small number of instances, these mills could be significant generators of income. A prime example of this is the mill associated with the castle at Carrick-on-Suir, County Tipperary, site of two tower houses joined by an early modern house. No doubt the closeness of a town and the fact that it was the caput of the earls of Ormond ensured that it was in constant use. In an ideal scenario, therefore, a water mill could be an appealing source of income that required minimal daily supervision. Tower house builders generated income through every means at their disposal, thus the building form was an investment as much as an expenditure.

Even if we concede that some of the mills referenced within these documents were tuck or fulling mills, then that is still evidence for the practice of the manorial economic activity of sheep farming, if the reference dates to before early modern colonisation. We have underestimated the resilience of certain aspects of the manorial economy into the later Middle Ages and after in Ireland. While we lack concrete forms of manorialism in other ways, such as landscape features from ridge-and-furrow ploughing or fishponds, some manifestations thrived in an Irish context as suggested by numerous references to both mills and manor courts in the extant documentation. It may be that Irish landholders picked and chose what aspects of European manorialism worked best for the specific conditions they found themselves in. A diversified agricultural economy would perhaps be preferred after the natural disasters of the fourteenth century, the events of that century highlighting the usefulness of alternate food and income sources should one be badly affected by pestilence. Focusing on the production of a single resource would be financially risky, and we know that the later Middle Ages was in general a prosperous period for Ireland, highlighted by the building boom of which tower houses formed a major part. Such economic diversification would explain the harnessing of aquatic environmental resources.

Notes

1 The comparative figures between 1479 and 1533 for County Dublin show a rise in the area under tillage from 30.4 to 34.9 per cent of agricultural land, for the same period in County Louth from 16 to 17.1 per cent, for County Kildare from 7 to 8.5 per cent and for County Meath from 10.5 to 12.5 per cent (Ellis, 2015).
2 See http://downsurvey.tcd.ie/down-survey-maps.php#bm=Corcumroe&c=Clare.
3 In other words, MacMurrough's territory, which was in the vicinity of south Wicklow and north Wexford (Nicholls, 2003).
4 The MacGillpatrick lands stretched along the modern boundaries of counties Kilkenny, Laois and Tipperary, and the O'Mores had lands in the vicinity of southern Laois to the west of the MacGillpatricks. O'Byrne's lands were in County Wicklow (Nicholls, 2003; Otway-Ruthven, 1968).
5 From a transcription of 1848. This is the same as BM Harl. 3756.
6 Such as the publication on the Nendrum monastic early medieval tide mill, a horizontal mill with millpond (McErlean and Crothers, 2007).

3

Rivers in pre-modern Ireland: Environment and economy

Having explored the land-based activities occurring in the vicinity of tower houses, what of the water? After all, Ireland is an island and is penetrated by countless rivers, many of them navigable at least to small boats, and lakes dot the interior. Water is therefore intrinsic to any study of historical landscape exploitation. Substantial numbers of tower houses stand within half a kilometre of water, whether this be sea, lake or river. This chapter examines the functions served by water at tower house sites, before the next chapter goes on to consider how many tower houses facilitated movement and connections along water-based routes.

It is not hard to understand why control of other money-making resources was essential to tower house occupants. For example, according to the *Civil survey* for northern and western Tipperary there was often at least one tower house per parish, with the land held by more than one person in the majority of cases. With so small an area to support a tower house and its inhabitants, it is of no surprise that other income-generating resources were relied upon, such as toll imposition and aquatic resource exploitation. The profits from these could be substantial, as O'Sullivan wrote: 'fishing provided food for rich and poor, an income for fishermen, shipowners and merchants and taxes for church and lay authorities' (2003: 462). The importance of water to castles has been investigated before, though such study pales in comparison to the number of works conducted on their terrestrial environments. A major conclusion of McManama-Kearin's castle-siting study (2013) was that proximity to water was a major influence on site choice, with the combination of water access and control of routeway junctions being particularly alluring.

Rivers as medieval boundaries

Rivers are, even today, extremely convenient boundaries. They are clear and easy ways to demarcate land, and this was no different in late medieval Ireland. Rivers marked counties, baronies and lordships, and as a direct consequence could be hotly contested spaces. Their liminality is attested to by their choice as sites for military negotiations, like those meetings conducted between the earl of Tyrone and the English Crown representatives, whereby they would converse from opposite banks of the river (e.g. CSPI, SP63/206, f. 156, 1599). There is therefore significant overlap between the use of rivers in all the ways outlined in this chapter and for territorial and/or defensive purposes. Indeed, the use of rivers as defensive features has overshadowed a more holistic understanding of their role in medieval cultures. This limited perception does not have repercussions just for the study of tower houses, as almost all of Ireland's inland towns were located on rivers which were both boundary and trade route. This is particularly apparent on the major medieval rivers of the Barrow, Nore and Suir (collectively the 'Three Sisters'); Munster Blackwater; and Boyne. That towns in the north and west of the country tend to have coastal locations has been suggested to be because the Anglo-Irish had a weaker command on the interior, meaning that a coastal location was necessary to compensate for the multiple functions rivers provided to landlocked settlements (Glasscock, 1987).

The function of rivers as boundary markers also places significance on their crossing points. Bridges and fords frequently were military flashpoints, as is reflected in a cursory glance at the names given to pre-modern battles. During the Tudor Conquest, the Gaelic-Irish O'Neill, earl of Tyrone, constructed many defences along the Ulster Blackwater between counties Armagh and Tyrone. The famous Elizabethan mapmaker Richard Bartlett commented that these were especially concentrated at river fords (O'Neill, 2013–14). A fortification was constructed in County Tyrone on the river by the Crown, which included a wooden bridge and stone tower (this stone coming from dismantling at Benburb Castle) through which a road passed. The intention was to construct a second fortification on the County Armagh side of the river, to provide further support to the Tyrone site (*ibid.*). Had it come to fruition, these structures would have probably resembled an adaptation of the 'bridge castles', or tower houses that commanded bridge access and crossing points. But, as will be discussed in chapter 4, to solely note the military strategic abilities of medieval bridges is to woefully underestimate their multifaceted role.

The greatest cultural and psychological manifestation of late medieval political instability in Ireland is the Pale, which was also a physical boundary. In the later Middle Ages, a ditch was constructed around the Pale heartland in the counties of Meath, Kildare and Wicklow, ostensibly to protect the city of Dublin. That tower houses formed part of this protective strategy is clear from the historical and archaeological evidence. The creation of a financial subsidy of £10 in 1429 to assist with defensive building construction in County Louth is sometimes taken as proof of the starting point for tower house building in Ireland (Leask, 1944). This 1429 subsidy proved so successful that it was extended not long after to more Pale counties. But even in the middle of the fifteenth century, it is unlikely that £10 would have motivated much stone building construction. This has been used as an explanation for the general small size and plainness of Pale tower houses. Leask used the example of Donore, County Meath, as supporting evidence for the usefulness of the grant. Indeed, Donore almost meets the prescribed minimum dimensions stipulated in the subsidy conditions, with internal ground dimensions of 6.3 by 3.9 metres. It is also an architecturally plain tower house on its exterior, the only feature of note being its one projecting circular turret. This tower house is located within metres of the River Boyne, but at a height. This provided defence as well as avoiding flooding, a practical consideration noted at many riverine tower house sites, where the benefit of unimpeded river access had to be weighed against possible flood damage.

Aside from the tower houses, a ditch was constructed in some stretches of the Pale, parts of which survive in the landscape today. Although hard to see from ground level, it is partially extant at Kilteel, County Kildare. This is an interesting settlement complex; as well as a tower house (figure 3.1), there is a medieval church around two hundred metres to the southeast, and 'castle bridge' is marked on OS mapping. This site was occupied long before the period of tower house occupation, as it was an early Christian ecclesiastical location. That the tower house had a role in controlling access is apparent from the attached gateway, aligned northeast–southwest. The main tower looks to have had a residential function, with a projecting turret to the northwest. Compared with other tower houses in the Pale, Kilteel is quite a large example, although it is architecturally plain. The peephole on the ground floor of the tower house, which would have allowed a gatekeeper to monitor entry, implies the main tower also had a role in contributing to Pale defence.

Kilteel's defensive role is further illustrated by its association with the Knights Hospitaller military order. Although mainly known for their activity in the Crusader States in the Near East, they were present in Ireland too. After a dispute with the king that potentially brought them into conflict with the master of the order, the Hospitallers in Ireland were coerced into carrying out attacks on the Gaelic-Irish O'Byrnes along the southern stretches of the Pale, in modern County Wicklow (Coleman, 2014). This was not a successful campaign, but the proximity

3.1 Kilteel Castle in County Kildare is an excellent example of a 'Pale castle'. It is located beside an extant stretch of the Pale ditch, as well as a preceptory of the Hospitallers. It has a distinctive architecture that allowed it to monitor those who passed through its gate.

of Kilteel Upper townland to the Wicklow Mountains meant that the complex formed part of the boundary between the Anglo-Irish and Gaelic-Irish. There is possibly a second gatehouse associated with the preceptory, just over a hundred metres to the east-northeast.

Other tower houses in the Kildare–Wicklow border region are less overtly part of the Pale defence system, and instead bear relation to other settlement features. It is probable, therefore, that defence was just one of a multitude of functions for these sites, even in such an apparently militaristic location. Threecastles tower house, just over six kilometres to the southeast of Kilteel, is sited about three hundred metres from the modern course of the River Liffey. This area is the site of the modern Poulaphooca reservoir, which obscures medieval water patterns. As the townland name implies, it is believed that there were originally three castles here, of which only one survives. A church and DMV at nearby Burgage indicate that defence was not the whole function of this region, but that it could support a population.

Further north in the Pale, in Meath there are fifty-eight tower houses listed with the ASI, particularly concentrated along the borders of the Pale (Davin, 1983). Analysis of tower house distribution in the Dublin area shows that there is a correlation with the physical boundary of the Pale, especially along its southern reaches in counties Dublin and Kildare (Murphy and Potterton, 2010). In several cases, murage grants (supposed to be for building or defending town walls) indicate that the tower houses had defensive roles. Athboy received a murage grant for building wall defences in 1446, Kells in 1468 and Nobber in 1436. Syddan's was redirected to castle building. This reflects the multifaceted use of tower houses within County Meath, since use of the grant on a tower house would have provided security on the frontier and visually commanded the countryside.

The Pale boundary was in many places formed by a river. The 1488 definition of the Pale as it ran through Meath used Laracor to Bellewstown by the River Boyne, then along the Leinster Blackwater from Athboy. As the Pale shrank over the course of the later Middle Ages, a process that involved the Anglo-Norman town of Trim becoming a frontier town, so more riverine tower houses became built expressions of the Pale boundary. By monitoring the fluctuating extent of the Pale we could add all those tower houses along the River Boyne. However, to do so would be a drastic oversimplification. For example, Newhaggard, which is located to the west of Trim, would have fallen on the Pale boundary, yet it was a profitable mill site. To mark Newhaggard down as purely a 'Pale Castle' would hide a significant socio-economic role. As here, other uses of medieval rivers may be overshadowed by their function as a convenient territorial boundary.

Rivers as a water source: Washing, tanning, cleaning

Rivers served a variety of other purposes in medieval Ireland, including providing water for basic household functions. Such uses of rivers are surprisingly difficult to document, and they accordingly receive scant treatment in the published scholarship. Medieval people needed water for cooking, brewing and washing, though the extent to which water was directly consumed is a subject of debate. Medical beliefs at the time certainly included an awareness of the correlation between water and pestilence (Hoffmann, 2010; Rawcliffe, 2013). Despite the perceived hazards, it is likely that people did drink the water, especially if they were poor enough to have other sources of liquid nourishment denied to them. Fresh running streams were viewed as the best source of water, and wells were also used. The *Liber primus Kilkenniensis* contains a 1337 complaint leading to the prohibition of washing clothing and animal intestines in the town's fountains.

The other roles of rivers are less clear (Hoffmann, 2010; Rawcliffe, 2013). Rivers would also have been needed for less pleasant activities, both industrial (such as in tanning, dyeing and animal slaughtering) and personal. The fort and bridge tower built on the Ulster Blackwater in County Tyrone during the Tudor Conquest is documented in plans, and one of these (Hayes-McCoy, 1964; National Archives of the United Kingdom (hereafter TNA): MPF 1/311) shows two drains running from the fort down to the river. One drain was crossed by a small bridge, and the other connected with a privy and carried the fort's waste to the river downstream of the site (O'Neill, 2013–14). This shows an awareness of the need to separate one's water source from one's waste water. Sites close to or on river estuaries would have struggled to obtain water that was not contaminated by saline, including their well water and the river water itself (Rawcliffe, 2013). It is fair to presume that tower houses on estuaries, as well as many of medieval Ireland's towns, would have struggled with this same issue.

There are multiple references to accidental drowning in English records, such as in coroner's rolls ('Coroner's records'; Rawcliffe, 2013). Many drowned when attempting to draw water, and there is no reason to doubt that the same hazards existed in Ireland at this time. Cleaning out weirs must have only added to this threat. At least once in London the holders of wharves along the River Thames attempted to impose charges on the city's inhabitants for access to fetch water from the river. This was derided as being particularly unfair, in part because of religious associations with the charitable provision of water (Rawcliffe, 2013). It illustrates the attempts by those holding capital in the medieval economy to exploit every financial opportunity that they could. In light of the impositions placed by tower house occupants for access to natural resources, it is not hard to see river access for basic needs as something that also would have been monitored, especially if it was sought by those who were not tenants or otherwise associated with the castle site. In the early sixteenth century, water supply conduits and cisterns in London were 'elaborately crenellated with stone battlements' (*ibid.*: 224). No doubt this was a social statement by those who funded the public works to provide daily water needs to the populace, and it reiterates the use of castle architecture in conspicuous consumption.

The correlation of fish weirs with tower houses

Like water mills, fish weirs are commonly encountered alongside tower houses in a number of sources, including the *Civil survey* and OS mapping. The survival of a substantial body of documents relating to fishing in the Lismore Castle papers further testifies to the economic importance of the fish weir. Although most of these fishing weirs were dismantled owing to government legal investigations and subsequent restrictions in the mid-nineteenth century, when conducting fieldwork at these sites today it is easy to imagine how a fish weir could have been ideally suited to the environment. These suppositions are supported by discussions with landowners, which often indicated both illicit and legal fishing practices close to these sites within living memory. References in the literature to fish weirs at tower houses are legion, in part thanks to the series of articles written by Arthur Went in the 1950s and 1960s, detailing the history of the fisheries of Ireland's major rivers.

There is continuity in the use of fish-weir sites, so that modern weirs identified on OS mapping often indicate historical uses in the same spot, even though the weir structure itself would have been replaced many times over. O'Sullivan's research found that 'there is even a striking correlation between the location of medieval fish weirs and post-medieval structures, suggesting that in the eighteenth or nineteenth century local communities used their knowledge of them when they decided to build weirs on the mudflats' (O'Sullivan, 2003: 466). This went so far as to include sites that had remained disused for many generations. Continued use may be our only significant clue as to original locations, as eel weirs, particularly, were frequently flimsy assemblages that did not remain in use for long (Went, 1956).

A number of these weirs could have served two purposes: both providing energy for water mills and catching fish. Went describes 'kiddles' or 'kidills' as stake fences set into a mill dam so that they could catch fish (Went, 1953). Other contemporary descriptions are less precise. 'Fisheries' is an oft-encountered description and seems to refer to a weir, while *gurgites* is a Latin word that most frequently refers to weirs, but which in some contexts might also mean watercourse. 'Gurges' and derivatives like *gurgitem* are often encountered in the Irish documentation, and it is not always clear from their context what structures they are referring to (Langdon, 2004; and see e.g. Trinity College Dublin, MS 1207). Consequently, they may refer to a weir or a weir and mill. Riverine weirs tended to look like large 'V's in the water and could catch fish moving up- or downstream. Again there is a multiplicity of terminology, with the term 'head weir' commonly found referring to an ebb or tide weir that could be used to capture salmon (Went, 1961). That Irish weirs might have looked different to English examples is hinted at in a late sixteenth-century indenture whereby the grantee 'at own expense would build and make stronger the salmon weir after the salmon weir of England' (NLI, MS 43,153/1).

Weirs are the most commonly encountered method of obtaining riverine fish in the historical documentation, but were not the sole way of doing so. Nets were also used. In 1532–33 the tower-house-owning Lynch family of Galway city were granted three fishing nets in Galway located between the bridge and the sea for catching salmon and other fish (*Irish fiants*: vol. 1). Traps could also be utilised. These include the large stone 'V'-shaped structures identified in Strangford Lough in County Down. These traps went out of use by the late sixteenth century, but might have once stood one or two metres high, and some ran for as long as 1.6 kilometres (McErlean and O'Sullivan, 2002; O'Sullivan, 2005). Wooden traps were used in this tidal region in the same places as the stone versions (McErlean and O'Sullivan, 2002).

The techniques used in constructing weirs differed enormously, depending on local traditions and the availability of resources. For instance, while weirs made out of wattle were historically common, this method of construction has faded from modern usage (Went, 1961). What all weirs had in common was that they were barriers through the water that deflected the fish into an opening where they would be trapped and caught (O'Sullivan, 2003). The largest may be associated with medieval religious houses, owing to their larger populations, but can also reflect commercial activity (O'Sullivan, 2003, 2005). Fish weirs may have declined in use throughout the course of the late medieval period, as marine fishing assumed dominance of the market (O'Sullivan, 2003, 2005). Whether the overall number of fish weirs declined over the later Middle Ages or not, their correlation with tower houses remained notable. Even if never caught in large numbers, freshwater fish had a considerable social impact. The elite-foodstuff status of river fish, salmon in particular, will have assured the demand and constant need for fish weirs.

Tenants associated with riverine tower houses had labour obligations corresponding to fishing as well as terrestrial agriculture. Fishing weirs needed to be checked and emptied twice a day when the fish were in season, necessitating that the tenants responsible for their maintenance lived close by (O'Sullivan, 2001, 2003). Emptying the traps and weirs would not have been carried out by the lord, but he would have at least received a sizeable income through levies imposed on fishermen tenants (O'Sullivan, 2001). Although more economical than fishponds, inter-tidal weirs needed annual rebuilding and total replacement every decade (Daly, 2014).

Fishing rights came in time to mean the right to trap and gather fish for lordly and household consumption, with the excess sent for commercial sale. Before fish became a full market commodity there was a midpoint where tenants collected the fish from the weir and gave the landowner the right of first refusal, a set cut of the catch and a fixed monetary rent for continued use of the weir (Hoffmann, 1996). We also find leases of weirs, and this arrangement dominated after the Black Death, when population levels meant leasing was the easiest and most practical way to ensure a steady income. Prime fish could travel great distances to reach market. In 1524 a group of merchants from the English port of Chester leased the salmon fisheries of the River Bann, in the middle of Ulster, from the earls of Kildare (*Crown surveys of lands*). No doubt this rent was unique to the political conditions of the day and may have been, at best, difficult to enforce in the later Middle Ages, when the Bann was firmly within Gaelic-Irish-controlled lordship.

Fishing weirs could be associated with monastic houses. This relationship has been recognised before, with O'Neill (1987) stating that the majority of weirs were under monastic control, and there is a strong general correlation of religious houses with rivers. Fifty-one of fifty-six Augustinian houses and eighteen of twenty-five Cistercian foundations were by a river, which they needed for domestic usage and to power their mills (Rynne, 2003). Fish weirs might be located at some distance from the monastic house itself. For instance, at Annamult in County Kilkenny, site of a tower house, there was a water mill and half an eel weir owned by the Cistercian house of Duiske at Graiguenamanagh (Went, 1955). Many monasteries leased their far-away weirs, retaining part of the fish as rent. For instance, St. Mary's Abbey in Dublin leased a fishery in Lough Ennel, County Westmeath (O'Neill, 1987). In northeast Ireland there is likewise a correlation of large stone fish traps with stretches of the coast controlled by the church: along the County Down coast traps were held by the Cistercian abbey of Greyabbey and by the bishop of Down (McErlean and O'Sullivan, 2002). There is also overlap of religiously held lands, tower houses and weirs, one example being

Dysart Castle in County Kilkenny on the lands of the Priory of Kells in Ossory (*Irish monastic and episcopal deeds*).

At the time of the Dissolution of the Monasteries, Richard Calffe gave half of the salmon he caught in a pool (*stagnus aque*) and four of every five salmon caught in the adjacent weir in the River Boyne to the monastery of Mellifont (Went, 1953). Usually fish weirs were leased in this way for cash (*ibid.*). Other religious houses leased their fishing rights in full, such as the grant by Jerpoint Abbey in County Kilkenny to Thomas Fossard in 1532. Fossard is documented as a merchant of nearby Thomastown, and he was given the 'water of Skerdan' near Kilgrellan (unidentified, but possibly close to Mount Juliet), with all the fishing in ponds or watercourses as well as all the fish in the Skerdan (*Irish monastic and episcopal deeds*: 69). As Fossard was a merchant, we can safely presume he sold the fish he caught at market.

The present study also shows, however, that this relationship was not exclusive to religious houses, and that many lay landholders controlled fish resources. In fact, the documentary references collected do not reflect an overwhelming control by religious institutions; instead, there is a strong seigneurial and tower house correlation. Indeed, by law all tidal reaches and fisheries of navigable rivers belonged to the king, and he retained the use of some of these. Magnates controlled weirs, but so too did important town residents, and merchants rented others (O'Neill, 1987).

The best documented river from historical Ireland is the Munster Blackwater, subject to extensive investigation by the earls of Cork. Official copies of many medieval deeds destroyed in the Four Courts fire relating to the river and the rights associated with it are now housed in the Lismore Castle papers collection in the NLI. The legal status of the fishing rights to the Blackwater was no doubt partly of concern because of the variety of fish therein. The River Blackwater contained salmon, trout and eel, as well as many other species (Went, 1960). Before the earl accumulated land in the river area, the bishop of Lismore held the salmon fisheries of the lower river, according to a 1478 document, while the earl of Desmond lost his tower houses and weirs in the attainder following the Desmond Rebellion in 1584 (*ibid.*). Sites specifically mentioned in the attainder were the Desmond manor of Strancally, corresponding with a tower house and 'the manor of Lisfinny lying upon the River Bride, and the fishing for salmon and other fish to be taken in the said river to the aforesaid manor belonging, one castle' (*ibid.*: 55). There is a second tower house on the River Bride associated with a historical fishing weir at Conna tower house, and on the Blackwater, Temple Michaell tower house was located by fishing weirs intended to catch sprats (Went, 1961). Salmon and eel fishings in conjunction with castles and mills are mentioned in the 1602 document forged between Raleigh and the earl of Cork, including Strancally (NLI, MS 43,087/5). The salmon, trout and 'other fresh fish' connected to the manor and castle of Mallow were listed in the earl of Desmond's sixteenth-century attainder, and a seventeenth-century document indicates that the fishings here were probably through a fishing weir (Went, 1961). O'Sullivan concludes that the tower houses of this region were specifically sited with control of navigation and the fisheries in mind (O'Sullivan, 2001).

Weirs were a nuisance for those who did not possess them. The barrier mechanism caused problems for boats trying to pass. In some tributaries, a fish weir or mill dam could cut off spawning populations (Hoffmann, 2010). Compromises were attempted in terms of boat navigation on rivers. Weir design could allow for navigation: 'The weirs on the Blackwater are not (like those at Limerick and many other places), flood weirs, extending across the whole river. ... The wings are staked and wattled, extend through that part of the river where there is least current, so as not to impede the navigation' (Went, 1960: 117).

Owing to the shallow depth of rivers, even along the navigable reaches, barges would have been the main vessel encountered. The interests of those holding rights to fish weirs clashed with those wanting to use the river for movement. Where complaints are made about obstructions, this is often taken by historians to indicate otherwise navigable stretches of river (Langdon, 1993). In 1537 the people of Clonmel in County Tipperary complained that the weirs along the River Suir between Carrick-on-Suir and Cahir were preventing boat access, and these protestations were reiterated in 1576 (Went, 1956). For compromise, it was stated that weirs could not extend past a certain distance, such as twelve feet for the River Blackwater in 1589, and an aperture of twenty-four feet for boats to pass through on the River Boyne was recorded in 1366 ('Cal. Carew MSS 451', cited in Potterton, 2005; NLI, MS 43,153/1; Went, 1953). Sometimes other clauses, such as one specifying a gap of seven feet from the river bank as a clear towpath for horses (presumably pulling barges), were added to these documents (Potterton, 2005; Went, 1953). That the waterways were fairly regularly obstructed despite this is apparent in the number of complaints regarding different rivers in the extant documentation. These include the River Boyne in Meath in 1435 and 1537 (Holton, 2001; O'Neill, 1987; Potterton, 2005), and the River Liffey outside Dublin (Murphy and Potterton, 2010). In 1366 the abbot of Mellifont was in trouble over his weir at Oldbridge. To remedy, it was demanded that he insert 'a certain free passage in that river from the town of Drogheda to the bridge of Trim, usually called a watersarde, twenty-four feet in breadth from the bank on each side of the river ... and that through that aperture, boats called corraghs, with timber for building and flotes had liberty to pass constantly free from Drogheda to the bridge of Trim' (Went, 1953: 22). That the abbot paid little attention to these instructions is evidenced by the same issue flaring up three years later (*ibid.*).

The Netterville family of Dowth tower house controlled a salmon weir on the River Boyne, which they fought to retain control over, including having it returned from the Crown in 1381 (Went, 1953). Such mentions support the interest of lay lords in asserting control over weirs. A number of other profitable weirs are cited in conjunction with tower house sites, including a weir on the manor of Slane in 1459, which the *Civil survey* indicates might be the weir at Fennor tower house; seventeenth-century references to a weir at Dunmoe Castle; three fishing weirs at Athlumney tower house; and a mill and fishing weir at Scurlockstown tower house. Trim town had several mills and at least one eel weir, while the previously discussed tower house and mill at Newhaggard were linked to the fisheries between there and Trim in 1544 (*ibid.*). The medieval town (home to several urban tower houses) of Ardee, County Louth, was likewise the site of mills and mill dams used for the taking of eels in 1304 (Went, 1959).

Along the River Nore, the occupant of Brownsford, County Kilkenny, had two salmon weirs, which seem to have been opposite his lands and thus presumably his tower house, in 1543 (Went, 1955). Shine has followed Edwards's interpretation that the Fitzgeralds who occupied Brownsford Castle controlled significant stretches of the rivers Barrow and Nore 'to the annoyance of the local fishermen' (Edwards, 2000: quote 70; Shine, 2011b). Dysart Castle was associated with a salmon weir, which according to the landowner was illicitly in use until the 1980s, and three fish weirs are documented in 1609 at the medieval town of Thomastown, itself in a location good for salmon and eels (Went, 1955).

This trend is mimicked in the other rivers of the Three Sisters network, and here again we find strong evidence for seigneurial control of these resources. For instance, in 1434 the earl of Ormond maintained that 'they shall permit the lord's fish to be taken and shall guard them and the said castle and do all other things which constables were anciently wont to do for the lord' at his castle in Carrick-on-Suir, County Tipperary (Went, 1956: 193). This site contains two tower houses within a significant castle complex, and the claim for the 'lord's fish' probably operated on a similar basis to the cut claimed by Gaelic-Irish lords controlling maritime fish shoals (*ibid.*). These weirs were particularly lucrative – a 1415 extent shows that the castle controlled seven salmon fishing weirs on the Suir, valued at £8. In comparison, the water mill was only worth 30s. (*Red book of Ormond*). Weirs were significant obstacles to boat passage on this river, too. The residents of Clonmel complained that the weirs between there and Carrick-on-Suir prevented safe navigation, but that they also prohibited fish movements (*ibid.*).

Considering the level of Crown interest in religious assets, it is somewhat surprising that documentary references to weirs are not more numerous than they actually are. The Tudor fiants document several religious sites that are associated with nearby tower houses, among them the Carmelites of Ardee in County Louth holding an eel weir (*Irish fiants*: vol. 1), and the rectory of Carlingford in County Louth controlling fishing on the River Carlingford (*Irish fiants*: vol. 2). However, there are just as many references to non-religiously owned fish weirs. One example is a grant of 'as many eels as shall be taken weekly in one day of 20 eel weirs there' in Galway city, where no religious interest is referenced (*ibid.*: p. 195, 1499).

The historiography has tended to focus on religious control of water resources in the medieval world (Arnold, 2012). The explanation most commonly cited for religious ownership of fishing engines is the sizeable population residing there, demanding significant volumes of fish for consumption on holy days when the eating of meat was prohibited. In contrast, it has been argued that consumption of freshwater fish must be associated with the aristocracy in medieval England (Dyer, 1994), and in Ireland there were as many, and possibly more, fish weirs controlled by tower houses than by religious institutions.

The correlation between riverine tower houses and fish weirs tells us about the social mentality of the tower house occupant. Most obvious is that securing a supply of fish was an important consideration. Even on stretches of well-stocked rivers, market supply of fish could be a problem, as indicated by the descriptions of fishermen being 'deforced' of their catch in Kilkenny city (*Liber primus Kilkenniensis*: 28 and 35), which sounds rather violent. The supply problem, combined with references to fish weirs, along the River Nore implies that local fish catches remained in the hands of a minority. In a tower house, the number of people resident would have been substantially smaller than in even a small monastery or abbey (even the garrison numbers cited within CSPI are to men numbering in the teens), and there would not have been the same emphasis on fasting as a regular lifestyle restriction. Therefore, the level of fish consumption at a tower house would have been much lower than at a religious foundation. So where did the fish go?

First, river fish being the most elite of the piscine foodstuffs, there would be significant social cachet attached to the possession of a fish weir and, more pertinently, to a steady and numerous stock of fish. Very few fishponds for the raising or even the storage of fresh fish have been discovered archaeologically in medieval contexts in Ireland. This conundrum led Murphy and O'Conor (2006) to suggest that Irish lords simply did not utilise fishponds to the same degree as their English and continental neighbours, and instead relied upon other sources for their fish stocks. The evidence uncovered here supports their conclusion, and it is proposed that fish weirs, in riverine, estuary and coastal locations, comprised those other sources. Whereas elsewhere in medieval Europe the fishpond stood as a symbol of lordly identity, along with the deer park and dovecote, it may be that a fish weir performed this function in Ireland. As O'Sullivan in his studies of the fish weirs of the Shannon estuary has noted, the same construction methods for fish weirs are seen in that region both before and after the Anglo-Norman Invasion. In other words, the arrival of a new stratum of society controlling land and river resources did little to change the material culture of the Shannon estuary (O'Sullivan, 2001). The continued reliance on Gaelic-Irish tenants has been suggested as the reason for this continuation of construction practice; however, it is also a possibility that over time the newcomers adapted to Gaelic-Irish social constructs (O'Sullivan, 2005). This would explain why fish weirs are equally associated with tower houses in Gaelic-Irish and Anglo-Irish regions, and those dominated by settlers of the early modern period: that the practicality and benefits of the fish weirs ensured their continuity.

Second, and relatedly, the feasting and hospitality expectations of medieval lords would have aligned nicely with a secure supply of freshwater fish. The high incidence of halls at tower houses and their social uses indicate that tower house occupants entertained to varying degrees. However, even the most ardent entertainer could not have used up all his fish-weir supply in that way. The most likely explanation is therefore that the excess not consumed was sold at market.

As with many other landscape features located at tower houses described in this volume, the economic profits from these fish weirs could be substantial. What we might have in tower-house-era Ireland, therefore, is a midway commercial point, in which excess would be sold at local market or the weir leased out to an intermediary for a set rent and cut of the catch. The latter relationship, one seen in the documentation, would have kept a good balance between the demands of income and daily necessity. A quick and easy way to move the catch to local market was ensured by being on the river. We do see stable references to salmon in the extant customs accounts. The huge price discrepancy between marine species and salmon ensured that salmon remained a luxury foodstuff (Hoffmann, 1996).

Eels could be almost as valuable as salmon, but stayed local and do not seem to have been much exported – only once do they appear in the Bristol records, for 1479–80 (O'Neill, 1987). Eels could be kept alive in special boxes with running water for long periods of time, and this may explain their movement overland by merchants from Athlone via Athboy and Trim in 1452. This convoy was attacked and the eels lost. The archbishop of Armagh was also sent many eels, according to the registers (*ibid.*). Fish must have been a significant trade item between Irish towns and their hinterlands. The fishing rights nearest towns were therefore well guarded, since they were the most accessible to market (*ibid.*), and this might explain the numerous references to weirs near and in towns extrapolated above.

Fishponds: Elite status symbol and food source

This research supports Murphy and O'Conor's (2006) assertion that the low incidence of archaeologically and historically identified fishponds is connected with more intensive exploitation of other riverine and marine sources. Although, the low number of identifiable fishponds might be due to their not being recognised by archaeologists in the landscape and during excavations (*ibid.*). Regardless, it is hard to imagine that fishponds would rival the oft-mentioned fish weirs. Fishponds may have served a different purpose; in England they provided a private supply of fish in situations where a lord or king controlled the rivers (Aston, 1988), but this was not the situation in Ireland. Ireland's island topography and extensive involvement with maritime exploitation may have ensured that fishponds did not dominate to the same degree as found elsewhere.

There are a small number of references to fishponds, which will have provided a source of freshwater fish to their owners. Fishponds were artificial ponds made to hold and/or raise live fish. That they were usually built responses to a scarcity of natural supply likely explains the Irish patterns (Hoffmann, 1996). Artificial fishponds elsewhere in Europe were mainly later medieval in date, and the fish they cultivated tended to be similar species to those found in rivers (Dyer, 1994; Hoffmann, 1996). Fishponds were very costly to maintain, ensuring that they remained the preserve of a wealthy minority. This also probably explains the Irish preference for river fish, since a fish weir was far less expensive and labour intensive.

To raise fish in fishponds needed multiple ponds with complex connections between them, which could resemble artificial lakes more than ponds (Hoffmann, 2000). In medieval England the documented ideal was three ponds over fifteen acres or two ponds over eight acres, of no more than 2.0–2.7 metres deep (Aston, 1988). Boggy land, of course frequently encountered in Ireland, could be ideal for fishpond construction, as it both provided a good environment for the fish as well as preventing easy theft of the pond contents (*ibid.*).

The small fishponds identified to date in Ireland, either archaeologically or historically, were instead for storage rather than culture (Hoffmann, 2000; Murphy and O'Conor, 2006). If they were close to the castle site, fish could be plucked out fresh for consumption. Ponds could also be a tangent to water mills or castle moats (Hoffmann, 2000; Steane, 1988). Again, these would not have been fishponds for the raising of fish, but rather storage measures, with fish being transported from these locations fresh when required. Ponds were not the only means of storing fish until they were consumed. In Scandinavia, fish were stored in large wooden boxes in lakes, and this technique could have been adapted to medieval Ireland's multiplicity of rivers and streams (Hansson, 2014).

Fish weirs ensured a more consistent engagement with the fish market – each catch could comprise numerous fish, too numerous for one castle household to consume fresh, and so the surplus could be sold. This could be an attractive quality to a tower house occupant, who could have both uses of sale and consumption from a weir, while requiring significantly less from tenants for upkeep of the weir compared to a fishpond. However, the two could also exist in tandem. In this way, fish caught at the weir that were surplus to requirements could be stored in a fishpond to keep them fresh until they were ready to be eaten. Fish movements in river and marine environments were seasonal, so the appeal of a fishpond was also that fish could be kept and enjoyed year-round (Chambers and Gray, 1988).

Most of the fishponds identified previously and as part of this study were through investigation of the historical record. In England this situation is reversed, with most medieval fishponds ascertained through archaeology rather than documentary means (Dyer, 1994). In Ireland, there has been some archaeological identification of post-medieval fishponds, such as the three fishponds beside the tower house/mid-seventeenth-century fortified house at Leamaneh in County Clare, although these are difficult to identify even when you know they are there (Murphy and O'Conor, 2006). Another rare instance comes from Killegland Castle in Ashbourne, County Meath. These may be the same fisheries noted at a mill in the *Register of the Abbey of St. Thomas Dublin*. The first-edition OS map indicates the presence of unusual earthworks at the site. Two distinct ponds, around eight to ten metres in diameter, were identified by excavators, who suggested that these were two fishponds linked by now-silted watercourses. Associated with the settlement complex is a pre-modern fording point that could have been taxed as additional income by the tower house occupant (*Database of Irish excavation reports*: 2002:1416, Ashbourne Town Centre, Meath; 2003:1346, Killegland, Ashbourne, Meath; 2003:1347, Killegland, Ashbourne, Meath).

3.2 Dunmoe Castle, County Meath, is located atop a steep outcrop above the River Boyne. Historical art shows it to have had circular corner turrets, with a later building attached to the right-hand side. At the base of the castle outcrop was a mill. A documented fishpond was possibly located in its vicinity.

Information from the written sources is still sparse. One example of a fishpond recorded in contemporary historical documentation is at Dunmoe, County Meath. Dunmoe is an early and large tower house (figure 3.2), though 2016 revisions in the ASI have it listed as a hall house, which is incorrect based on the nineteenth-century sketches by Du Noyer (see figure 3.3). Two such sketches depict a clear verticality, while three circular corner turrets (the fourth presumably having collapsed by that time) are depicted in two further images (Du Noyer, c. 1815?). Dunmoe overlooks the Boyne River, next to a medieval church. An assignment for dower in 1415 records that there were a water mill, weir and fishery at the castle, but also a 'stank', or artificial fishpond (*Inquisitions and extents*). Field survey could not identify these fishponds, but it seems probable that the ponds would have utilised the watercourses associated with the water mills also listed there. The medieval mills at Dunmoe are probably underneath the post-medieval stone mills on the

3.3 *Dunmoe Castle on the Boyne below Navan*, by George Victor Du Noyer. Du Noyer (1817–69) was an artist and antiquarian. He drew several scenes of Dunmoe Castle in County Meath, of which this one best depicts the site prior to further loss of building fabric.

site, now in a ruined condition, thus in keeping with other sites with evidence for continued site usage. This would mean that the medieval fishponds referenced might have been located in a densely wooded area at the base of the castle outcrop, and may even have been built over by a third mill which is in this location. The fishponds might alternatively have been on the floodplain at the base of the castle, with their profiles and outline subsequently destroyed by repeated river flooding.

Kilcrea Castle in County Cork may have had a small pond immediately to the west of the tower (see figure 3.4). A depression around five metres across was formed when the (possibly earlier) moat and ditch around the site were altered. A pond in this location would have made for a pleasing view for those inside. Presumably, fish would have been stored in this pond, for the social message as well as the convenience and practicality. Similarly, the millpond at Ballynacarriga Castle in County Cork could have doubled up as a fishpond.

A further obstacle to secure identification could be the shape of the pond, with no standard shape or design dominating examples. The shape of linear ponds means they could easily be confused with other earthwork features. Linear fishponds were longer than they were wide, as the name suggests, with this design aiding in the trawl of the pond using nets, and minimising the opportunity for fish to escape at the sides (Chambers and Gray, 1988). Fishponds could also have multiple uses – as

3.4 This image of the west face of Kilcrea Castle in County Cork is taken from the perspective of a possible fishpond identified during fieldwork. The remains of a double-headed ogee window on the top floor indicate that the interior hall would have had a bucolic view over the pond and beyond.

millponds as previously mentioned, but also as moats (Roberts, 1988). The incidence of extant moats at tower houses is low, particularly when compared with the numbers of bawns as external defensive features.

A disincentive for fishponds will have been the costs involved, which may have not appeared attractive compared with the market value of fish. For instance, the fishponds constructed in Limerick between 1211 and 1212 cost over £33, a massive outlay (Murphy and O'Conor, 2006). We must not overlook the sizeable number of lakes across Ireland either, as these would have maintained a steady supply of fish. At Lough Gur in County Limerick, the neighbouring lough was so 'full of river fish' that the lough was simply written as a 'fishery' (*Desmond survey*: p. 152, 388, MS f. 5).

Income generation: Maritime fishing, tolls and taxes

Although the bulk of this chapter has focussed on activities taking place along rivers, emphasis should also be placed on the contribution of marine fish to the economy and diet of later medieval Europeans. Marine fish species dominated the market and were accessible to a far wider range of people than were freshwater fish. By the later Middle Ages, sea fishing from a boat was the most popular way of catching fish (O'Sullivan, 2001). Herring was one of the most affordable and widespread options. Distance from the coast did not diminish marine fish consumption, and, despite costs of transport, this fish remained less expensive than freshwater varieties (Dyer, 1994). Most medieval people consumed marine fish, and consequently control of these resources was financially attractive. Several scholars, including this author, have commented on the correlation of tower houses with control of maritime fish resources. Attention has tended to focus more on the Gaelic-Irish lords who profited from the fishing industry, but recent research has shown that lords in Anglo-Irish-dominated areas were just as keen to exploit the maritime environment (McAlister, 2016). Demand stretched across the European continent, meaning that Irish-caught fish found a wide market.

From around 1450, herring began appearing in huge numbers off the coast of Ireland. Unpredictable in their movements, the herring had probably been forced southwards through the changing climate patterns of the onset of the Little Ice Age, and Irish tower house occupants were willing to exploit them (O'Neill, 1987). A reference from the CSPI says that the fish in the Irish Sea were 'so plentiful all the year round with cod and ling that a whole army might be victualled from the fishings there' (Butlin, 1976: 164). Herring had to be treated within twenty-four hours so that they didn't lose their flavour, which meant that shore facilities were required (O'Neill, 1987). It is this requirement for shore facilities that particularly allowed tower house dwellers to act.

Herring dominated the national and international fish market, but it was not the only fish species exploited in Ireland and, thus, associated with tower houses. Hake was another important Irish fish. A significant commodity before 1400, the sea fisheries were further developed after that date. Most hake were caught between Wexford and Cork, and the maritime tower houses of this region have been proposed to be linked to the profits of this fishing (e.g. Ballyhack Castle, County Wexford) (O'Neill, 1987). Cod were also fished in the North Atlantic, though it has been suggested that Ireland had little role in this during the fourteenth century, and that it was not until the fifteenth century that western Ireland, especially Galway, was used as a stop-off point by Bristol-based fishermen en route to the Icelandic fisheries (*ibid.*). It is unsurprising, considering the evidence presented above, that tidal river estuaries were especially profitable places for exploiting fish reserves. In the River Shannon estuary, herring were caught by net and then hauled ashore, as were the higher-priced salmon (Went, 1981). The profits from these fisheries funded building projects in the region (O'Sullivan, 2001).

Fishing was also a seasonal activity, and was undertaken along with other commercial ventures and agriculture to provide a year-round income (Gillespie, 1985). Its seasonality was dependent on climatic conditions like water temperature as the fish migrated to their spawning grounds (Kowaleski, 2010). In the Irish Sea, at least, there was a substantial range of fish species present, which made the fishing seasons less distinct than in other parts of Europe. This meant that good fishing was present nigh on year-round (*ibid.*). The precise quantities and times of year depended on location, though. For instance, on the northeast coast, herring and mackerel did not overwinter close to shore. Overall, fishermen in this region would have been active for on average four months of the year (McErlean *et al.*, 2002). Fairs were timed to coincide with the peak migration of herring past that point along the coast (Kowaleski, 2010). Flavin noted from the Bristol accounts that sailings from Ireland with fish tended to coincide with fairs, and to exploit the Lenten market. She noted that in one year thirty-one per cent of the annual trade with Ireland took place in the month of March, and seventeen per cent in just one day (9 March) (Flavin, 2004). These patterns are notable in the Chester accounts too.

The biggest limitation to an examination of maritime fishing is that it has left little trace, either as a landscape consideration – in material remains or landscape alteration – or in the documentary evidence, even when compared with riverine fishing. On a small scale, fishing was important because 'in return for a small capital investment in boats and nets, the catch, once marketed, provided much needed cash in the rural economy' (Gillespie, 1985: 67). This situation is well summarised by Gardiner's investigations into fishing settlements in England. He found that such settlements often had no waterfront structures that would survive in the archaeological record. Similarly, a lack of financial investment aided this deficiency of permanent facilities, and contributed to the dearth of written evidence. Instead, boats were drawn up at the mud at the edge of a river, or dragged up onto the shore. He concluded that a fishing settlement 'was simply a location with access to a road or track at which goods could be transferred to and from the land' (Gardiner, 2007: 85).

Some attempt has been made to identify these liminal spaces in Ireland, and they have been particularly associated with tower house sites. Such 'coastal access points' include steps, slipways, platforms and niches carved out of rock. Unlike sandy landing places, these sites have the potential to be physically identified, since they involve permanent alterations to natural features. They provided land access for those arriving by boat, particularly where the local topography favoured sheer rock faces over sandy beaches. These locations may have facilitated illicit activity, since they were by nature more inaccessible than landing places, but also could have served more mundane functions, like access to freshwater supply. Rock-cut steps are especially associated with access to castle sites, an excellent example being those to Dún na Seád Castle, in Baltimore, County Cork (Kelleher, 2013).

Unlike the situation with trade, where some attempt to identify goods and networks can be made through the evidence left by official merchants, maritime fishing was a more marginalised social activity. It has been found in Exeter in England, for example, that fish were predominantly marketed by artisans and retailers, rather than by merchants. Those who traded fish also sold other goods, suggesting that they were small town traders with a diverse range of interests. This is not to underestimate their importance to the local economy though, as the sale of fish provided ties between Exeter and the settlements comprising its hinterland (Kowaleski, 1995). The situation in southwest England is important to consider when dealing with fishing in Ireland, since the surviving historical evidence tells us that a considerable amount of Irish fish was exported to this region, especially from its southern and eastern coasts.

A significant volume of Irish fish may not have been caught by local fishermen, but rather by visiting fleets from England or even further afield, who used natural bays and harbours for shelter and processing (Nicholls, 1987). Evidence from the *Kildare rental* indicates that this practice was more widespread than first thought, and applied to both Gaelic-Irish and Anglo-Irish regions. That the foreign vessels were numerous is attested to by legal attempts to restrict the numbers fishing in 1465 (except north of Wicklow, which fed the Pale) and in 1449–50 off Baltimore, County Cork (O'Neill, 1987). The Irish fisheries lagged behind other parts of Europe in terms of commercialisation. By the late fourteenth century, the hake fisheries were becoming increasingly commercial in their orientation. English ships left their southwestern ports in late May and June, laden with salt, and returned from the southern Irish coast in late August and September with lightly salted and partly cured fish. The fishing fleets left the same origin ports in September to capitalise on the herring shoals, coming back in November or December (Kowaleski, 2010). The ability to travel for considerable periods of time over longer distances to obtain fish was assisted by a new process that allowed a light salt cure on board the vessel, followed up onshore with a more rigorous treatment (*ibid.*).

This has led some historians to conclude that the export of fish was, when considered overall, so significant in the late medieval period that exports to locations such as Flanders were large enough to overtake hides (Childs and O'Neill, 1987). These possibly vast numbers of barrels of fish are further obscured by re-exporting. One example in the English documentation refers to the herring of Sligo, yet there were very low numbers of ships from western Ireland arriving, indicating that local catches were assembled and then re-exported from a separate location (Childs, 2000).

By the sixteenth century the level of fish exports was attracting Crown attention. In 1515, Henry VIII proposed that a third of fish should be left to the Irish home market, ostensibly to prevent a shortage, but probably to increase the price and thus provide a greater customs return. Around this time, too, there were unsuccessful attempts to tax the foreign fishing vessels that visited Ireland, who would have ordinarily informally paid duties to the local lord of the area in which they fished. In 1601 a further Crown attempt to profit from the Irish fishing industry was made, with every barrel of herring or salmon requiring inspection, and, on being found satisfactory, stamped with the queen's seal upon payment of 3d. This was in addition to a tax of one night's fishing on every boat each fishing season. These attempts to gain control did not work, however, and the most efficient method for the monarchy to profit remained the farming of the customs to locals, where a customs farmer paid a flat rate to the Crown to buy the customs collection rights, and could then keep that income for himself (Longfield, 1929). Had they been successful, these measures would have had the effect of removing informal duties paid to the local lord of the area in which fishing was being conducted, a practice that would have negatively affected the income of tower house occupants.

In the later period of tower house construction, it is impossible to tell what damage to the fishing industry might have been caused by political events. In the sixteenth century, the destruction of crops may have encouraged fishing as an alternative local food source. As with the appeal of creaghting as a moveable consumable, the tools for catching sea fish comprised a low level of investment. Fish traps and fish weirs would have been more sensitive to such deliberate destruction, being permanent structures. Similarly, if population levels were as low as some maintain (e.g. Gillespie, 1985) then fishing would have had the advantage of requiring less manpower than did arable agriculture. The fact that fishing by natives is not mentioned in official sources by colonisers could have its origins in English interpretations of what it meant to occupy a place. The transitory nature of fishing, requiring limited alteration of the landscape, possibly means that it was considered in a similar manner to pastoral agriculture and therefore was subject to political interpretation and design. However, English colonists in the sixteenth century were keen to propose fishing as a feature of any land grants in Ireland, and may have seen the possibility of profit from this activity in the native use of fishing resources. For example, Walter Devereux, Earl of Essex, when proposing his colonisation, had the 'pressing' establishment of fishermen and a fishing industry as the second item on his list of instructions for his executors in Ireland, after the sending of soldiers (CSPI Tudor: 'Instructions for John Norris and Edward Waterhouse by Walter Devereux, earl of Essex, 2 December 1573'). As a consequence it is difficult to form any concrete conclusions based on late sixteenth- and early seventeenth-century writings on the fishing industry, since the sources have a notable bias from the desire for personal gain, no doubt influenced by a pre-existing knowledge of the volume of fish controlled by Irish lords, owing to the significant amounts entering the English marketplace.

Research has been done into the role of fishing at sites associated with tower houses in southwest, west and southeast Ireland, and by this author for northeast Ireland as a component of doctoral research, later summarised in a 2016 article. Observed in all these areas was the siting of tower houses so as to allow the monitoring of shipping and control of fishing-fleet movements and fisheries (Breen, 2005; Loeber, 2001; McAlister, 2013, 2016; McAuliffe, 1991; Naessens, 2007, 2009). The seigneurial claim to fish shoals was not limited to Ireland. In Devon in southwest England men played lookout for the fish from atop high rocks, signalling from here to men in boats who rowed out to the indicated location. The lord would then take one-third of this catch (Kowaleski, 2010). Elsewhere, and in other circumstances, lords claimed a cut from each boat of their fishing tenants (*ibid.*).

The use of fortifications like tower houses in controlling the movements of fishing fleets appears to have been well recognised at the time. In the sixteenth century, apparently, over six hundred Spanish boats might be found off the south coast, so that 'there was a proposal in 1572 to fortify one of the islands in Baltimore Harbour "in which the

Spanish lie aground during the time of their fishing" and to collect customs from them and from the Biscayans' (O'Neill, 1987: 34). Breen found that control of fisheries was particularly important to Gaelic-Irish lords in his study of the southwest, although such fishing was mostly undertaken by visiting fleets with little input from the local population, who would have instead fished to satisfy a local market. Rather than directly engaging with the local economy, fishermen paid dues directly to the O'Driscoll lords, who were resident in tower houses. The O'Driscolls charged 4*d*. to any vessel for sheltered anchorage, while fishing boats were taxed an additional 19*s*., a barrel of flour and salt, a hogshead of beer and a dish of fish three times a week for use of the fishing grounds and sheltered anchorage. It was concluded that most fish processing would have been done on board, rather than at onshore facilities (Breen, 2001, 2005). This is in contrast to the stipulation that a further 8*s*. 6*d*. was charged for drying the catch onshore (Breen, 2005). The landing of catches was common elsewhere in Ireland (McAlister, 2016; Naessens, 2007; Nicholls, 1987).

The tower house, therefore, was a place to receive these dues, a location from which to monitor fishing and processing, and a visual reminder of lordly interests during this pursuit (Breen, 2001, 2005). Evidence for this role comes from the entire country's coastline, from the southwest around to the Irish Sea. It is easy to see how collecting such tolls could have become a highly profitable endeavour for tower house occupants, as this control amounted to a monopoly. Lords reserved provisioning of the visiting fleets for themselves; this included 8*d*. for every cow killed and 1*d*. for every sheep or pig (Breen, 2005). Doubtless this was in addition to the raised prices charged to the visitors for purchasing the provisions in the first place. Lords also claimed precedence and special rates on trade items, with 'butts' singled out, no doubt referring to wine imports. This shows that complex economic systems were in place and that lords were well versed in taking advantage of them (*ibid.*; O'Sullivan and Breen, 2007).

It was not just the O'Driscolls who charged in this way in this part of Ireland. In Ventry Bay in County Kerry in 1482 the earl of Desmond had to intervene in a dispute between members of the Treunt families over the Dingle fishing dues. It was concluded that 'Richard Treunt was to have the anchorage charges imposed on ships anchoring in the bay of Ventry. Richard was to receive two-thirds and Philip Treunt one-third of charges imposed for fishing in the bay, for using the shore, for salting fish, or for drying the nets' (O'Neill, 1987: 34). In the early sixteenth century, Spaniards paid £300 per annum to MacFineen Duff of Ardee for the ability to fish in Kenmare Bay, again in County Kerry.

Fishermen from Kinsale had to pay a rent for the huts at Cape Clear where they cured the fish. All in all, the Biscayans and Spaniards gave up a sixth or a tenth of all the fish they caught between Baltimore and the Blasket Islands. In exchange, they received protection for their vessels. McCarthy Mór claimed 2*s*. 6*d*. from every ship that either fished in his territory or landed with merchandise within his lands (Breen, 2005). References like this indicate the large amount of fish and the profitability of the market to tower house occupants. A tall and visually imposing structure like the tower house was the ideal mechanism for asserting authority.

Dunmanus in County Cork is located atop a rocky prominence on the inside of a small bay where multiple modern boats lie anchored. The height of the natural rock, along with its own five stories, gives it commanding views all around. Unusually, Dunmanus looks to have a small 'secret' anchorage, about thirty metres to the east-southeast. This small tidal inlet now has its access from the bay bisected by the modern road. It would have been deep enough for a small and light boat like a galley. As the inlet curves behind the tower house, it may not have been visible at water level from the bay or the sea beyond. This would create a private and hidden anchoring point for the tower house occupant's vessel. The tower house itself has an unusual, uneven Z-shaped plan. The turret projecting in the north face is slightly higher in its western corner than its eastern. This is because of the site topography, but it may have also increased uninterrupted visibility. A similar design is employed at Jordan's Castle in County Down. Dunmanus tower house looks very large and imposing when viewed from the bay and sea approaches, but smaller from the private haven (see figure 3.5). The unusual Z plan may therefore be a deliberate optical illusion used to intimidate strangers approaching by sea.

In the Shannon region of the southwest, takes of cuts of the catch are recorded. The Abbey of St. Senan on Scattery Island was taking five hundred herrings once a year from every herring boat to fish there by the time of Dissolution. The abbey further kept the right to one thousand oysters from each boat; these rights were later transferred to the mayor and citizens of Limerick (Went, 1981). In 1541 the castle of Limerick had the right to one hundred oysters from the River Shannon from each vessel carrying them that accessed the city (*ibid*.). The coarb (a layman officer of the monastery) of Inneskatty took the right of one thousand oysters from every boatload travelling to Limerick every year (Went, 1961–63). The rights to oyster beds could be held from quite far away, such as those at Ballybrickan and Ringaskiddy near Cork that were possessed by the Priory of St. Catherine in Waterford (*ibid*.).

3.5 This composite image shows three different perspectives of Dunmanus Castle in County Cork. This uneven Z-plan tower house seems to have been deliberately designed to present different faces depending on who was approaching. From left to right: view from the bay to the front of the tower house; view from the perspective of those approaching by sea – the tower house appears noticeably larger from this angle; the tower house when viewed from the private, 'hidden' anchoring point – this appears the smallest.

Although many references come from the south and southwest, this activity was not exclusive to that region. In Galway, or more specifically Naessen's study area of Iarconnacht, the same pattern of visiting fishing fleets existed. Of these, Naessens thought that most came from southwest England, since one-third of the population there was engaged in fishing, and also from Spain, as an adjunct to the Galway wine trade (Naessens, 2007). Tower houses in Galway Bay, as at Oranmore, had small harbours that would have served as adjuncts to both the fish and wine trades. At Muckinish, County Clare, are two tower houses at opposite ends of an inlet. Both sites are well placed to control fish traps in the landscape today. Presumably the modern traps indicate previous usage. Muckinish West is located on a narrow neck of land, where it commanded the inlet entrance as well as the sea routes. Muckinish East is located towards the back of the inlet. Probably the former controlled access to this very well sheltered haven and fishing ground, whereas the latter controlled the grounds directly and could monitor anyone anchored there (see figure 3.6).

Naessens (2007) identified features required for foreign fishermen: political stability, safe anchorages, availability of shore facilities and a supply network, particularly of fresh water. Iarconnacht was well placed to take advantage of the visiting fishing fleets – its greatest natural

3.6 This is one of two tower houses at Muckinish, County Clare, commanding sea routes and sheltered anchorages. This tower house is the plainer of the two and is located at the back of the inlet, but has a better command of the fishing grounds still present and used by fishermen today.

feature was its many bays, havens and anchorages, in common with much of the Irish coastline (Naessens, 2009). Tower houses were specifically sited in locations from which the best economic return could be made from fishing, a crucial part of occupant income in this region, since lords could make as much from taxing fishermen and merchants as from directly engaging in trade (*ibid*.). The imposition of such duties on fishermen was aided in a practical way by tower houses, as they controlled freshwater supplies and victualling networks, as well as maintaining a visual presence on the water (*ibid*.). The importance of tower houses in the control of fishing in this region is not only attested to by their siting within the landscape, but also in contemporary documentary evidence. This includes an instance where the necessity of an effective site for a tower house is stated in bardic poetry; one poem in particular speaks of the effort required to build a tower house, before the monument was relocated elsewhere to form a better base for preying on vessels (*ibid*.).

Moving northwards, the O'Donnells of Donegal were known as the 'Lords of the Fish' for their ability to control revenue from fishing and shipping (Ní Loingsigh, 1994). Tower houses in counties Donegal and Sligo commanded extensive views over maritime routes, and were on many occasions placed next to harbours and other landing places. A prime example is at Easky in County Sligo, which commanded the sea, an anchoring point and entrance to the River Easky. Economics in the form of trade, rather than political considerations, was a motivating factor behind such a distribution (*ibid.*). This interpretation is confirmed by documentary references to castles in County Donegal controlling access to salmon fishing grounds, fords and havens (CSPI: vol. 10, SP63/208/2, f.0024, 1601).

In Carlingford, County Louth, on the east coast in 1425 fishing rights were granted for the mease (a quantity unit of fish, especially herring, usually numbering 500–630 fish) of the castle (Gosling, 1992). By the sixteenth century it was noted that both natives and aliens were sailing to Carlingford because of the abundance of herring there (*Crown surveys of lands*). O'Neill (quoting from CSPI) states that an English fishing fleet of six hundred vessels was operating in the vicinity of Carlingford in 1535. Again, no mention is made of the place in England from which this fleet came. The fishermen of the fleet reportedly offered to make three thousand men available for the Lord Treasurer's campaign in the area for two or three days (Childs and O'Neill, 1987; O'Neill, 1987). Although these numbers seem far-fetched by sixteenth-century military standards, this bit of evidence does illustrate Carlingford's extensive involvement in the Irish Sea fishing industry.

Smith's study of medieval Dalkey, an east-coast port settlement located slightly to the south of Dublin city with a multiplicity of tower houses, led him to state that even the town's role as outport for Dublin did not displace the primacy of fishing in the local economy (Smith, 1996). Murphy and Potterton in their study of Dublin's economy found that most lords exploited the foreshore of their manors by placing customs on those who used the havens abutting their lands. The fish exacted by a lord were often the best fish, becoming known as 'the lord's fish', and lords exercised their rights to buy more fish at a reduced price. Murphy and Potterton found that the religious houses in particular, which controlled most of the County Dublin shoreline, were 'zealous in guarding their rights' (Murphy and Potterton, 2010: 397). In many cases fortifications were constructed to aid in the overseeing of coastal rights, the merchant tower houses at Dalkey providing secure storage as well as controlling the settlement (*ibid.*). The wealth that could be accumulated from harvesting the herring shoals can be witnessed at Dalkey, where a number of tower houses were linked to people involved with collecting fishing revenues (Smith, 1996).

This could also explain the comparatively high number of six tower houses in Ardglass, County Down, one of the highest densities in the whole country. This observation might even be extended to a wider geographic remit across the entire country: coastal regions, and towns in particular, often have a higher density of tower houses than inland areas. In Ardglass, the *Kildare rental* records dues for the custom of the fishing there:

> of every shipp with a topp that fishit, yf they do dry fish upon lande 10s and yf not but 5s Item every pickarde [picard, a type of barge or boat often used in fishing] other ship without a top, yf he dry fish upon lande 6s 8d yf nott 3s 4d Every vessell having a bote for ankerage 4d yf he have none 2d A cheff ffish [chief fish, a cut of the catch] to the castell of every fyssher as oftyn as he cumyth with fish Of every bote taking hering a meyse [mease] to the castell (*Crown surveys of lands*: 311)

Presumably, similar charges would have been in place at other tower house sites, since they have a strong association with anchorages and landing places and are proximate to fish shoals.

Colfer (2013) convincingly argued that many of the tower houses in Wexford had a mercantile function, dominated in particular by involvement with the herring fishing industry for which Wexford was well known. Ballyhack, site of a commanding tower house, with Nook Castle located around the bay, is on the Three Sisters river estuary, so potentially those sites with access to both marine and riverine resources made the biggest economic profit since they could avail themselves of a diverse species base (see figure 3.7). Monastic extents for the Cistercian abbey of Dunbrody taken at the time of the Dissolution state that there were nine fishermen in eight cottages with two boats at Ballyhack. The extent further details the toll to be paid for fishing by those resident outside Ballyhack: a cut of the fish, with hake especially mentioned (*Extents of Irish monastic possessions*). A Tudor-era fiant states that the people of Ballyhack paid their tithes in fish, indicating that fishing activity dominated (*Irish fiants*: vol. 2). Wexford is also well known for its role in fishing because of the inhabitants' involvement in establishing the Newfoundland fisheries in the early modern period. The migration of the herring shoals had a big impact on the Irish fish trade: those who made their livelihoods from fishing these shoals in Wexford pre-empted decline of the fish stock by following the migration of fish to the New World (*Documents illustrating the overseas trade*). This problem was likely encountered across the country, albeit to a lesser degree; another shift in emphasis to the Atlantic World away from the medieval Irish Sea region.

It need not have been coin or luxury goods that were given in return for fish. Fine cloth might have been a popular item of exchange for fishermen from England, while trade goods like wine, iron and military arms were popular exactions from foreign fishermen (O'Neill, 1987). But these items will be even more ephemeral in the already sparse

3.7 Ballyhack Castle, County Wexford, was a religiously owned tower house. It is set back from the present-day ferry ramp, but presumably overlooked the documented medieval ferry. Ballyhack was a successful fishing village during the tower house period.

documentation. Hides were also sought at the same time as fish, and trade in hides could have served as an adjunct to fishing since the smaller boats used in fishing could access more maritime havens and thus come into contact with more Gaelic-Irish with hides to sell (*ibid.*).

Large quantities of salt were required to preserve fish. The salting, or alternatively the drying, of fish required large open spaces on shore if the vessel was not big enough for it to be carried out on board. This would have been an issue particularly for foreign fishermen, who needed to preserve their catch before a long journey home. A light salting might have been all that was possible on board (Kowaleski, 2010). It is highly probable that the smaller vessels visiting the Irish Sea coast of Ireland from England would not have had such on-board facilities, although some boats within the fishing fleets reportedly sailing to the west coast from Iberia may well have, since this was a longer sea journey. Salting and drying could be done at a port town, as is implied by the charges levied at Ardglass, or at 'cellar settlements', where a small collection of huts at a good landing place was used as a base for treating fish catches (Fox, 2001). A tower house would have formed an excellent focal point for such a cellar settlement. It therefore could be that tower houses are our only standing evidence for the profit-making fishing activity. The use of tower houses to extract income from maritime fishing is therefore evident from every coastal region of the country, regardless of ethnic landholding patterns.

Conclusion: Tower house exploitation of aquatic environments

A number of significant conclusions have been reached over the course of this chapter, with implications for wider socio-economic studies of medieval Ireland. One is the dominance of fish weirs and fish traps over fishponds, for which there is little archaeological or historical evidence. O'Sullivan found that the same fish traps were in use along the River Shannon both before and after the establishment of the Anglo-Norman colony. He took this to mean that the same groups of people remained living in the area (O'Sullivan, 2005). It could also indicate that the new lords found the weirs and traps to be less labour intensive and costly than fishponds, and yet more productive overall, and so adapted to the existing technology of the Gaelic-Irish. Of course, further examples of fishponds might be uncovered through archaeology, but it seems probable that Irish lords mostly extracted fish from rivers and the sea rather than raising them in artificial ponds. The size of the known fishponds suggests they were more for storage of fish than breeding, and so the two systems of pond and weir could have happily coexisted.

As elsewhere in Europe, though, weirs and the obstructions they and water mills presented were an issue in Ireland. While the same level of documentation does not exist for these legal conundrums in Ireland as for elsewhere in the British Isles or Europe, the concerns expressed are the same. In turn, this may account for a slight over-representation of fish weirs within the surviving historical documentation.

Less work has been done across Europe on lordly control of water resources compared with religious control, but the evidence that has been summarised here for Ireland suggests that control was heavy, whether religious or seigneurial. While there is significant evidence for religious involvement with water exploitation in Ireland, it does not supplant or potentially even rival that of lay landholders. Once we bring tower houses into the picture, as there were fewer ecclesiastical tower house occupants than secular (though there were religious tower houses, both as part of monastic complexes as at Bective and Newtown Trim, both in County Meath, and occupied by bishops and other senior churchmen, like Kilclief in County Down), then a fuller picture of lay control of fish resources is presented. Despite the traditional association of religious houses with fish, lay lords were not behind in terms of exploiting this income potential.

Again, when compared with European-wide studies, there is limited evidence for communal activity in the control of aquatic resources in Ireland, though this could be a symptom of the lack of documentation. Despite this, it is more likely that the political decentralisation of the later medieval period gave Irish landowners the opportunity for multiple avenues of additional income, which at times was the opposite of English and European patterns. The imposition of tolls, charges and taxes for as many things as could be charged for – including drawing water; catching fish from river, lake and sea; and space for processing – was not an activity solely reserved by the Gaelic-Irish lords as they asserted their autonomy during the Gaelic Resurgence of this time period. Instead, there is conclusive evidence that these same activities were occurring in Anglo-Irish areas and within the borders of the Pale. The activities taking place within the Pale were not that different than elsewhere in the country, so the rule of the city of Dublin may not have had such an impact outside the immediate city limits. This lack of effective external and central control gave lords and gentry across the island of Ireland new opportunities to generate personal income, which they then chose to display or re-invest in new building projects, including tower houses. Here, therefore, we see conspicuous consumption in action alongside the tower house as a necessary means of forcing economic and social control over a geographic area. Thus, the foreign fishermen trawling offshore fishing shoals would not forget the presence of a controlling authority, since the built manifestation of that authority would have been visible to the fishermen whilst visually monitoring them. The involvement of tower houses in controlling harbours and fishing was universal around Ireland's coastlines. They were used for this purpose from southwest Ireland all the way around to the Irish Sea.

Other tower houses, including those in counties Clare, Galway, Westmeath, Leitrim, Cavan, Fermanagh and Tyrone, controlled inland water. Tower houses located on or in lakes could control land- and water-based resources. In this way they could form manorial centres with water meadows convenient for grazing cattle, and the lacustrine fish providing both food and income, as at the riverine and maritime tower houses described above (O'Sullivan, 1998). How tower house builders made their money, therefore, seems to have varied considerably depending on local circumstance and opportunity.

4

Movement, transport and communication: Tower houses and waterways

Tower houses created and sustained diverse economic networks. In particular, this was accomplished through siting on communication routes, especially water based, and interaction with transport networks. A significant proportion of transport and communication occurred via water in later medieval Ireland. Not only was this cheaper than land-based transport, but it helped navigate politically unstable territories, since protection and effort could focus on specific places. It was also a response to Ireland's topography, which in many places necessitated circuitous land routes. That is not to say, however, that in some areas land movement did not dominate. In the flat, fertile and politically more stable lands, such as in County Meath, people did travel using terrestrial roads. This would have offered more flexibility than river and sea routes, since paths could be altered and a wider range of destinations accessed. Goods and materials were moved from agricultural estates to the ports and towns via these local networks. Limited information from the west of Ireland, combined with comparative evidence from England, indicates that raw and unworked materials from agriculture and woodlands would first be moved to a manorial or administrative centre, used as a bulking point, before they were removed to a port. Often this centre corresponded with a tower house.

A correlation between tower houses and points on communication routes has been observed across Ireland (Murtagh, 1988, 2011; Naessens, 2009; Shine, 2011b, 2015). McManama-Kearin (2013) goes so far as to propose revising Malcolm's (2007) criteria for castle siting, from the most prominent concern being a site that was defensible to being one that was located on a major routeway. This siting can be interpreted as having a defensive motivation, albeit this is only part of the picture.

Some tower houses were located by land approaches to urbanised places; many others were sited to control causeways, bridges, roads (both terrestrial and maritime), ferries, fords and crossing points. The precise relationship appears to have varied widely from place to place; for example, in County Down only two tower houses have been identified as controlling causeways (Mahee Castle and Sketrick Castle), yet the majority overall were located by deep-water anchorages. Tower houses also could have a function within networks without actually playing a direct economic role in them: they could be used by sailors as beacons, or as lining-up points marking safe navigation, or tower houses might be located at safe havens. These networks may have operated between tower houses as well as unilaterally, requiring a certain level of elite interdependence. This may be indicated by intervisibility between tower houses – where they are positioned so as to be viewable from one another. This in turn might explain the regular spacing of tower houses along some routes.

We are again reliant on piecing together details from a variety of sources. Where the mid-seventeenth-century *Down survey* mapping survives at the barony or parish level, we can often see depictions of features like bridges and roads. The *Civil survey*, too, sometimes references the presence of crossings and bridges, though not always as its emphasis was on identifying profitable land use. The first-edition OS mapping can sometimes be useful, but really the most information can be garnered from investigating the landscape surrounding tower houses and comparing it with the available written evidence. Sometimes communication features survive in the modern landscape, or are indicated by continued site use. In other places we need to work with more ephemeral information, like the positioning of a tower house that appears odd in a modern-day context. These cases can indicate now-disappeared features that were important in the Middle Ages, such as wooden bridges. The susceptibility of such temporary constructions to adverse conditions is seen in the multiple records of wooden bridges being swept away by floods, including along the River Boyne in 1330, where only the few stone bridges were left standing, and at Fermoy in County Cork in the seventeenth century (Ellison, 1983; Lewis *et al.*, 2008; Rynne, 2018).

Mechanisms of travel in pre-modern Ireland

The attraction of riverine and maritime transport is readily apparent when we consider travel speeds in the Middle Ages. Oxen could travel on average at 3.2–4 kilometres an hour (Landers, 2003). In contrast, medieval sea-faring vessels could sail at between three and six knots (*c.* 5.5–11 kilometres an hour) 'speed made good' – in other words, after limiting factors such as wind direction are taken out of the equation (Hutchinson, 1997; Langdon and Claridge, 2011). Barges plied medieval rivers alongside the smaller vernacular currachs. Indications from legal documents are that barges were towed by animals, but they also would have utilised the tides when in estuaries. This was slower than marine transport, but, when contrasted with carrying items on pack animals, the volume that could be moved was substantially higher. In addition, so long as the towpath was not impassable, the animal could move along it faster than along a road where the local topography would have been more variable than a flat river bank. Barges moved commercial levels of goods, while the small size of the currach means that it was suited to the transport of people and to river fishing.

Without an accurate reconstruction of medieval Ireland's terrestrial environment, we cannot precisely compare the efficiency of different types of transport. This problem is further amplified by Ireland's topography, which is hugely localised in its differences, and by political conditions that would have made some transport options safer than others. If we apply the English evidence, despite these issues, we see that there was a significant cost differential between water- and land-based movement. This in turn influenced the distances individuals were prepared to travel. In England, small-scale sellers were willing to travel six to fourteen kilometres for goods, at times going up to twenty-four kilometres, depending on the specific good being marketed and the method of transportation. In Ireland, the journey distance was probably higher, especially when it could be facilitated by river (Holton, 2001). For specific undertakings, like purveyance (the requisition of provisions for the king's military campaigns), the distance travelled overland per day could be between sixteen and fifty kilometres. River transport was about half the cost of road, while sea movement was even cheaper. Masschaele (1993) has calculated the cost ratio between land, river and sea transport at 8:4:1, although that would have been altered depending on water access and the size and weight of commodity moved. Jones (2000) has argued that the discrepancy between land and water transport was even greater, estimating the former would have cost over ten times the latter. Such costs will have ensured that bulky items were moved by water as much as possible. In medieval Ireland, such bulky items included agricultural produce such as grain, bundles of animal hides, timber, and barrels of fish and wine.

The interplay between cost ratio and difficulty in overcoming physical obstacles might explain the patterns noted by Potterton at Trim, County Meath. Most items for sale within the town were valued according to cartload or horse load, with the exception of timber, which was valued by boatload. The movement of timber using the Boyne is supported by other documentation, such as the 1234 grant by Walter de Lacy to the monks in Drogheda of timber from his forest at Trim, which stipulated that they 'may carry it by the river Boyn or otherwise' (*Calendar of the*

Gormanston register). An account of provisions sourced for Ardmulchan manor at Trim market hinted that these goods may have gone downriver (Potterton, 2005). However, most murage grants consulted used horse loads as a unit of measurement, raising questions as to whether this was a standard measure rather than reflecting how local transport was conducted. The burgesses of the towns of Trim and Drogheda had the right of passage along the river, which would imply a good deal of activity spread among a varied group, in contrast to the documentary account (*ibid.*).

The Boyne was not the only navigable river used to move timber – there are references to firewood transported along the River Liffey to its south, and along the River Slaney in County Wexford (Colfer, 2013; Murphy and Potterton, 2010; O'Neill, 1987). Waterford obtained its timber by water using barges, with extra men required if travelling to The Rower on the River Nore in County Kilkenny to obtain it (*Archives of the municipal corporation of Waterford*). The River Blackwater running through counties Cork and Waterford was also used for shipping timber (NLI, MS 43,153/1). Even smaller rivers like the Loobagh were used for transporting bulky essentials, as testified to by the rent due from the extant tower house at Kilmallock, County Limerick, whose lessee was to bring wood and fuel to the earl of Desmond when the latter was resident in town (*Desmond survey*).

The reliance on river transport for timber might also be a symptom of the chronic shortage of wood by the seventeenth century (Murphy and Potterton, 2010). The other bulk item for which water transportation might have been favoured, which is especially pertinent to this study, is building stone. The cost ratio was more apparent in shipping this item: past nineteen kilometres' distance travelled, the cost of transport by land exceeded the cost of the building stone (Gardiner, 2007). We have evidence for stone quarrying near some tower house sites, such as that from the cliffs next to Minard's Castle outside Dingle, County Kerry, but a very small proportion considering their overall numbers (see figure 4.1).

Naturally, a downside of river transport is that it has a set route, and this may at least in part explain the predominance of items carried by cart and animal at Trim. More upmarket and luxury items such as were sold at the important regional fair and markets at Trim probably came from Dublin, as medieval Ireland's main city and political hub. They may have travelled from further afield, based on a few mentions of continental merchants attending the markets. Travelling to Trim from Dublin by sea to Drogheda and then up the River Boyne would have effectively been two sides of a triangle, so whenever political conditions allowed (which must have been most of the time considering the central

4.1 Minard's Castle in Kilmurry, County Kerry, outside Dingle, is located atop a cliff above a stony inlet. It has excellent views along the Dingle Peninsula coastline and could have monitored sea traffic. To the rear of the image are sea cliffs that show evidence of quarrying. The stone of the cliffs looks to be the same as that the tower house was constructed from.

placement of Dublin, if not Trim, within the ever-shrinking Pale) an overland route may have been preferred. On the other hand, one cannot ignore the convenience and cost savings associated with water transport, which have led Murphy and Potterton (2010: 475) to deduce that 'Despite the lack of evidence for grain being brought into the city [Dublin] by water, the location of many manor centres close to navigable rivers and to the coast suggests that it should not be discounted as a possibility.'

Hinterlands: The connection between rural and urban sites

Flavin has suggested that by looking at where people mentioned in the Bristol port accounts (discussed in more detail in chapter 6) came from, we can get some idea of river-based hinterlands. We can then match up the places mentioned with specific sites. The Bristol accounts record Ballyhack in County Wexford, but also Clonmel on the River Suir, Kilkenny city on the River Nore and New Ross on the River Barrow near the junction with the Nore, as well as Passage East at the estuary. As these towns lie on navigable stretches of a river, this displays the use of rivers for distribution of goods inland, including to Gaelic-Irish areas.

The coastal port and the navigable river acted in tandem to increase the hinterland and its accessibility. For instance, the River Ilen, flowing inland from Baltimore in County Cork, enabled a 'two way trade between the terrestrial and coastal communities', since the larger sea-going vessels would communicate with, and unload to, smaller boats (Kelleher, 2007b: 132). Tower houses along this river therefore had a key role in overseeing the movement of goods (*ibid.*). Oldcourt Castle is one of the few tower houses still standing along the Ilen River estuary. It has good visual command along the river, and the proximity of a modern boat club to the site shows the river was readily accessible from it. It also makes use of a rare rocky site among tidal mudflats.

The medieval port of Drogheda is located at the mouth of the River Boyne, and this location enabled communication both within the Irish Sea zone and with the fertile interior through the movement of barges along the Boyne (Bradley, 1997). Control of river crossing points influenced the location of high medieval motte earthwork castles (Graham, 1975). Based on this, Graham argues, the implication is that cementation of power over the region by the Anglo-Normans encouraged the economic and spatial development of Drogheda. He states that 'Little is known of road communications in the medieval period but it may be assumed that they were poor. Because of this, the River Boyne, which was then navigable, was an important means of transport between the interior of Meath and the town of Drogheda at the river's lowest bridging point' (*ibid.*: 238).

Galloway has identified the extent of Drogheda's hinterlands in the early fourteenth century, based on purveyance accounts. He concluded that Drogheda's grain hinterland was dominated by the Boyne. Even further reaching was Drogheda's demand for wood, a proposition backed by Potterton's evidence from Trim. Drogheda's hinterland may have stretched even farther, into Gaelic-Irish areas, to obtain wool and hides for export. While this study is informative, purveyance was a specific need demanding a different approach to agricultural food acquisition than the everyday operation of trade along the river. The king's representatives needed to travel to as many markets as they could as quickly as possible to compulsorily purchase the desired produce. The bought goods then needed to be removed quickly and as cheaply as possible, as the goods were being shipped to Crown armies in the field (Langdon, 1993). The Boyne facilitated this activity by aiding rapid transportation of bulky items (Galloway, 2015).

This scenario was within the comparatively politically stable Pale. It stands to reason that, outside of the Pale, endemic low-level violence rendered land travel more hazardous, especially to merchants transporting sought-after goods. There are several references within the registers of the archbishops of Armagh to providing safe passage for merchants and traders travelling through Gaelic-Irish areas. The effectiveness of these notes of safe passage can be debated, but that these foreign merchants appealed to the highest-ranking church official in Ireland indicates the fragmented nature of the Gaelic lordships at this time, as well as the risks involved in this occupation. Presumably merchants reasoned that the archbishop was the one man who stood any chance of being able to control the actions of Gaelic-Irish lords and their followers. That this approach was not always successful is attested to by mentions of attacks on caravans, with the merchants themselves sometimes murdered (Potterton, 2005).

A number of tower houses are located along the banks of the Boyne, such as Carrickdexter, Fennor and Dowth. These have commanding views along the river as well as ready access to the water. Significant areas of land surrounding the river were under the control of a handful of important monastic sites until the Dissolution of the Monasteries, in particular the abbeys of Bective and Mellifont. The politically and socially centralised force of these two abbeys negated the presence of tower houses by removing lay individuals seeking to cement their social status through construction. This is not to say that tower houses were not built on religiously controlled lands here – there is at least one tower house at Bective Abbey. This tower house appears to pre-date the Dissolution, too, although remodelling seems to have been undertaken by the Geraldines afterwards (Geraldine Stout, personal communication).

Drogheda was not the only medieval port located at the mouth of a river with a number of tower houses along it. Waterford lies at the mouth of the Three Sisters rivers, and there were several other regionally important river ports along these rivers, including New Ross, Carrick-on-Suir, Thomastown, Kilkenny city and Athy. Waterford in the later Middle Ages and early modern period was the dominant Irish port trading with Bristol. It was particularly well positioned to capitalise on the wine trade and its interior distribution: ships entering the Irish Sea halted there and the Three Sisters river system dispersed wine inland, as well as transporting bulky agricultural goods for export (O'Neill, 1987). The southeast of Ireland was particularly associated with wool production in the Middle Ages. Waterford was connected with ten major Cistercian abbeys through these river routes, a religious order particularly renowned for sheep husbandry. Movement along the river could be quick: a shallow-draught barge could travel from Kilkenny city to New Ross in a day (*ibid.*). Waterford obtained wood in 1508–09 from The Rower (*Archives of the municipal corporation of Waterford*), a location proximal to several tower houses, including Coolhill Castle, an excellent example of a circular tower house.

Isolated references reflecting goods distribution along rivers include the abbot of Holy Cross Abbey in County Tipperary, located close to the tower houses of Ballynahinch, Castlelake and Golden, receiving wine via the River Suir (O'Neill, 1987). A later document from the seventeenth century references Golden's right to hold a fair (*Irish monastic and episcopal deeds*).

Two significant rivers run through County Wexford, also in the southeast of Ireland: the Slaney and the Barrow. Wexford is also a coastal county, ensuring its reputation in the marine fishing industry. More than one in three tower houses in this county were located directly on freshwater sources; ninety-four per cent were situated within half of mile of fresh water (Jordan, 1991).

A similar pattern existed in western Ireland along the River Shannon, on which the port town of Limerick lies. Vessels wishing to sail up the river had to clear customs, and the levying of duties on goods sailing up the river was undertaken at Carrigafoyle Castle, at the mouth of the estuary. Carrigafoyle is a good example of a sectionally built tower house (Donnelly, 1998). It has an excellent visual command along the coast and into the river estuary, as well as being located by good anchorages. Other tower houses sited along the river acted as beacons and places of surveillance (Mac Curtain, 1988). Using Carrigafoyle allowed ships to bypass the port of Tralee, to sail on to Tarbert or Limerick itself (*ibid.*).

A significant number of tower houses were located along the Shannon, especially along its southern banks. This may have been encouraged by landholding patterns and cooperation between the local families, such as the 'close ties' between the Knights of Glin and the earls of Desmond. That tower houses 'were given to' subordinates implies that some, if not most, of the tolls and taxes they collected at their sites were submitted to their Desmond lords (*ibid.*). Unfortunately this premise is not possible to validate.

The pattern is again witnessed along comparatively more minor rivers with regionally significant roles. The status of a river does not necessarily reflect the importance of ports located at the junction between river and sea. A good example is Youghal in County Cork. Youghal appears regularly and consistently in the Bristol trade accounts. The River Blackwater is tidal as far as Lismore, meaning that harnessing the tide ensured quick access to the interior. Although the usual range of items is listed in the Bristol accounts for export, Youghal had a special emphasis on the wool industry (Frame, 2012). It is no surprise that there were a number of tower houses regularly spaced along the length of the Blackwater. These tower houses are mainly on the County Cork side of the river, and include Temple Michael, Strancally and Camphire. Their siting might be related to an underdeveloped potential hinterland on the County Waterford side of the river, caused by a wide estuary which could only be crossed by ferry (Kelly and O'Keeffe, 2015).

Within the *Bristol Port book* entries after 1575, we can ascertain mentions of five other places in southeast Ireland associated with Youghal: Kilmallock, Mallow, Cork, Limerick and 'Carleon' (the last unidentified to date) (*Bristol's trade with Ireland*). Of these places, only one, Mallow, is accessible by river from Youghal, which indicates that either cargoes were transferred to smaller boats for coastal trading, or goods were moved overland. The former is more likely, since there was no natural land-based routeway to the interior along the River Blackwater from Youghal (Kelly and O'Keeffe, 2015). Cork and Limerick both would have been best reached by sea (*Bristol's trade with Ireland*). However, the route between Cork and Limerick is noted as being potentially dangerous (O'Neill, 1987). River transport, therefore, if available, must have appeared especially attractive.

Riverine tower house distribution and siting

The commanding height of some tower houses gives the impression of site selection for defence. For example, this author discussed the siting of Audley's and Ardkeen castles in an article for *Speculum*, where both castles were located at a height, with steep drops on several sides. Fieldwalking at these sites showed that a land approach ran from below the tower house at the water's edge. Comparison of observations from field survey with OS and Admiralty mapping reinforces the interpretation that the site was approached from boat anchorages, since deep water is located mere metres offshore. This granted unimpeded access to the water. As at nearby Jordan's Castle, on-site survey showed that the most impressive architectural aspects of the tower houses were oriented towards those approaching from the water, not from land (McAlister, 2016). This is a repeated trend in other landscapes. The tower houses of the Suir, Barrow and Nore rivers usually have the largest and most ornate windows facing out over the water. As well as providing the best view for those within the tower house, the placement of these windows indicates that the biggest architectural investment was reserved for features that the largest number of people would see, as they used medieval Ireland's busy waterways. Well-placed tower houses defended stretches of these rivers. The Three Sisters rivers, as well as the Munster Blackwater, passed through Anglo-Irish, magnate (in the form of the Ormond and Kildare lordships) and Gaelic-Irish lands, making a unified strategy nigh impossible.

Considering the risk to life and property presented by late medieval and early modern Ireland's political climate, the attraction of a well-defended river-based highway is readily apparent. Rivers, as fixed routes, shared the same vulnerability as overland transport in that certain points could be targeted. The residents of Clonmel in County Tipperary complained in their liberty court in 1514 that they were being attacked as they used the River Suir to travel to Waterford city. Another individual was robbed when transporting merchandise to Clonmel by boat along the River Anner. The complainants also noted land-based attacks along the 'King's Way', the route of which was not described (*Calendar of Ormond deeds*: 1509–47, vol. 4, 'Liberty court of Tipperary 1514'). By the 1350s it was already dangerous to travel along the River Barrow without 'a considerable armed guard' (Frame, 2012: 141). Here, the risks of travelling by river and by land were similar. Attacking a barge on a river reduced the possibility of men and goods fleeing, since a boat was stuck in one place on the water. Conversely, this may also have been an attraction for trade and transportation, as a set route could be more easily defended. The major rivers of medieval Ireland could boast market towns at intervals that served both economic and defensive purposes. This could explain the siting of a smaller number of tower houses at a height, commanding extensive views up and down the river.

An excellent case study to illustrate such site selection is Coolhill Castle, County Kilkenny, on the River Barrow (see figure 4.2). Most tower houses surveyed along the banks of the River Barrow were on low-lying ground. Coolhill, sited atop a cliff rising above the River Barrow, is therefore very unusual both for the region and the country as a whole. Coolhill stands directly above the river, but has a sheer drop from the front of the tower house down to the water. A footpath could be observed along the face, permitting access to the river, but it is rather

4.2 Coolhill Castle in County Kilkenny is a good example of a circular tower house. It is located directly above the River Barrow, atop a steep cliff. It has excellent views of the surrounding countryside and river approaches.

perilous and not a route that would be taken with bulky or heavy goods. Perhaps steps like those at Baltimore in County Cork once assisted movement but do not survive (Kelleher, 2013). Coolhill Castle has impressive views over the Barrow valley as well as a sizeable stretch of the river itself. As it stands in contrast to the observed pattern at tower house riverine sites, it is suggested that Coolhill Castle was located so as to visually control the river and movement along it. From its height, any trouble at the river below would have been easily spotted, making it a kind of watchtower. Coolhill Castle had the ability to monitor an even wider area on the strategically important route between Kilkenny city and New Ross, both important marketplaces. Its commanding position above the river would have also acted as a deterrent to poor behaviour.

An interesting and unique structure is Ship-pool Castle in County Cork. Located on the banks of the River Bandon between Kinsale and Bandon, it is a split-level tower house with the entrance on the ground floor from the riverfront, but on the first floor from the other side. This split-level design allowed the tower house to be built into the steep bank rising up from the river. This must have been a complicated site to build in the absence of any flat ground, reflecting that the overarching consideration in siting the tower house was proximity to the river.

Water could be harnessed to control access to the tower house, as opposed to the tower house controlling access to the water. The most obvious example of this is a moat. Moats like those at Kilcrea Castle in County Cork would have originally been fed by a diversion channel from the nearby river. Even at tower houses in Ireland, more sophisticated approach routes were sometimes created by redirecting water features. Sweetman commented of Fiddaun Castle, County Galway (see figure 4.3), that the water-filled channel running between the two lakes on either side of the tower house and the bawn 'protects the whole complex' (Sweetman, 2000: 169). This channel runs in front of the modern mock 'gatehouse', so has to be crossed before passing through the gatehouse. Probably an original feature at this point is the raised area along which the castle is accessed, which runs between the two lakes and their adjacent boggy land, visible on some aerial photographs as a straight-line shadow (e.g. CUCAP: ALN023). The raised routeway passes through this watery landscape to the side of the enclosing bawn and the medieval gatehouse, through which the interior was reached. As the modern gatehouse obviously would not have been there at the time of medieval occupation, the waterway alone would have controlled initial access to the site. The controlled access also provided the most architecturally striking approach to the tower house, as well as the most visually pleasing landscape: only from this direction do the two lakes on either side

Movement, transport and communication

4.3 Fiddaun Castle, County Galway, is a well-preserved tower house and bawn. This image shows the perspective of those approaching along the proposed raised access way. Visitors would have passed to the right-hand side to enter via the gatehouse.

unfold, and there is a bartizan (a turret projecting from the castle corner) on the bawn corner before reaching the gatehouse. There is a more unusual bastion, a feature rarely seen on tower house bawns, on the opposite side, but this appears to have been a later addition.

The tower house's role in coastal transport and networks

Water-based transport in later medieval Ireland was not only conducted by river. Instead, a large proportion of regional and national communication was undertaken using maritime routes. Obviously, international transportation occurred this way. Maritime distributions of tower houses are observed right across the country. The control of fish resources had significant overlap with the command of anchorages, landing places and other maritime communication points. This is in part because fresh fish in an age before refrigeration needed immediate treatment for preservation, and that usually required shore space close by.

A significant number of tower houses were in coastal locations, not solely within Gaelic-Irish territory, though the literature has tended to focus on these. At the county level the correlation can be even more apparent. The majority of County Kerry and County Down tower houses are located on the coast. Kerry tower houses controlled communication, trade and travel routes, and fishing (McAuliffe, 1991). In other counties the numbers are less overwhelming, but no less convincing. County Cork tower houses likewise have a strong coastal distribution, with a particular association with promontories, such as those by inlets (Sweetman, 2000). In County Galway many sites are inland, in agriculturally fertile areas, but those in the west are particularly inclined to be located close to the sea or a river, with an additional preference for siting on rock observed (*ibid.*).

Within this coastal distribution, a large number of tower houses are sited to control either an anchorage or a landing place. In County Down, all tower houses with a coastal setting controlled such a feature. Even at rural sites, the number of ships that might use these anchorages could be substantial. The 'Queen's fleet' is recorded as anchoring 'directly opposite' Carrigafoyle Castle, County Kerry, while this tower house was also accessible to an army marching by land, showing the tower house's excellent location at the juncture of land and sea routes (AFM: 1580, vol. 5, p. 1733). Lord Deputy Mountjoy was instructed to station his fleet at Kilclief Castle, County Down, in 1599 (CSPI, 1599–1600, vol. 8, 'Report by Sir Ralph Lane to the Earl of Essex'). In addition to this direct correlation, a great number of coastal tower houses across Ireland have visual command over maritime sailing routes, such as those along the coast of County Sligo that watch over movement into Sligo Bay and town. Even those set back some distance from the shoreline – like Carrowbrickeen Castle at just over one kilometre, or Doonnagore Castle in County Clare, six hundred metres from the coast and atop a cliff – could have wide-ranging views along coastal access routes.

A Dutch chart made in the early seventeenth century to identify possible pirate bases notes prominent and sizeable anchorages with an anchor pictograph. Many of these correspond with notable tower house densities, including along Strangford Lough in County Down. The coastline is not represented accurately, but the relations of the anchorages to it are. Some castles are specifically marked along the County Wexford coast, although since there are a number of coastal castle sites along this stretch and the coastline is not depicted precisely, it is difficult to equate those drawn with any specific buildings (Voorbeijtel Cannenburg, 1935).

Landing points at tower houses could also have been used in elite communication, as is possibly implied by the presence of internal boathouses at Mahee and Sketrick castles in County Down (Jope, 1966).

Historical references suggest that goods moved into national trade routes before they were prepared for international export (*Red book of the earls of Kildare*; *Letters and papers ... of the reign of Henry VIII*: vol. 2; McErlean *et al.*, 2002; TNA, TN/PO7/III/36). First observed in

County Down, this pattern – from analysis of the mentions of inland and lesser sea ports in conjunction with nationally important ports in the extant customs accounts – appears to have applied throughout the island. In this way, the practice of coastal trading converged on the nearest major maritime port, with tower houses providing stop-off and consolidation points along the way (McAlister, 2016).

We can also get an indication of what places formed units within these maritime networks through other sources, including landholding patterns and related rights. For instance, the customs for the ports of Ardglass and Strangford in the northeast of the country belonged to the earls of Kildare, some of the most influential landowners in Ireland in the later Middle Ages until the Silken Thomas revolt under Henry VIII, when they lost favour. The caput of the family was further south, in County Kildare, meaning there is over one hundred miles between the two places. County Down coastal connections stretched northwards as far as County Antrim from Drogheda, to obtain wood for boatbuilding (Galloway, 2015). Strangford and Ardglass would have been middling-sized ports at the time, so such communication networks would have been much farther reaching for more important ports and wealthier hinterlands.

The system of outports, too, added complexity to these networks. Possibly the best known of these is Dalkey in County Dublin, which served as an outport for Dublin city owing to the limitations of the latter's harbour, which was silting up. The convergence of many transport connections, and the income associated with this, is reflected in the density of tower houses in this port town – there were seven tower houses, alongside town fortifications (Smith, 1996). As it was a dependent port of Dublin, there are no independent trade accounts surviving for Dalkey, which adds further obscurity to an already difficult avenue of investigation. The relationship was not an official one, but important nonetheless: 'unloaded cargo was stored in the fortified town houses prior to removal to Dublin by pack or cart animal' (*ibid.*: 48).

The development of a formalised port hierarchy assisted this process. An Elizabethan statute allowed for overseas trade only at designated ports where there were Crown officials (Breen, 2007a). This process accelerated and became more politicised in the seventeenth century, with ports actively seeking to designate neighbouring ports as their 'creeks', an official category according lesser status. This is seen at New Ross, for example, where both Waterford and Kilkenny sought to designate it as their port. New Ross increasingly came to be dominated by their interests, even though it had a deep harbour better suited to the larger vessels of the seventeenth century (Brian Donovan, personal communication). This aggressive acquisition of status is also implied by Belfast's relations with Carrickfergus, whose customs rights it purchased in 1637 (Robinson, 2000).

Much of this coastal trading will have involved smaller boats making frequent stops to collect or disperse a cargo, including at the small settlements clustered around rural tower houses. Coincidental documentary survivals, such as that allowing the people of Clontarf, County Dublin, the right to fish in Carlingford Bay in County Louth without having to pay tithes or other tolls, enable us to see what must have been common connections for somewhat substantial distances along Ireland's coasts (*Irish fiants*: vol. 3).

Tower houses as navigation aids

An even more ephemeral means of engagement for tower houses came in the form of assisting navigation. Tower houses and churches with steeples would have been the only multi-storey buildings in much of medieval Ireland. Their height would have made them immediately recognisable by people, and from substantial distances, so their use as markers is a logical step. Identification requires a different mindset: 'shore features, such as church towers, are commonly regarded as part of the landscape but the way they figured in the seascape also needs to be appreciated. The siting of prominent structures may have been influenced by navigational considerations' (Hutchinson, 1997: 164). There is documentary evidence to suggest that in Britain at least the setting of lights for seafarers was an ecclesiastical duty (*ibid.*).

It is feasible to consider that some of the tower houses may have been located with similar considerations in mind. Mac Curtain (1988) suggests as much for the tower houses of the Shannon estuary, citing several as beacons, whether for public good or to benefit the lord who held the right to wreck. We can get an indication of their use as marking points when we look at modern sailing directions and admiralty mapping. Often tower houses are mentioned as back markers – that is, the bigger point behind a smaller front marker that could be made of something impermanent. When sailors lined the two up, this marked a course of passage for a sailing vessel.

Although discussed in regard to motte castles, specifically along the County Down coast, intervisibility may have been in response to Scottish and Gaelic-Irish shipping that could have had an economic and political impact on the nascent Anglo-Irish economy (O'Sullivan and Breen, 2007). Intervisibility could also serve navigational needs. In the same county, Angus Rock provides an excellent transit point when lined up with either a modern beacon lighted on the northern point of the rock, or, more pertinently, with Kilclief Castle (see figure 4.4). It is also recommended to use Kilclief Church (located to the rear of the castle) in

4.4 Kilclief Castle in County Down is located at the rear of a sandy beach on the approach routes to Strangford Lough. It is documented as being an anchorage for fleets of ships. It was constructed by John Sely, Bishop of Down, sometime between 1413 and 1441.

transit with, or aligned with, 'a clump of trees' when leaving the lough in a southerly direction (*Admiralty Chart of Ireland*, 1988; Kean, 1995). It may not be coincidence that the tower house can be used as a navigational aid, considering that its original occupier was John Sely, Bishop of Down. Pilots could have rowed out from either of the local port towns of Portaferry or Strangford, both sites of tower houses which commanded their respective harbours, to meet ships intending to pass through the Narrows, to guide them safely in. The Narrows is an appropriately named tidal passage passable when travelling in the same direction as the tide. Since vessels may have had to wait up to eight hours for a favourable tide, it follows that vessels wishing to enter Strangford Lough would have anchored at a nearby location, such as Kilclief Castle, to await the turning of the tide. Likewise, those vessels desiring to leave the lough would have had to wait at a similar location to the north of the Narrows. This is supported by antiquarians who mention that Audley's Roads was used as a waiting point for vessels going northwards, while Ballyhenry Bay, near Portaferry, was used for vessels going southwards (McErlean *et al.*, 2002; Smith, 1744). Audley's Roads anchorage is commanded by Audley's Castle, and the tower house was also used for navigating the approach to the anchorage (Cormac McMullan, personal communication). This may in part explain the tower house's unusual siting at a height. Ships anchoring thus could have been taxed, providing additional income. It is hard to see how use of tower houses simply as a navigational aid could have resulted in direct financial profit.

Cowd Castle in neighbouring Ardglass is an interesting architectural conundrum (see figure 4.5). It is questionable whether Cowd Castle could have provided a residential function, as it is one of the smallest tower houses in the entire country, with no internal evidence for inhabitation, such as fireplaces, latrines or even permanent stairs. Cowd Castle may instead have been used either as a lighthouse or as a marker for entrance to the harbour. Since access to the roof was difficult it seems improbable that Cowd Castle was used as a lighthouse, as that would have necessitated regular and unimpeded access. That Cowd Castle had a special function in monitoring Ardglass harbour is further supported by a field-of-fire diagram developed by McNeill. This shows that most of the power that could be fired from inside was directed towards the southern approaches to the harbour, with a lesser amount covering the harbour itself. No firing cover was provided at the angles facing Newark/Ardglass Castle or the town (McNeill, 2005). We would expect to find the harbour and town the best defended areas, since they are where most of the goods and people would have been concentrated. That the area of fire cover is instead directed away tells us something about the priorities of the builder, and the function of the tower house within the communal operations of the town.

Control of ferries and causeways

The locations of riverine networks can be indicated by the presence of ferries, causeways, fords and bridges. Correlation between tower houses

4.5 Cowd Castle is located beside the now much-altered Ardglass Castle/ Newark in Ardglass, County Down. It is one of the smallest tower-house-type structures in existence, but examination of the building fabric suggests it was a commercial building and was not used as a residence.

and these facets of communication routes is observable right across Ireland. Command of these routes would have provided the tower house occupant with an additional, or perhaps primary, income through the levying of tolls for the use of 'his' routeway. Adherence was enforced by the might of the defensive-appearing structure itself. There was often overlap between the different means of broaching the nodal point: bridges in disrepair could be replaced temporarily with ferries, which were more easily tolled than bridges from a legal standpoint, until enough money had been raised to reinstate the bridge (Cooper, 2006). A problem with historical ferry identification is that we rely solely on written documentation or oral history, since ferries will not leave archaeological remains. They might also traverse considerable distances, not just in lieu of a bridge or ford, for a river crossing. Farmers in County Kilkenny in 1537 complained that the ferry from Waterford was being blocked by weirs at Jerpoint and Inistioge, showing that there was a public service running along the River Nore (Bradshaw, 1974).

Control of ferry operations was 'a common manorial monopoly', although, as with trade customs collections, the service may have been farmed out (Gardiner, 2007: 97). The one exception to the law forbidding tolls to be placed on road users in England was made for ferries, as 'owners of ferries were allowed to charge for passage. The result is that ferries were profitable and therefore ferries appear in the records as assets to be argued over' (Cooper, 2006: 132). To illustrate, the income comparison is given for Nottinghamshire in England, where a fishery was worth 26s. 8d. and a ferry across the River Trent valued at £6 13s. 4d. As fishing rights were subject to legal actions, it is surprising that we do not have more documenting of ferry rights, since there could be competing ferries at the same or nearby crossings to fight for business (ibid.). Ferries, of course, made for a slower crossing than bridges and they could be deadly, as attested by occasional references to drownings (e.g. AFM: vols 4, 5; Cooper, 2006).

In County Down eight sites have been identified that potentially controlled crossings. Of these, five controlled ferry crossings, alongside two at causeways. Historical and medieval ferry routes might be indicated by the presence of modern-day ferries, such as that crossing The Narrows, the tidal entrance between Strangford and Portaferry. Both towns have tower houses located by the harbour, and the modern ferry docks within metres of both. Ferries would have been needed at much-used crossing points too wide for a bridge, such as at river estuaries. Other examples of tower houses located at potential medieval ferry crossings include Castle Island and Quoile Castles on the Quoile River estuary in County Down, and Ferrycarrig on the River Slaney in County Wexford.

In County Wexford, Ballyhack Castle fulfils a number of criteria under discussion in this volume – it is located on the River Barrow estuary, a ferry route, was known for fishing activity of both marine and freshwater species, and it has been convincingly argued that it was built and owned by the Cistercian religious order (Colfer, 2013). Ballyhack had a ferry running between the settlement of the same name and Passage East on the other side, again run by the Cistercians (ibid.). The tower house is located about a hundred metres to the northeast of the modern ferry ramp. That this crossing point was valuable from a defensive perspective is attested to by the presence of the seventeenth-century star-shaped fort at Duncannon about three and a half kilometres to the southeast. Although later in date, by 1645, when it saw a successful Confederate siege, the fort was 'commanding control over Waterford Harbour and the inlet of the Barrow towards New Ross. During the Confederate Wars, Duncannon Fort was a strategically vital stronghold, as it offered potential control of a major channel of communication between Waterford Port (and by extension New Ross) and Continental Europe' (Cronin, n.d.). By extension, the tower house potentially could have fulfilled a similar role at a prior date. This further supports the multifaceted functions carried out by the tower house.

In the case of Ferrycarrig Castle, again in County Wexford, the historical ferry does not survive. As is implied by the place name, this was historically the site of a ferry river crossing, stretching back to before the time period when tower houses were constructed, to at least the high Middle Ages. Its existence is attested to in documentation including 1307 and 1324 inquisitions (cited in O'Conor, 1993) and it was presumed by scholars that it operated in the vicinity of the tower house and ringwork castle (the ringwork is located on the opposite bank). The tower house has an unusual raised site above the river, although access is not steep nor treacherous (see figure 4.6). Instead, the tower house at Ferrycarrig is well located for a commanding view

4.6 This view of Ferrycarrig Castle, County Wexford, is taken from the sandy landing point on the opposite bank of the River Slaney, from whence a possible medieval road proceeded. Located by a modern bridge, the tower house historically controlled a ferry crossing along a major road.

over the River Slaney and its estuary, as well as having ready access to the water. Colfer (2013) has written that its position at a narrow point in the river meant that it protected travel between Enniscorthy and Wexford at a place that was vulnerable and open to attack. Not only does the tower house rise above the river, but it commands the modern Dublin to Wexford town road approach, and back in the Middle Ages would have been located to control an important land-based routeway into the Anglo-Norman colony in Wexford (*ibid.*). Again based on the available high medieval documentation, the modern road seems to follow (at least at this point) the route of a much earlier road. Nowadays, the road meets a concrete bridge (the remains of an earlier modern bridge may stand next to it) to cross over the river.

Considering the tower house's location at the junction of road and river, it would have made a good site for one end of the ferry crossing, and would have commanded the overall crossing. This route is reflected in the 1780 image reproduced in Colfer's *Wexford castles* (2013), which shows the ferry mid-crossing, with people waiting for it underneath the castle. From a practical perspective, it would have been nearly impossible to pass the tower house without being observed, and so it would have made an excellent place for the administration of tolls. The added advantage of building the tower house here to collect ferry tolls was that it would – partially, at least – recoup the financial losses incurred from the initial construction of the tower house. From the proposed launching site, the river current appears very strong, and the water moves from this point south-southeasterly to the opposite bank, where there is a small sandy beach. Beaches were often used in the Middle Ages as a good place at which to draw up boats, to avoid the expense of building permanent landing features (Fox, 2001). It is again likely no coincidence that a medieval-era road running past the castle park to the medieval parish church of Carrick, seven hundred metres to the south of the ringwork (O'Conor, 1993), commences at the rear of this small beach (Emma Arbuthnot, personal communication). It is part of an earlier lordly, designed landscape, including a legally defined forest starting on the bank opposite the tower house (Orpen and Brooks, 1934).

Ferrycarrig tower house is architecturally very plain, with little exterior ornamentation. Most windows are small, as generally encountered at tower houses, but the most impressive and largest windows are oriented towards downstream and the land access route coming from the northeast. This has been interpreted as having particular meaning at tower house sites, since it is in these specific places that effort, time and money are concentrated. These larger windows probably indicate places that the builder wanted people to see, and people to see out of. Framing the landscape has been discussed in an English context (see Creighton,

2002), with pleasant views desired from high-status rooms and interior halls. It is suggested here, then, that these large windows served multiple functions, including being the best place to observe movement and those approaching from a distance. Distant approaches would not be visible from most tower house windows, which are usually narrow slits. The larger windows therefore also reflect the lord's own interest in monitoring his area of command. At Ferrycarrig, the communication route brought travellers along the road to the tower house at the ferry crossing, users being deposited by a continuation of the same road on the opposite side, and this movement could have been closely monitored by those inside the tower house.

A reference exists for a ferry at Ballinlaw Castle in County Kilkenny on the River Barrow, and at Kinsale, County Cork, site of one extant tower house (*Inquisitions and extents*). Ringrone Castle could have had a good view over the ferry serving the town of Kinsale, as well as the entrance to the Bandon River. As the castle is located at a height, it would not have directly interacted with the ferry. The ferryman across the River Boyne at Drogheda was described as 'a poor little fisherman [who] used to wait with a little boat', indicating informal activity (AFM: 1592, vol. 6, p. 1921). At Athlone the bridge was temporarily replaced by a ferry in the early fourteenth century (Bradley, 2007), reminding us that a variety of methods could be used to control and cross rivers. The bridge and ferry might even have co-existed, as is implied at Carrick-on-Suir, County Tipperary. A bridge is documented near the mill and castle there around 1470 (*Calendar of Ormond deeds*: 1413–1509, vol. 3), but a ferry is also mentioned prior to this date in 1412 and 1434 (*Calendar of Ormond deeds*: 1350–1413, vol. 2, deed 420). One particular entry provides interesting detail as to the connections between castle and ferry. In 1434 the earl of Ormond let to Annota Walshe and her son Thomas the custody of the castle of Carrick and the ferry there. The ferry was expected to be used to provide fuel for the earl's castle of Carrick, and both persons were to permit the lord's fish to be taken, as well as guarding that fish and the castle (*Calendar of Ormond deeds*: 1413–1509, vol. 3). Mac Curtain (1988) states that the earl of Desmond gave tower houses to men who had a duty in return to collect tolls from ferries, bridges and movement through passes. That enforcing crossing charges was profitable is evident by the magnate lord ensuring he delegated the task.

'Bridge' tower houses

Another method of physical and visual control of routes and networks was the siting of tower houses by bridges. This had the benefit of strategically defending the bridge, and thus any road access via it, in addition to the waterway below. In an English context, mapping grants for bridge maintenance (pontage) shows that bridges were located at the nodal points of national roads, thus displaying their role in connecting terrestrial networks with riverine ones (Cooper, 2006). The construction of bridges assisted in integrating the road system in England, and a similar process may have occurred in Ireland (Langdon and Claridge, 2011). Quoted in John Bradley's article on the bridge at Athlone is a line from a letter from the dean of Armagh to Lord Deputy Cecil summarised in the CSPI, that 'All Connaught [has been] tamed by the building of the bridge of Athlone' (Bradley, 2007: 173; quote reproduced here from CSPI: vol. 1, SP63/22/1, p. 347, 1567). This is not necessarily a bridge function that occurs to the modern mind, but reflects their historical significance in security, or, as Bradley terms it, that bridges were 'a raw statement of government power' (Bradley, 2007: 173). The antiquarian William Wilde wrote that 'at every ford and pass, or bridge, if such existed at the time, some castle was erected' (1849: 38), which might be stretching reality somewhat, but nonetheless reflects a visible correlation.

Tower houses placed at or near bridges served a security role, but this was as economic as it was political. Where there was fortification at either end of a bridge, it provided the ability to control both land and river access (Harrison, 2004). Tower houses tended to be occupied by individuals and their households; they were not a security system maintained across the country by a single organisation (such as the Crown). This inherently implies personal, or at most magnate, interest in managing the Irish system of bridges. Episodes of heightened bridge-building activity accompanied general building booms, which implies renewed construction of bridges in line with the later medieval Irish building boom that tower houses formed a part of (*ibid.*). Others have disagreed somewhat as to the political context that bridges represent, proposing they were a symbol of increased state power, possibly at the expense of fords and ferries (Langdon and Claridge, 2011). In England, bridges tended to be built for the public good, rather than for private gain, which explains the location of many bridges in towns, and complaints about their poor maintenance (*ibid.*). Several publications have discussed the funding of bridges, with a combination of charitable giving (Brooks, 2000; Harrison, 2004), endowments (Harrison, 2004) and guild obligations (Brooks, 2000) prevalent. Many bridges were communal endeavours, even in rural areas, as they had a role in maintaining economic activity (*ibid.*). Towns in particular seem to have been eager to obtain grants for bridge maintenance, to ensure merchants were not deterred from trading there (*ibid.*; Cooper, 2006).

That is not to say that lords did not have a say in bridge management. Bridge upkeep could be the responsibility of vills, the lord of the manor, those with labour obligations or a combination (Harrison, 2004). In Ireland, bridge building remained a 'matter of individual initiative' until the eighteenth century (Rynne, 2018: 94). Lords had a lot to benefit from a bridge: 'A new bridge transformed a region so that the river no longer formed a barrier or natural frontier; it enabled both banks to be effectively integrated into one lordship' (Brooks, 2000: 21). On a more mundane level, bridge maintenance was 'a straightforward estate investment' (Harrison, 2004: 194). But while bridges might be located on a lordly estate, and benefit it, there is limited documentary evidence for direct financial exploitation of bridges. What there is tends to refer to public bridges on public roads, not those located on private roads (*ibid.*). We do know a toll was charged at the bridge at Athlone, monitored by the impressive castle there, though it is not a tower house (Bradley, 2007). The pontage grants issued by the English Crown tend to be very formulaic, and so cannot tell us much about the administration of tolls (Cooper, 2006). The indication is that tolls were complex and depended on what was being moved. They are consistent in that they were assessed on goods to be sold, and the quantities imply that merchants rather than small-scale customers were the targets, as does the option of a weekly flat rate for bridge usage (*ibid.*; Harrison, 2004). These tolls were only supposed to be temporary grants, in place until sufficient funds were raised for the necessary repairs. We have no extant records for tolls charged at bridges in Ireland, but the similarity of the English bridge tolls to those claimed towards murage in late medieval Trim, County Meath (Potterton, 2005), indicates that we should expect similar extractions for use of bridges and ferries.

Historians studying medieval bridges in England have looked to the *Patent rolls* for records of pontage. Cooper provides a useful summary at the back of his volume that includes Irish grants up to 1400 from the *Calendar of patent rolls*. Drogheda is mentioned thrice (in 1228, 1229 and 1317), Cork received grants in 1284 and 1318 alongside a licence to apply murage tolls to bridges, and a grant was made for the bridge running between New Ross in County Wexford and Rosbercon in County Kilkenny in 1313. The grant for Bennettsbridge in County Kilkenny in 1285, which went to the burgesses of Kilkenny (presumably the city), is most interesting for this study (Cooper, 2006). The pontage grant for Cork in 1318 is the last one listed for Ireland, even though Cooper's list runs for a further nine pages, until 1399. That the last recorded Irish grant comes at the start of the fourteenth century is telling when placed against the political and social backdrop of that traumatic century. It is unlikely that after 1318 Ireland found itself without need to maintain bridges, rather it seems probable that no more requests were made. However, these pontage grants were always expensive to obtain and for smaller bridges it would never have been financially worthwhile to pursue this option (Harrison, 2004).

The year 1318 comes close to the start of the most impactful events of the fourteenth century. It also coincides with the start of the tower-house-building epoch. The historiography has held that the later Middle Ages were a period of decreasing centralised political influence in Ireland, standing in contrast to increased Crown involvement following the Tudor Conquest. It is completely believable, then, that such requests for pontage dried up during the middle of the fourteenth century, and then were not re-instigated as the colony went into decline. In most parts of Ireland, areas of Anglo-Irish and English influence included, locals administered their own taxes and tolls with little fear of repercussion, so it is not a stretch to conclude similar behaviour was applied to bridges. Back in an English context, the number of legal cases regarding illegal toll collection indicates that most bridges located on public roads were not privately administered for personal profit (Harrison, 2004). It is easy to question how effective any such legal action would have been in late medieval Ireland, especially in the areas of Gaelic influence, and considering the ease with which tower house occupants were demanding fishing taxes. Cooper (2006) has determined that most grants for pontage were made at times of royal weakness. In England in the early Middle Ages, before royal grants were made, it is presumed that people just set up a toll booth and charged for bridge use without consulting the king's representatives (*ibid.*). It is entirely reasonable that this tradition was reasserted in Ireland. That might explain the 'bridge-building spree' commenced by the earl of Cork in the seventeenth century. This has been interpreted as to assist with administration of his estates and colonial military strategy, since he did not charge for their use (Rynne, 2018). At a more local level, his charitably built bridges would have removed valuable income from competitors, as well as their control over the landscape.

A further complication is that, of course, not all bridges were made of stone, as timber bridges would have been a far less expensive option. Stone bridges overwhelmingly dominate the contemporary historical evidence as well as the modern published material. Despite this, most European medieval stone bridges had wooden predecessors (Brooks, 2000). The comparative price probably goes some way to explain the absence of timber bridges from historical documentation across Europe, but unfortunately these bridges also rarely survive in the archaeological record – or must be carefully identified from their foundation levels if they do, in waterlogged soil (Brooks, 2000; Harrison, 2004). The AFM describe a bridge being built out of wicker across the River Avonmore in County Wicklow that was strong enough to allow both foot soldiers and cavalry to cross, and it then being allowed to float downstream to prevent others using it (AFM: vol. 4). This indicates that bridges could be ephemeral in construction method while still being effective. They also were susceptible to being replaced at a later date with a stone bridge, or were even viewed as interchangeable with a ferry: the earl of Cork built a timber bridge at Fermoy, County Cork, to replace a ferry crossing, and this was in turn superseded by a stone bridge (Rynne, 2018).

Ben Murtagh has written most extensively on what he has termed 'bridge castles', including sites at Athy in County Kildare and Thomastown in County Kilkenny. The 'fortified houses' (Bradley and Murtagh, 2003: 210–1; the issue of terminology is discussed here in chapter 5) in Thomastown were likely funded by trade, mainly of bulky wool and hides, with goods travelling up the navigable stretches of the River Nore by barge. Thomastown's location ten miles downstream of Kilkenny city, one of medieval Ireland's most important inland towns, also aided its economic development. The use of Dundry stone in the construction of the fortified houses/tower houses in Thomastown reflects a connection with Bristol, as well as the usefulness of the Three Sisters rivers in transporting goods, especially heavy and bulky ones, inland. Thomastown is not the only location on these rivers where Dundry stone has been identified, it is also known at Athassel in County Tipperary and Inistioge and Kilkenny city in County Kilkenny (O'Neill, 1987).

Murtagh has argued that the fortified houses in Thomastown reflect late medieval control of trade by a handful of merchants. These fortified houses were also used to shelter their profitable goods, Murtagh making a direct comparison with the warehouses of Ardglass, County Down (Bradley and Murtagh, 2003; Murtagh, 1988). The Bridge Castle at Thomastown, sometimes referred to as Sweetman's Castle (Murtagh, 1988), is a good example of a riverine tower house located in an urban inland port. It has an oblong-shaped chamber on the ground floor, entered from the river, that is reminiscent of the interior boathouses located at Mahee and Sketrick castles, both maritime tower house sites in County Down. Murtagh has interpreted this chamber as an excellent location for goods storage and easy loading from the quay. Furthermore, he stated that the ground floor could have been leased out separately to a merchant for additional income, as at the Tholsel in Drogheda (*ibid.*). Vernacular urban houses in medieval Ireland often had part of the ground floor turned over to commercial use, so it makes sense that tower houses, which bridged the vernacular–elite building divide, might have too (Bradley, 1995). That usage has been suggested by this author for Strangford Castle in County Down, similar to the arrangement of homes above ground-floor shops in medieval timber-framed buildings in England. Murtagh made a direct comparison of the Bridge Castle at Thomastown with the undercrofts in medieval buildings in Southampton (Murtagh, 1988).[1] He believes that the plain interior of this tower house indicates that the whole building initially served a warehouse function, with a conversion to living quarters taking place in the sixteenth century (*ibid.*). Brady's Castle in Thomastown is located on the river and has a vaulted ground floor that is believed to have been for storage (Bradley and Murtagh, 2003; Murtagh, 1994).

What is described as an 'outwork' at the Bridge Castle, lying between the tower house and the river quay, could have functioned either as a bawn or as a hall-like warehouse (Murtagh, 1988). A similar arrangement can be seen in Audley's Castle in County Down. Here, a stone building within the castle bawn is located between the tower house and the water, interpreted as a warehouse based on interior-space-usage calculations undertaken by Eadie (Eadie, 2009, 2015; McAlister, 2016). It would be illuminating to apply Eadie's methodology to this structure to see what social functions could be accommodated within the building.

The Bridge Castle appears to have once been mirrored by another tower house on the opposite bank which projected out into the river. These two combined to provide control from opposing river banks. Although the current bridge is of eighteenth-century date, the river narrows here, making it an appropriate place for the medieval bridge mentioned in the documentation. Defending the bridge was an important security role as this was the road to New Ross, a major medieval river port downstream (Murtagh, 1988). In addition, the tower houses could defend the river, movement along it and the mercantile activities taking place within the town.

Murtagh has convincingly argued that the Bridge Castle at Thomastown is only one of many riverine tower houses to fulfil this duty: he also cites the Bridge Castle over the River Suir at Thurles, County Tipperary, and the White Castle over the River Barrow at Athy, County Kildare (*ibid.*). Athy was an inland port, as the River Barrow was navigable up to that point, and this enabled connections with New Ross and beyond. The town was situated outside of the Pale during the later Middle Ages, but the historical references to Gaelic-Irish attacks and its proximity to both earl of Kildare and earl of Ormond lands made it a flashpoint site for conflict (Murtagh, 2011). Consequently, it is specified as controlling access to the 'patrie' – ancestral lands – and its inhabitants (*Crown surveys of lands*: 152). As an inland port, it aided contact between geographically disparate Anglo-Irish areas (Murtagh, 2011). The White Castle is another example of these 'bridge castles'. A map preserved within the Cotton Collection in the British Library illustrates that originally another castle was located on the opposite bank of the river, supported by a written reference to two castles in the *Civil survey* (*ibid*.). Like at Thomastown, these two tower houses could work in tandem, as well as independently, to control road and water access through the town.

An old, presumably wooden, bridge has since disappeared outside Cashel, County Tipperary, across the River Suir where Castlelake and Ballynahinch castles would have been located to control it. Although no bridge is depicted on the first-edition OS map, local landholders state that the wooden bridge was there until around the 1930s. The placement of the tower houses would indicate that there was a crossing point here. Castlelake and Ballynahinch are like Athy and Thomastown in that a tower house was built at either end of the crossing point to best control access and, presumably, extract a toll from those using the bridge. At Ballynahinch the purported bridge was located at the base of the tower house, the tower house itself being located on the flood line. To the north of the tower house, over a natural rise, are the remains of a medieval church and graveyard. These are comparatively quite distant from the castle site, around five hundred metres. Fieldwalking, aerial photography and DEM suggest that the two settlement sites lay along a hollow-way. This medieval track would have continued on to the river crossing from the modern-day road. A medieval road would have passed along the west side of the tower house; thus, the building could monitor both road approach and river crossing. Castlelake tower house is directly opposite on the other bank of the river. The historical flood plain explains why it is set back from the river bank, as at Ballynahinch. Castlelake was incorporated into later buildings as construction material, but the presence of these ruined buildings gives us a site location for the tower house. Continuing on the aforementioned road to the other bank would bring the medieval trackway in front of the site of Castlelake.

A number of tower houses along the Blackwater River and its tributaries in counties Cork and Waterford may have controlled a fording point or bridge. What is puzzling is the proximity of the tower houses to these crossing points, while they are not located at or on the bridge or ford, unlike the other examples cited. Lisfinny Castle is located overlooking the River Bride, yet the modern bridge is about seven hundred metres to the southeast. Conna in County Cork, again on the River Bride, is situated at a height atop a rocky outcrop along the river bank. Conna is about six hundred metres from the modern bridge. In both these instances the distances involved suggest that the modern crossing point might not reflect the historical one, or that there was another factor at play that explains the greater than usual distance between them. We might expect to find a relationship more like that at Conva, County

Cork, on the River Blackwater. Conva Castle is highly visible from the bridge, two hundred metres to the southeast. Built at a height above the river, its positioning is excellent for visual command over a large area, including the land as it slopes down to the bridge.

The location of these tower houses atop bluffs and cliffs overlooking the crossing points might indicate instead that they sought visual control, if not direct control. There are also many weirs and fishings mentioned in the early modern documentation; although, strangely, not many are marked on the first-edition OS mapping. In County Limerick, the tower house in the town of Glin controls the historical bridge over the Glencorbry River, which it sits next to. Field survey has suggested that this bridge stood atop an earlier fording point, and that might explain why no bridge is marked on the 1600 drawing of the siege of the castle.

Many more tower houses were located close to, but not upon, bridges. Good examples of this come from Slane, County Meath, where Slane Castle and Carrickdexter Castle are located slightly downstream of the bridge spanning the River Boyne, while Fennor Castle overlooks it from the opposite bank. This bridge is historical, and parts of it even today are taken as indicating a mid-fourteenth-century date (Seaver, 2005). Slane Castle is now a later rebuilding, but the *Down survey* shows this was preceded by a tower house and bawn. It has been theorised that the tower house represents an elite relocation from the nearby Hill of Slane, to be closer to the river crossing (*ibid.*). Possibly these three tower houses did not need to be right by the bridge, as the *Civil survey*'s mention of an old castle being on it might indicate that it once had a bridge-end tower with fortified gate (*ibid.*). However, the proximity of three tower houses no doubt sent an effective message even without on-bridge construction.

Leighlinbridge, County Carlow, has an excellent position for monitoring bridge traffic (see figure 4.7) (Murtagh, 2011). Ellis has written that the constables of Leighlin and Athy illegally levied customs on the substantial trade that developed between Kilkenny and New Ross and between Carlow, Castledermot and Athy (Ellis, 1986). Owing to the prominent positioning of tower houses at bridges in both of these places, we can see the physical method of extortion. The Gaelic-Irish lord McMurrough also levied customs on river traffic north of New Ross,[2] where a number of previously discussed tower houses are located along the river banks (*ibid.*). Further surveyed examples exist at Golden in County Tipperary, and Newtown Trim (Saintjohns) and Castlejordan, both in County Meath. In the case of Castlejordan, we know the tower house controlled a bridge crossing over the River Boyne from the depiction of this on the *Down survey* mapping. The other tower houses have locations on or by historical stone bridges.

4.7 Leighlinbridge Castle in County Carlow is an excellent example of a 'bridge castle' – that is, a tower house located by a bridge to regulate and toll those crossing. The modern bridge shown here is on the site of an earlier bridge.

It is unfortunate that no Irish examples of fortified bridges survive, as a number of them once existed. McNeill (1980) has suggested that they slightly resembled the Pont Valentre at Cahors in France, based on the description of the fourteenth-century bridge at Coleraine over the River Bann, which had towers at either end for imposing and collecting tolls.

Tower houses at fording points

Other tower houses were located by fording points, though they have not been discussed much in the literature. Many fording points were probably later replaced by bridges. A significant number of tower houses along the Blackwater River in counties Cork and Waterford control a fording point (ASI). A ford is recorded in the *Civil survey* at Dunmoe, although this contrasts with the Boyne INSTAR project conclusions that the castle may not have controlled a ford at this point because the river is fast flowing here (Lewis *et al.*, 2008). However, there are historical references to the parson of Ardmulchan sharing responsibility in the fifteenth century for the upkeep of the stone 'Babe's Bridge' at Ferganstown, which is just over a kilometre upstream of Dunmoe Castle (*ibid.*). Wilde mentions this bridge in his description of Dunmoe Castle, noting it stood below the point of the castle (Wilde, 1849). Likewise, the authors of the INSTAR report conclude that Castlerickard and Killyon's being settlements on opposite banks implies a crossing point there (Lewis *et al.*, 2008). This conclusion might have wider applications.

Not only did many tower houses control river fords, but there is evidence in the landscape that these fords were originally part of medieval road networks. This might indicate the kind of road to be expected: in England, bridges tended to be located on major and secondary roads (except along the lower reaches of a river, where a ferry was more apt). On minor roads there were some bridges, but many more ferries and fords. We might deduce that fords were located on roads of middling importance. Many fords were located alongside bridges, and used contemporaneously. This could be because the bridge was too narrow for carts to use, or simply for water access for animals (Harrison, 2004). In the pastoral economy of Gaelic Ireland, it is not hard to see why fords could have been the more attractive prospect for a river crossing. Fords were often used to get around ferry and bridge tolls (*ibid.*), but the presence of tower houses at many fords indicates that this was not so much of an option in an Irish context, or at least was a usage that came to be exploited by tower house builders.

Crossing points may have disappeared over time, but the remnants of roadways are sometimes visible as lumps and bumps in the surrounding fields, as at Newhaggard in County Meath, where a short stretch of a hollow-way runs away from the river. Newhaggard sits just a few metres from the river's edge on a slight rise, the closest point to the river that did not regularly flood. The tower house is located perfectly for control of this routeway and where it met the river. While no concrete evidence has been unearthed for a fording point here – beyond the landowner reporting seeing odd alignments of stones when the river was at an extremely low level – there is support for the medieval road passing by the tower house. The *Down survey* parish and barony maps depict the roadway between Trim and Clonard running in front of the tower house. Higher-resolution aerial imaging from ArcGIS shows what may be two sides of a hollow-way. More importantly, this imaging matches the mid-seventeenth-century map.

Tower houses at roads and passes

O'Donovan writes in the *Ordnance Survey letters* that a number of castles were located by old roads (O'Donovan, 2001). Specific mention is made within the *Civil survey* to those tower houses that controlled important strategic routes, such as the passes, commanded by Rosse and the unidentified site of 'Ballinah' Castle,[3] into County Cavan from Meath (*Civil survey*: vol. 5). Cavan was Gaelic-Irish-controlled territory, and so any site that had the potential to restrict access and thus hold off raids would have been highly valued.

The most famous manifestation of this access control was the Pale. Parts of the Pale boundary were formed by rivers, but in places it was a divide made of banks and ditches, such as at Kilteel in County Kildare. There is a notable density of tower houses along the Pale boundary, no doubt for a range of reasons, including communal defence. Another reason might be connected to the possible use of Pale banks as roadways (Murphy and Potterton, 2010).

Further research in this area might ascertain the correlation of known tower houses with historic roadways, although medieval roads may not survive in the modern landscape either. Indeed, it was only through geophysical survey and excavation at Killeen Castle that the remnants of the medieval roads to Trim and Tara were discovered, the castles at Killeen and Dunsany sited so as to control communication on these routes. Baker commented that these sites would have mostly been controlling trade along the routeway, as well as access to settlement centres in the vicinity. Elite control of the roadways, she believes, is reflected in the local saying that 'Travellers in Meath should beware for if they are not robbed by the Lord of Killeen, they are sure to be robbed by the Lord of Dunsany' (Carty and Lynch, 2000: 69; cited in Baker, 2009: 34). In a similar scenario to the bridge castles, Killeen Castle was not only positioned to control roadways, but was also sited on a rocky outcrop overlooking the River Skane to the east (Baker, 2009).

Identifying precise road networks is difficult, if not impossible, but general overviews can often be ascertained more readily. This can include comparing known castle sites with modern roads that are probably continuations of much more historical roads. For example, we have a reference to land in Scurlockstown, County Meath, that stretched along the royal road (*via regali*) (*Register of the Hospital of St. John*). The site of the tower house at Scurlockstown is on a road that runs near the banks of the River Boyne, and only two hundred metres from today's main road between Trim and Piercetown, north of Dunboyne. Possibly this royal road is one of these two roads. Only one road is mentioned by Wilde in conjunction with Scurlockstown Castle, but he notes the command the tower house had over it (Wilde, 1849). That one road runs alongside the river course might be particularly telling about how tower houses were used to control multiple methods of communication.

The *via regali* noted in the *Register of the Hospital of St. John* was a *via regia*, which was a major road that connected baronies and boroughs. It was probably unpaved and in very variable condition along its length, which ran in County Meath from Drogheda through Slane to Navan and from Slane onto Skreen, Ratoath and ultimately Dublin (Seaver, 2005). This was a public road, and people could travel along it freely;

private roads could be exploited by the enterprising to charge tolls, which was technically illegal on public roads. We have no idea of how many private roads existed here or elsewhere in the country, or where they ran. Scurlockstown, within the Pale, may have had its public-road rights protected by its location within the English sphere of influence, but the king's law did not run so meticulously guarded outside of the area proximal to Dublin. However, no records of tolls being charged for using a private or semi-private roadway have been discovered to date.

The eighteenth-century Taylor and Skinner's road maps give us an indication of the location of medieval roads. Many of these remain in use today. Many others appear to have been more ephemeral in nature. Josias Bodley, writing in 1602–03, recalls a visit to Lecale in County Down. He arrived at Newry, the main English town in the south of the county, before making his way northwards. This land-based journey was not without its hazards, and Bodley recounts getting lost along the road on a number of occasions, even with a guide, writing at one point that they 'were compelled to go on foot, leading our horses through bogs and marshes, which was very troublesome, and some of us were not wanting who swore silently between our teeth, and wished our guide at a thousand devils' (Bodley: 331). One has to wonder why he didn't travel by water for the longer part of his journey, as his destination, Downpatrick, was located along a navigable stretch of river. There is a high incidence of tower houses in Lecale with control of anchorages. Perhaps Bodley was avoiding the water; although if he was, the reason is not given. That Bodley mentions having to dismount and resort to foot travel reflects the extremity of the situation, for overland transport even in Ireland would have been by packhorse (O'Neill, 1987). If a horse could not pass, the roadway must have been very underused.

Associated with Killegland Castle is a pre-modern fording point that could have been taxed for additional income by the tower house occupant. A similar set up may be observed at Macetown, where a tower house (now rubble) once stood. Here, a deserted settlement covering almost eight acres has been identified, with rectangular house platforms on a grid pattern fronting onto sunken trackways. The edges of the deserted settlement are defined on two sides by a mill race (*Database of Irish excavation reports*: 2003:1347, Killegland, Ashbourne, Meath; 2006:1497, Killegland, Ashbourne, Meath; Murphy and Potterton, 2010).

A location by a river, with street frontage, or at the junction of roads or bridges would have been the best place for mercantile activity (Murtagh, 2011). A large number of tower houses are located in places like this. The sheer number of tower houses sited in this way makes it unlikely that all of them were merchant owned. Instead, a rural location probably enabled a profitable engagement with the wider economy by local lords and gentry. A location by a communication point allowed for both physical control of the landscape and a potential income source.

Terrestrial, riverine and maritime routes may not have overlapped to any great extent, each serving as the most efficient method for its particular region, if the English evidence can be applied. The fourteenth-century English road system rarely had roads running near the coast, which suggests that instead water was employed. The relative usage will also have depended on what was being transported,[4] the terrain and availability of waterways (Hutchinson, 1997; O'Neill, 1987). On the other hand, the only method of goods transportation referenced in Kilkenny city's murage grant is 'every horse load of sea fish' (*Liber primus Kilkenniensis*: 120). This seems an odd method of transporting marine fish inland, considering the presence of the River Nore. Perhaps movement was obstructed by the frequently mentioned weirs and mills along this river, or the 'horse load' may have just formed a convenient standard measure.

Considering how much of Ireland's medieval settlement was accessible by either sea or navigable river, the incidence of terrestrial roadways may have been low. An added complication would of course have been the political conditions of the day, which would have made travellers an easy target. Regardless, we do know that so-called 'grey merchants' travelled around Gaelic-Irish areas gathering goods to sell, while other, usually town-based, merchants journeyed specifically to the Gaelic-Irish chieftains to conduct trade (O'Neill, 1987). These merchants will have transported themselves and their wares by whatever means were necessary and, considering that several of the Gaelic-Irish lordships were inland, they must have travelled overland extensively.

Conclusion: The tower house as nucleus of water-based communication

Most identifiable tower house occupants were local lords, meaning that commercial maritime networks were not controlled solely by merchants in late medieval Ireland. Interesting recent publications suggest that many tower house builders were members of the gentry class, with tower house architecture used as part of a greater scheme of social aggrandisement (Oram, 2015). It is impossible with the state of extant documentary material to determine the builders and occupants of the vast majority of tower houses, so comparative studies are invaluable. The observations made in Oram's edited volume regarding the extensive economic exploitation undertaken by tower house occupants therefore tells us about gentry social roles by extension. Primarily, it indicates that members of the gentry class were eager to present themselves as the new elite, but also that they had an interest in financial engagement. Should we have more data, it would be interesting to compare and contrast the economic positioning of gentry tower houses vis-à-vis magnate tower houses. It appears that the late medieval gentry in Ireland, if we can base this on tower house distribution, had an economic income base much wider and more diverse than high medieval castle builders, who drew their wealth mainly from the land.

If we take the now-accepted academic view that castle design made use of a widely understood visual language to convey meaning about its inhabitants, then the simple issue of a castle's placement within the landscape becomes central (e.g. Creighton, 2002; Johnson, 2002). The time and money saved through communication and transportation by water, in comparison to overland transport, enabled lords to live in the locations they found most favourable. This might be represented by a commanding view over the landscape, or proximity to designed landscape features like deer parks and rabbit warrens. That so many tower houses are located on water suggests two things: first, that what was regarded as the central location in the lord's estate was not necessarily at the geographic centre, on land, but in proximity to the aquatic resources; second, that a visual connection with the water was an integral part of elite identity. Water also makes an impressive backdrop for a castle, as has been observed at other castle sites by Johnson (2002). That a water-based location might have been chosen for defensive reasons is negated by the ease of access to these sites from the water.

Taken as a whole then, there is conclusive evidence for the use of both riverine and maritime tower houses as facilitating sometimes very extensive transport and communication networks. Such interactions could take a number of forms, ranging from defending bridges and fords to keeping watch over a stretch of river. Tower houses might have been deliberately built in places where they could control a small part of a bigger economic machine. The reasons behind these uses of tower houses are likely manifold. Defence will have been an issue, as was visual and practical control over territory. Rights will have been asserted using these buildings, and a very attractive income could be made by exploiting the siting. A sizeable number of tower houses therefore should be viewed as points representing their owners' wider understanding of the outside world and interactions with it.

Notes

1 Murtagh refers to Faulkner (1966), 'Medieval undercrofts and town houses', *Archaeological Journal*, 123, 120–35.

2 Hore and Graves, 'Southern and eastern counties', cited in Ellis (1986).
3 'Ballinah' was presumably in the townland of that name, but there is no archaeological site corresponding to the castle and bawn in the *Civil survey*.
4 For example, in England, it cost as much to take a tun of wine forty to fifty-four miles by road as it did to bring it by sea from Bordeaux, and that imbalance must have been even more apparent in Ireland.

5

'Urban' tower houses

While, at first glance, the distinction between rural and urban might seem obvious, the reality is far different. The proliferation of settlements officially designated as 'rural boroughs', with burgesses who held special legal rights shared with urban residents, implies that a number of urbanised places were spread across Ireland. In reality, very few of these boroughs became truly urban places. Instead, the title was used as a promise of improved social station to lure new settlers to the country. Towns were created by the Anglo-Normans with the intention of funnelling trade through them from the rest of the territory they controlled (O'Brien, 1988). The Irish port towns thrived financially in the tower house era, in spite of difficult political circumstances. Indeed, Ireland is described as having been in 'substantial economic recovery' at this time (*ibid.*: 25). The influx of money into Ireland's urban places and the control of this activity by a small and interrelated mercantile community explains, at least in part, a late medieval building boom that included tower houses. It also included tower-house-type structures. As has been discussed, sometimes confusing terminology is employed to skirt categorisation issues. This pattern of enthusiastic building also transcends space – differences in urban and rural architecture have been repeatedly discussed in a late medieval English context (for example, see the brief summary in Grenville (2008)) – but tower houses are common to both environments in Ireland. There must have been something universal in their appeal and functionality.

Even if most boroughs remained rural in essence, we know of several urban locations that evolved out of agricultural and manorial centres. A borough might not have been a town, but a town had to have been a borough (Graham, 1988b). Some have gone so far as to say that the town was a manorial 'outgrowth' (Bradley, 1985: 38). These towns originating in castles were small in population, with Nicholas estimating that 'the total population of most agglomerations consisting simply of castle and suburb would scarcely exceed 1000–1500' in the more industrialised Low Countries (Nicholas, 1996: 28). It is highly likely that Irish examples were even smaller. Urban tower houses would have been built after the town's establishment, so town development, if not origins, can be associated with them.

Medieval towns in Ireland were smaller and fewer in number than elsewhere in Europe at this time, though their role in later medieval economic development was substantial (Galloway, 2015). Several definitions of what constitutes 'urban' in medieval Ireland have been proposed, all of which would work within the tower house framework. John Bradley, one of the foremost scholars of urban medieval Ireland, defines a town as:

> a settlement occupying a central position in a communications network, represented by a street pattern with houses and their associated land plots whose density is significantly greater than the settlements immediately around it ... it incorporates a market place and a church and its principal functions are reflected by the presence of at least three of the following: town walls, a castle, bridge, cathedral, a house belonging to one of the religious orders, a hospital or leper-house close to the town, an area of specialist technological activity, quays, a large school, or administrative building, and/or suburbs. (Bradley, 1985: 35)

Graham finds two issues with Bradley's conclusions: first, that they presume these features existed contemporarily with one another, and, second, that they separate the inseparable. In other words, that the distinction between rural and urban is often not as clear cut as theory makes out (Graham, 1988a, b).

Functionality may have separated a town from a village – a town produced materials with support from the local rural economy, sometimes referred to as its hinterland (Clarke, 2013). Reynolds has argued for a more integrated town–country approach, defining a town as a permanent and comparatively dense settlement with a population working mainly outside of agriculture. It held a relationship with a hinterland from whence essential goods were drawn (quoted in Wall Forrestal, 2015). The role of the hinterland and the interdependence of town and country are consistent in recent historiography, witnessed in publications like Giles and Dyer's edited collection *Town and country in the Middle Ages: Contrasts, contacts and interconnections*, as well as others (Giles and Dyer, 2005; Kowaleski, 2014). Another take on defining the town stresses inhabitants' occupations (Graham, 1988b). However, Ireland lacks the surviving documentation necessary to identify occupations at the local level, so this definition is arguably not as useful (*ibid.*). Dyer has suggested we focus more on use of space, including building density and marketplace prominence (Dyer, 2013a).

Places included here as towns have tended to be defined as such following a composite of many of these methodologies. The model of occupational differentiation has been somewhat followed, since by taking the urban tower house as this publication's focal point, the social group most examined is the merchants. The mutually supporting nature of town and country is emphasised throughout this volume. The demand of trade and exchange centred on the port towns was also felt at a local rural level. Taking tower houses as a focus by default creates an adapted 'kritirienbundel', a model list of defining urban features first proposed by Max Weber, to define a town, by giving pre-eminence to the presence of a castle. Town walls, discussed below, play a less defining role in this definition. It is argued here that there is less of a dichotomy between public and private urban spaces, more of a sliding scale. Towns founded by lay elites tended to be at sites where good opportunities for profit existed, whether this be at the crossing of routeways or, ideally, where people were already unofficially meeting to exchange items (Dyer, 2013a). It is not surprising, then, that most of the late medieval urban tower house sites are at towns where opportunities for profit were ample.

The control of land-based movement

The preceding chapters have examined the usefulness of the tower house in controlling land- and water-based routes. It is only apt that we enter the urban space through the medium of the trade route, as the mainly agricultural goods once did. Many of the so-called 'bridge castles' previously discussed were in towns. The significant port towns of later medieval Ireland tended to be located on the junction of river estuary and sea. All 'roads' led to the towns, where more tower houses were located, to capitalise. Therefore, the towns formed the loci of an integrated network of roads and rivers, which at the coastal towns, connected to the wider world. Specifically, it was the *via regia* that formed the major land routes that connected baronies and boroughs. These were probably unpaved for the most part and, even though their width was supposed to have been set by legislation, their dimensions are likely to have differed wildly. Alongside the navigable rivers, these roads connected the interior to the port towns, and the port towns to inland market towns via the settlement hierarchy. For instance: one routeway ran from the north of Drogheda, a major trading port on the border of counties Louth and Meath, through Slane (which was also located on the navigable River Boyne), onwards to Navan (likewise on the Boyne), while another branch travelled on to smaller inland settlements like Skreen and Ratoath, before linking to Ireland's capital city, Dublin (Seaver, 2005).

To return to the issue of the interdependence of town and country: Galloway's study of urban hinterlands shows the varying spatial areas needed to support a medieval town, the precise area dependent on the good required and the means of transport. In his study of Drogheda, for example, he examined timber and grain. He found that timber needed to come sizeable distances, necessitating movement by river, while grain was transported in that way when its movement needed to be expedited (Galloway, 2015). Likewise, in Waterford the city's official remit stretched as far as Inistioge in County Kilkenny, about thirty-five kilometres away, and encompassed the tidal reaches of all the Three Sisters rivers (Galloway, 2011). The influence from these cities could 'subsume' the smaller economies of the local towns.

This means that the economic benefits accruing from supplying the towns could be felt over fairly considerable distances. Tower houses were built manifestations of this income as well as being forms of investment in it, since they provided secure storage and a business venue. Naessens has proposed that rural tower houses were employed as bulking points for cumbersome agricultural commodities in trading networks, as he noted in his case study in County Galway (Naessens, 2009). For this function to be served by tower houses, a bulking area would have been needed either in the tower itself, or within the castle complex.

The tower houses of medieval Ireland's urbanised settlements

The incidence of urban tower houses in the modern landscape has much to do with the fortunes of the town in the intervening period. Far higher numbers appear in near-contemporary sources like the *Civil survey* than can be counted today. Urban places with multiple extant sites tend to be those that underwent infrastructural neglect in the post-medieval period. Ardglass is just one example of where an abandonment phase has allowed the survival of much of the late medieval fabric (O'Sullivan and Breen, 2007). Even considering the loss of many urban tower houses, too many remain to give an exhaustive list here; instead, this chapter highlights a select number from across the country. One estimate has the number of extant urban tower houses at thirty-seven; the original number will, of course, have been many times higher (Murtagh, 1989). For example, only one example survives of a reported eight in Naas, County Kildare (Murtagh, 1985–86). That urban tower house examples come from across the country and a variety of contexts is worth noting. This includes from the Pale, from 'contact zones' and from Gaelic-Irish areas. Tower houses are known in towns with both long and short histories, that developed economically in the later Middle Ages, and those originating in early medieval and Anglo-Norman settlement. Urban tower houses tend to be smaller than their rural counterparts (aside from St. Leger's Castle in Ardee, County Louth), reflecting their smaller building plot. Some have remarked that urban tower houses were less decorated than rural ones, but this is contradicted by heavily ornamented examples like the Mint in Carlingford and Lynch's Castle in Galway. It has tended to be accepted by castle scholars, too, that urban tower houses could have a wider range of functions than those at rural sites. It is almost taken for granted that urban tower houses could have had the usual castle functions of defence, residence and administrative centre, but they could also have had storage functions, as well as symbolic currency (Smith, 1996). In the last decade or so, there has been a willingness to view tower houses as having been, in part, working buildings. This recognition commenced with the maritime examples, with a view that they could have been adaptable to marine-based economies (O'Sullivan and Breen, 2007).

Preservation is an issue affecting the survival of all tower houses, rural and urban, alongside their contemporary features like mills and street plans. Perhaps affecting urban tower houses more than their rural relatives are the modernising renovations that often obscure earlier building fabric. We can see good examples of this in the insertion of large modern windows in the urban tower houses of Ardee in County Louth and Youghal in County Cork. It has been suggested that the urban examples originally looked closest architecturally, and in terms of their dimensions, to the '£10 Castles', such as Donore in County Meath. In turn, this indicates that urban tower houses might come early in the tower house chronology (Murtagh, 1985–86). Presumably, their small size was also due to spatial constrictions within the walled towns. What follows is a description of urban tower houses from a range of contexts from across Ireland, to provide case studies for further discussion of specifically 'urban' features and functions.

Athboy, County Meath: Athboy was within the Pale, in the region included within the £10 Castle grant of the fifteenth century. Athboy has no extant tower houses within the present-day town, though documentary evidence shows that they did historically exist. We have two interesting examples, however, only a few kilometres outside the town at Causestown and Fraine. These sites are located between the town and the modern border with County Westmeath. Therefore, their potential role as Pale defences and outworks of the town might be pondered.

Athboy itself is on a fording point of the Athboy River, and is a boundary point (Shine, 2011a). References indicate that a settlement already existed at Athboy at the time that the Anglo-Normans settled there. It then became a manorial caput and the centre of the barony of

Lune (Bradley, 1988–89). In 1407 Athboy was granted the right to form a merchant guild. It was one of the four walled towns of Meath and was supported by murage grants, for which we have documentation dating from 1306, 1446 and 1462. It was still noted as walled by the late sixteenth century (*ibid.*; Shine, 2011a). Although, as stated, there are no standing remains of tower houses within the modern town, the *Civil survey* has thirteen castles listed. From at least 1338 it was a market town and borough.

Its subscription to defending the Pale indicates it was one of the wealthier towns of the region by 1423 (Bradley, 1988–89), and this could be where the neighbouring rural tower houses come into play. At the very least, they highlight the interconnectedness of town and country. Being on the edge of the Pale, Athboy was fairly regularly attacked by the Gaelic-Irish. Causestown Castle is two and a half kilometres southwest of the town, while Fraine Castle is roughly three kilometres to its south. Fraine is an interesting example as it clearly still shows hall foundations immediately to the east of the ruined tower, as well as the remnants of a field system to its south and east.

Athboy highlights the relationships that existed between town and country in medieval Ireland and illustrates that urban tower houses cannot be studied in isolation, but rather as contributing to the socio-economic whole. It is worth remarking, too, that the proximity of rural tower houses could have negative ramifications for town inhabitants, though these issues seem to have been less frequent than the positive interactions. One such example is the complaints made by the people of Youghal, County Cork, that they were being attacked from an unnamed castle located four miles upriver (CSPI: vol. 5, SP63/5f.231, 1562). There are several tower houses located outside the town of Youghal along the River Blackwater, including Temple Michaell, Strancally and Camphire. The many tower houses in County Limerick, similarly, were at times employed to 'annoy passage' between towns and disrupt trade by land and river (CSPI: vol. 9, SP63/207/3, f. 285, p. 241, 1600).

Slane, County Meath: The modern town of Slane reflects an eighteenth-century plan; the medieval town was probably congregated closer to the bridge. Slane was first referred to as a borough in 1370 (Bradley, 1988–89), but it could be categorised more accurately as a village with an agricultural outlook. It is mentioned here because it controlled a bridge along an important riverine communication network and had religious sites of some significance, including the 'College'. Fennor Castle sits on the high point of the ridge, commanding the prospect over the bridge, on the bank opposite where the medieval village was probably located. Originally a tower house, it now shows signs of having been adapted into a fortified house sometime in the seventeenth century. Upstream is Carrickdexter Castle (sometimes listed as Slanecastle Demesne), again only a couple of kilometres outside the presumed town and with command of the approach routes into it. Like Athboy, then, Slane highlights the interlinked nature of town and country as well as showing how urban influence could stretch into agricultural areas.

Trim, County Meath: An Anglo-Norman foundation, Trim boomed in the fourteenth and fifteenth centuries, before declining in the sixteenth as it became a frontier town in the shrinking Pale (Hayden, 2009). Finds from excavation indicate that Trim had craft producers and a market economy (Beglane, 2009). The marketplace may have been substantial, with different products sold in different areas (Potterton, 2005). Place-name and surname evidence shows craft activity, such as cloth dying, but merchant is the most frequently encountered occupation in the surviving documentation (*ibid.*). Trim is best known for its large Anglo-Norman castle, though several tower houses are recorded in the town, including Nangle's Castle. This building had a garden running down to the navigable river. It may have been part of the Augustinian priory in the town, but has also been interpreted as a merchant's residence owing to this location (*ibid.*).

Newtown Trim, County Meath: Only a couple of kilometres downstream is Newtown Trim, which was deliberately developed in hopes of its developing into a town (Bradley, 1988–89). Standing remains indicate it was once wealthy, although it is largely abandoned today (*ibid.*). Several tower houses are associated with the settlement. On one bank of the river was the foundation of the Augustinian canons, with tower house. On the other side, the priory of the Crutched Friars is recorded as possessing two tower houses. One of these controlled the bridge crossing between the two sides of the River Boyne. These form excellent examples of religiously connected tower houses. They also reflect the role of tower houses in suburban development. The Augustinians, in common with the other mendicant orders, tended to establish their houses outside town walls. This extra-mural construction may be due to lack of space inside the town for new foundations, or to cater to those approaching the town. As Newtown Trim was established with the intention of growing a town, these houses may have taken advantage of lower land costs in the failed attempt, while still being close to the major secular and ecclesiastical settlement of Trim.

Ardee, County Louth: Ardee was on a fording point of the River Dee, which may have been a focal point of routeways by the Anglo-Norman period. The main street in Ardee is wide enough to have been used as a marketplace. Indeed, the sale of certain goods – like geese, eggs and fish – was mentioned in 1450 (Bradley, 1984). It also has a bridge, which was present by 1306 when the town received a pontage grant for repairs in stone (*ibid.*).

Ardee has aspects of a well-preserved medieval town, including the largest urban tower house in Ireland, St. Leger's Castle (Bradley, 1995). It projected into the street, enabling it to control access up and down the street, and this may have included access to the marketplace (Murtagh, 1989). It is likely that Ardee had numerous tower houses, of which two survive inside and one outside the walls (Bradley, 1984; Murtagh, 1989). The latter tower house is described by Bradley as 'extra-mural', thus connecting it to the town even though it physically stood outside it. It might have belonged to a religious house, which would explain its unusual location (Bradley, 1984). It has since been substantially altered, and forms part of outbuildings to a later house. Unfortunately, one aspect of the medieval town that is not well preserved is the town walls. These are documented through murage grants in the fourteenth and fifteenth centuries, though little of the walls stand today, and none of the mural towers (*ibid.*). We know that the walls enclosed a large area, but we do not know if the whole of this was built up throughout the town's history. The walls may have enclosed gardens and orchards as well as the denser urban part (*ibid.*).

Dalkey, County Dublin: Dalkey's medieval history is closely interlinked with that of Ireland's main city, Dublin. Dalkey is probably the best known example of an outport, as it was the landing place for goods bound for Dublin. There are a number of tower houses linked to people involved with collecting fishing revenues (Smith, 1996). Seven tower houses, three extant, were built in this town, and Murtagh believes their function was to store goods and defend them against the incursions of the Gaelic-Irish striking from nearby County Wicklow (Murtagh, 1988). Although there is some documentation for the Dalkey tower houses, none of it references merchant occupants aside from the suggestions of family names, but the two functions may not be mutually exclusive (Bradley, 1998). In many cases fortifications were constructed to aid in the overseeing of coastal rights, the merchant tower houses at Dalkey providing secure storage as well as controlling the settlement (*ibid.*). As at Fethard, below, two of the urban tower houses here are located by the church (O'Keeffe, 1999). This could reflect a merchant seeking status by association, or perhaps there is a correlation between the merchants and religious landholding. Indeed, the two need not have been exclusive, as is suggested by the presence of crosses at medieval marketplaces and ready access between marketplaces and churchyards (*ibid.*). In many Irish towns, the marketplace is located to the east of an older ecclesiastical centre, possibly because the graveyard was used for a market until a 1308 ban on this use (Lennon, 2013).

Kilmallock, County Limerick: Kilmallock has a largely well-preserved medieval fabric, including one tower house (see figure 5.1). This tower house is located in the centre of a major thoroughfare, which was its original location as it is described as being in the centre of the street in the late sixteenth century (*Desmond survey*: MS f. 15d), and has a passage running through the ground floor. This situation must have been somewhat unusual even for the time, since it is specifically remarked upon. The town's late medieval wealth can be attributed to its association with the Desmond earls (Lee, 1965). The tower house is only a few metres from a stone-built medieval house, and near the modern footbridge across the river to the Dominican friary. It is likely that this is only one of many tower houses that once stood in the settlement, based on comparative evidence and the town's association with a powerful family. Lee writes that 'at one time there were several castellated mansions inhabited by wealthy families, all built of hewn stone and communicated by gateways with the streets' (*ibid.*: 150–1). However, there is no citation given to support this statement and we do not otherwise find references to 'castles' within the town until the seventeenth century. It is probable that there were extra-mural tower houses, based on the descriptions from the *Desmond survey* of the castle at Courtruddery, which was close to the town walls in the north but does not stand today. There are also a mural gate and stretches of extant town wall. The town was walled by the close of the thirteenth century. It was extensively destroyed in 1571 but was rapidly rebuilt after (Lee, 1965).

Youghal, County Cork: Best known for its early modern associations with the likes of Sir Walter Raleigh, Youghal was an important late medieval port on the south coast. It has a number of well-preserved medieval sites, including one tower house as well as several medieval town gates and a good stretch of town wall. It also has medieval religious buildings that remain in use today. Youghal is discussed below in more detail regarding an unusual document that survives in the Lismore Castle papers of the earls of Cork, stating what uses residential mural towers could have.

Fethard, County Tipperary: Fethard is one of the best preserved medieval towns in Ireland, and has two tower houses. It had a marketplace, and looks to have had a bridge (Bradley, 1985). The fortified gate depicted on Madam's Bridge in the nineteenth century would have provided clear yet controlled access to the marketplace. This bridge tower resembled a tower house in its architectural design, but with access cut through the ground floor (O'Keeffe, 1999, 2003). The town may have been founded with ecclesiastical patronage from Cashel, but was walled from the late fourteenth century at the latest (O'Keeffe, 1999). Several tower houses in the town were squeezed into short plots

'Urban' tower houses

5.1 Historical references demonstrate that this tower house in Kilmallock, County Limerick, was located in the centre of the main street. It is a good example of an urban tower house, which are often smaller than their rural counterparts. Many urban tower houses do not survive in the modern landscape.

in order to be near the church, including Court and Edmond castles (*ibid.*). Edmond Castle may have been the residence of the priest, since it incorporated part of the communal town walls and was flush with the churchyard, thus providing direct access. That both these castles were deliberately sited is indicated by their orientation: the lower floors open onto the street and the upper look towards the church (*ibid.*). The two levels did not directly communicate with one another, instead the upper levels were accessible from the rear using external stairs. This is reminiscent of medieval commercial plans – with shop or warehouse on the ground floor and residence above – and lends credence to the theory that these were merchant-owned tower houses. There is no indication that this was a later adaptation, but rather that they were originally constructed in this manner. The ground floors could also have been rented out to a third party for income (*ibid.*). The split levels controlled movement, particularly entry. This has been interpreted as an expression of the built language of privilege and financial wealth (*ibid.*).

O'Keeffe has described the arrangement here as 'unusual' for Irish urban tower houses, yet it is reminiscent of the possible split layers of Strangford Castle in County Down and the row of commercial properties known as the Newark in Ardglass in the same county. This author wonders if more detailed study of building fabric in other urban tower houses would lead to the identification of further examples. These urban towers could be a fortified version of the numerous timber-framed urban merchant houses of England (and that presumably existed in Ireland, but for which no example survives into the modern era).

Strangford, County Down: Strangford Castle has two entrances. One of the entrances, enlarged from its previous state and then restored, is on the ground floor in the northeast wall. The second entrance is in the same wall, towards the north angle and at first-floor level, and appears on the outside as a small splayed opening. This first-floor entrance is difficult to identify from the exterior as alterations have obscured the original stone. Inside the castle, however, its existence is attested to by the presence of a draw-bar socket, leading Jope to conclude that it 'is the sole feature obviously to survive reconstruction of the tower in the later sixteenth century; dating possibly to the fifteenth century, it is the only instance of a first-floor entrance to a tower-house surviving in County Down and, indeed, in the north of Ireland' (Jope, 1966: 253).

Strangford exhibits several features indicative of a dual-entrance tower house in the stricter sense of the term – i.e. having two entrances in use at the same time. While Sherlock observed in his study that dual-entrance tower houses usually had one entrance directly above the other, presumably so that both could be covered by a machicolation, in some cases one entrance was set to one side, as is the case at Strangford. He further notes that in dual-entrance tower houses the principal internal stair does not begin at the ground floor, rather at the floors above, and has suggested that where wooden flooring was used, access between the ground and first floors must have been by a ladder through an ope (small opening) cut in the floor (Sherlock, 2006). Of course, there is no surviving wooden flooring to attest to this at Strangford, but where the ground floor was covered by a vault a similar hole was cut through the vaulting to provide access between the storeys. Strangford Castle contains no stone internal stairs, unusual for the region, so would have had wooden ones. Likewise it had no stone vaulting, so the flooring was also timber, as indicated by the presence of beam holes.

The overwhelming majority of such dual-entrance tower houses occur in counties Cork and Kerry, but one exception is the Mint in Carlingford, County Louth. As at Strangford, the Mint had two entrances in the rear wall (if we take the wall facing the medieval street as the front). The first-floor entrance was possibly accessed by a wooden extension (Gosling, 1992). Sherlock believes that the decision to build a dual-entrance tower house was for defensive, domestic or pragmatic reasons, or a combination of all three. It may have been for damage limitation against raiding, where the ground floor could be comparatively easily raided, deterring the effort of accessing the upper floors and thus providing a 'firewall' for the upper floors. The dual entrances could have been for social reasons, so as to separate a service ground floor from the domestic upper floors (Sherlock, 2006). Sherlock rejects the notion that dual-entrance tower houses were dual-functionality tower houses, providing a public and commercial function at ground-floor level and a residence above. In contrast, this study finds correlation between medieval dual-function buildings, well known from English contexts, and Irish tower-house-type buildings. These findings mirror O'Keeffe's conclusions from his study of the built fabric of medieval Fethard.

Carlingford, County Louth: Like Dalkey, Carlingford profited from the financial proceeds of fishing, sufficient to warrant two upstanding tower houses as well as fragments of others. It also has a Tholsel (a public building that could serve a variety of purposes as needed, including town hall, market house or courthouse), town gates and an Anglo-Norman castle. Of the standing tower houses, the Mint is a dual-entrance tower house and Taaffe's Castle has an attached hall or warehouse.

Carrick-on-Suir, County Tipperary: Two towers survive, incorporated into the building fabric of the earl of Ormond's fine early modern house at one end of the town on the River Suir. Presumably these towers were utilised prior to the construction of the grander (and undefended) house.

Within the town, Main Street was the broadest street and this probably indicates it was the marketplace. Fourteenth-century pontage grants testify to the presence of a bridge from this date, and there are also references to quays located on the north river bank (Bradley, 1985; *Calendar of Ormond deeds*: vol. 3, 1413–1509).

Ardglass, County Down: Ardglass has a large and sheltered harbour with six known tower houses scattered at locations close to the waterfront. Of these, three have been proposed as port buildings – shops, warehouses and potential navigational aids – with a fourth, Jordan's Castle, having dual functionality (commercial and residential). The establishment of Ardglass is thought to be the result of efforts by Janico Dartas, a Gascon who followed King Richard II to Ireland, who took advantage of the isolation and potential autonomy of Ardglass from both London and Dublin. Ardglass was made a borough in 1442 and a customs port in 1467–68, although it probably had its origins as a customs port long before that date (Martin, 1981). Janico Dartas appears to have been a man closely connected in trade – in 1395 a consignment of cauldrons was granted to him in lieu of payment of customs. No mention is made of where these cauldrons came from, although it is probable that they were manufactured in either Chester or Bristol (O'Neill, 1987). In 1408 Dartas was assigned the task of building a 'nave de guerra' (warship) at Drogheda.

Ardglass Castle, also called the Newark, is listed as one of Dartas's possessions in his *Inquisition post mortem*. Through excavation, McNeill (2005) identified partitioning of the interior, reminiscent of a row of shops. Ardglass may have had a permanent role as a market town, since the Newark provided a market environment year-round. There would need to have been a large and wealthy hinterland to warrant market-based exchange as a permanent feature. The commercial functions of the Newark were long hinted at before McNeill's excavation provided conclusive results, with Jope in his *Archaeological survey* (1966) reckoning it a warehouse. Westropp, writing about depictions of Ireland on Italian maps, said: 'When we read of Henry IV establishing a trading company at Ardglas, and see the remains of its extensive fortified "factory," we no longer wonder at the appearance of the other-time obscure little place on the maps after 1450' (Westropp, 1912–13: 364–5). That is to say, even places we consider unimpressive and unremarkable today could have historical significance that may only be uncovered through diverse investigative methods.

The smallest of all the tower sites, Cowd Castle, may have functioned as a navigational aid and watchtower (McNeill, 2005). Margaret's Castle is another example of a small urban tower house, though it is much larger than Cowd Castle. It stands at just under 7 by 6.5 metres in ground dimensions. The small size of Margaret's Castle is possibly a result of the reduced space available in the late medieval town of Ardglass, and no ancillary buildings have been identified. Even at the more average-sized Jordan's Castle in the town, excavation by Gardiner found that the building had been crammed into a small plot and had a pathway squeezed in alongside it, connecting to the main streets (Gardiner, 2005).

Galway, County Galway: Galway thrived on international trade with continental Europe. Still standing today are two tower houses, both associated with merchant activity. One of these is close to the modern-day quays, while the other, known as Lynch's Castle, is located further inland on the main street. The latter has impressive stone carvings on its façade, which makes the observer think a statement was being made. These finely carved windows are mainly original, but are mostly not in their initial locations (Newman Johnson, 1998). A third tower house survives in a very fragmentary state within the King's Head public house, near to Lynch's Castle. Galway city also has extant medieval churches.

This section has focussed on a mere sampling of urban locations with a variety of relationships with tower houses – some still have multiple tower houses within their fabric, others have only documentary reference to those within the urban confines and instead have extant examples close by in their rural hinterland. There are other types of tower houses that have not been discussed here: the solitary tower houses still standing in several smaller market-type towns across Ireland. These include Buttevant in County Cork, where the tower house stands in a prominent position on the main street, and Ballingarry in County Limerick, where it sits on a small plot to the rear of the main street. In this latter instance, it may be that the road layout was realigned in the post-medieval era, and that the street was originally slightly closer to the front of the tower house.

Taking the evidence as a whole, we can ascertain some common features that regularly occur in Ireland's towns where tower houses are located. These support the contention that, when defining a town from the perspective of material culture and built environment, a melding of the various theories is most illuminating. This is true despite the serious problems presented by low survival rates of medieval building fabric. In all cases a notable level of post-medieval destruction has taken place, and there are few documentary references to compensate. Brief and passing references to a multiplicity of tower houses in the likes of the *Civil survey* are not so useful in studies like this, where the precise location of the tower house gives us major insights into their original form and function.

Many of the locations described above had associations with trade. Several were known port towns, and in late medieval Ireland these tended to have coastal distributions. Others were located on rivers. The role of the tower house in controlling the nodal points of communication and economic networks along navigable waterways is relevant again here. Urban tower houses are frequently mentioned alongside bridges and fording points. Yet again we can see the tower house association with controlling crossing points between routeways, both riverine and terrestrial. The control of routeways appears to have been a decisive motivator in the location of towns, as well as of specific tower houses, as evidenced by Graham's studies of Anglo-Norman town planning in eastern Ireland. Urban tower houses may have been doubly useful in exploiting this association.

There is evidence for more diverse occupations in these late medieval towns than in the surrounding rural areas. This tends to fall into one of two distinguishing characteristics: either the tower house is located near to a marketplace or the main street is of sufficient breadth to host this function, or the tower house is associated with merchant occupancy. Although the evidence for a diversity of craft-based production is still fairly sparse, places having undergone significant excavation – like Trim – aside, the job of merchant was one predominantly associated with urban environments.

Although tower houses are frequently emphasised as rural monuments, a systematic study like this shows that they are known from almost all late medieval market and port towns, from all corners of the country. It is only right, therefore, that tower houses from now on be considered both a rural and an urban phenomenon, with the flexibility in their functions accounting for their prevalence across many other social divides. This lends credence to the central premise of this entire volume: that the great number of tower houses between the fourteenth and seventeenth centuries can in large part be attributed to their ready adaptation to a wide variety of purposes and social backdrops.

The tower house as merchant residence

Ireland's merchants were small in number and interconnected, leading to one historian describing them as 'urban patriciates' (O'Brien, 1988: 22). They also seem to have been wily, with attempts to keep financial gain within their own hands hinted at when we read complaints to the Crown regarding hyperbolic economic stresses (*ibid.*). Their incomes could be considerable, and this returns us to the issue of conspicuous consumption and social emulation. Within Hanseatic towns, the artefactual evidence is that urban residents attempted to emulate the material culture and style of the merchants. Scholars have gone so far as to suggest that these merchants 'dictated contemporary design taste' and brought new craft methods into the regions in which they settled (Gaimster, 2014: 73).

Although we are, rightly, warned against making sweeping statements regarding the emulation of lordly habits by the emerging capitalist class (or vice versa) in the later Middle Ages, it is hard not to ponder this dynamic when we are faced with the architectural evidence. A good instance of this comes from Thomastown, where the residences associated with its merchants strongly echo specific and unusual features found at the nearby Anglo-Norman Grenan Castle, founded by a follower of Strongbow – Richard de Clare, the second earl of Pembroke – a leading figure in the Anglo-Norman Invasion of Ireland. A merchant of new social standing could do worse than claim a visual connection with some of the earliest Anglo-Norman settlement of the region. Urban locations thus provided 'perpetual canvases for both the display of wealth and the expression of political influence' (O'Keeffe, 1999: 9).

The construction of 'fortified merchant houses' occurred across the country. These were called castles by contemporaries, did not form part of the town walls but were focussed on the main streets of the town. Murtagh calls them the rural tower house's 'urban relative', and says they demonstrated prestige and wealth to the community (Murtagh, 1988: 536). Merchant families thrived on trade after the mid-fourteenth century in Ireland, so they 'enjoyed an importance out of all proportion to their numbers' (*ibid.*: 550). These merchant families used their money to build fine tower houses on the river or street front through which to conduct their business (*ibid.*). In the discussion of urban tower houses town by town, above, several listed have traditionally been associated with, or attributed to, mercantile families. This is potentially in contrast to Scottish urban tower houses, which were usually constructed as town houses by the rural gentry (Creighton and Higham, 2005: 71).

In the case of Jordan's Castle in the town of Ardglass, we have archaeological evidence for the mercantile function in the form of an attached warehouse with macrofossil remains indicating a storage usage. Such proof is rare, and the attribution is usually tentative and tied to often vague references to a medieval merchant family. It is through this means that Jordan's Castle earned its name. The earls of Kildare farmed out the customs of Ardglass, one of several town custom collection rights they possessed, for periods of time. This included in 1524, when collection of customs was granted to three men, one of whom was Thomas Jordan of Drogheda (*Crown surveys of lands*: 252). Possibly the same Thomas Jordan, or a close relative sharing the name, appears in the *Crown survey* of 1540–41. Here it is stated that the manors of Ardglass and Strangford with their appurtenances were occupied by Thomas Jordan of Drogheda, merchant. Presumably it is the family name of this individual that was lent to 'Jordan's Castle', the mercantile occupation of its inhabitants reflected in the stone warehouse.

Slightly further north, Rowland White was a Dublin merchant who was lord of the barony of Dufferin, County Down (Morgan, 1985). Any tower house he resided in or constructed was therefore merchant occupied, although whether he conducted any business from this dwelling is unknown. The original building of Killyleagh Castle was a tower house dating from the approximate period of the White lordship, and therefore may be one such site. Bangor in County Down was one of the last built tower houses, as it was noted as being under construction in 1637 (Jope, 1966). It is, unusually, a site for which we have limited evidence for a residential role, and instead its purpose is overwhelmingly associated with merchant activity. It was constructed in a Scottish architectural style, and provided accommodation for visitors as well as operating as a customs house. Bangor was probably built in this style because the port's trading links would have been almost exclusively with Scottish ports (Jope, 1951; McAlister, 2013). Since it served as accommodation for visiting mariners, this architectural style may have also been chosen to make its visitors from Scotland and northwest England feel at home, thus encouraging their return business.

Other urban sites are generally accepted by scholars as representing merchants' abodes, among them the tower houses of the Mint and Taaffe's Castle in Carlingford, County Louth (O'Sullivan and Gillespie, 2011). We are more secure in the connection of Lynch's Castle in Galway city with the merchant family of the same name. An individual named Germyn Lynch took pilgrims to Santiago de Compostela in Spain in one direction, and brought wine in the other, in the later fifteenth century (Bradley, 1995; O'Neill, 1988). The builder of Lynch's Castle may have been the extremely wealthy merchant Dominick Duff Lynch, based on the merchant marks of the Lynch family on this tower house as well as on other medieval buildings in the town, including the neighbouring St. Nicholas's Church. This gives the tower an estimated construction date in the early 1500s (Newman Johnson, 1998). It also provides an example of prestige and wealth being communicated through expensive and expansive building projects.

There were at least four tower houses along the quays at Thomastown, including the Bridge/Sweetman's Castle and Brady's Castle, which are both still standing. These were located to take advantage of the wool trade moving along the river by barge. They are all associated with merchant owners, although unlike the cases above that is presumed on the basis of internal arrangement (Murtagh, 1988).

Merchant-held tower houses need not have been exclusively urban in location. Documentation attests to merchants acquiring land in the country, this possibly accelerating over the course of the sixteenth and seventeenth centuries. The evidence collected for this study contrasts with Bradshaw's conclusions on the impact of the Dissolution of the Monasteries on mercantile landholding in Ireland. He stated only one example of a merchant using newly acquired religious possessions as a means to increase social standing (Bradshaw, 1974). However, he conceded that Dublin merchants had by this time longstanding interest in monastic property, particularly in taking advantage of less desirable lands on the outskirts of the Pale where speculation was possible (*ibid.*). That merchants obtained grants of rural landholdings is testified to by such events as the 1541 grant of 'Anee' (Knockainy) in County Limerick to merchants from Kilmallock (*Irish fiants*: vol. 1); the numerous deeds of land in counties Meath and Louth preserved by the Dowdall family, whose members included many merchants (*Dowdall deeds*); and the earls of Ormond assisting Waterford merchants in 'colonising' the lands north of the River Suir in County Kilkenny (Galloway, 2011). Rural property acquisition by merchants may have been a statement of social ascent to the point where it sometimes altered their lifestyle and activities. For instance, in 1586 it was commented that many Galway merchants had 'relinquished their mansions in towns and keep themselves in the country' (Gillespie, 1991: 21). Aside from being granted land outright, merchants may also have leased tower houses in rural areas, as indicated by an entry in the AFM that 'Teige took Dunbeg, one of his own castles, from a Limerick merchant, who had it in his possession, in lieu of debt' (AFM: 1598, vol. 6, p. 2091). All these sites listed are associated with tower houses, though their construction and occupation cannot be conclusively linked to these merchants.

The 'townhouse' issue: Defining the urban tower house

Several terms have been employed in the literature to describe these urban residential buildings. This author has been consistent in preference of 'tower house', since it is argued that they are part of the same tradition as the rural examples. Tower house contemporaries used the term 'castle' to describe all incarnations of tower houses, although 'fortalice' and derivatives are sometimes encountered, and, once, the perplexing 'battlle halle' (*Dowdall deeds*: p. 263, entry 586).[1] Other scholars have been more cautious in their terminology, preferring to avoid the issue by the use of descriptors like 'fortified town houses', or the rarer 'town-castle' used by Etienne Rynne. The main reason for this appears to be that these urban sites sometimes predated the Pale's '£10 castles' by more than a century, and calling them tower houses would challenge the thorny issue of tower house origins.

Urban examples are first referred to in 1310 beside Usher's Quay in Dublin (Bradley and Murtagh, 2003). Bradley and Murtagh have made studies of two of the so-called 'fortified town houses' in Thomastown, County Kilkenny. Their physical and functional similarities with urban tower houses elsewhere, including those discussed here, raises questions as to the chronology of the monument type, as well as the limitations of categorising monuments without a holistic approach. We are also unfortunate that, owing to the high levels of building destruction in consistently urban areas, such 'fortified town houses' are documented but none survive. Our evidence is therefore incomplete.

We know that Brady's Castle is of an early date because of the use of dressed Dundry stone in the windows, which went out of style around the year 1400 (*ibid.*). While many scholars have looked for an early origin date for tower houses, the evidence thus far has been inconclusive. Limited evidence for early rural tower houses comes from Tyrellspass in County Westmeath, which was dendrochronologically dated to 1410, alongside the defended towers added to religious buildings (*ibid.*). Barry has argued that towers in the city of Dublin had early construction dates, supported by references such as that from 1289–90 to a tower held by William Sweteman beyond St. Audoen's Gate passing to 'William le Deveney's' and a 1284 grant to a tower near the Ostman's Bridge (*Calendar of ancient records of Dublin*: vol. 1, p. 107). Other thirteenth- and fourteenth-century references to Dublin's towers imply they were mural towers and no specific ownership is cited. The named individuals in the examples given were probably receiving mural towers, too, and thus influence over tower house evolution cannot be directly attributed to them. The argument that some aspects of castle architecture, particularly machicolations, evolved from their ecclesiastical purposing has been discussed by Bonde (1994). Many tower house builders were also religious patrons, as the architectural similarities between Lynch's Castle and St. Nicholas's Collegiate Church in Galway city indicate (Newman Johnson, 1998).

Although the focus of this book is not on the religious life of medieval buildings, there is definitely some overlap between the religious and tower houses. This could be the simple construction of tower houses by lay people on confiscated monastic lands after the mid-sixteenth century. The church did have residential church towers which show basic similarities to tower houses. Some of these are very small, and some are appended to one end of the church. Cross East in County Mayo, which has been ascribed as a tower house in the ASI, is a residential church tower attached to a medieval church, while Cashelboy Castle in County Sligo is located only 5.3 metres from a wall enclosing a graveyard and ruined medieval church (see figure 5.2). The College in Slane, County Meath, had a tower house for a rectory. 'This practice stresses that in smaller boroughs lords endowed the church with buildings comparable to the

5.2 The plain and overgrown Cashelboy Castle, County Sligo, is located within a few metres of a medieval parish church and graveyard. The tower house is the building to the right; the church was attached to the graveyard enclosing wall and is to the left of the picture. It is likely that this was a tower house occupied by a parish priest.

residences of wealthy burgesses in large settlements such as Dalkey, county Dublin, and Thomastown, county Kilkenny' (Seaver, 2005: 88).

A possible religious influence aside, Bradley and Murtagh share with this author the observation that the 'form' of Brady's Castle is similar to that of rural tower houses (Bradley and Murtagh, 2003). Suggestions that such urban tower-house-type buildings owe their origins to the earlier hall houses of rural Ireland have been debunked by O'Keeffe's findings from Fethard, County Tipperary. Here, the split functionality of the Fethard towers is cited as evidence against this evolution (O'Keeffe, 1999). Rather, we should include urban examples clearly within the tower house category, regardless of indication of a very early date for some of them. We have been seeking evidence for late thirteenth- and early fourteenth-century date in a structural type famously bereft of striking architecture, so such caution as exhibited by 'fortified town houses' seems unnecessary. The tower house was a magnificently multifaceted building in terms of its potential functionalities. That it was used by merchants successfully in urban locations for several purposes, including storage, residence, display, defence and commerce, could in part explain its ready adaptation in the countryside.

Both of the extant Thomastown examples have similar dimensions to the '£10 castles' of the Pale, though they were not as tall (Bradley and Murtagh, 2003). Brady's Castle is located on a burgage plot leading down to the River Nore, Sweetman's Castle sits near a bridge across the same river, and a third is known to have been mere metres away from Brady's but is no longer standing. At Brady's Castle the stair turret at the northwest corner was a storey higher than the wall walk, which is similar to the style of Jordan's Castle. That feature at Jordan's Castle has been interpreted by this author as intended to increase visibility of the water to assist in the control of approach routes (Bradley and Murtagh, 2003; McAlister, 2016). At Brady's Castle this would have enabled control of river communication. Again, as at Jordan's Castle, window placement indicates that either a laneway or a single-storey building was located on the southwest. It has been interpreted as being the residence of a wealthy merchant family, with a prominent street location and ready river access (*ibid.*). The ground floor contained vaults – two or three bays forming separate chambers – and, again, a commercial function has been inferred: 'The vaulted ground floor was almost certainly used for storage and it recalls the account in 1295 of the seizure of 300 hides belonging to a Flemish merchant "in the cellar of Richard le Marshall" at Thomastown' (*ibid.*: 209). Both of the standing 'fortified town houses' in Thomastown had easy river access, with the ground floors being ideal for goods storage since loading and unloading could have been carried out from them (*ibid.*). These are reminiscent of the internal boathouses at two tower houses in County Down.

Town defences and tower house communal functions

One defining element of the medieval town was its walls. These both physically and metaphorically separated it from the rural world outside. However, not all late medieval Irish towns had walls. Or, at least, not masonry walls; they might well have had a bank topped with wooden palisades. Lack of masonry walls was not necessarily indicative of a lower urban rank (Creighton and Higham, 2005). While most of the towns discussed above were walled, a few were not, such as Ardglass and Strangford in County Down. The presence of walls therefore cannot be taken as a necessary attribute of a town. But there was a difference between unwalled and walled towns: a town wall could serve as a mental barrier, since it demarcated more subtle social distinctions like burgage tenure (O'Keeffe, 1999).

Walls tended to enclose the town itself; there may have been suburbs outside the walls in some cases. The area enclosed varied and cannot always be taken as an indicator of population. Dublin's walls contained an area smaller than its presumed population, necessitating fairly expansive suburbs (Clarke, 1998). The tower houses at Newtown Trim might indicate a transition of this settlement from rival to suburb. Ardee in County Louth has walls enclosing an area that either was significantly larger than the anticipated population or included orchards and gardens. Town walls tended not to run alongside river banks in Ireland, presumably because that would have interfered with critical river access. Exceptions to this rule existed at Carrick-on-Suir and Clonmel, both in County Tipperary (Bradley, 1985). Instead of walls, a chain may have been drawn between the river banks to prevent unapproved movement along the river (Creighton and Higham, 2005).

Town walls were financially supported by murage grants. We have numerous pleas for murage grants surviving from the later Middle Ages, and an impression is generally given of poor upkeep. Revenue owing to the kings of England regularly had to be waived to support town wall repairs because of the threat of attack from outside, often by the Gaelic-Irish (O'Brien, 1988). Complaints of poor trading conditions have been interpreted as being mainly exaggeration, so these appeals may have been part of a wider attempt to reduce merchants' communal obligations and line their own pockets, as complained about the Munster ports by the Leinster ports (*ibid.*).

Money for wall upkeep could be directed to specific towns within a region. For example, there were five walled towns, as well as seven smaller unwalled settlements, in County Meath. The unwalled towns tended to form the caput of subinfeudated lands, and were market centres. They were at strategic locations and all had borough status (Graham, 1975). Tolls from other towns in Meath were directed to Trim, with the implication that the money went towards Trim's wall upkeep (Potterton, 2005). Trim's walls were punctuated by gates, including the Water Gate in the west that may have controlled river traffic, and the Sheep Gate, the name of which suggests either the wool trade, or a corruption of cheap (as in cheap merchandise) or ship (*ibid.*). A gate was an expensive addition, but a useful investment since it could be used to control access and collect tolls. It also tended to be from mercantile tolls that murage funds were raised. Most urban gatehouses were rectangular, though in larger towns twin-towered gates were built – for example, St. Laurence's Gate in Drogheda (Bradley, 1995).

Many town walls were plain, as adding gates or mural towers would have substantially raised construction costs. Despite an initial presumption that this would have deterred many of the smaller Irish towns, several do seem to have had mural towers. One such survives from Athboy in

County Meath, not a town of serious significance in the Middle Ages. According to Bradley, only in the wealthiest towns like Dublin, Limerick and Cork were these mural towers used for habitation (*ibid.*). However, this description may be too limited, as in smaller towns with regional economic importance these towers and gates would have needed nigh continuous occupation to have a truly effective function (O'Keeffe, 1999). That they were commonly inhabited may partially at least explain the cost required for upkeep and the regularity of murage grants (*ibid.*). Elsewhere in Europe it was common for administrative officials to reside in town gates (Creighton and Higham, 2005).

We have concrete evidence of this dual residential and communal function from Youghal in County Cork. This comes in the form of a nineteenth-century transcription of an earlier deed on the reverse of manuscript 43,153/8 in the National Library of Ireland. No original is included and this may have perished in the Four Courts fire, as many of the documents within this collection are transcripts of deeds later destroyed. The agreement dates from 1616 and is between Edward Coppinger and John Wilson, both residents of the town of Youghal. It granted to Wilson:

> the use of the Quay Tower or castle together with the use of all the rooms cellars chambers and appurts [appurtenances] thereinto belonging situated ... upon the south part of the quay of Youghal aforesd [aforesaid] having only and always excepted that upon occasion of his Majestys service and for the better defence of the sd [said] town the Mayor and Bailiffs of Youghal aforesd and such others as shall be directed and nominated by the said Mayor or Bailiffs to the use of the said tower for his Majestys service as often as the like occasion is offered shall have free ... and regress with the interruption of any person into the sd tower or castle for the using charging or discharging the two brass pieces of ordnance called sackers they which pieces belonging to the sd corpor[ation] to have and to hold the said tower or castle with the apps [appurtenances] ... and if in case of fail that the key of the lock of sd tower could not be had as often as there shd [should] be occasion to use the said Brass pieces for his majestys service and for the service of the sd town that then so often as the said key is missing as aforesd that it shall be lawful for the mayor and bailiffs of Youl [Youghal] aforesd for the time being to break up the door or doors of the said tower and enter thereunto for the using of the said pieces in manner as aforesd and if any of the sd doors be so broken the same shall be made up at the cost of the sd mayor and bailiffs in as good fashion as the same were at anytime ... and that after the end of the sd term the sd 2 brass pieces together with the quiet possession of sd castle or tower shall be yielded and delivered up by the sd John Wilson ... to warrant and defend the sd tower or castle.

'Urban' tower houses

This is a fascinating document for a number of reasons. Looking at the maps for Youghal contained within the *Irish historic towns atlas*, the description suggests the 'Quay Tower or castle' was not one of the documented tower houses, but rather a larger mural tower. Firstly, this indicates that a portion of a communal structure could be privately leased and held, and, secondly, that there were mural towers of sufficient size for this in Ireland. Thirdly, the defensive aspect appears to have mainly rested on the artillery pieces atop the roof and not in the tower inherently, as evidenced by the suggestion that the front door is to be broken down if the key is not to hand. This is additional evidence for the lack of militarism within towers and tower houses. However, it is worth noting that this document dates from 1616, towards the conclusion of the tower house era, and therefore a different emphasis will have existed in the fourteenth century, prior to widespread and effective use of gunpowder technology. This structure may have been the same as one that served as the port's blockhouse and was later converted to a storehouse (Kelly and O'Keeffe, 2015). This shows that the mural tower had a commercial function too. The site may be the larger tower depicted on the projecting pier from the town walls in 1633 in *Pacata Hibernia* (see figure 5.3). This map shows two projecting artillery pieces on either side of this tower, and it is the only one on the water side to have these depicted.

The role of residential towers in walled towns could veer close to the tower house: evidence for Creighton's statement that 'many town walls embodied the ambitions of elite sectors and other minority stakeholders in urban society' (2007: 45, 56). He describes this as their 'secret history', an example being the 'wall' of Bridgwater in England, which was in actuality just the joined back walls of stone houses (*ibid.*). On the other hand, supposedly private tower houses could serve purposes usually fulfilled by communal defences. One example comes from Thomastown in County Kilkenny, where the Bridge Castle protected the bridge, meaning that the tower house had the dual functions of commercial building and communal defence. Another is Dundalk, County Louth, where fortified houses controlled movement up and down the streets (Murtagh, 1988). This control of access might also be witnessed at Ardee in County Louth, where the large St. Leger's Castle projects well into the street.

The tower house in business and trade: Warehouses, internal storage and meeting spaces

Better documented in recent years has been the arrangement of internal spaces within tower houses, including some telling information about

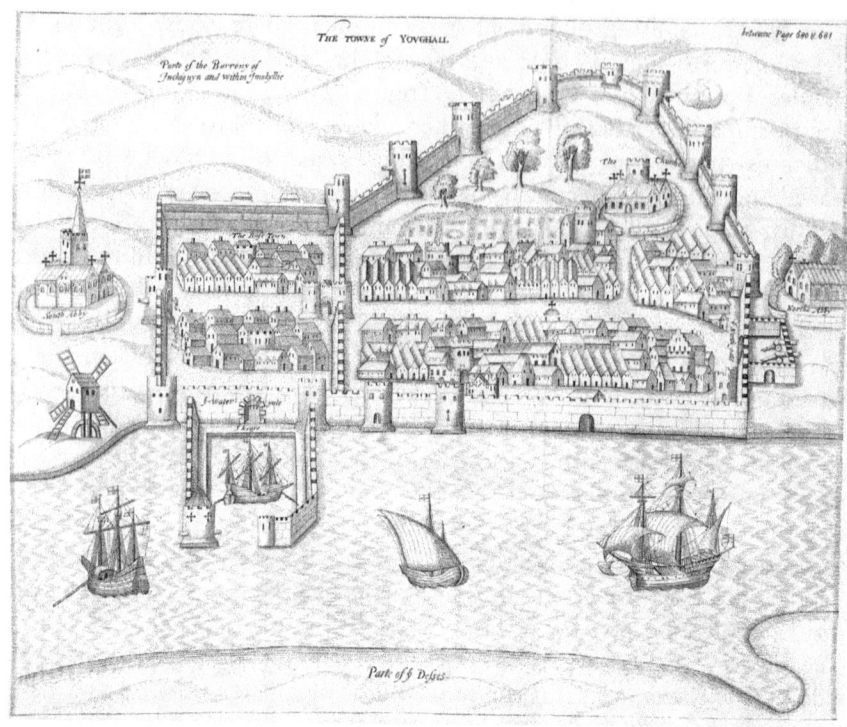

5.3 The 'Quay Tower or castle' described in a 1616 agreement is probably illustrated in this 1633 map of the town of Youghal, County Cork, from *Pacata Hibernia*.

commercial and mercantile uses. Although Irish towns in the late Middle Ages were small in terms of their area, making all components of the town proximal to one another, tower houses were frequently located on the main streets and, therefore, near to marketplaces and the areas of business. Lynch's Castle in Galway city is one of the most central buildings within the medieval walled town (Newman Johnson, 1998). This might be in contrast to seigneurial castles in an English context, where it was observed by at least one scholar that there was no relationship between castles and the marketplace, although castles were regularly enough inserted so as to control trade routes (Slater, 2015). By extension, Irish tower house builders must have been able to obtain land plots close to the marketplace, potentially indicating long-standing land interests within the town. Properties tended to be smaller and more densely packed the closer to the marketplace in several medieval Irish towns, including Carlingford in County Louth (O'Sullivan and Gillespie, 2011). Even in planned towns, demand will have resulted in compression and subdivision of the best plots over time, unless the prohibition of this was specifically enforced.

While this is one difference between the Irish and English urban evidence, a similarity might come from internal arrangements in buildings. In England, urban houses were residences as well as workplaces. Descriptions of 'shops' could refer to workshops, places of sale or even storerooms, and these were frequently located within the home (Riddy, 2008). A common layout was to have the hall on the first floor, above a ground floor used for retail, production and storage (Rees Jones, 2008). More complex arrangements are known, too, such as merchants' private warehouses with vaults for wine storage and dual entrances, with access to a wharf on one side and a shop with frontage on the other. In King's Lynn, merchant houses tended to have split functionality, with residence oriented to the landward side of the building and warehouses towards the quays and between the street and the river (Hutchinson, 1997). Outside of merchants, Kowaleski discusses in Exeter how butchers were provided with specially constructed stalls to sell their wares – not just meat but hides and leather, which had a variety of uses and buyers within a town with a diverse occupation (Kowaleski, 1995). The modern street name 'Booth/e Street' tends to originate from the use of the ground floor of medieval Irish houses as shops, or booths (Bradley, 1995).

We have an extreme example of mercantile use at the Newark in Ardglass. This was identified through excavation as a row of shops by McNeill (2005). This means that it was not truly a tower house, since it did not provide either a residential or an administrative function. It does illustrate the overlap between tower houses and commercial buildings though, particularly in terms of appearance. Again, taking us back to the issue of display through architecture, the choice of crenellations and other distinctive castle-type forms was deliberate. What value was there to make these additions to a two-storey row of shops? The practice might be more common than thought: the builders of the Newark may not have needed to look far for their inspiration, with a plethora of urban split-functionality tower houses to choose from. Religious buildings were often fortified in late medieval Ireland, particularly church towers. These architectural flourishes were also used on lower-status buildings, which can appear remarkable to us today. An example comes from the Dominican priory in Carlingford, County Louth, whose outbuildings are documented as appearing fortified, like a tower house (O'Sullivan and Gillespie, 2011). Early sixteenth-century water-supply conduits and cisterns in London were 'elaborately crenellated with stone battlements' (Rawcliffe, 2013: 224). This must have been a deliberate statement by those who funded the public works. For castle architecture to be used on outbuildings and water conduits must mean it had a symbolic language of its own, or was more approachable than heretofore appreciated. One possibility is that castle architecture was used to project conspicuous consumption, although the reasons for this in a Dominican priory are not immediately clear. Again in an English context, both in municipal and ecclesiastical buildings licences to crenellate were sought. In religious buildings the goal was apparently also the projection of nobility, while burgesses used it to denote a free borough and thus privilege (Coulson, 2016b). Coulson attributes wanton crenellation to a pervasive chivalric culture limited not just to nobility (2016a).

It has been questioned by Eadie (2009) whether tower house occupants would have been prepared to spend a third of their available internal space in storage, but the comparative evidence indicates that this was not a concern as storage was a function integral to the building. It perhaps also explains why verticality was necessary. The merchants of Chester, in response to the threat of arson from the neighbouring Welsh, stored their most valuable goods in 'secure stone undercrofts', as masonry and tile roofs were the best prevention against urban fire hazards (Rawcliffe, 2013: 170). This description sounds very similar to the barrel-vaulted ground floors found in tower houses from across Ireland, in counties Down, Tipperary and Kilkenny. Murtagh (1988) has suggested that the ground floors of fortified houses in Thomastown were used for storage, based on comparison with the identified warehouses at Ardglass. The Bridge Castle at Thomastown has a vaulted ground-floor chamber entered from the river, making it ideal for loading cargo arriving by boat.

The potential split functionality at Fethard in County Tipperary, Strangford in County Down and Carlingford in County Louth has already been discussed. These sites all had two entrances, and this study has indicated that there are many more tower houses with that arrangement. Newman Johnson's architectural study of Lynch's Castle in Galway city found evidence for two entrances, which he compared to many other sites in County Cork, including Belvelly and Downmacpatrick. These two latter sites were also surveyed by this author, but the two entrances are not immediately apparent and require some investigation. Consequently, other examples have probably been overlooked. Eighteenth-century descriptions of medieval houses in Galway record different people holding the ground and upper floors (Newman Johnson, 1998).

An internal boathouse was first identified in the *Archaeological survey of County Down* at Sketrick and Mahee castles in County Down, based on the alignment of their barrel-vaulted ceilings at ground floor level. In both cases entry to the long, narrow, barrel-vaulted chamber was through an entranceway several times larger than those commonly found at tower houses. The locations of these island tower houses mean it would have been possible to drag a boat up from the water. The boats that could have been housed in either of the two cannot have been very large, however; the ground dimensions of Sketrick's being only 9 by 2.5 metres (Jope, 1966: 250). These boathouses are similar to the chambers in the tower houses of Thomastown and the free-standing late medieval hall at Trim Castle, and would have been suitable for storage of goods as well as housing small boats.

Aside from this specific feature, identifying medieval storage facilities is a difficult undertaking. Claridge and Langdon (2011) found that merchants responsible for grain purveyance used a range of storage places, including *hospitia* (storage complexes for people and goods) and designated parts of larger structures. This led them to argue that regular mercantile requirements were amply catered for at *hospitia* at strategic economic points. When needed, as during purveyance campaigns, both commercial and private granaries could be employed (*ibid.*). The upshot of this analogous study was that, in extreme conditions, goods were accommodated within the storage facilities identified at tower houses. Tower houses' ground-floor chambers were usually badly lit, meaning that storage was one of the few functions this storey was suitable for (Eadie, 2009; Leask, 1944). Documentary references to goods storage tell us that bulk agricultural produce was being stored near to the point the purveyance goods were bought, and it is usually concluded that the ground floor of a tower house was being referred to.

Recognition of this storage function in urban tower houses has come from examples focussed on the east coast of Ireland, though there is no reason not to presume that this function extended southwards and westwards as well. Taaffe's Castle, an urban tower house believed to have been merchant occupied, had a ground floor that opened onto the harbour front, aiding its identification as a storeroom. There was no direct access from the rest of the tower house to the storeroom, and its original entrance may have been secured by the still-extant machicolation (Gosling, 1992). Storehouses are referenced in documentation from Carlingford in the late sixteenth century, but it is unknown whether these were sole-function, independently standing structures, or whether the storage units at sites like Taaffe's Castle might be included in the designation (O'Sullivan and Gillespie, 2011). In Dalkey, the main outport for late medieval Dublin, cargo from the vessels in port was stored in the tower houses before being transported to Dublin overland. This has led to presumptions that the tower houses were built by Dublin merchants to control the activities mediated by the town (Smith, 1996). In seventeenth-century Waterford city, many houses had cellars opening onto the street, which provided for both mercantile and domestic use. A shop or display area was incorporated into the upper levels alongside the residence, a layout described as mirroring the tower houses (Breen, 2007a).

Even small towns could have municipal warehouses as part of their efforts to equip themselves for commercial activity, alongside the more commonly encountered toll booths and bridges (Dyer, 2013a). Storage space could have been rented out separately to the residence above, as is documented at the Old Tholsel tower house in Drogheda and suggested at Fethard. Murtagh further believes the upper storeys of the Bridge Castle were used as warehouse space, as indicated by their austere original internal appearance (Murtagh, 1988). He has further questioned whether the 'outwork' abutting the Bridge Castle was an attached hall, as at Taaffe's Castle in Carlingford (*ibid.*). Thanks to Gardiner's excavation at Jordan's Castle, we know that these attached halls could have been warehouses for storage rather than feasting halls. Structures standing independently of the tower within the castle complex may also be too hastily interpreted as feasting halls, and instead might indicate warehouses or storage. This is particularly true for any urban sites, but also applies to rural ones. This author had presumed Audley's Castle in County Down had a hall until Eadie's conclusion that a width of around five meters is 'much too narrow to be considered as a hall, as a formal seating arrangement would not fit here' (Eadie, 2015: 120). The proximity of urban examples, as at Jordan's Castle, suggests a storage use.

Not all tower house ground-floor chambers had the access required to store large and bulky items. This became apparent during the excavations of Jordan's Castle in Ardglass between 1998 and 2000, when the archaeologists attempted to store wood planks in this room but were prevented by the tight angle providing access. Consequently it can be deduced that it would have been similarly difficult to store items such as barrels and packs of hides during the occupation period. There is no evidence above ground for the stone storehouse at Jordan's Castle; it was only discovered through the course of excavation by Gardiner. He suggested that the storehouse was constructed at the same time as the tower house, since a window in the tower house's east face was located so that the attached building would not obstruct it. Gardiner also proposed the building's use as a storehouse on the basis of a drainage channel in its floor. This drain would have allowed water to run out of the building and down the slope the site is constructed on, which would alleviate any problem of damp and prevent stored items getting wet (Gardiner, 2005). The efforts made to keep the storehouse dry further suggest that the goods stored here were agricultural in nature and would spoil easily, such as grain and hides. This contention is supported by grain analysis undertaken as part of the excavation, which found evidence of a number of crops on site (*ibid.*).

At the lowest level, informal business activities could have been accommodated within a tower house. The tower house would have provided a more amenable environment in which to conduct business than the shorefront, for example. As Eadie said, 'If we locate an area suitable for feasting, we can imagine more public business matters taking place in the same location' (2009: 144), although there would be business matters that required more privacy. There might have been a chamber specifically for that purpose, or it might perhaps have doubled up as the lord's bedchamber. As regards identifying a suitable place for public business matters, this room would need to have been spacious enough to seat numerous people, and it would have to have been heated. Eadie believes that the business room would not necessarily need to have been decorated, since those doing business would not require the same symbolism as other guests because they would be of the same status as the occupier (*ibid.*). This latter point may be questioned though, as much of business relies upon pretence and ostentation. For example, a lord seeking to do business with a merchant to sell his produce (or vice versa) would have wanted to show his wealth for the psychological impact when coming to an agreement. Through his ostentatious display he would have shown that he was not relying on the success of this deal and could wait to sell the produce while he found a better bidder. Social aggrandisement would surely have also have played a part, since even men of the same social status would be inclined to form partnerships with men charting the same social course.

In the Dublin Assembly Roll of 1492, the merchant Reynold Talbot was granted the tower located between the New Gate and Gormond's Gate in Dublin city, so long as he roofed it with oak timbers. John Marcus, also a merchant, had the tower over the 'fish slip' (*Calendar of ancient records of Dublin*: vol. 1, p. 290). In the same year, a goldsmith was granted the tower over the Dame's Gate (*ibid.*). These are tantalising glimpses of how mural towers could be utilised, even more so since we have merchants specifically mentioned. It is a pity that no detail was provided as to how these individuals intended to use their towers.

Conclusion: Not just a rural phenomenon

Although they are usually studied as facets of rural life, this chapter shows that tower houses were a familiar sight in towns as well. When we look at the issue of defining settlement from a tower house perspective, we find they transcend all late medieval settlement types. Indeed, in an urban setting, tower houses can be taken as evidence for occupational diversity, itself sometimes cited as a criterion for defining the town. However, their dominant location in smaller unwalled market towns, like Slane in County Meath, does complicate this interpretation. As we have seen, too, tower houses could provide a home for commercial functions in otherwise agricultural rural lordly settings. The multifunctionality of tower houses must have lent to their broad appeal.

While they are known from both rural and urban contexts, the possibility has been raised that the inspiration for the rural tower house lay in the urban examples. Some believe that chronologically early urban tower houses do not meet the criteria to be described as such, but from the perspective of function and usage used here, the buildings are the same. While desiring to steer clear of the thorny debate surrounding tower house origins, it is foolish to ignore the evidence, and other scholars have actively sought to establish a fourteenth-century timeline for the monuments.

This chapter has shown that there are potentially good parallels to be made between the Irish and English urban evidence. That has not been a given throughout this volume. For instance, the breakdown of centralised authority before the Tudor Conquest allowed privatisation to develop. This is a socio-political trend not seen in more rigidly controlled areas of western Europe. With the lack of surviving remains of medieval urban fabric in Ireland, including timber-framed houses, we might look across the Irish Sea for similarities in spatial arrangement. Several potential cases of split functionality have been presented here, with the ground-floor chamber used for various service and economic functions (boathouse, storehouse, shop, workplace) and the residence in the storeys above. Future research should consider communal defences in Irish towns more in tandem with the historiography of castle studies. The document describing the use of the 'castle' at Youghal shows how residence and communal defence had overlap in the form of mural towers in town walls. There is obviously significant overlap between mural towers and tower houses, and this also highlights that communal and private use were not mutually exclusive, but either could be adopted for temporary periods of time in response to specific events. If communal fortifications could have a private residential role, then the reverse also has implications to consider.

Part of this might overlap with the issue of buildings serving as a social statement. We might explore the status that came with contributing to communal defence, perhaps as a sign of participation in the good of the town. The borrowing of castle architecture by buildings like the Newark, and even Bangor to a lesser commercial extreme, tells us that this had a symbolic message that would have been readily understood by contemporary observers. This is reminiscent of the suggestion made by Coulson of the symbolism of crenellations in creating and establishing lordly identity (Coulson, 2016a, b). For the same reason, merchant builders of tower houses might have sought in that way to raise their social profile to advance towards the ranks of the landed gentry. We presume merchants copied the architecture of the nobility and exclude the possibility that the reverse was also the case. Perhaps we presume society in late medieval Ireland was more rigid and class conscious than it actually was. There is limited evidence for merchants within landholding families. While the evidence is later in date and from a newly landed family, the Hamiltons – who came to hold significant land and property in seventeenth-century County Down – counted a merchant among their number, who may have facilitated trade with their landholdings. Sir James Hamilton's younger brother Gavin was apparently a merchant in Glasgow, and obtained a lease along the River Bann, near Coleraine, where he was successfully exporting goods to Scotland before being killed prematurely when one of his boats overturned (Lowry, 1867).

The transport of goods along routeways connected the rural and urban, and also the country tower house and town tower house. In both manifestations, defended storage and commercial spaces could be, and were, provided. This means that trade goods were controlled along their entire journey, from point of exploitation to urban management. These goods were overwhelmingly agricultural in nature, as we have already seen, ranging from wool, to grain, to fish. Although neither exotic nor exciting, there was usually demand for these items elsewhere in the medieval world. Therefore, it is the humble tower house that ultimately (if indirectly) connected peripheral Ireland economically and geographically to the wider world, as is explored in the next chapter.

Note

1 Used to describe a castle in Carlingford, County Louth, *c.* 1590. The appendage of 'halle' might suggest Taaffe's Castle or a similar structure was being referred to.

6

Tower houses, late medieval Ireland and the connection with the wider world

This chapter offers a brief summary of Ireland's trading activity, and relates this to the built environment, explaining how tower houses facilitated the contact of their occupants with the rest of the medieval world. In this book we have followed the role of the tower house step by step as our perspective has broadened from the site specific, to the local, to the regional and, now, to the wider world. Throughout the tower house construction period, international trade was the main means through which people communicated with the world outside their daily living space. It was through trade, too, that people understood the world and their place within it; whether through receiving books recounting other times and places, such as the 'Cato and Puerile books' exported to Ireland from Bristol in the sixteenth century, or through personal economic connections to the New World. Imports to Ireland in the later Middle Ages were in large part driven by tower-house-occupant demand. Over the course of the tower house period, medieval people's world increased in size and scope. The later Middle Ages brought greater and more complex economic connections with the rest of Britain, but also with the continent. This knowledge of the outside may not have affected tower house occupants across Ireland evenly – the bias in the written record emphasises the longer-standing routes between southeast and east Ireland and England. The less-documented parts of the country may also have increasingly engaged with the European continent. As the last geographic landmass in temperate waters, Ireland had a role to play in expanding European interests westwards, and in integrating an Atlantic World.

The central role of the tower house in every aspect of the socio-economic environment has been stressed. Tower houses provided a manorial, settlement and administrative centre upon which to focus agricultural activity. Agricultural materials made up the greatest proportion of Ireland's export items, but the greatest percentage of export by volume, overall, was fish. Tower houses controlled the movement of these items to ports and dominated the skyline of medieval towns, and can be taken as a built manifestation of wealth from trade. In addition, they were extremely useful in facilitating interactions and so should also be accepted as a manifestation of cultural coexistence. The apparent simplicity of the tower house allowed for many different internal functions to facilitate these goals, including its use for storage and as the workplace of merchants.

Ireland's trade was well established long before the advent of the tower house. An Irish Sea province evolved throughout the early and high Middle Ages into 'one of the great trading areas of northern Atlantic Europe' (Hudson, 1999: 40). Within this were three particular routes: connecting the southwest of England with the southeast of Ireland; the northwest of England, Wales and the Isle of Man with the east of Ireland; and a north–south route running past Ireland's west coast and communicating between Galicia in the south and Iceland and the Baltic to the north. These same routes were in operation by the late Middle Ages and are the subject of much of the following discussion.

Colfer (2013) has stated that the tower house was a creation of the manorial economy. This is true, to a certain extent, but it is the trade networks originating in this economy that sustained them. Late medieval Ireland was both a commercialising economy and an urbanising one, and these trends were especially marked in port towns (Galloway, 2015). As Agnew said, 'the rapid growth of a port is a sure indication of the existence of a stable and prosperous merchant community' (1996: 1), and, as we have seen in the preceding chapter, this 'prosperous merchant community' liked to build ostentatiously. This building accompanied the growth in economic activity: the construction of tower houses is built evidence for an increasing reliance on goods exchange for income, accompanying a change in the relationship between lords and their tenants (Britnell, 1996). A decentralising political authority encouraged local entrepreneurism – manifested in the tower house, which could be used in a variety of ways to force tolls and make a statement of command. The later Middle Ages was therefore a potentially prosperous time for Ireland, as local lords and great magnates took over the duties exercised by the Crown in other parts of Europe.

The impact of political change on trade, and by extension on the tower houses, in the early modern period (up until the cessation of tower house construction in the mid-seventeenth century) is more contentious. Some scholars have argued that trade expanded thanks to the imposition of a central government. A centralised economic and political system meant that merchants no longer had to negotiate individually with local lords and port towns, so the costs of trade were suddenly reduced

(Gillespie, 1991). It may have been the custom previously for merchants to purchase the right to exclusively trade within a lordship, and the requirement to compensate a tower house lord was now removed (Nicholls, 1987). Indeed, many ports, if not elsewhere in the country, profited from open warfare as points of embarkation for soldiers and provisions. Following the Tudor Conquest of Ireland, the opening decades of the seventeenth century were an economic boom time until the catastrophic years of the 1641 Rebellion and Confederate Wars (Gillespie, 1991). However, it should be noted that this prosperous experience was not universal. Carlingford in County Louth is one coastal port that did not experience the growth that many other ports did at this time (O'Sullivan and Gillespie, 2011).

Overview of Irish trade, c. 1300–1650

Medieval Ireland's main export items were agricultural and marine in nature: grain, fish (especially herring), wool, cloth and cattle hides. The activities that produced these items are associated with tower houses. Sheep farming increased in popularity over the high Middle Ages, with the result that Ireland produced large quantities of wool. Much of this was woven into a coarse woollen cloth for export, probably both as a cottage industry (cloth woven for mostly local or personal use, or cloth that was collected by 'grey merchants' and brought to towns for sale) and in the cloth industries in towns. Irish-made mantles (heavy woollen cloaks, also known as 'falling' or 'falding'), in particular, were well known and desired throughout Europe. The linen trade started to develop in the fifteenth century, although little is known about linen cloth or yarn production since it was a very low status occupation, and thus not commonly recorded (O'Neill, 1987). By the sixteenth century, however, large quantities of linen yarn were being exported, and these volumes only increased in the following centuries (*ibid.*). The amount of cloth being exported from Waterford by the mid-sixteenth century indicates that a sizeable textile-production industry must have developed there (Flavin, 2004).

Cattle hides also formed a large proportion of Ireland's exports. These were exported from all over the country (O'Neill, 1987). Merchants as far away as Dublin desired the right to collect customs from shipping hides from the west in the sixteenth century (*Irish fiants*: vol. 1). Presumably this income could be substantial. Castles may have had a particular role in production of hides, since they were specifically mentioned in a statute from Galway: 'if anny gent[leman] of the country shuld salte or ocupie any hides in his own town or castell ...' (*Archives of the town of Galway*: 406). This suggests that tower houses could be centres for this business in terms of collection as well as creation of hides. Similarly, quantities of other animal skins were exported. It has been suggested that these skins were shipped 'undressed', with processing being carried out upon arrival (O'Neill, 1987). This is perhaps reflected in the commonly encountered use of 'fell' (with the wool or hair still attached) to describe these skins and fleeces in the customs accounts.

The (arguably) extensive Irish woods also facilitated the export of timber. Irish timber was highly prized, especially with the increased deforestation of England from the thirteenth century. This timber was mainly exported as planks or boards, although it would have also been used in the manufacture of barrels and casks for containing other goods for trade (*ibid.*). The variety of timber products exported from southeast Ireland can be witnessed particularly in the *Welsh Port books*, where they formed one of the dominant imports from Ireland. Demand for high-quality timber was not just limited to Ireland's nearest trading partner; Aquitaine imported timber from the southeast and south in particular, as did Normandy (Everett, 2014).

Fish is a difficult to enumerate but extremely valuable contributor to the late medieval trading economy. The dominance of herring indicates that Ireland profited from changes in seawater temperature, 1330–1600 having the highest bottom-water temperatures in the North Atlantic of the last five thousand years (O'Sullivan and Breen, 2007). In the fourteenth and fifteenth centuries, herring shoals were concentrated in the western Baltic and off the coast of eastern England. By the mid-fifteenth century herring had begun to migrate into the North Sea, the Irish Sea and off the coasts of west and south Ireland. This movement continued throughout the sixteenth century. Because the erratic migratory patterns of these shoals meant they were not a consistent or year-round presence, their appearance in any place was rigorously exploited. Along with the need, for religious reasons, to eat fish on approximately one-third of the days of the year, this made herring one of Ireland's chief exports in the later Middle Ages (O'Neill, 1987). By 1572, apparently, more than six hundred Spanish fishing ships were active off the Irish coast (O'Sullivan and Breen, 2007). In 1569, fishing fleets off the southwest coast were described as also transporting hides and tallow, indicating that fishing did not preclude other economic participation (Breen, 2005). This diversity is reflected in the surviving port accounts from England, discussed below, which only on very rare occasions list a ship carrying only one or two types of goods. Cod was plentiful in the North Atlantic, while hake was concentrated off the south coast of Ireland (O'Neill, 1987). Eels seem to have been eaten by all levels of society and, unlike most other fish, could be kept alive in special wooden boxes for a considerable amount of time (*ibid.*).

Until the fifteenth century, at least, one of Ireland's main exports was grain. Grain was in demand as food for campaigning English armies, for supplying marcher castles, for when English supplies were running short and at the English abbeys (*ibid.*). Crown restrictions were intermittently placed on grain as an export to ensure garrison supplies; a particularly inclusive one from 1602 at the end of the Nine Years' War banned the export of corn and grain, beef, lard, bacon, butter, tallow, wax, wool, tanned leather, hawks, hobbies, horses, staple wares, and gold or silver coined or in bullion (*Irish fiants*: vol. 2). However, 'the perilous position of the declining colony in eastern Ulster increased its dependence on supplies arriving by sea from the farmlands of Louth, Meath and Dublin' (O'Neill, 1987: 21), meaning that international grain exports were not as universal across the country as exports of hides, wool and fish, so the impact of export restrictions is moot. Grain exports may have focussed on the Pale in particular, as grain supplies being transported to Carrickfergus, Carlingford and Greencastle came from Drogheda's hinterland (*Calendar of the patent rolls*: 1392–96, vol. 5, 'Licence, for two years, for James Boys ... August 5 [1376]'). Drogheda is a good example of a Pale town which continued to deal in the trade of grain consistently throughout the later medieval and early modern periods (Galloway, 2015).

Tower houses enabled these agricultural and marine items to make their way to the port towns for cargo bulking and export. Imports would have reached them in return, using the same communication networks. Wine, salt and iron comprised a significant proportion of Irish imports, and all of these will have found a ready market at the tower house. Wine, iron and most of the salt needed for the fishing industry were imported from the continent, either directly from European ports or re-exported via the larger English ports. Many luxury goods were imported from Britain, including cloth and wine (Sherborne, 1965). The cloth recorded as coming from England was probably of a fine woollen variety. Other imports included silk, soap, honey, spices, sweets (such as almonds and dates) and high-quality wax (for seals and candles) (O'Neill, 1987). Josias Bodley's account of his visit to Lecale in 1602–03 hints at the goods that were imported at wealthy households like tower houses towards the end of the Nine Years' War. He visited a Master Morrison at Downpatrick, and there consumed such foodstuffs as Spanish wine, French wine, spices and tobacco. In addition, Bodley and his friends ate high-status foods from the immediate region, such as venison, goose, veal, game and other more common meats.

International-scale trade only occurred at specific places. The 'Great custom' of 1275 lists eleven ports in Ireland: Galway, Limerick, Kerry, Cork, Youghal, Waterford, Ross, Wexford, Dublin, Drogheda and Ulster, though these refer not just to the town proper, but the coastlines and hinterlands of each (O'Sullivan and Breen, 2007). This clarification has potential import for the study of tower houses, as Breen and O'Sullivan noted that this designation would have aided in the economic development of the surrounding region. The 'Great custom' also shows that ports of the southeast dominated trade, with those of the west and northeast taking a secondary role (*ibid.*). By 1402 distinction was made between the 'large sea ports' which were engaged in long-distance trade and the 'small creeks' that played a role in local and coastal trading as part of a three-tiered system that further evolved during the Tudor period (discussed in Jarvis (1959); applied to an Irish context in Breen (2007a); O'Sullivan and Breen (2007)). These same port towns align with a high incidence of tower houses, although, as described in the preceding chapter, many of these survive as documentary references only.

As Ireland's closest geographic neighbours, England, Scotland and Wales always exerted economic influence. This was particularly so in those parts of Ireland closest to these countries and depended on ethnic make-up, with those identifying as Anglo-Irish more likely than the Gaelic-Irish to trade with England rather than the continent. The degree of involvement was also dependent on the time period and, by extension, political events. 'The economic dislocation caused by the rapid and sizeable decrease in population in England after 1348 led to a new reliance on Irish resources, and to efforts to integrate more closely the economies of both sides of the Irish Sea' (Smith, 2013: 41–2). According to concerns expressed in the fourteenth and fifteenth centuries about ability to keep up with fee-farm payments due to the English Crown, Irish international trade was supposedly at risk, largely owing to a need to defend the port towns from both land and sea. However, these claims were much exaggerated (O'Brien, 1988). The merchants of Ireland's port towns profited from political instability in England and a lack of oversight. By the early modern period, though, England was reasserting dominion. In this way, while continental European pottery dominates assemblages from Gaelic-Irish southwest Ireland in the later Middle Ages, by the seventeenth century the finds are overwhelmingly English in origin, as a material culture side effect of the Plantation (Breen, 2007b).

Returning to the Middle Ages, Dublin was settled after the Norman invasion by citizens of Bristol, while Youghal was also colonised by people from this English city (Kelly and O'Keeffe, 2015). This will have ensured a close connection between the two cities in the early years of their settlement, and one that probably continued throughout the medieval period. It has been surmised that Bristol merchants funded the Anglo-Norman Invasion in order to gain control of Irish trading connections

(O'Sullivan and Breen, 2007). Bristol was the chief port for Irish trade with England, and possibly all trade, throughout the tower house period (Kowaleski, 2007), and after around 1600 the English ports came to really dominate Irish trade. While the volume of Irish trade with England and with Bristol in particular increased over this time, Waterford's share of that trade increased also. In 1516–17 Waterford controlled nineteen per cent of Irish trade with Bristol, and this had increased to fifty-eight per cent by the 1540s. Fish dominated this trade, comprising a little over half of Irish exports to Bristol by the early sixteenth century, although this was a reduction from over three-quarters at the end of the fifteenth century (Breen, 2007a). Hides, sheep skins and wool were increasingly important exports from both southern and eastern Ireland by the seventeenth century (*ibid.*). Once we look within these broad descriptions, interesting patterns and events turn up which have significant insight for the study of tower house society.

It is hard to tell from the written record to what extent vessels belonging to English fleets operated in Irish waters, as large parts of their cargoes, especially their fish catches, were not subject to customs. In addition, because the 'indigenous merchants' recorded in the documentation included the Anglo-Irish from the 'English' towns of Ireland, as well as the native English and Welsh, these merchants only paid duties on a limited range of exports from Ireland, including hides and wool (Childs, 1982, 2000; Down, 1987; *Ireland-Bristol trade*). This probably, at least in part, explains the preponderance of Anglo-Irish names in the accounts; it is very rare to find a Gaelic-Irish one (Childs, 2000). However, as we have already and consistently seen, the Gaelic-Irish were involved in Ireland's economic activities, especially providing the facilities and goods comprising the trade. Even in predominantly Gaelic-Irish areas like Galway, the merchants, popularly known as the 'Tribes' of Galway, tended to view themselves as separate from those living around them, even if they were happy to conduct trade with those neighbours. In turn, this may have insulated them from the strife that affected the surrounding countryside (Prunty and Walsh, 2016). The records are incomplete for Bristol, as 'particular' accounts are missing for the middle of the fifteenth century. The Welsh accounts commence at the end of the sixteenth century and are less numerous, meaning that trade records are piecemeal for the period when tower houses were being constructed (Carus-Wilson, 1967; Childs, 2000). Bristol, overall, remains the best source of information – it has the most detailed accounts of any English or continental port (Flavin, 2011).

No late medieval trade accounts for Irish ports survive either; the closest we have is an account from the early seventeenth century that survived in a regional English archive. This is useful to some degree in reconstructing the trade patterns of the later Middle Ages, but that reconstruction is still educated guesswork. To compound the documentary problems, the archaeological record can be very quiet from the later Middle Ages for the Irish port towns. For example, the Lady Lane excavations in Waterford turned up very little fifteenth-century material, and the same pattern was found for Cork. This supports the contention that Cork was especially badly hit by the Black Death (Barry, 1987). In addition to this problem, the types of items being exported – raw materials and half-finished goods – could be moved over long distances but will be under-represented in the archaeology because their organic nature means they do not survive. When studying a maritime culture we are best focussing on the areas in which most activity took place – waterfronts and harbours – and on underwater sites like shipwrecks (Gaimster, 2000). We must be wary of drawing significant conclusions from the limited number of pottery sherds and small artefacts that have survived, and from the terrestrial location of most excavations in Ireland's port cities.

We are even more unfortunate to have only limited accounts from Chester, one of Ireland's major trading partners. Only in 1559 was Chester brought into the national customs system, as it was a palatinate port with special administrative rights. Before 1559 Chester kept local records, but these are 'obscure' and fragmentary (*Chester customs accounts*). These accounts cover only hides, wine and iron, as those were the only taxable goods until Chester was incorporated into the English customs system. Wine customs had been in place since the late thirteenth century, iron since 1464–65 and hides from 1537–38 (Driver, 1971). Consequently, we are left with piecemeal records for Ireland's trade with Chester. The accounts from Bristol have been partially published, but the body of materials for this port, held within TNA, is intimidatingly large. Luckily for a study such as this, where the trade records themselves are less useful than the social implications that can be deduced from them, the regular annual samplings published by Flavin and Jones are perfectly insightful. This large publication includes years from the 'particular' accounts, what was recorded increasing in detail up to the annual surveyor's accounts for the Port books. Comparing the two types of documentation highlights what might be missing. Ireland dominated Bristol's international trade, in no small part because of the tendency in Irish trade for many merchants to collaborate in putting a cargo together in a comparatively small consignment and in smaller vessels in terms of their burden capacity (*Bristol's trade with Ireland*). Going through the annual accounts, a further trend is apparent: we see two or three ships arriving from and departing for the same port on the same day, presumably to assist with security and to manage risk.

Continental contacts

The 'new custom' of 1303 included wine, which means there are some records of Ireland's wine imports through Chester. However, there are only nine entries where a specific place in Ireland is mentioned, over a 140 year period. Gascon wine is specifically mentioned in several of these, and in one instance a wine trader is cited as coming from Bordeaux. Dublin and its outport of Howth (though this relationship may have been contested; see 'Rights to customs at Howth 1481–2', in *Calendar of ancient records of Dublin*: vol. 1) dominate the limited record, with Drogheda appearing twice and Waterford once. More telling, perhaps, is that by the sixteenth century, most of the ships traveling with wine to Chester were coming from Spain, presumably with Spanish wine (*Chester customs accounts*). The market shift from French to Spanish wine tallies with the loss of English lands in France, also implying that wine imports were direct from Spain to Ireland rather than re-exports via England, as re-exports were French until the loss of lands there. Longfield (1929) stated that the wine shipped from England to Ireland was of poor quality; the better wine arrived directly from the continent. The multiplicity of Spanish fishermen in Irish waters supports this direct trading connection. An exchange of wine for fish would have been in the best interests of both groups. It may also explain the emergence of Galway and other ports of southern and western Ireland, if they were profiting on the back of this wine trade with Iberia, since these regions of Ireland were more accessible for sailors coming from the south. This scenario is supported by an isolated reference to a ship of Kinsale, County Cork, in 1404–05 carrying 'white Spanish wine' (*Chester customs accounts*: 112). The income from control of the continental wine trade could be substantial, as is implied by the struggle between the earls of Desmond and Ormond over the prise wines (the special charge due on wine imports). In 1495–96 the prise wines of Ireland had been worth over £93, and the dispute between the earls reached the point that the Crown took temporary control of the prise wines for Youghal and Kinsale in 1562, before ultimately awarding it in 1569 to Ormond (McCormack, 2005).

Certainly, when we look at the Bristol evidence we continue to find limited involvement of Irishmen with the continental trade. This affected Irish exports, too, for we find few mentions of obviously Irish products on ships setting sail for Portugal, Spain or France, aside from the occasional dicker of hides (also observed by Flavin (2011)). This indicates that the major market for Irish-produced goods was England. Childs has commented that England produced sufficient hides and wool for its own needs, and did not import them from Ireland. Instead, Ireland exported these items to Flanders, while England preferred fish and cloth (Childs, 2000). Longfield has argued that the English were eager to control the trade in hides and wool, but the greatest demand came from Spain, followed by France, the Netherlands and Italy (Longfield, 1929). Irish cloth found in Navarre in Spain possibly came via Bristol (Childs, 1978). Perhaps Ireland had its own connections with Flanders and France – there is some evidence for Irish vessels using western England as a haven en route to those parts of the continent (Childs, 2000).

Bristol was trading with southern and southeastern Ireland mainly, and we see the occasional oddity in the accounts that indicates a lot more was taking place than first meets the eye. Although references are few, the specific items arriving as imports to Bristol from places that otherwise did not conduct extensive trade with it suggest that these were re-exports from Ireland, having first landed in that country directly from the continent, rather than excess unsold items returning (*ibid.*). In the 1516–17 particular accounts, no port of origin is specified but olive oil and wine were imported at Bristol from Ireland, while the sole ship arriving that was registered at Wicklow was laden with herring, salmon and wine (*Bristol's trade with Ireland*). The wine here may have made its way down the coast from Dublin before being re-exported. In 1545–46 a ship registered to Dublin entered with a cargo solely made up of salt (*ibid.*). Again, this may have been what was not needed locally, and was so sold on.

More intensive trade with the continent might be indicated by some anomalous entries for County Wexford. Again in 1545–46, a ship registered to Wexford town arrived with olive oil, while in 1550–51 a ship associated with Ballyhack, a coastal town controlled by the Cistercians discussed previously for its fishing and ferry associations at the tower houses of Ballyhack and Nook, arrived in Bristol with skins, cloth and wine (*ibid.*). In 1595 ships were travelling to La Rochelle in France, looking to return with salt (CSPI: vol. 5, SP63/183, f. 96, 1595). The recovery of pottery sherds originating in Spain, France, Portugal and the Netherlands, as well as England, from excavation of the Ballyhack tower house garderobe chute supports the existence of economic connections with the continent (Colfer, 2013). By the second half of the sixteenth century, Wexford was regularly sending shipments of sack wine, a white fortified wine imported from Spain or the Canary Islands (*Bristol's trade with Ireland*).

The most detailed Port books presented, from 1600–01, have a separate section for wine imports, and here we see four ships importing wine arriving from Waterford (*ibid.*). These trends are mirrored on a lesser scale in the *Welsh Port books*. A small number of continental goods (wine and iron, with 'seck' and French wine occasionally specified) being shipped from Ireland to Wales indicate that Ireland may have obtained these goods directly from the continent. Wales had its own connections with Bristol, which suggests that it was not simply a case of re-export from Ireland. Instead, the shipment of several cargoes of wine from Waterford to Wales implies that an independent route existed between Ireland's biggest port in the southeast and the continent. Gilbert, in his introduction to the *Great parchment book of Waterford*, states that Waterford's trade beyond Ireland, England and Wales was with Flanders, Spain and Portugal (*Archives of the municipal corporation of Waterford*). As trade details are not contained within the volume, there is limited supporting evidence for this statement. Connections between that port and Italy are implied by a court case where a man was found guilty of concealing a Florentine merchant and his goods in 1441–42 (*ibid.*). Although not observed from Bristol, there are very isolated references to Irish ships sailing between Wales and the continent, such as a Dublin vessel going from Llanelli to La Rochelle with a cargo of coal (*Welsh Port books*).

These shipments indicate that the volume of goods was too sizeable and their movement too frequent to be simple excess being returned. Rather, they demonstrate there was a connection, now obscured, between Iberia and the southeast of Ireland, and not just western Ireland. That there were also connections with France can be seen by the turn of the seventeenth century. French wine was exported from Youghal; a merchant of Wexford transported coal from Bristol to La Rochelle; a Dublin merchant had a cargo of salt aboard a ship arriving from La Rochelle (*Bristol's trade with Ireland*). Tellingly, we have a vessel registered at La Rochelle going to Dublin with Newfoundland fish, testifying to the emergence of new transatlantic routes and Ireland's role within them, even though we might suppose Ireland already had fish sufficient for its own consumption demands (*Bristol's trade with Ireland*). Aside from this last entry, it is worth reiterating that the Bristol accounts become more detailed over time, so that entries occurring later in the sixteenth century do not necessarily indicate new patterns, but might actually be older trends suddenly exposed.

Fewer examples of this trade can be inferred from the Chester accounts, but the odd entry hints at Irish vessels going directly to the continent from further up the east coast than Waterford. An illustrative example is the single entry of a ship from Dublin traveling to Chester from (La) Rochelle in France, transporting 'bay salt' (*Chester customs accounts*: 95). Large quantities of salt were required to preserve fish, and most would have been imported from the Bay of Biscay, as local production could not have met demand. There were salt pans at Dundrum in County Down in the early thirteenth century, as well as possibly at Loughinisland, also in County Down, but even combined these could only have served a very localised need. There is limited evidence for salt panning by the Cistercian houses located in that county; the salt was exported to mother houses in northwest England (Carville, 1981; McNeill, 1980). It is extremely improbable that the volume of salt produced by these pans could have supported the whole local industry. Instead, imported salt, most likely from the Bay of Biscay, must have supplemented local production (*Admiralty examinations*; O'Neill, 1987).

The amount of salt brought in from La Rochelle would further support that Ireland's continental trade was mostly with France (Kearney, 1955). Indeed, the southeast of Ireland was easier to reach than the west of England from the Bay of Biscay (O'Neill, 1987). We know from the customs accounts at Bordeaux that Irish ships sailed this route, but unfortunately their precise ports of origin are not stated (*ibid*.). Ireland's exports to France and Spain are not easily identifiable, although Kearney (1955) claimed that St. Malo was the main port receiving cargoes of Irish hides.

Exports to England: Pre-modern Ireland's main market

The most complete accounts for Chester and its associated port of Liverpool survive for 1565–66. Exports are dominated by agricultural goods: animal skins, especially sheep and 'brock' (sheep killed by accident or disease), but also the more infrequent rabbit, marten and fox; lower-quality cloth and the famous Irish mantle; wool and wool flock; and tallow. These are all agricultural and bulky items, perfect for transportation along the network of local exchange routes characterised by Irish rivers and controlled by the ubiquitous tower house. Fish was a major Irish export yet rarely appears, in large part because it would not have been subject to the same duties and taxes. Where it is mentioned it is usually herring. Exports appear to have been very similar to Bristol in the fifteenth century, according to Childs's (1982) study of the manuscript accounts – fish, skins and cloth. Very revealing, too, are the references to corn exports from eastern Ireland in 1404–05. These are not frequent but of sufficient number to reinforce the argument, presented first in chapter 2, that the extent of arable agriculture in the era following the Black Death has been underestimated, and that late medieval Ireland was a more mixed agricultural economy than is often realised. Corn came from Drogheda and the ports of Rush and Malahide to the north of Dublin (*Chester customs accounts*; O'Neill, 1987). This shows that, at least within the boundaries of the Pale, cereal cultivation remained common enough to allow for the export to England of surplus, and this in the generation following the Black Death, a time traditionally thought to be of manorial contraction in Ireland. The 'corn' exported was probably wheat, barley or oats (Longfield, 1929).

The rise in prominence of grain by the seventeenth century is attested to by analysis of charred plant remains. In line with evidence in the early seventeenth-century Irish Port books, oats were the most common cereal type found at Gardiner's excavations at Jordan's Castle, followed by barley. These grains were present throughout the period of the port's activity, from the fifteenth to the eighteenth century. The deposits dating from the fifteenth century contain fewer grains than the later ones (Gardiner, 2005). Thus, it is probably fair to say that grain remained a staple export throughout the period.

An unexpected export item from Bristol to southeast Ireland might illuminate agricultural practices outside of the Pale. Over several years we see oft-repeated entries for large values of 'beans' being imported into Ireland. This has been interpreted as the importation of a foodstuff (Childs, 1982; Flavin, 2011), as Ireland imported lower-quality cereals such as rye, but also malt and peas (Longfield, 1929). This, of course, indicates that beans were not being grown in sufficient quantities for Irish demand. However, the usual method of three-field crop rotation, the method most associated with manorialism, used legumes like beans during a fallow period to restore soil fertility. Consequently, this system created large amounts of beans, which could be consumed by human or beast. That southeast Ireland was importing beans therefore indicates that it was not practising crop rotation. Coupled with the amounts and diversity of products originating in pastoral agriculture (both cattle and sheep), we can understand why historians, relying on the written documentation, stated that pastoralism was really Ireland's economic mainstay outside of the Pale. However, the evidence presented in chapter 2 details a significant number of water mills in this same region, and these in a set-up similar to a manor, with the mills associated with a lord's tower house. These water mills were probably for grain grinding, therefore their presence tells us that the economy cannot have been exclusively pastoral. So, since mixed agriculture was being practised to some degree, we might conclude that the normal method of crop rotation was not being utilised. It is possible that instead the rundale system was most extensive, even in those areas that were previously under Anglo-Norman control, as much of the Three Sisters river catchment area was. In turn, this could explain the lack of ridge and furrow remains. Alternatively, the prevalence of beans being shipped to Ireland could simply have been a means of filling up the cargo hold. Ships coming to Bristol from Ireland carried bulky agricultural goods, but the return voyage was transporting mainly small luxury items, and so the extra space may have been filled with beans rather than leaving it empty.

The occasional bean imports might reflect annual changes in crop yields, with the imports brought in to supplement local supply. Other entries reflect a bad harvest rather than consistent under-production of crops: the *Welsh Port books* document some imports of wheat and other grains to Ireland, and butter and cheese were imported from Carmarthen to Dublin one year. Pastoral items were not normally in any shortage in Ireland, and this is a rare entry. By extension, annual output fluctuations in Ireland could also explain the occasional references to grain and bean imports.

Comparison with Irish exports to Bristol is instructive. The dominant export to southwest England was fish. White herring and hake are the two most frequently encountered, but also amounts of red herring, salted fish, salmon, eels and pollock. Fish comprised the overwhelming majority of cargoes during the most buoyant period in the Ireland–Bristol route, between winter and Easter. No doubt this is when demand was greatest, to coincide with Lenten obligations. Outside of the Lenten season, more complex cargoes of agricultural goods are evident, particularly compositions of hides, wool and cloth. Early in the calendar year, the cargo composition of vessels sailing for Bristol resembles that of Chester more closely. This does not necessarily mean that Chester did not import fish or that all Irish fish went to Bristol. Indeed, the regular and frequent references to herring exports to Wales indicate that demand for fish existed along the British coast (*Welsh Port books*). The culprit for such discrepancy in the written record is likely bias in accounts reporting and creation: unlike luxury and long-distance trade items, which were taxed (wine being the best example), fish were not always subject to duties.

This lacuna can sometimes be rectified through study of the archaeological record. As one example, in the early-seventeenth-century Irish Port books there is a lack of mention of exports of barrels of fish. This stands in direct contrast to the fish-bone finds in a seventeenth-century deposit at the Jordan's Castle excavations. Analysis of these bones found that all the species present were likely to be saltwater varieties. The small number of the bones indicates that the warehouse was used for storage of barrels rather than as a processing centre (Gardiner, 2005). An alternate possibility for the assemblage is that fish were not being exported and that this sample represents what was consumed directly on site. This would also explain the absence of fish from the documentary sources. A further explanation for the lack of written reference to fish exports could be owing to the erratic migratory patterns of the herring shoals. The historical accounts suggest that herring shoals had stopped migrating to this part of Ireland by the early seventeenth century and did not return until the eighteenth century, although the economic repercussions of the returned plenteous herring shoals were arguably not felt in the town of Ardglass until the first decades of the nineteenth century (Lewis, 1837).

The limited archaeological evidence supports the argument that the lack of fish in the official written documentation (i.e. the Port books and customs accounts) is due to bias in the original record-keeping rather than a supply shortage. For instance, a sixteenth-century shipwreck excavated in Drogheda harbor, one of Chester's main trading partners, was carrying barrels of herring (Galloway, 2015). Occasional references found in other contemporary documents provide evidence that fish exports are under-documented and under-represented in the extant government accounts. In the mid-sixteenth century, visiting fishermen lived in the dissolved Dominican priory in Carlingford, County Louth (*Extents of Irish monastic possessions*). Much of the herring caught in Carlingford was sent to Cornwall in southwest England, while September and October are mentioned as being 'safe' months to visit the northeastern ports of Ireland. References such as these reinforce the conclusion that herring dominated Irish fish exports (O'Sullivan and Gillespie, 2011). If fish was used as a synonym for herring, then the small number of official entries in the records from the second half of the sixteenth century can be explained by a reduction in fish exports due to the migration of shoals away from the Irish Sea coasts. We also cannot discount the possibility that the Henrician Reformation affected fish consumption patterns in England, with knock-on effects felt on the Irish fishing economy.

Owing to herring's irregular migratory patterns, the Irish fish export trade was speculative, metaphorically feast or famine. The one exception to this was salmon. Salmon had year-round demand owing to its high status and the species' migratory predictability. The fluctuation in volume of the Irish fish trade was amplified by fair times. Bristol's fairs were held in July and January, and these events would have given Irishmen access to a maximum of continental goods, including those brought to the Bristol fairs from other English ports (Flavin, 2011). The Irish economy was well developed to meet seasonal demand from its outside markets. Its seasonality meant fishing could be undertaken along with other commercial ventures and agriculture to provide a year-round income (Gillespie, 1985). Consequently, both maritime and terrestrial activities could co-exist at tower houses.

Fishing was a profitable commercial activity. Although not included in many official port records, government interest in its financial contribution is attested to by efforts in the reign of Henry VIII to increase the price of fish, to thus provide a greater customs return. Had this Crown attempt been successful, the income of tower house occupants would have been negatively affected, as it would have removed the practice of paying informal duties to the local lord of the area by fishermen, as discussed in chapter 3. Instead, the most efficient way for the Crown to profit remained the farming of the customs (Longfield, 1929).

Completely different patterns arise in the *Welsh Port books* that document the late sixteenth and turn of the seventeenth century. Trade here is nigh exclusively between Wexford and Milford in south Wales, although Dublin makes a numerous and sudden appearance after 1600. Here we see boatloads of herring being shipped from Wexford to Wales. As the Welsh accounts usually do not specify destination, we are instead reliant on the imprecise analysis of where vessels were registered. However, this at least allows us to see that trade was being conducted in ships attached to Ireland, and Wexford in particular, not only those in Welsh or English hands. The second most dominant Irish exports to Wales were timber products, while salt, wool and flocks were lesser exports (*Welsh Port books*).

Imports to Ireland: The items of consumption

Imports were mainly small luxury goods, alongside manufactured items and the essentials of iron and salt. The proliferation of luxury goods suggests a period of consumerism and financial confidence throughout the tower house era. This increased confidence is similarly reflected in the increased range of luxury imports traversing the Irish Sea over the duration of the sixteenth century (Flavin, 2011). Flavin analysed the Bristol accounts and found that there was diversification in terms of cost and quality of individual items (for example, differently priced combs) as well as a new range of previously unknown goods (*ibid.*). Imports of luxuries were stable throughout the year, in contrast to Ireland's export patterns. We see goods such as foods and spices (raisins, currants, prunes, saffron, aniseed and liquorice are all regular mentions), soap, cloth of higher quality than that produced in Ireland, dress fittings, diverse 'small wares', and 'merchandise' with regularity.

These items, many of which came over long distances via re-export, would have been expensive and their purchase must have been mainly by the social ranks occupying the tower houses. Flavin, in her article on increased consumption patterns in sixteenth-century Ireland, attempted to explain the upsurge in luxury items as demand created by English colonisation and increased numbers of soldiers, while also acknowledging this was a period of economic growth for Ireland (*ibid.*). When merchant place of residence begins to be listed in customs accounts we can gain some insight into inland trade networks, and Flavin interprets this evidence as showing that the elites across Ireland at this time had a shared material culture (ibid.). We can consequently make an educated guess as to where the bulk of these luxury goods ended up: at tower houses and in their vicinity. We might therefore imagine the attire of our tower house occupants, and the interior of tower houses to a lesser extent, but especially when dining with guests, to be reflective of these trade items. Fashion was just as appealing for those residing inside the Pale as outside it, and cheaper versions of popular items must have been sought by those less financially solvent but yet wishing to appear in fashion (ibid.). This is naturally not a peculiarly Irish trait: medieval people used material culture in a variety of ways – as a form of emulation, for advancement, and to visually show control and belonging. The tower house notably meets all these demands. It is, of course, not the only built manifestation to do so from this period – the 'cultural signature' of the Hanse was expressed through both their built environment and their domestic goods (Gaimster, 2000, 2005, 2014). Nor does this indicate a process of acculturation to English appearances, for a typically 'Irish' style remained dominant, witnessed in diverse items of material culture from mantles to tower houses (Flavin, 2011). The popularity of the Irish mantle throughout Europe reminds us that fashion transcends ethnic and national divides. Along with death and taxes, it seems that another human universal is that an income surplus will result in increased spending on frippery. The tower houses themselves are part and parcel of this overt spending and consumption.

Hops were another constant import to Ireland from Chester – used then, as now, in beer production – and this may have met a southern English taste (ibid.). Exceptions to the rule of luxury and manufactured items are natural materials not commonly found in Ireland. In this way we have numerous cargoes comprising only coal travelling to Dublin (*Chester customs accounts*). Coal became a popular fuel during the sixteenth century, when it was used by the wealthy (as implied by the volume imported to Carrickfergus in the early 1600s; see Sweetnam, 1986). Before then, fuel needs were served by the local woods; even scrub wood and furze could provide ample fuel. We also have the import of knives and sword hilts, presumably as militaristic statement items and reflecting the higher quality of weapons production outside Ireland. Iron (and, by extension, nails) and salt also appear with regularity, as does alum, a dye-fixing agent used in cloth manufacture.

Imports from Milford in Wales were almost exclusively coal and culm (i.e. coal dust). A lower volume of trade between Beaumaris and Wexford and Dublin was mostly imports of slate (*Welsh Port books*).

Presumably, slate was needed for roofing during the building boom. The outright domination of coal in the Welsh accounts (*ibid.*) suggests that these Irish import patterns were specific to the sixteenth and seventeenth centuries, as it is another definitively early-modern-period type of good, its extraction only developed from the middle of the sixteenth century. This might in turn suggest trading connections between Ireland and Wales were lower, or at least different, in the later Middle Ages.

Trading patterns: An Irish Sea world

The ranges of import and export items were largely uniform across Ireland, with no one good controlled by or the expertise of a particular port. Three exceptions exist. First, that Drogheda appears to have maintained a closer relationship with Liverpool than with Chester. Second, fish was dominated by Wexford, at least in the documentary record. While other places exported fish, including Rush in County Dublin with 'white fish', Dublin with 'dry fish', and both Dublin and Howth with salmon, Wexford dominated the herring trade (*Chester customs accounts*). Both the red and white varieties were specified, but perhaps most interesting is an entry for 'small Newfoundland fish' from Wexford (*ibid.*: 89). The famous Grand Banks fisheries expanded greatly from 1615 onwards but, prior to this, migratory fishing communities fished them, and this included many Wexford men (Kelleher, 2013). Wexford's association with Newfoundland was well established by the second half of the sixteenth century, and demonstrates Ireland's ability to prosper through exploiting the emerging Atlantic World economy.

Third, the merchants of Athboy in County Meath and Ardee in County Louth exported only yarn. Both Athboy and Ardee were discussed in the previous chapter, examining urban tower houses, and it is not too presumptive to surmise that the tower house residents were the same individuals who regularly appeared in Chester. Yarn, too, could be easily stored. Large quantities of this linen yarn were demanded by industry in the vicinity of Manchester (Longfield, 1929). Imports were more diverse, and included hops, iron and cloth, as well as small luxury goods. A fascinating small study could be made of one individual – a merchant of Athboy by the name of Katherine White. A female name is a rarity in the accounts, and the frequency with which White's name appears in the *Chester customs accounts* indicates that she had a sustained interest in Athboy's trade and did not simply make a single investment. Women are seldom mentioned in Bristol, and the handful who do manifest are usually described as 'widow'. So Katherine White, by extension, may have been a widow left a trade business or capital for investment by a deceased husband.

Another odd person appears in Bristol records – a Tessicke Berii, listed as an alien merchant of Youghal (*Bristol's trade with Ireland*). The merchants detailed in the Ireland–Bristol trade are all 'indigenous' merchants: those considered 'English' in Ireland, also known as the Anglo-Irish (*ibid.*). Berii was therefore originally from outside the British Isles, and his ascription 'of Youghal' indicates that he was foreign born but resident and trading in that town. This was a rare incidence as such aliens had strict conditions placed upon them, possibly as an act of protectionism for local businessmen (Holton, 2001). This was witnessed in Kilkenny city around 1529, when it was proclaimed that no merchant resident in the town could receive a foreign craftsman or his son in service to be trained or apprenticed. The penalty for doing so was a steep fine of 100*s*. (*Liber primus Kilkenniensis*). That 'foreign' here refers to those originally from outside the British Isles is indicated, since this term is not employed anywhere in the volume to describe the Gaelic-Irish living around the town. Often, restrictions on who could trade in Irish port towns seem to have been at the discretion of the town government, as in Kilkenny, but also in Carlingford, County Louth, where a 1570–71 charter stipulated that no foreign merchants could be active in the town unless permitted by the corporation (*Irish fiants*: vol. 2). At times though, the activities of foreign merchants could reflect international relations. In the same year, a Galway merchant was granted a special licence from the English Crown allowing him to trade with the French, Spanish, Portuguese, Flemish or Scots for wine, salt, iron, hops, grain and merchandise. The reason given for this exception was that the cessation of trade with 'strangers' had stopped trade with the town, and so led to Galway's impoverishment (*ibid.*).

Another interesting issue is that many named in the Chester–Ireland trade route were not professional merchants, but artisans moving goods associated with their trade. Tailors, skinners and ironmongers occasionally appeared in the accounts. These were exclusively English residents and their wares comprised only part of a cargo. Indeed, most cargoes at this time were provided by a number of investors, mainly to minimise the financial impact of loss, but this also must have made trade an option for those of comparatively more limited financial means, like wealthy artisans, since they did not need to sponsor an entire ship. Every person listed as from Ireland in the Bristol accounts was described as a 'merchant', suggesting that this occupational diversity had not reached Ireland, at least by the seventeenth century. The economic role of Irishmen was waning by the beginning of the Tudor Conquest. From 1594–95, the number of merchants connected to a named place in Ireland dramatically dropped off, and the number of merchants tied to places in England increased accordingly. It looks as though the trade routes were increasingly in the hands of the English, as a result of their influence in Ireland more generally. Some trade items seem to have catered more to English tastes, especially cider shipped to Sligo (*Bristol's trade with Ireland*). The sudden uptick in timber products exported from Wexford in 1600–01 is suggestive of the woodland clearance most often associated with the period following the Tudor Conquest. In Wexford's case this started early, with restrictions placed on timber export in the 1560s (Longfield, 1929), as Wexford was reportedly supplying timber for the Scots to build ships during the Nine Years' War (De Courcy Ireland, 1987). Other scholars have argued that timber products mentioned in the English trade accounts were coming from Gaelic-Irish areas, for Anglo-Irish regions had surely already been exploited (Everett, 2014). But this argument seems vastly oversimplified in light of the evidence in the records for economic cooperation between Ireland's ethnicities, money effectively 'greasing the wheels' of any potential ethnic rift.

When we analyse the places associated with trade between Ireland and England we can see that separate systems, or networks, existed across the Irish Sea that connected certain regions of Ireland with her neighbours. These may have continued in existence from the early Middle Ages. Hudson, in his study of the early medieval Irish Sea zone (1999), proposed that Chester and Bristol maintained separate economic links with different parts of Ireland. It should be noted that conclusions are tentative, as before 1575 the accounts document only that a ship was coming from or going to 'Ireland'. The numbers given below from before this date apply only to where the ship was domiciled. As can be seen once merchant origins and destination are included, a much more complex economic network immediately becomes apparent.

For Chester, we find that Dublin provides the majority of references, with sixty-eight per cent of imports to Ireland and sixty-four per cent of exports. Drogheda trails in a distant second, with Waterford and Wexford picking up a handful of cases each. In Bristol, the impact of the Tudor Conquest can be seen, as trade overall declined noticeably from 1545 to 1575. Waterford was Bristol's leading trade partner, apart from one year, when Youghal took that position. The ports of Dublin and Drogheda do not appear in large numbers, indicating that their relationship with Chester was close to exclusive. This exclusivity is supported by the references to Chester and its inland trading partner of Coventry in the collection of documents comprising the first volume of the *Calendar of ancient records of Dublin*. One of many documents regarding mercantile activity in that city is a complaint that London merchants were being unfairly restricted by Dublin's residents, who were preventing them from selling their goods either inside or outside the city. Combined, this evidence strongly suggests that Irish ports traded with those they were closest to on the other side of the Irish Sea.

The total number of ships plying these routes is impossible to ascertain, in no small part because of to the popularity of the most common vessel names, *Mary* and *Katherine* (Childs, 1982). Other port towns fluctuated in their connections, as new places assumed more economic and political importance following the Tudor Conquest. This indicates that while we can utilise records up until the mid-seventeenth century and take them to be largely indicative of late medieval socio-economic activity, in many other areas the same cannot be said when examining international trade. There are numerous dangers in doing so: most notably the apparent disparity between exports from the fourteenth to the seventeenth centuries, as well as the change in port primacy. We therefore must take the application of the evidence contained within the 1614–15 Irish Port books to late medieval times with hefty scepticism. The only surviving Port books for Ireland are the years 1614–15, which are in the Temple Newsham collection held at the West Yorkshire Archive Service (copy at PRONI, Belfast, MIC 199/1).

We see little of the third major trade route having an impact on Ireland – that running from the continent along the west coast. This is in contrast to the increasing number of depictions of this coastline on continental portolan maps throughout the fifteenth century (O'Neill, 1987). Galway is only referenced a handful of times in the Bristol accounts, and was as often the residence of a merchant utilising another port's facilities as it was a destination entry in its own right. Similarly, Limerick only appears as a merchant residence with any frequency in the Bristol Port books. Yet the scale of wealth represented in building in the west testifies to a level of income that must have stretched far beyond the imposition of tolls and informal fishing duties.

That individuals from the west could be active on a more impressive scale is exemplified by Germyn Lynch (see figure 6.1 for the eponymous tower house), who held land in Galway but was listed repeatedly as a goldsmith of London, showing that his career encompassed the opposite ends of the two countries (O'Neill, 1988). This was not his sole geographic connection – Lynch also turned up in Kinsale after a voyage from Portugal, before taking pilgrims to Santiago de Compostela (*ibid.*), and then in association with a Bristol ship destined for Iceland. O'Neill commented how few Irish merchants were engaged in trade with Iceland, that we are aware of, which is in contrast to the early medieval evidence. It would, however, be sensible for a Bristol ship bound for Iceland to use Galway as a sheltering and stopping-off point, which possibly explains Lynch's involvement. Indeed, O'Neill noted that the expansion of the

Connection with the wider world

6.1 Lynch's Castle in Galway city is a highly decorated example of an urban tower house. Although the decorative features have been relocated since its medieval manifestation, it was obviously architecturally impressive originally. It is connected with the prominent merchant Lynch family.

Icelandic cod fisheries attracted fishers from southwest England, who travelled via western Ireland and who probably helped to economically grow Galway city (*ibid.*). This in turn might be an elusive hint at an under-documented route affecting the west coast in the late Middle Ages.

That the Crown had some control over the economic activities of Galway city by the sixteenth century is witnessed in the Tudor-era fiants. As early as 1525–26 the fees of Galway were granted to Robert Cowley, a Dublin merchant; set at 2s. for every last of hides shipped. This grant was previously held by the Lynch family (*Irish fiants*: vol. 1). Later, this custom on hides was granted to another merchant of Dublin, Thomas FitzSymon. FitzSymon also received eel weirs, other weirs, places for nets, parts of income from mills, 'a little fort' and 'a great fort' (*ibid.*: p. 101, entry 129). Some level of integration with the English political economy, and a nationwide Anglo-Irish one, is displayed here.

As mentioned earlier, a merchant of Galway was granted a special licence from the English Crown allowing him to trade with the French, Spanish, Portuguese, Flemish or Scots because the lack of foreign trade had hurt Galway economically (*Irish fiants*: vol. 2). In 1579, apparently, 'Divers strange vessels have been in all these western havens, and have sold their wines and departed' (*Calendar of the Carew manuscripts*: 228). Again, this implies the use of Galway port by continental merchants. Therefore, that Galway is mentioned only infrequently in the English port accounts indicates trade was being conducted with other countries, probably on the continent. Hardiman hinted at this activity in his *History of Galway*, writing that the volume of wine imported there in the sixteenth century surpassed anywhere in the country. The Galway focus on wine imports, he stated, necessitated 'vaults and stores at Athboy' in County Meath, en route to the east-coast ports, if travelling overland (Hardiman, 1820: 79). Generally, Galway's statutes sought to preserve the interests of the town freemen to the detriment of others, including the local Gaelic-Irish, and in 1540 it was stated that freemen of the city were permitted to sell victuals to Spaniards and Frenchmen without paying customs (*Archives of the town of Galway*). This suggests foreign sailors and merchants were visiting the town.

Another impression garnered from consulting the English and Welsh accounts is the interconnectivity of Irish ports. Aside from the Dublin merchants with interests in Galway, on the opposite side of the country, people from both Dublin and Drogheda appeared in the records for the other with regularity. The smaller-scale merchants from the likes of Ardee and Athboy used vessels leaving from both of these east-coast ports. The people of Clontarf, north of Dublin city centre, were given the right to fish in Carlingford Bay off County Louth without paying tithes (*Irish fiants*: vol. 3). That Dublin's influence stretched northwards along the coast as far as the Ulster ports is seen in occasional mentions such as that of the *Mary* of Lusk, County Dublin, sailing to Ardglass in County Down (*Welsh Port books*). This indicates that Irish coastal trade was very well established and well integrated, as suggested by the tower house evidence. Coastal trade fed into riverine trade, especially on the tidal estuaries where Ireland's main sea ports were located. In this way the hinterlands of ports probably overlapped to a degree, as is also implied by a lack of exclusivity in which port towns inland merchants utilised, according to the Port books. Coastal trade would go unrecorded, even in English customs documentation, but it has been estimated that it might have contributed up to seventy per cent of a port's income (Kowaleski, 1995). Coastal trade could also shelter and protect the local economy from tempestuous international events (*ibid.*).

A possible example of two overlapping hinterlands is Dingle and Limerick. This can be attributed to a difference in the geographic extents of their local lordships. Dingle was the main port for the earl of Desmond in Kerry from the late thirteenth century, when it commenced exporting fleeces (O'Brien, 1988). Ships stopped there before proceeding on to Carrigafoyle, and thence Tarbert and Limerick. Several lordships clustered along the banks of the River Shannon, and this, combined with the coastal trading routes, explains the proliferation of tower houses in this region (Mac Curtain, 1988). Carrigafoyle tower house is an interesting site, as it and the surrounding bawn were once their own sheltered island in the river, and boats could approach under the walls. The attractiveness of approach by water is borne out by the proximity of higher ground, atop which sits a medieval parish church, overlooking the tower house completely, making the tower house location far from ideal from the perspective of defence. We are reliant on historical maps and depictions to see the island site today, however, as the riverbed is now dry. Coastal trading will have favoured some items over others, especially the bulkier items like hides. Such trade was further facilitated by, for example, the confirmation provided by the Exchequer in 1313–14 that magnates could send hides from port to port without paying customs dues (O'Neill, 1987).

At times even small trading points interacted with mariners from international locations. For example, in southwest Ireland much of the exchange of local tower house dwellers probably came from visiting fishing fleets (Breen, 2005). These fishermen travelled there from England and from continental Europe. As fishermen paid tolls to tower houses for the right to fish, to take shelter and for fish-processing facilities, in a society with low levels of circulating currency like Ireland it is easy to see how such tolls would have been met with international trade goods like wine and salt. Salt would have been brought on the fishing vessels regardless, as it was necessary for fish curing, while wine was in demand across the medieval world. Finds of continental European pottery from excavations support this contention, with shards originating in France or Spain recovered at Dunboy tower house in County Cork (*ibid.*). This indicates extensive local contact with what were probably Spanish fishing fleets (O'Sullivan and Breen, 2007).

The Irish Sea system was highly integrated. Again isolated mentions, but insightful nonetheless, are to several merchants from Trim, County Meath, with a barge from Caernarfon in Wales (*Chester customs accounts*). This is the sole reference to merchants from Trim, a town frequently discussed here since it was one of the major Anglo-Norman foundations of the Pale. That inland merchants were involved in Irish Sea trade indicates a well-developed network. Likewise, a handful of Wexford-registered ships were trading between different Welsh ports (*Welsh Port books*). The Bristol accounts document a similar interconnectivity within the southeast, with ships registered to one town sailing to another with cargoes belonging to merchants from sometimes four different places from across the southern portion of Ireland. The sudden appearance in the Port books from 1575 of inland towns tells us that merchants resided in Kilkenny and Clonmel in particular, as well as Kilmallock, Tallow, Cashel and Callan. Kilkenny had a merchant guild that was well established by the fourteenth century (*Liber primus Kilkenniensis*). Waterford had coastal and inland connections with Callan, Carlow, Cashel, Clonmel, Fethard, Kilkenny, Kinsale, Ross, Wexford and Youghal (*Archives of the municipal corporation of Waterford*). All of these places were intricately connected via the navigable waterways of the great rivers of medieval Ireland, with tower houses facilitating every step of the way. Presumably, these merchants were also represented within the earlier accounts, but the bias in the record of the 'particular accounts' did not preserve them. These inland merchants were mainly exporting items from pastoral agriculture. This economic activity can be linked to tower houses, as described in chapter 2. However, the numbers of inland merchants were paltry compared to the numerous citations of merchants from coastal ports and towns, especially Waterford.

Hudson and Ditchburn think it unlikely that extensive trade was conducted between Ireland, particularly the north, and the Isle of Man, as their pastoral agricultural bases were too similar (Ditchburn and Hudson, 2015). However, the island did not produce sufficient quantities of wheat to be self-sufficient, so this could have come from Ireland, and Man was a probable stopping-off point for journeys within the Irish Sea (*ibid.*). This role is supported by the significant number of ships registered to Ballaugh in the Isle of Man going to and from Ireland listed in the *Welsh Port books*. These entries indicate that if Man was not a stopping-off point, then there was a somewhat integrated economy (*Welsh Port books*).

Historians have suggested that hides were traded with continental Europe, in particular with Flanders and Pisa. Trade was also conducted with Chester and Bristol in England; Bordeaux, La Rochelle and Calais in France; Spain; and Portugal. Wine, iron and salt were imported both directly from the continent, particularly the Bay of Biscay, and by way of re-export from English ports, such as Bristol and Chester. Strangely, it is through the hints in the English accounts that we can infer Irish–continental activity. Childs has argued that Flanders was Ireland's main market for hides, albeit impossible to enumerate (Childs, 1982: 33), while Longfield thought there less demand from Flanders than from Spain (1929). O'Neill agreed with Childs, but thought that a large amount also went to Gascony in exchange for wine, with further quantities being shipped to Pisa. He estimated the total annual volume exported to the continent between 1300 and 1500 as between 1,300 and 1,500 hides, collected from all over the country (Childs, 2000; O'Neill, 1987). The export of hides was not limited to Gaelic-Irish areas, as there are some mentions from the port of Drogheda of the export of hides to Flanders and to Spain in the later fourteenth century, though this also probably indicates increased economic integration between Gaelic-Irish and Anglo-Irish areas (Galloway, 2015).

Wool was demanded by the textile manufacturers of the Low Countries, and Irish wool exports, particularly from the southeast, are documented throughout the fourteenth and fifteenth centuries, mostly through Calais (O'Neill, 1987). Irish cloth was generally of low quality, but this did not reduce demand for it, even seemingly in the great textile centre of Flanders. Irish cloth was not prohibited for sale in Flanders, in contrast to English-made cloth, so long as it went via the staple port of Bruges (Nicholas, 1976). The most likely import from the Low Countries to Ireland was finished cloth, the demand for which led Childs to the conclusion that 'it is quite possible that at this date [i.e. the late fourteenth century] Flemish trade ran close to English in its value to Ireland' (Childs, 1982: 33).

By the fifteenth century, Dublin, and to a lesser extent Kinsale, was maintaining Irish wine-trade contacts with Bordeaux, before that region was lost by England. In the early fourteenth century business had been more brisk, with the southeastern Irish ports commanding the trade (*ibid.*). Mentions in surviving documents become even rarer after the Hundred Years' War, and Childs has argued that Iberian shipments did not compensate for the loss of French contacts. She conceded that continental connections likely overshadowed English ones in the west, suggesting links between Galway and Portugal in particular (*ibid.*).

This continental trade integrated itself with the coastal trade. Again, it is the isolated reference that hints at more. In 1306 the *Nicholas* of Downpatrick was wrecked off Portmarnock, north County Dublin. This vessel was carrying a cargo of wine, wax, pots, jewels and spices (*Calendar of the justiciary rolls*: 'Pleas of the Crown at Swerdes', 1305–07). The composition of the cargo indicates that these imports, probably purchased in Dublin, were landed from the continent, before being reloaded and traded with Ulster through coastal trade routes. Continental routes, more so than the Irish Sea ones, probably fed into the wide range of coastal trading networks, since the items acquired from Europe tended to be those deemed more essential to medieval elite lifestyles: wine for consumption, salt for sale to the fishing industry and iron for a whole host of purposes. Ireland had minimal direct interaction, we think for geographic reasons, with the Mediterranean. Similarly, relations with the Hanseatic League were infrequent, even with Hanseatic-controlled Iceland (Childs and O'Neill, 1987). Of course, the belief here is that indirect trade via the continent or England could expand these connections even further.

Scottish and English colonisation in the early seventeenth century has been suggested as marking a period of growth in the ports, particularly those in Ulster where colonisation had perhaps the greatest impact (Gillespie, 1991). This interpretation argues that trade in sixteenth-century Ulster was not a major commercial force owing to underpopulation. Also, 'as immigration from Scotland and England increased both the labour force and the proportion of productive land in Ulster, a rapid rise in the number of inland fairs and markets, coupled with gradual improvements in communications, made this produce easier to market' (Agnew, 1996: 2). The economic growth of Belfast was primarily based upon the export of linen, which trade largely bypassed that of Dublin (Truxes, 1988). Trade from the colonies legally had to come via England, which boosted those Irish ports closest to England at the expense of those furthest away. Prosperous port towns also needed a productive hinterland. Agnew reasoned that the growth of the Ulster ports in the early seventeenth century was primarily assisted by the development of more inland markets (Agnew, 1996). Initially, the ports of the western coast of Ireland, particularly Galway, were those most affected by transatlantic trade. Kelleher, in her study of Baltimore in County Cork, noted that a number of vessels would stop at ports on the south coast of Ireland for provisioning before crossing the Atlantic (Kelleher, 2007b). In time, Cork, Dublin and Belfast increasingly came to dominate.

Tower houses at small ports: Between rural and urban

Late medieval Ireland's port towns were the focal points from which a complex network of economic connections originated. The evidence is sparse, but researchers have long suspected that the multiplicity of smaller ports along Ireland's coasts acted as centres for coastal trade. Coastal trade acted as a hinterland in many respects. For example, Carlingford in County Louth in the northeast would have funnelled goods from south Ulster through to the major port of Dublin. This coastal trade expanded during the Nine Years' War as supplies were ferried up and down for the armies. By the early seventeenth century, a route moving grain between Ulster and Dublin was well established, taking precedence even over travel between the former and Scotland, as it was not as dependent on good sailing conditions and was therefore faster and less expensive (Gillespie, 1985).

Ports also functioned as outports for other settlements, for varying reasons. Best known is Dalkey, which served as Dublin's outport owing to difficulties accessing the latter's harbour, but this system was known elsewhere. For instance, Youghal in County Cork served as the outport for the inland, but riverine-sited, town of Clonmel in County Tipperary (Breen, 2007a). Prosperous port towns needed a productive hinterland, and Galloway has ably demonstrated how this hinterland varied hugely depending on what goods were being transported (Galloway, 2015). Agnew reasoned that the growth of the Ulster ports in the early seventeenth century was assisted by the development of more inland markets (Agnew, 1996). Medieval towns like Fethard, County Tipperary, were economically connected with major coastal ports. For Fethard, this was the port of Waterford (O'Keeffe, 2003). A diverse hinterland provided both export materials and a market for imported goods, and probably insured against market fluctuations to some degree. For example, while Carlingford's main income probably rested on fishing, it was also well provided with timber, turf, salt, limestone and grain from its hinterland (O'Sullivan and Gillespie, 2011).

Many settlements abutted Gaelic-Irish regions so as to facilitate networks. 'The fifteenth century saw the rise of other towns that fulfilled this role along the edge of the Pale, including Longford, Cavan and Mullingar, and Carlingford may have benefited from an increase in trade from this source' (O'Sullivan and Gillespie, 2011: 3). Despite a tendency to view the late medieval and early modern periods in Ireland as violent, inter-ethnic economic cooperation was widespread. An example is the production of coinage for local use, such as that created by the O'Reilly lords of Cavan to facilitate trading links between them and the Pale (*ibid.*). This is a more optimistic view of 'O'Reilly's money', which O'Neill stated consisted of forgeries of the poor-quality English coins made by the Gaelic-Irish of Louth and Meath (O'Neill, 1988). Other semi-legal and illegal mints were in operation elsewhere across the country, operated by Gaelic-Irish and Anglo-Irish alike (*ibid.*).

An interesting avenue for future research would be the role of Irish port towns in facilitating long-distance travel, particularly that associated with pilgrimage. Evidence for this might be ephemeral, however, such as the dedications to St. James (of Compostela) at Carlingford in County Louth that suggest it was a centre of pilgrimage travel (O'Sullivan and Gillespie, 2011), and the occasional reference to ships transporting pilgrims to Santiago de Compostela (O'Neill, 1988). Boom times were during holy years, when we might even find less-significant Irish ports engaged in this travel. For instance, in 1477 a London-based man transported pilgrims from New Ross to Santiago de Compostela in a huge ship, a 320-ton carrack (*ibid.*).

The small towns discussed in previous chapters had an essential role to play in the maintenance of trade. The much-debated Irish borough, whether it developed into a town or not, had the innate right to hold a market (Graham, 1988b). Much of the trading activity at this level across Ireland must have been in reality closer to exchange, especially since those engaged would not have had full-time employ in trade and therefore cannot be described as either merchants or traders. These small markets enabled peasants to obtain cash if needed for rent or tax, and to offload surplus agricultural goods (*ibid.*). In due course, their combined goods will have formed the larger cargoes discussed below. Burgesses had the exclusive right to buy and sell in their market without paying tolls (*ibid.*).

Rural tower houses slotted in easily in the lower levels of the developing port hierarchy, as they could readily serve as both administrative centre and storage facility (Breen, 2007a). We have documentation of mercantile enterprise even at small rural locations. Ringhaddy Castle in County Down was held by the Gaelic-Irish Brian McArt in 1594, with the intent of facilitating trade with Scotland, as the tower house sits on the western side of Strangford Lough, which opens into the northern Irish Sea. A rare documentary reference, albeit from the later period of tower house occupation, from the CSPI mentions up to twenty barques a week anchoring under Ringhaddy Castle's walls with supplies for the rebels, including munitions, cloth, wine and aqua vitae (CSPI: vol. 11, 'The Lord Deputy and council to Secretary Cecil, 26 October 1602'). The site was found to have a pier and 'hard', or landing area, to assist with the handling of vessels (O'Sullivan and Breen, 2007). Underwater excavation duly focussed on this landing place. An underwater ledge by the jetty meant that it would have been accessible at both high and low tide, although larger vessels such as the barques would have anchored slightly offshore at the deep-water Ringhaddy Sound (referred to as a 'road' in CSPI) and had their passengers and goods ferried across. The underwater excavation at the site corroborated the historical evidence, finding items such as north Devon ware pottery, bottle fragments, musket balls and corroded iron (Breen, 1997). These artefacts reflect the type

Connection with the wider world

6.2 Mahee Castle, County Down, is one of two coastal tower houses in this county with internal boathouses. This boathouse is located on the left of the building – a wide, barrel-vaulted area running between the front and rear of the tower house. It allowed for a boat to be pulled up directly from the water, where it could be unloaded and protected.

of goods stated in the historical documentation as being imported by the rebels, and, as the excavation focussed on the landing place, came from this precise area. This excavation revealed the economic needs of warfare, yet also demonstrates how, by the close of the Nine Years' War, attentions were already shifting to new settlement plans and economic profit.

Only a few miles to the north of Ringhaddy Castle, excavations at Mahee Castle (figure 6.2) found quantities of pottery, mostly of late medieval date but with no suggestion made as to its origin, and slag that might indicate the import of metal for working (*Database of Irish excavation reports*: Down 2001:315, Mahee Castle, Mahee Island). This site is documented because of late-sixteenth-century attempts to use it in colonisation. The proposed settlers, Brown and Burrows, stated that they wanted the site's emphasis to be on trading activities, their bargaining tool being the promise of an annual customs return of £5, roughly half that of Carrickfergus (CSPI Tudor: 'Petition of Thomas Brown and

Thomas Burrows to Queen Elizabeth, Endorsed 1571'). Expecting such a customs return was overly optimistic, but it does reflect how new colonists viewed tower houses as tools in economic development.

At Inch, near the county town of Downpatrick in the barony of Lecale, river dredging in 1992 uncovered timbers belonging to either a bridge or a jetty. These timbers underwent dendrochronological dating, with one found to have a date of 1529 ± 9 years, the other 1564 ± 9 years (*Database of Irish excavation reports*: Down 1992:035, Quoile River at Inch Abbey). Metal detecting at the site also found a bronze weight box with sixty brass disks and part of a set of miniature weighing scales. It is deduced, therefore, that prior to the Tudor Conquest some level of economic activity was being undertaken at a landing place outside the county town of Downpatrick. This site is further upstream on the Quoile estuary than Ballintogher, noted in the early-seventeenth-century Port books and identified as equating to Castle Island tower house (it is called 'Balentogher' Castle in a 1641 deposition of Lieutenant Edward Davies), which lies on the Quoile River side of the townland (*1641 depositions online transcript*: 'Examination of Edward Dauies'). No mention of trade activity at Inch is made in all the seventeenth-century historical documentation consulted. It could be that trade at Inch was incorporated into the returns for Ballintogher, although as Ballintogher is around four kilometres away, it seems unlikely that the two were confused. Indeed, since Inch lies on the outskirts of Downpatrick it could be that any customs collected there would have been listed under Downpatrick. Another explanation is that with economic changes after the mid-sixteenth century, Inch ceased to be used as a point of trade.

Economic motivations were of course major incentives for colonisation in the sixteenth and seventeenth centuries. The tower house's role in this has been documented elsewhere (Lyttleton, 2007; McAlister, 2015). Part of colonisation plans involved establishing ports. For example, in the reprinted 'Life of the learned Sir Thomas Smith ...' it is stated that Smith knew that the Ards were 'lying well for trade by sea' (1698, reprinted in Lowry, 1867: 25). This period consequently witnessed the creation of new port towns, not all of which were successful, and many of these were to detract trade from the previously successful medieval ports (McAlister, 2015). This new potential was recognised also by Anglo-Irish inhabitants with closer connections to medieval trading. Rowland White, a Dublin-based merchant, was also lord of Dufferin, the lordship including Ringhaddy Castle. White's interest in trade and settlement is stated in his work *Discors touching Ireland* (written c. 1569), even if it was not provably acted upon (Morgan, 1985). All of these aspiring colonisers knew the importance of harnessing trade to ensure success, and this focussed on environmental resource exploitation. Specifically, timber, fish, corn and manufacture were mentioned (*ibid.*). It is little wonder that the historiography of environmental resource exploitation in Ireland, and of woodlands in particular, has emphasised the destructive efforts of early modern colonisation based on such documented statements.

There are, frankly, far too many tower houses associated with landing places in maritime areas, even within the small sample of around two hundred surveyed for this project, to discuss them all here. Suffice it to say that these tower houses come from the entire coastline of the country and transcend ethnic divides. Local trade and exchange took place at these tower houses throughout the country. This was not just directly with the elites, but also with the wider populace in the form of fairs and markets. Exchange would have taken place informally throughout the countryside, but the densest activity was probably by the coast, as many of the fairs of longest duration were in coastal regions, where they were easily supplied (Holton, 2001). This may partially explain the high density of coastal tower houses. In addition, many of the imported goods enumerated in this chapter will have made their way to market stalls and urban shops, some of which were located on the ground floors of tower houses.

Gaelic-Irish trade

O'Sullivan and Breen would include much of Gaelic Ireland under the heading of 'smaller trading points'. This is not to say that the Gaelic-Irish did not export and import goods, but rather that 'it was on a different scale and not centrally controlled. Exportation was on a more localized scale and facilitated on a casual basis' (O'Sullivan and Breen, 2007: 193). 'Cultural interchange' rather than economic infrastructure was key to this (*ibid.*). A lack of representation of the Gaelic-Irish in medieval maritime history is compounded by absence from the annals. War fleets comprise the few nautical mentions in the annals, as trade was probably too mundane to warrant note, except on very rare, 'newsworthy' occasions (Flanagan, 1988: 502).

Breen has debated to what degree the Gaelic-Irish were directly involved in international trade. He also believes their direct involvement in maritime fishing was minimal, that they were content instead to gather profit from international fishermen, although this study has found that interpretation a bit limited. Breen has argued that the Gaelic-Irish lords resident at tower houses relied upon galley-type vessels, employed foreign ships for trade, and chartered transport for pilgrimage or specific cargoes from such international locations. He stated that there were no waterfront facilities capable of servicing the larger vessels characteristic of international trade in Gaelic-Irish southwest Ireland (Breen, 2001; see also Kelleher, 2007b). The trade in hides was perhaps particularly dependent on cordial relations between Ireland's ethnic groups since most hides must have made their way to the coast from the Gaelic-Irish lords' great cattle herds (O'Neill, 1987). The timber and firewood trade likewise seems to have been controlled by the Gaelic-Irish, with aid of the navigable riverways (*ibid.*). In the 1560s there were Gaelic-Irish merchants at Armagh, who conducted their business within the O'Neill lordship, and it is probable that more Gaelic-Irish merchants operated, at least out of the inland market towns (Nicholls, 1987).

Piracy, smuggling and illicit activity at tower houses

The extent and impact of piracy on the national and local economies is impossible to ascertain before the Plantation era. That Ireland's multitudinous harbours and landing places, many commanded by tower houses, would lend themselves well to illicit activity is certain. We have some evidence for Gaelic-Irish lords maintaining fleets of oar-propelled galleys and pinnaces, which they arguably did not use to participate in trade directly themselves, but rather to engage in piracy and the exploiting of trade. They were, in essence, waterlords, rather than landlords (Kelleher, 2007a, b). Smith comments that illicit activity was well embedded within Irish trade:

> The legislation of 1569–70 to control Irish trade was intended to protect the established port towns, on whose loyalty the state depended. But, together with the activities of the new royal customs officers, it led to a wave of smuggling, which the authorities, in practice, had to tolerate. It is arguable that Irish overseas trade after 1569 was largely in the hands of merchants, who were technically smugglers, operating from places outside the reach of the state, often with the connivance of customs officials. (1996: 52)

The very nature of piracy and smuggling, however, means that records were not kept in the first place, and these activities would only be mentioned if something of significance was caught, or when they were known to be practised on a damaging scale. That the combined illicit trade operating out of Ireland could be detrimental to the English economy is testified to by an act of 1430, when:

> The sheriffs of Bristol, Cornwall, Devon, Gloucestershire, and Somerset and Dorset were ordered to confiscate the ships of Irish and English merchants and fishermen who came to England from Ireland, particularly

from the ports of Dublin, Drogheda, Waterford, Cork, and Limerick, with uncustomed goods because, it was said, heretofore such merchants and fishermen 'laded ships and other vessels with salt fish and divers other wares in arms of the sea, "crikes" and elsewhere in ports of Ireland, and when so laded have sailed therewith by night and by day out of Ireland to England without payment of the custom due, concealing and unlawfully stealing custom to the value of 100 or 300 marks a year'. (O'Brien, 1988: 23)

How successful the authorities were at halting illicit trade is moot. Smuggling occurred especially when there was an incentive to do so – goods that were only subject to poundage, or a five-per-cent duty, were less likely to be smuggled, since the profit margins from avoiding payment were not so great as to outweigh the risk of being caught. Grain, which had prohibitions placed upon its movement, was one exception (Flavin, 2011), and no doubt wine was another, as it was subject to fluctuations in international relations. Wine prices in Ireland were supposedly fixed by law, which surely will have acted as incentive (O'Neill, 1987). Also, wine was only supposed to be imported at particular, designated places. In Connacht, this right was reserved for only Galway and Sligo (*Irish fiants*: vol. 2). This will no doubt have encouraged illicit activity, since the distances between such designated ports were great.

That piracy in the Irish Sea was an issue of international proportions is witnessed in the creation of charts of Ireland in 1612 for the Amsterdam admiralty to combat the threat. The Dutch did not have extensive direct trading links with Ireland that we know of, so the commission seems to be in response to pirates using Irish havens as bases. A 1611 account of a Dutch attempt to deal with pirates records them operating off the Portuguese coast before the Dutch fleet proceeded to southwest Ireland to await the pirates there. However, they ultimately did not find any (Voorbeijtel Cannenburg, 1935). Evidently, Irish-based pirates could range over to the continent, and the specific mention of activity near Portugal indicates wine may have been at least part of the goal.

Convenience must have played a role. The staple-port system meant that trade formalities were supposed to be completed at Dublin, Drogheda, Cork or Waterford. This meant that merchants travelling, say, from Galway or Limerick had to 'undertake the dangerous coastal voyage' to Cork before venturing on to the continent (O'Neill, 1987: 63). It is extremely likely that they aimed to avoid making this journey whenever possible (Hardiman, 1820; O'Neill, 1987). Consequently, the secure storage space and protective command over harbours provided by tower houses must have meant these buildings lent themselves extremely well to smuggling.

Even at a local level, illicit fairs and landing places and forestalling – the act of buying up goods before they reached the marketplace at a reduced cost to then sell on – were remarked upon. Such complaints are documented for Waterford (Galloway, 2011). They are also discussed at Dublin's outport of Dalkey in the ordinances by the Common Council of the City of Dublin (*Calendar of ancient records of Dublin*: vol. 1). Dalkey, as the landing point for Dublin, must have enticed forestallers attracted by the distance between the two. Wine, iron and salt are the three goods specifically mentioned, indicating that illegal activity focussed on continental items, where the greatest profits lay. In Kilkenny, forestalling of grain was mentioned in 1422, whereas provisioning of fish was more of a problem in fourteenth-century Kilkenny city, with frequent references to ensuring supply for sale in the predetermined place (*Liber primus Kilkenniensis*). A particular problem was the violent theft of fish directly from fishermen, resulting in fines and punishments for those found guilty of the offence (*ibid.*). Evidently, despite Kilkenny being on a major river stocked with fish and navigable to the sea, fish supply was uncertain. Forestalling is the most commonly encountered complaint at Ireland's port and market towns overall, so it must have been the most frequent abuse practised.

Given the readiness of tower house owners to charge visiting fishing fleets, no doubt similar deals would have been calculated for other items. The particular lure of smuggling grain might partially explain the discrepancy between its record in the surviving written documentation and the number of water mills and the pollen record indicating more mixed agriculture than historians have heretofore accepted. As tower houses are a characteristic of decentralised political authority, unrecorded and unregistered trading must have been epidemic, and it is even possible that occupants were completely unaware that, technically, a proportion of proceeds were thanks to the distant and ineffectual state. We might suspect therefore that Ireland became even more attractive in the later Middle Ages for the enterprising from across the western European seaboard, since profit could remain largely 'in house'. The goods exchanged must resemble those in the overall trade with Britain and the continent – fish and agricultural products in exchange for wine, iron and luxury goods. Smuggling was probably small at the individual level, but could be significant when all incidences were combined. For instance, the *Calendar of ancient records* mentions that in some towns fishermen were allowed to sell their catch directly from their vessels at the quayside without having to pay tolls, although later documents indicate this right was usually reserved for town burgesses, with merchants in Galway able to sell only after passing through the customs house (*Archives of the town of Galway*; *Calendar of ancient records*, cited in Holton,

2001). Tower house residents could also profit from siding with the government to stamp out illicit dealings; for example, in 1583 Fineen O'Driscoll took action to prevent piracy (Kelleher, 2013). In the decentralised political atmosphere of late medieval and pre-Plantation Ireland, tower house dwellers were often free to act as best benefited their individual interests or, at worst, in the interests of their lordship.

Outside of the Pale and the major ports, occasional references to extreme events are all that hint at illicit activities on the seas. For example, the archbishop of Armagh was captured in Dublin Bay by pirates, and taken to Ardglass on the County Down coast. This indicates that lawlessness was rampant even in this part of County Down, a region mostly held by the Anglo-Irish that the Pale administration might consider marginally more civilised (Childs and O'Neill, 1987). Once we enter the seventeenth century, piracy is better documented and, indeed, 'occurred under the umbrella of a plantation policy that was being played out among politicians and government officials, Old English elites, New English aristocrats, entrepreneurs, merchant venturers and ordinary settlers' (Kelleher, 2013: 347–8). Southwest Ireland in particular, the setting for many tower houses with an overt role in controlling maritime and fishing activity, became an option for relocation for the lawless expelled from England wishing to take advantage of expanding Atlantic trade routes (*ibid.*). At this later period, coming at the tail end of the period of tower house construction, piracy was an integral part of the local economy for extensive areas of Irish western coastal regions. Presumably, this capitalised on an earlier trend making use of the myriad landing places, many of which were readily marked out by the presence of those tower houses. Customs and tolls from trading could be controlled by lords on an official basis as well as this theorised unofficial collection. For instance, in 1515 Gerald, Earl of Kildare, received the ports, creeks, fishings, maritime wreck, wharves, tolls and customs from merchandise, goods, and fish of Strangford town, Lough and Ardglass in County Down (*Red book of the earls of Kildare*). By the middle of the same century these rights were being distributed regularly by the Crown, including in 1558 to a William Brabazon (*Irish fiants*: vol. 1). In this part of the country, by the sixteenth century, the Crown therefore had enough control to extend this right.

Conclusion: The tower house in the 'glocal'

Examining the items most commonly found in trade accounts allows us to analyse how tower houses were the enablers of contact between Ireland and the wider world. As has been seen in the preceding chapters, exports could be housed within tower houses. These export goods were predominantly agricultural items, as elaborated in chapters 1 and 2. It was stated in the Introduction that one scholar viewed the tower house as the creation of a manorial economy (Colfer, 2013), but we have also witnessed that it was the surplus of this economy that enabled their proliferation over the course of over two centuries. We may need to rethink the agricultural manorial economy as inherently subsistence, for, as the documentation shows, ample excess was leaving the country every year. In turn, imports were in large part driven by tower-house-occupant demand: the elites of Ireland, who tended to reside in tower houses, consumed luxury items, and these were the mainstay of Irish imports. Salt and iron were another two major imports, and these were needed by those living around tower houses as well as those within them. Discussion in earlier chapters has shown how tower houses were involved in transport routes, including the movement of trade goods. Here, again, the issue of coastal trading was returned to, with it forming a significant, if under-documented, aspect of the successful support of international trade. Similarly, we have seen that inland communities were home to merchants who connected with the coastal port towns to bring trade to the interior. Trade, therefore, will have reached every tower house in Ireland.

It was through international trade that Irish people encountered the world beyond their daily living space. Foreign goods must have been noticeable even inside these daily living spaces, especially in the tower houses where the wealthier elements of late medieval society resided. Tower house inhabitants understood the world around them through their consumption of goods. In turn, they knew that the agricultural and fishing economy of the area where their castle was situated provided their social position. Over the course of the tower house period, people's world increased in size and scope. This is in large part owing to the complex economic connections linking tower houses with the ports, and thence to England and the continent. Further places were reached by Irish merchants, and goods of greater quality and range permeated the home market in turn. Although the evidence is still slight for regular contact beyond Iberia, perhaps some cargoes of hides were shipped to the Italian city-states and with the Hanseatic League. Ireland was very much a part of the medieval North Atlantic trading system. As the Middle Ages concluded, as the last geographic landmass in temperate waters, Ireland had a role to play in expanding European interests westwards and in integrating an Atlantic World.

The port towns are responsible for a high incidence of tower houses. Tower houses can be taken as a built manifestation of wealth from trade, including in such port towns as Galway and Youghal, where some still stand. Not many exceptions could be found to the statement that every nucleated settlement in late medieval Ireland featured at least one tower house. Not merely defensive residences, tower houses provided a multiplicity of functions from public and private meeting spaces to secure storage. It was not just the tower houses in nucleated settlements that had a role in trade and thus the larger world: rural maritime tower houses were frequently the sites of international exchange, if not trade in the strictest sense. With regularity, tower house lords in rural areas were given salt and wine in exchange for fishing rights by visiting vessels from England and continental Europe.

Another fascinating conclusion has been the evidence that ethnic and national differences were overlooked in order to participate in trade. This is not a new discovery: Kowaleski proposed that a common purpose among mariners cut across these lines and united them by occupation (Kowaleski, 2007). This may explain why previous scholars' attempts to distinguish tower house builders by correlating ethnicity with architecture have failed. The economic system behind international trade ensured inter-ethnic cooperation. A small cadre of wealthy merchant families residing in the port towns, many of whom we believe utilised tower houses as their places of residence and business, controlled links out of the country. However, their prosperity, alongside that of their towns, was dependent on a good relationship with the rural Gaelic-Irish and Anglo-Irish alike. Economic necessity and attractive profits led to interdependence between Gaelic-Irish and Anglo-Irish, which effectively removed ethnicity as an obstacle to doing business (O'Neill, 1987). In turn, the usefulness of the tower house in facilitating these interactions must be recognised, and interpreted as a sign of cultural co-existence, rather than the friction it is traditionally claimed they represent.

This chapter has shown that a lot more was going on than the historical record tells us. The documentation is biased in that it mostly survives only from the one English port of Bristol, and only in any detail from the late sixteenth century. Anomalous entries discussed above raise suspicions that Ireland was better integrated with the medieval global economy than scholars may have been willing to concede, or that the bias of the sources indicated. Trade also tells us about the rest of the medieval Irish socio-economic climate. It shows that fishing was a steadfast component of the economy. It provides further evidence that more cereal cultivation was being undertaken in the later Middle Ages than historians have recognised.

Tower houses represent increasing economic confidence – their boom correlates with the diversification of importation of luxury and manufactured goods. Many of these items were destined for the expanding ranks of the 'elites', including cadet branches of major medieval families and an emerging gentry class. As has consistently been seen, these people were displaying their social upward mobility through construction. In addition, there was increased percolation of consumption to new sectors of society, characterised by cheaper versions of consumer goods. Consumption and construction tied the Irish wealth-accruing classes with their European counterparts. The international socio-economic trends following the Black Death did not exclude this westernmost island. The difference between the new social classes in early modern capitalistic societies and their Irish cousins was that the Irish used the tower house as a visually understood manifestation of their statement of belonging to the world at large. The use of building to make such claims is not peculiar to Ireland; it is better understood within the more capitalistic Hanse, Italian city-states and the colonies. As this chapter has shown, even the geographically peripheral Irish knew how to harness primary economic activity for capitalistic profit. Proto-capitalistic trends were inclusive in their reach.

At the very end of their construction lives, tower houses found a useful function as outposts of colonisation. A central component of colonisation within Ireland was establishing new ports to rival the medieval ones. Colonisation also had an impact on what was being exported. Export goods were becoming more diverse but were markedly natural in origin – for example, horses and linen yarn appeared with increased regularity. Colonisation also affected how Ireland participated in trade routes. The seventeenth century saw the end of the three separate areas in the North Atlantic and Irish Sea of the early Middle Ages remarked upon by Hudson. Instead, Ireland became integrated within an Atlantic World economy. All of those who economically participated in Ireland, regardless of ethnicity, obviously saw the natural environment as something to be exploited for their own gain. Although colonisation is often credited with the destruction of the Irish woods, the exploitation of natural resources had a long and profitable history in Ireland well before this event. Although environmental resource exploitation did not reach the critical levels of today (Nedkvitne, 2016), that is probably only because of a lack of technological capability and low population levels, rather than an interest in environmental sustainability. Irish exports were nigh exclusively natural raw materials, while the country's imports had manufactured goods as a significant component. This indicates that people had sufficient income from natural resources that they were not forced into industrialisation, beyond the manufacture of specific items as cloth and mantles, whose peculiarly Irish style was part of their market appeal beyond the island. Tower houses, we have seen throughout this book, were exceptionally well placed to enable this environmental exploitation and maximise financial profit.

Conclusion: The social, economic and environmental contexts of the Irish tower house

This book, the first to ever be published focusing solely on the tower house, has spent little time describing its architecture or attempting a typology. This may cause consternation among some, but an overarching aim has been to broaden the relevance and appeal of the tower house outside of a narrow group of castle enthusiasts. Tower houses are a remarkable monument type; their number and distribution enables us to study the worldview and agency of medieval and early modern people from a variety of social backgrounds. We have been able to catch an elusive glimpse of the lives of lordly elites, merchants, peasants and fishermen. A multiplicity of functions could be encompassed by the tower house, affecting both its residents and those around it. It is crucial that we contemplate all of these possible functions alongside one another and consider how they overlap, otherwise we miss what makes tower houses fascinating buildings. They served diverse roles in their contemporary societies, and this multiplicity is believed to be the reason behind their success.

Tower houses are present in all settlement types from both late medieval and early modern Ireland. They have been most studied in rural settlement, and could be well adapted to such a context. We find them being constructed by Gaelic-Irish, Anglo-Irish and early modern settler. This might reflect similarity in usage not just of the building form, but also the economic basis. It is possible that there was little difference between the agricultural practices of the Gaelic-Irish and Anglo-Irish by the later Middle Ages, when we consider the types of exports leaving the country, as discussed in chapter 6, alongside the prevalence of water mills, considered in chapter 2. Combined, this evidence suggests the continuation of a mixed agricultural economy rather than a wholesale switch to pastoralism. It was tentatively proposed that three-field crop rotation was not practised as part of this mixed agriculture, but instead the rundale system was more common, based on the importation of legumes. Perhaps further study through palynology will provide a clearer answer to this question. This was a kind of adapted manorial economy, evolving from Anglo-Irish areas in the high Middle Ages. However, tower houses are known from places where emphasis was on pastoral agriculture and fishing. A diversified agricultural base may have provided the income necessary to build in stone. The rural context for the tower house therefore seems to be as basic and as general as anywhere with sufficient economic activity to produce surplus. This reflects the same flexibility in purpose of the tower house that was expressed in their sheer numbers.

As well as this long-established relationship with rural settlement and agriculture, the social context to tower houses benefited from the governmental laxity of the later Middle Ages, though not the open warfare of the Tudor Conquest. There was more than simple, low-level endemic violence, characterised by raiding, in this era. Instability from a lack of authoritative central government meant that there was no supervision of what were usually Crown rights in other places. Tower house inhabitants made significant income from seemingly inconsequential enterprise that is under-represented in both the archaeological and historical records. In particular, attractive levels of income could come from control of the fishing industry and from the imposition of tolls wherever movement was restricted. There is also the distinct possibility that smuggling between continental Europe and Ireland, based at the tower houses, was lucrative. Control of these water resources was often in the hands of lords, not just religious landowners as has been emphasised in other European-based studies. Another peculiarity is that commercial networks were not controlled solely by merchants, or even at the local level by artisans. Instead, participation may have been wider, with gentry and nobility alike holding an income base much more diverse than their high medieval castle-building contemporaries. Unlike at high medieval elite castle sites outside Ireland, tower house dwellers maintained fish weirs and fish traps rather than fishponds. The traps and weirs served much the same symbolism as the ponds, but were cheaper and easier to manage and produced enough fish to sell or lease out the rights. Defensive concerns have been over-valued when discussing the interaction between tower houses and water. The best examples of this are the tower houses following the Pale boundary. This alignment with the stated extent of the Pale has led to the interpretation that they were located for protection. What has been largely ignored is that much of the Pale follows important medieval rivers like the Boyne and Liffey. As is showcased here, rivers were major generators of wealth and power in medieval Ireland, therefore we cannot simply equate the locations of these sites to defence of the remnants of the Anglo-Irish colony. Their contexts are far more complex.

Alongside the more numerous rural tower houses, this book has also discussed urban tower houses. One of the issues surrounding the study of these buildings has been the early dates attributed to them (Bradley and Murtagh, 2003), which are in advance of the established tower house chronology. This has led to scholars categorising these early examples as other than tower houses, using terms including 'town houses'. Many are listed in the ASI as 'house – fortified house'. They have fallen foul of the same enthusiasm for categorisation held by many archaeologists and architectural historians. It is contended here that the functions of these early urban examples were the same as the later tower houses universally recognised as such. Several scholars have debated the origins of tower houses, and while there is largely agreement as to the likelihood of their existence prior to the early fifteenth century, proof of this has been frustratingly elusive. It is suggested here that we turn to the towns for an answer. The functionality of mural towers could have been residential and overall very similar to tower houses, as was illustrated by the usage of the Quay Tower in Youghal. We have been willing to concede that tower houses were inspired by gatehouses in high medieval masonry castles, but are reluctant to accord the status of 'castle' to more modest forms of fortification. This raises yet another issue – that we tend to view castles as inherently private in nature, and do not attribute the term to communal defences. Rather than seeing these two roles as dichotomous, we should view them as points along a spectrum that reflects real-life use. Social status may have accompanied a contribution to a town's communal defence, in that it reflected a commitment to the good of the town. Such a perception may have been especially relevant to those involved in town government, or those looking for favour from the town, as merchants would have been.

McNeill (1997) has commented that it appeared unlikely that there was sufficient wealth in small Irish towns to warrant as many tower houses as there were, giving the specific examples of Ardee and Carlingford, both in County Louth. Yet this study has shown that income was generated from a multiplicity of sources, and might have been sufficient to support tower house construction even in what appear to be unfavourable circumstances. These tower houses in small towns were part of the web of interconnections between rural and urban Ireland. Goods were transported along riverine, maritime and terrestrial routeways, and tower houses were located all along these to control and assist movement. In all tower house locations, defended storage areas could be provided, either interior or exterior but within the castle complex.

Commercial spaces, too, could be supplied at many. This enabled the control of trade goods along their entire journey, beginning with their exploitation through farming or fishing, through to their being bulked for ship cargo. Throughout this process, the tower house had connections with the outside world; such connections could be distant and indirect, but contact was filtered through these routes.

Tower houses, therefore, are visual manifestations of economic confidence among all ethnicities in Ireland. As well as controlling the landscape they exploited, they display a belief in the ability to master this control and this landscape. We might go so far as to state that they are overt signs of conspicuous consumption, and that this consumption was common across the rural–urban 'divide'. Chapter 6 looked at what items were leaving and entering Ireland, and highlighted some of the ways these affected the inhabitants of tower houses. Irish imports were dominated by manufactured and luxury goods. Their purchasers must have been numerous among the tower house class, for they represent the wealthiest across the country and it is logical to conclude that the wealthiest purchased the most. This consumption was not limited to townspeople; merchants were located inland, too, and had well-established relationships with ports. Consequently, luxury goods made their way across the island, and may even have reflected a shared material culture (Flavin, 2011). Small items would have been displayed within tower houses and upon their occupants, again making a visual statement of those occupants' belonging in the world and among the community of tower house builders. There again does not seem to have been an ethnic distinction, with suggestions that a typically 'Irish' style was dominant even towards the end of the sixteenth century, when we might anticipate changes in material culture accompanying warfare and colonisation (ibid.). Tower houses can be included in this visible statement of an Irish style of consumption and display.

Most of the documented goods reached Ireland, and the tower houses, from England. But this is reflective of a documentary bias rather than reality on the ground. Conclusive evidence for extensive economic connections outside the Irish Sea zone is minimal, but there are some tantalising hints. These indicate that there was contact with France and Iberia in particular, and with Italy and Flanders possibly to a lesser degree. Later in the tower house era, Ireland increasingly became part of an Atlantic World, with a role in supporting transatlantic travel, but also sharing colonisers with the New World. Despite being geographically on the western periphery of Europe, it is not accurate to describe late medieval and early modern Ireland as socially, economically or environmentally peripheral. Instead, it was well integrated within the Irish Sea region in particular, but also with economic powerhouses located

Conclusion

further away. Tower houses provide a fantastic example of the 'glocal', a theme increasingly of interest to academics of the Middle Ages.

A number of hypotheses were presented in the Introduction that the rest of the book aimed to address. It remains to assess how successful that goal has been. Perhaps foremost was the contention that a multidisciplinary methodology could illuminate an under-documented period of history. Historical documents and the archaeological record, particularly fieldwork at over two hundred individual tower house sites, were primarily utilised. Methods and theories from geography, especially historical geography, and art history were also employed to a lesser extent. The destruction of historical records has led to an emphasis among historians of medieval Ireland on religion and politics. However, it has been possible to develop more information on economic activity using the few surviving trade materials in conjunction with assessment adapted from landscape archaeology. Likewise, a combination of tools can tell us about agricultural practices. However, in this area we come across one of the biggest obstacles to interdisciplinarity – when the sources contradict one another. With careful reasoning and assessment of the benefits and limitations of each, it is usually possible to forge a median path. Indeed, often the bias of one source type complements the other. The further upside of using tower houses to conduct this methodological assessment is that they provide concrete points upon which to focus efforts. They also enable precision in making conclusions, since specifics and examples can be called upon. Despite the successes in this regard presented here, it is imperative that the methodology be developed and tested by other scholars working in fields with similar limitations. They might feel inspired by the confidence of tower house builders to engage in forms of economic participation not previously their remit in tackling historical data sources or archaeological sites usually outside their purview.

Turning to the building form itself, it was initially proposed that tower houses were physical manifestations of a more diverse society in the era following the Black Death. This more complex society, not simply the three estates never leaving their narrow occupational remits, also had more money than before. People chose to make statements through building projects that would be immediately understood by their contemporaries. There may have been few restrictions on this desire for monumentality, aside from potentially the will of a more powerful lord, or the size of a pre-existing urban land plot, as discussed in chapter 5. In the countryside, the only physical limitation may have been the location of a parish church and perhaps an earlier castle. The placement of these two earlier features might explain possible site migration, whereby a tower house was situated closer to peasant settlement, as presented in chapter 1. These tower houses were built by anyone who could afford the outlay, whether they were local lord, churchman or merchant. Furthermore, the outlay may only have been temporary, if the building were positioned so as to generate some continued income, such as through tolls.

In this way, a tower house was also an investment. It was frequently a real investment, but it could also be one figuratively, such as in the form of conspicuous consumption. A theme running throughout this book has been the eagerness with which those who participated in the Irish economy, regardless of their ethnicity or social background, viewed the natural environment as something to be exploited for profit. Tower houses are distributed across the country in places where they were proximal to the most valuable raw materials. As many have pointed out before, castles in Ireland are very rarely located more than five hundred metres above sea level, beyond which the productivity of the land was low. It could well be, too, that with population decline after the Black Death, previously marginal uplands could be largely abandoned. Tower houses located at lower altitudes and in more fertile landscapes reflect mixed agriculture, owing to less demographic pressure to retain land suitable for crop growing exclusively for that purpose.

Location aside, the building itself could be used in many different ways. This was particularly true of the ground floor, even if there were not two entrances indicating split usage in function. The placement and orientation of the more ornamental features also reflect both literal and figurative investment. We often find the largest and most impressive windows overlooking the places where control could be exerted, including ferry crossing points and navigable river stretches, but also from where these architectural features could be best viewed by those outside the castle. Often this control of view incorporated an aesthetically pleasing landscape, pleasant for the residents and their guests looking out from the hall at a height. Proposing that tower houses were used as statements of social belonging and status acquisition is nothing new. Both material culture and the built environment have been seized as means of displaying social prominence and the holder's view of their position in the world throughout time and place.

These displays of social and economic confidence are closely interlinked, therefore. Not always have such actions have been taken as representative of the Middle Ages. Instead, there is usually more willingness to view these in association with colonisation in the early modern globe. The argument presented here that they do represent confidence can consequently be interpreted in several ways. Tower houses could represent a transition from medieval to modern. Even removing the sixteenth- and seventeenth-century colonists from the equation, the buildings do reflect new landholders and landholding patterns. They might also reflect a new post-plague reality of breakdown between the social estates that had characterised the feudal era. Maybe that description was always inaccurate when applied to medieval Ireland. Certainly, when we look at the tower house, the activity of the medieval 'those who work' is well represented. The display of confidence could be a trend peculiar to Ireland. Ireland, after all, was colonised in the high Middle Ages by the Anglo-Normans, an event not experienced in most other parts of Europe. Among academics today, some refer to Ireland's modern socio-political landscape as 'post-colonial', which is more in common with other colonised parts of the early modern globe than Europe.

There is also evidence weighing against the dominance of modern features during this transition. It is evident that much of what we have considered 'high medieval' in character continued in use well into the later Middle Ages. The most overt manifestation of this is, of course, in the use of an accepted vocabulary of castle architecture in new buildings (i.e. the tower house itself). This is in a period past the time when much of England and continental Europe had moved beyond castle building, and instead their elites were constructing undefended mansion houses. To continue utilising a medieval architectural form indicates a medieval outlook and view of oneself in the world. The economy of Ireland also remained distinctively medieval, with raw materials and partly worked goods dominating exports, arguably until the second half of the seventeenth century, though that was changing in certain places before this date.

The modern legacy of the tower house

Tower houses were constructed in decreasing numbers after the first decade of the seventeenth century. Few are known to have been constructed in the 1630s (for a discussion of the decline in popularity see McAlister (2015)). Of course, just because tower houses were no longer being built by the mid-seventeenth century does not automatically mean that they were also no longer occupied. Instead, it is extremely likely that many tower houses continued to be inhabited and, in many cases, updated for years after. Of course, there is the oft-heard story that Cromwell's forces obliterated this or that castle. While documented in some cases, most of this is folklore and reflects the low opinion held of the man across Ireland.

Determining dates of eventual abandonment is difficult and these seem to have varied widely. Presumably, many tower houses were abandoned even in the era during which they were constructed. The later history of most is not documented, though for a few it is, and we can estimate longevity if a tower house was built into another, later building. The antiquarian writers have provided much of the historical evidence for tower house occupation in the modern period, as they tended to comment if a family was still using its tower house as this fell within their sphere of interest. For example, William Wilde wrote in 1849 that Liscartan Castle in County Meath was still partially occupied, and even sketched a picture of how it looked. Based on Smith's description of Kilclief Castle, County Down, in 1744 as being 'entire' and roofed with thatch, it would appear that this tower house was still in use in the mid-eighteenth century (1744: 24). The same author wrote that Portaferry Castle in County Down was 'inhabited by Andrew Savage' (*ibid.*: 46). Other written sources might testify to occupation. In the case of Quoile Castle, County Down, a wall tablet located in the church at nearby Saul was erected in memory of John West, who died 16 February 1866, the 'son of John West, born in Quoile castle, 1727, died 1787' (Jope, 1966: 248). Thus it appears that the West family occupied Quoile Castle at least into the eighteenth century.

We can also easily look for architectural evidence of post-medieval occupation. As an example, Walshestown Castle in County Down is both confirmed by the antiquarian writer Samuel Lewis as being the residence of one R. F. Anderson at the time of his writing in 1837 and has architectural remnants of this inhabitation. The windows in Walshestown Castle were expanded from their medieval appearance and sash windows were inserted, presumably around the time that it was occupied by Anderson. Based on site survey, Walshestown Castle formed a feature within the once-impressive Victorian gardens attached to Myra House. It appears likely that the tower house was used recreationally by the occupants of the later 'big house'. The extensive modernisation undertaken at some point in the 1800s at Kirkistown Castle, again in County Down, likewise implies later occupation. This modernisation was presumably to allow for continued occupation, as in 1744 it was the residence of Mrs Lucy Magil, 'the Widow Savage' (Smith, 1744: 67). Modern comforts were added to this tower house, coincidentally also one of the last dateable tower houses as it was constructed in 1622, including inserting sash windows and fireplaces, redecoration in pseudo-Gothic style, removal of spiral stairs for straight stairways, a new porch, new room subdivision, and ill-fated attempts to buttress the tower against subsidence (Jope, 1966).

An interesting future project, perhaps well suited for postgraduate research, would be to examine occupation patterns of castles and tower houses in the modern era. From a handful of references to widows living in tower houses, while the rest of the family lived in the proximal 'big house', they may have found particular usage as dower houses. This

Conclusion

C.1 Leamaneh Castle in County Clare is one of many tower houses with a later building attached. In this case, part of the tower house has been rebuilt into the early modern fortified house to the left of the image. Leamaneh commanded a designed landscape, including fishponds.

repurposing might be evident countrywide, as it was observed in County Down during doctoral research by this author and also in the barony of Shanid, County Limerick, by Mac Curtain (1988).

A sizeable cohort of tower houses have an early-modern-period building attached to them, whether simply as an add-on with entrances knocked through (as at Ballinlaw Castle, County Kilkenny) or with a more concerted effort at integration (as at Leamaneh Castle, County Clare; see figure C.1). This enabled the tower house to readily adapt to more modern living standards and conveniences, while still providing an image of a long-standing connection and claim to the land. This claim of longevity was especially important in Gaelic-Irish society, where 'having demonstrable connections through time with the place where you lived was an essential social value' (FitzPatrick, 2009). Another fascinating study would be to examine the use of later building additions by the New English as opposed to the Gaelic-Irish, to determine to what extent these changes reflect ethnicity. Distribution across the country would also be an enlightening investigation. In County Meath, for instance, there is a noteworthy element of site continuity both from the high to later Middle Ages, and from then on into the early modern period. Several tower houses in Meath are located near earlier medieval earthwork castles. In the case of Rathmore, the tower house is built into the north side of a motte and is entered from it at first-floor level. A number of tower houses are attached to later stone houses, most of these being of seventeenth- and eighteenth-century date. Examples include Athlumney and Carrickdexter, which were expanded in these later centuries with larger stone houses built onto the original tower houses.

It is very difficult to enumerate the instances where a later building contains small remnants of an earlier tower house as part of its fabric. It is entirely possible that most people living in such houses have no idea that some elements are medieval in date, especially if no recognisable features are visible. In some cases there is awareness thanks to continued family occupation or particular interest in house history, such as at Ballyduff in County Kilkenny and Ballymaloe in County Cork. The best means of identifying these sites might be through building survey, but this would be hard to implement and ascribe a particular direction to.

At several points in this book the high level of tower house destruction has been raised. This destruction was particularly far-reaching in urban contexts and in counties like Meath and Kildare, which have both excellent farmland and proximity to Dublin. The appeal of dismantling tower houses will have been their excellent building stone. Carved and designed features may have been removed for display inside modern 'big houses', a complaint heard with frequency during fieldwork from farmers with tower houses on their land.

Of those still standing, the largest number of tower houses today are within agricultural communities and often within farmyards. In this way, their original rural context has not altered much. These farmyard tower houses are in varying states of preservation. They are regularly used as agricultural out-buildings. Throughout the course of fieldwork, farmers expressed frustration over their attempts to 'improve' the buildings. Much of this was well intentioned on both sides: the farmers wished to restore something of the old impressiveness of the building, while the Monuments Service needs to ensure that damage is not inflicted unwittingly. It is fortunate that most landowners have an interest in their built heritage, but less so that they are unsure as to what actions they can take. Perhaps an educational-outreach campaign would be beneficial, focusing on what protective measures could be taken by landowners with minimal effort and expense. The National Monuments Service already maintains a presence at major agricultural events, and published a series on monuments in the *Farmer's Journal* (National Monuments Service, 2012). This included a one-page article on tower houses, though unfortunately there was little on good management practices ('Ireland's Tower Houses'). Preservation is a worthy goal, though restoration is problematic. It is difficult to ensure the careful inclusion of original features while also inserting modern conveniences, and to enact this precise balance requires enormous financial investment.

Funding for archaeological sites is also currently limited, and it remains to be seen how effective it is. The Green, low-carbon, agri-environment (GLAS) scheme is the current agri-environment scheme that is part of the Rural Development Programme 2014–20. The overall goal of the programme is to 'address the cross-cutting objectives of climate change, water quality, and biodiversity' (*GLAS – proposed new agri-environment scheme*). Within this framework, archaeological sites have low priority, and only rank at all if the farm fits the environmental criteria. Obviously, the number of tower houses that can benefit from this scheme will be small. The financial recompense for those participating is also minimal, with payments of around €120 to €146. Regardless, it would be illuminating for future preservation efforts to accurately gauge the effectiveness of the GLAS scheme.

Future research directions

Castles, and tower houses as part of the castle grouping, loom large in the public imagination. This is especially true in Ireland today, as so many of them are easily visible from major routeways, whether that be motorway or train line. Tower houses could therefore provide an excellent educational tool for the public, and this element of ensuring their preservation should form a priority of future research efforts. It would be especially beneficial and effective if this could be accomplished in conjunction with state organisations.

Another extremely worthwhile future project would be to examine the Irish tower house within its European and worldwide context. Tower houses have suffered too long from a type of Irish exceptionalism, whereas we know that similar small towers were built across Europe and in other global regions. The intention of chapter 6 is to assist in setting the stage for such an expanded study. The possibilities of international comparison have been highlighted by recent conferences, and resulting publications like Oram's edited volume based on two of the Tower Studies conferences (2015). A start could be readily made by first undertaking nuanced comparison with the already well-studied towers from Scotland and the north of England, before expanding the remit geographically further. In particular, this scholar posits that if we take a maritime and economic perspective across these tower distributions, some extremely insightful conclusions could be made about shared lived experience across the European Middle Ages and beyond.

This leads well into a theory proposed above that deserves rigorous testing: that tower houses display economic confidence more characteristic of the colonial early modern globe than the medieval. This could indicate that social structures in late medieval Europe were drastically shaken by demographic shifts following the Black Death, perhaps even more so than currently recognised. More work could examine the impact on landholding patterns and standards of living, particularly from an archaeological-science perspective. Pollen analysis and isotope studies more overtly focussing on identifying landscape alteration in the later Middle Ages could remove a lot of ambiguity among historians over economic transformations. Similarly, osteological and isotopic studies of late medieval skeletal remains seeking to identify changes in lifestyle could transform our long-held beliefs regarding the lived experience. It would be even more insightful were these conclusions made with comparison to other parts of Europe, since Ireland had an established history of colonisation by the end of the Middle Ages. In 1988, Anngret Simms attempted a comparison between high medieval Irish colonisation and that in the Baltic and Eastern Europe (1988a). It is unfortunate that this study has not been much advanced in the last thirty years. It is suggested that tower houses could prove an enlightening vehicle to extend this work, since, as has been witnessed here, they provide a focal point upon which to focus investigations and make precise observations of change in their vicinity.

Many readers will no doubt have noticed the lack of detailed consideration of the use of tower houses by members of the church and other religious personages and institutions. To include this would have made the book simply too broad in scope, as a significant minority within the examined corpus of tower houses were located in association with a religious foundation. A complication arises in that landholdings were not consistently in either religious or secular hands throughout the period of tower house construction. Even leaving the major event of the Dissolution of the Monasteries aside, which brought significant previously religious lands into lay possession, the primary-source research conducted here has indicated that land was frequently leased by religious houses to local lords or merchants, and granted in reverse. In consequence, Irish landholding of the fourteenth to seventeenth centuries was fluid, and it was predominantly undocumented. Reactions to the Henrician Reformation could be ably assessed using tower houses. Liddiard (2005) observed in England that church control of extensive tracts of land tended to lower castle numbers. This may be the pattern in Ireland, too, but unlike in most parts of England castles were still being constructed past the mid-sixteenth century. It seems reasonable to suggest that the

Dissolution of the Monasteries might have encouraged tower house building, since it brought new land to the secular market.

There are a number of examples of tower houses built on formerly monastic land that we already are aware of, such as Bective in County Meath, subject of recent excavation and publication by Geraldine and Matthew Stout, and Annamult in County Kilkenny. Annamult Castle was constructed on the monastic lands of Graiguenamanagh Cistercian house, though not in the best location within that property. An issue here would be securely dating the tower houses to either before or after the mid-sixteenth century. The benefit of the Stouts' work has been that the evidence from excavation has been brought to bear (Stout and Stout, 2016). We also need to acknowledge that many religious men will have desired to have a tower house, if their position brought them sufficient status and wealth. Good examples of this are Kilclief in County Down, built by the bishop of Down, and Mountgarrett in County Wexford, constructed by the bishop of Ferns. This probably explains the tower-house-type structures attached to the end of a few churches, or found within mere metres of them. Cross East in County Mayo is a residential church tower attached to a medieval church which has been ascribed as a tower house in the ASI, while Cashelboy Castle in County Sligo is located only just over five metres from the wall enclosing a graveyard and ruined medieval church. A study of religious tower houses would consequently be a valuable contribution to the literature. Religious and secular architectural styles might hugely overlap in the later Middle Ages, and there has even been some confusion of church towers with tower houses in the past. Bonde (1994) has written of fortified churches, and has argued that much that is accepted as castle architecture – for example, machicolations – had an earlier use in religious architecture.

Again, more recognised outside of Ireland are deliberately designed landscapes around castles. To date, few apart from O'Keeffe have attempted to identify designed landscapes at Irish castles, and even less attention has been paid to their possible existence at tower houses. Yet, as we have seen here, tower house occupants were exceptionally canny when it came to controlling their surrounding landscapes and at siting their buildings so as to maximise profits. It is no great stretch of the imagination, therefore, to suggest that designed landscapes existed at tower houses. Indeed, one possible designed landscape has been identified by this author at Kilcrea Castle in County Cork, in association with the Franciscan friary, and will be the subject of a forthcoming article. One possibility to be explored in this work is the role of buildings as displays of patronage: Kilcrea, like Claregalway Castle in County Galway, is located next to a Franciscan house, and so the foundation of a mendicant order in tandem with the tower house may be conveying a dual social and religious message.

The tower house was a remarkable building. Surviving examples may not look like much today, in their various ruined conditions, and indeed their architectural plainness and small size can encourage their dismissal. Instead, this volume has showcased the variety of functions this simple building could perform within late medieval Irish society. Tower houses were both rural and urban, occupied by lords and merchants, and utilised by both Anglo-Irish and Gaelic-Irish. Not only did they transcend ethnicity and socio-economic status, they played a formidable role in connecting medieval Ireland to its place in the world.

Appendix: Sites referred to in text

Tower house name	County	Sites and Monuments Record code
Anbally	Galway	GA057-001----
Annamult	Kilkenny	KK023-084001-
Ardee (extra-mural)	Louth	LH017-009----
Ardkeen	Down	DOW 025:005
Ardmayle	Tipperary	TS052-034009-
Athlumney	Meath	ME025-032001-
Audley's	Down	DOW 031:006
Aughnanure	Galway	GA054-002----
Ballingarry	Limerick	LI029-106----
Ballinlaw	Kilkenny	KK044-012001-
Ballyduff	Kilkenny	KK032-006----
Ballyhack	Wexford	WX044-009001-
Ballymaloe	Cork	CO089-004001-
Ballynacarriga	Cork	CO108-051003-
Ballynahinch	Tipperary	TS060-059001-
Bangor	Down	DOW 002:003
Barryscourt	Cork	CO075-018001-
Bective	Meath	ME031-026001-
Belvelly	Cork	CO075-030----
Bourchier's/Lough Gur	Limerick	LI032-022034-
Brady's, Thomastown	Kilkenny	KK028-040010-
Bridge/Sweetman's, Thomastown	Kilkenny	KK028-040005-
Brownsford	Kilkenny	KK033-028001-

Tower house name	County	Sites and Monuments Record code
Bullock Harbour	Dublin	DU023-020001-
Bunratty	Clare	CL062-001004-
Buttevant	Cork	CO017-053002-
Camphire	Waterford	WA029-033----
Carrickdexter/Slanecastle Demesne	Meath	ME019-033002-
Carrick-on-Suir	Tipperary	TS085-004001-
Carrigafoyle	Kerry	KE002-045----
Carrowbrickeen	Sligo	SL013-029002-
Cashelboy	Sligo	SL018-029001-
Cashlaundarragh	Galway	GA058-045001-
Castle Island	Down	DOW 031:034
Castleboy	Down	DOW 025:016
Castlejordan	Meath	ME052-005---- ME052-004----
Castlelake	Tipperary	TS060-116001-
Causestown	Meath	ME029-010----
Claregalway	Galway	GA070-036----
Conna	Cork	CO046-001----
Conva	Cork	CO034-037001-
Coolhill	Kilkenny	KK033-027001-
Cowd, Ardglass	Down	DOW 045:023
Cratloekeel	Clare	CL062-018----
Cratloemoyle	Clare	CL062-021----
Cross East	Mayo	MA121-107002-
Dalkey	Dublin	DU023-023014- DU023-023010-
Dardistown	Westmeath	WM013-099----
Derrymaclaughna	Galway	GA070-065001-
Donore	Meath	ME041-008----
Doolin	Clare	CL008-059002-
Doonnagore	Clare	CL008-087001-
Downmacpatrick	Cork	CO137-009001-
Dowth	Meath	ME020-018----
Dún na Seád/Baltimore	Cork	CO150-036002-

Appendix

Tower house name	County	Sites and Monuments Record code
Dunboy	Cork	CO128-001002-
Dunmanus	Cork	CO139-015----
Dunmoe	Meath	ME025-018002-
Dunnaman	Limerick	LI030-012----
Dysart	Kilkenny	KK032-004003-
Dysert O'Dea	Clare	CL025-095002-
Easky	Sligo	SL011-020----
Fennor	Meath	ME019-036002-
Ferrycarrig	Wexford	WX037-027----
Fethard	Tipperary	TS070-040005- TS070-040002-
Fiddaun	Galway	GA128-052----
Fraine	Meath	ME029-017----
Galway (city)	Galway	GA094-100044-
Glenogra	Limerick	LI031-038004-
Glin	Limerick	LI017-022001-
Golden	Tipperary	TS060-097001-
Hatch's, Ardee	Louth	LH017-101015-
Jordan's, Ardglass	Down	DOW 045:020
Kilclief	Down	DOW 031:006
Kilcolman	Cork	CO017-041001-
Kilcrea	Cork	CO084-022001-
Killeen	Meath	ME038-012----
Killegland	Meath	ME045-005----
Killyleagh	Down	DOW 024:030
Kilmallock	Limerick	LI047-022008-
Kilteel	Kildare	KD020-006----
Kinsale	Cork	CO112-034006-
Kirkistown	Down	DOW 025:007
Knockainy	Limerick	LI032-141003- LI032-141002-
Leamaneh	Clare	CL016-032002-
Leighlinbridge	Carlow	CW012-070003-
Liscartan	Meath	ME025-009001-

Tower house name	County	Sites and Monuments Record code
Lisfinny	Waterford	WA028-013----
Lynch's, Galway (city)	Galway	GA094-100043-
Mahee	Down	DOW 017:004
Margaret's, Ardglass	Down	DOW 045:022
Minard's	Kerry	KE054-063----
Mountgarrett	Wexford	WX029-009----
Muckinish East	Clare	CL003-008002-
Muckinish West	Clare	CL003-002----
Nangle's, Trim	Meath	ME036-049013-
Newark/Ardglass	Down	DOW 045:021
Newcastle Lyons	Dublin	DU021-017002- DU020-003006- DU020-003007-
Newhaggard	Meath	ME036-017----
Newstone	Meath	ME003-017002-
Newtown Trim	Meath	ME036-049013-
Newtown Trim/Saintjohns	Meath	ME036-049012-
Nook	Wexford	WX044-001----
Oldcourt	Cork	CO141-116----
Oranmore	Galway	GA095-110----
Portaferry	Down	DOW 032:003
Poulakerry	Tipperary	TS084-019----
Quoile	Down	DOW 031:009
Rathcannon	Limerick	LI039-027002-
Rathmore	Meath	ME024-018001-
Rathvilly	Carlow	CW004-009----
Ringhaddy	Down	DOW 024:012
Ringrone	Cork	CO125-001----
Scurlockstown	Meath	ME037-011----
Ship-pool	Cork	CO111-010----
Sketrick	Down	DOW 017:008
St. Leger's, Ardee	Louth	LH017-101018-
Strancally	Waterford	WA034-034----
Strangford	Down	DOW 032:001

Appendix

Tower house name	County	Sites and Monuments Record code
Taaffe's, Carlingford	Louth	LH005-042005-
Temple Michaell	Waterford	WA037-014001-
The Mint, Carlingford	Louth	LH005-042008-
Old Tholsel, Drogheda	Meath	LH024-041006-
Threecastles	Wicklow	WI005-031----
Walshestown	Down	DOW 031:008
White, Athy	Kildare	KD035-022010-
Youghal	Cork	CO067-029008-

References

Primary sources

1641 depositions online transcripts, www.1641.tcd.ie, accessed 27 November 2018.
Annals of the four masters, https://celt.ucc.ie//published/T100005A/index.html, accessed 20 March 2018. Cited as AFM.
Annals of Ulster, https://celt.ucc.ie/published/T100001A/index.html, accessed 20 March 2018. Cited as AU.
Archives of the municipal corporation of Waterford, in the manuscripts of the marquis of Ormonde, the earl of Fingall, the corporations of Waterford, Galway, &c., ed. John T. Gilbert, HMC 10th report, appendix, part v, (London: Her Majesty's Stationery Office (HMSO), 1885). Cited as *Archives of the municipal corporation of Waterford*.
Archives of the town of Galway, in the manuscripts of the marquis of Ormonde, the earl of Fingall, the corporations of Waterford, Galway, &c., ed. John T. Gilbert, HMC 10th report, appendix, part v (London: HMSO, 1885). Cited as *Archives of the town of Galway*.
Bodley, Sir Josias. *A visit to Lecale, in the County of Down, in the year 1602–3*, https://celt.ucc.ie//published/T100074/index.html, accessed 22 March 2018. Cited as Bodley.
Bristol's trade with Ireland and the continent 1503–1601: The evidence of the Exchequer customs accounts, eds Susan Flavin and Evan T. Jones (Dublin: Four Courts Press, 2009). Cited as *Bristol's trade with Ireland*.
Calendar of ancient records of Dublin in the possession of the municipal corporation of that city, ed. John T. Gilbert (Dublin: Joseph Dollard, 1889). Cited as *Calendar of ancient records of Dublin*.
A calendar of material relating to Ireland from the High Court of Admiralty examinations, ed. John C. Appleby (Dublin: Irish Manuscripts Commission, 1992). Cited as *Admiralty examinations*.
Calendar of Ormond deeds, 6 vols, ed. Edmund Curtis (Dublin: Irish Manuscripts Commission, 1932–43), www.irishmanuscripts.ie/servlet/Controller?action=digitisation_backlist, accessed 3 March 2018.
Calendar of state papers relating to Ireland, 11 vols (London: HMSO, 1860–1912), all available at https://archive.org. Cited as CSPI.
Calendar of state papers Ireland Tudor period 1571–1575, ed. Mary O'Dowd (Kew and Dublin: Public Record Office and Irish Manuscripts Commission, 2000). Cited as CSPI Tudor.

References

Calendar of the Carew manuscripts: 1575–1588, https://play.google.com/books/reader?id=KwMVAAAAQAAJ&printsec=frontcover&output=reader&hl=en&pg=GBS.PR23, accessed 11 March 2018.

Calendar of the Gormanston register circa 1175–1397: From the original in the possession of the right honourable the viscount of Gormanston, eds James Mills and M. J. McEnery (Dublin: Royal Society of Antiquaries of Ireland, 1916). Cited as *Calendar of the Gormanston register*.

Calendar of the justiciary rolls, or, Proceedings in the court of the justiciar of Ireland preserved in the Public Record Office of Ireland, Edward I, part 2 (1305–1307), ed. James Mills (London: HMSO, 1914). Cited as *Calendar of the justiciary rolls*.

Calendar of the patent rolls preserved in the Public Record Office: Richard II, vol. 5 1391–6 (London: HMSO, 1905), https://babel.hathitrust.org/cgi/pt?id=mdp.39015008966072;view=1up;seq=7, accessed 23 March 2018. Cited as *Calendar of the patent rolls*.

Chester customs accounts 1301–1566, ed. K. P. Wilson (Liverpool: Record Society of Lancashire and Cheshire, 1969).

The Civil survey, A.D. 1654–1656, 10 vols, ed. Robert C. Simington (Dublin: Irish Manuscripts Commission, 1931–61). Cited as *Civil survey*.

Coroner's records, in Emilie Amt (ed.), *Women's lives in medieval Europe: A sourcebook*, 2nd ed. (Abingdon: Routledge, 2010), pp. 155–7.

Crown surveys of lands 1540–41 with the Kildare rental begun 1518, ed. Gearóid Mac Niocaill (Dublin: Irish Manuscripts Commission, 1992). Cited as *Crown surveys of lands*.

Desmond survey, https://celt.ucc.ie//published/E580000-001/index.html, accessed 9 March 2018.

Documents illustrating the overseas trade of Bristol in the sixteenth century, ed. Jean Vanes (Bristol: Bristol Record Society, 1979). Cited as *Documents illustrating the overseas trade*.

Dowdall deeds, eds Charles McNeill and A. J. Otway-Ruthven (Dublin: Irish Manuscripts Commission, 1960).

The Down survey of Ireland, http://downsurvey.tcd.ie/down-survey-maps.php, accessed 20 January 2018. Cited as *Down survey*.

Extents of Irish monastic possessions, 1540–1541 from manuscripts in the Public Record Office, London, ed. Newport B. White (Dublin: Stationery Office, 1943). Cited as *Extents of Irish monastic possessions*.

Gernon, Luke. *A discourse of Ireland, anno 1620*, ed. Caesar Litton Falkiner, Corpus of Electronic Texts ed., www.ucc.ie/celt/published/E620001/, accessed 11 July 2014. Cited as Gernon.

Inquisitions and extents of medieval Ireland, eds Paul Dryburgh and Brendan Smith, List and Index Society vol. 320 (London: National Archives, 2007). Cited as *Inquisitions and extents*.

Ireland-Bristol trade in the seventeenth century, www.bris.ac.uk/Depts/History/Ireland/datasets.htm, accessed 11 July 2014. Cited as *Ireland-Bristol trade*.

The Irish fiants of the Tudor sovereigns: During the reigns of Henry VIII, Edward VI, Philip & Mary, and Elizabeth I (Dublin: Éamonn de Búrca for Edmund Burke, 1994). Cited as *Irish fiants*.

Irish monastic and episcopal deeds A.D. 1200–1600, ed. Newport B. White (Dublin: Stationery Office, 1936).

Kilkenny city records: Liber primus Kilkenniensis: The earliest of the books of the Corporation of Kilkenny now extant, ed. Charles McNeill (Dublin: Stationery Office, 1931). Cited as *Liber primus Kilkenniensis*.

Letters and papers, foreign and domestic, of the reign of Henry VIII, ed. J. S. Brewer (London: HMSO, 1920). Cited as *Letters and papers ... of the reign of Henry VIII*.

National Archives of the United Kingdom, Kew, MPF 1/311, Map of Blackwater Fort, County Tyrone, Ireland, showing the governor's house, storehouse, cour de guarde, huts, cannon, armed men, stockade and surrounding country. No scale shown. Endorsed: 'Apr. 1598. Platt of Dongannon'. Cited as TNA, MPF 1/311.

National Archives of the United Kingdom, Kew, TN/PO7/III/36, order for the Attorney General to report on the case where Robert Cogan, John Pitt and William Massam, agents of the farmers of the Irish customs, claimed that the customs of Strangford and Ardglass were in the hands of the countess of Kildare, and that her lessees have lowered the duties there to draw shipping away from the neighbouring ports. Cited as TNA, TN/PO7/III/36.

National Library of Ireland, Dublin, MSS 2301–2562 and 11,044–73, Ormond family papers. Cited as NLI, MS#.

National Library of Ireland, Dublin, MS 2656, maps by Richard Bartlett, 1601. Cited as NLI, MS#.

National Library of Ireland, Dublin, MSS 41,981, 41,985, 43,087/5, 43,142/3, 43,153 and 43,308, Lismore Castle papers. Cited as NLI, MS#.

Public Records Office of Northern Ireland, Belfast, D3078, Leinster manuscripts. Cited as PRONI, D3078.

Public Records Office of Northern Ireland, Belfast, MIC 199/1, Port books for Strangford, Arglasse, Killough and Dundrum, 18 January 1614–29 September 1615. Cited as PRONI, MIC 199/1.

The red book of Ormond, ed. Newport B. White (Dublin: Stationery Office, 1932).

The red book of the earls of Kildare, ed. Gearóid Mac Niocaill (Dublin: Irish Manuscripts Commission, 1964).

Register of the Abbey of St. Thomas Dublin, ed. John T. Gilbert (Dublin: HMSO, 1889).

Register of the Hospital of St. John the Baptist without the New Gate, Dublin, ed. Eric St. John Brookes (Dublin: Irish Manuscripts Commission, 1936). Cited as *Register of the Hospital of St. John*.

Trinity College Dublin, MS 1207, medieval estate deeds.

The Welsh Port books (1550–1603), ed. E. A. Lewis, Cymmrodorion Record Series no. xii (London: Honourable Society of Cymmrodorion, 1927).

Secondary sources

Aalen, F. H. A. (1978). *Man and the landscape in Ireland* (London: Academic Press).

Admiralty chart of Ireland 1988, Glucksman Map Library, Trinity College Dublin.

Agnew, Jean (1996). *Belfast merchant families in the seventeenth century* (Dublin: Four Courts Press).

Archaeological survey of Ireland, National Monuments Service, www.archaeology.ie/archaeological-survey-ireland, accessed 20 March 2018. Cited as ASI.

References

Armstrong-Anthony, Sinead (2005). 'From Anglo-Norman manor to plantation estate: An archaeological survey of Monasteroris, County Offaly', in James Lyttleton and Tadhg O'Keeffe (eds), *The manor in medieval and early modern Ireland* (Dublin: Four Courts Press), pp. 105–31.

Arnold, Ellen (2012). *Negotiating the landscape: Environment and monastic identity in the medieval Ardennes* (Philadelphia, PA: University of Pennsylvania Press).

Aston, Michael (1988). 'Aspects of fishpond construction and maintenance in the sixteenth and seventeenth centuries', in Michael Aston (ed.), *Medieval fish, fisheries, and fishponds in England* (Oxford: Archaeopress), vol. 1, pp. 187–202.

Baker, Christine (2009). *The archaeology of Killeen Castle, County Meath* (Bray: Wordwell).

Barrett, James H. (2016). 'Medieval sea fishing, AD 500–1550: Chronology, causes and consequences', in James H. Barrett and David C. Orton (eds), *Cod and herring: The archaeology and history of medieval sea fishing* (Oxford and Philadelphia: Oxbow Books), pp. 250–72.

Barry, Terry B. (1987). *The archaeology of medieval Ireland* (London: Routledge).

Barry, Terry B. (1988). '"The people of the country ... dwell scattered": The pattern of rural settlement in Ireland in the later middle ages', in John Bradley (ed.), *Settlement and society in medieval Ireland* (Kilkenny: Boethius), pp. 345–60.

Barry, Terry B. (1993a). 'The archaeology of the tower house in later medieval Ireland', in H. Andersson and J. Wienberg (eds), *The study of medieval archaeology: European symposium for teachers of medieval archaeology, Lund 11–15 June 1990* (Stockholm: Almqvist and Wiksell International), pp. 211–7.

Barry, Terry B. (1993b). 'Late medieval Ireland: The debate on social and economic transformation', in B. J. Graham and L. J. Proudfoot (eds), *An historical geography of Ireland* (London: Academic Press), pp. 99–122.

Barry, Terry B. (1996). 'Rural settlement in Ireland in the middle ages: An overview', in Jan Klápště (ed.), *Ruralia I* (Turnhout: Brepols), pp. 134–41.

Barry, Terry B. (2000a). 'Excavations at Piperstown deserted medieval village County Louth, 1987', *Proceedings of the Royal Irish Academy*, 100C3, 113–35.

Barry, Terry B. (2000b). 'An introduction to dispersed and nucleated medieval rural settlement in Ireland', in Jan Klápště (ed.), *Ruralia III* (Prague: Institute of Archaeology), pp. 6–11.

Barry, Terry B. (2006). 'Harold Leask's "single towers": Irish tower houses as part of larger settlement complexes', in P. Ettel, A.-M. Flambard Héricher and T. E. McNeill (eds), *Chateau Gaillard 22: Chateau et Peuplement Colloque de Voiron 2004* (Caen: Publications du CRAHM), pp. 27–33.

Beglane, Fiona (2009). 'Meat and craft in medieval and post-medieval Trim', in Michael Potterton and Matthew Seaver (eds), *Uncovering medieval Trim: Archaeological excavations in and around Trim, County Meath* (Dublin: Four Courts Press), pp. 346–70.

Beglane, Fiona (2016). 'The faunal remains from Bective Abbey', in Geraldine Stout and Matthew Stout (eds), *The Bective Abbey Project, County Meath: Excavations 2009–12* (Bray: Wordwell), pp. 126–69.

Beglane, Fiona (2018). 'Forests and chases in medieval Ireland, 1169–c. 1399', *Journal of Historical Geography*, 59, 90–9.

Bonde, Sheila (1994). *Fortress-churches of Languedoc: Architecture, religion, and conflict in the High Middle Ages* (Cambridge: Cambridge University Press).

Bradley, John (1984). 'Ardee: An archaeological study', *Journal of the County Louth Archaeological and Historical Society*, 20/4, 267–96.

Bradley, John (1985). 'The medieval towns of Tipperary', in William Nolan (ed.), *Tipperary: History and society* (Dublin: Geography Publications), pp. 34–59.

Bradley, John (1988–89). 'The medieval towns of County Meath', *Ríocht na Midhe*, 8/2, 30–49.

Bradley, John (1995). *Walled towns in Ireland* (Dublin: Country House).

Bradley, John (1998). 'The medieval boroughs of County Dublin', in Conleth Manning (ed.), *Dublin and beyond the Pale: Studies in honour of Patrick Healy* (Bray: Wordwell), pp. 129–44.

Bradley, John (1997). *The topography and layout of medieval Drogheda* (Drogheda: Old Drogheda Society).

Bradley, John (1999). 'Rural boroughs in medieval Ireland: Nucleated or dispersed settlements?', in Jan Klápště (ed.), *Ruralia III* (Prague: Institute of Archaeology), pp. 288–93.

Bradley, John (2007). 'Sir Henry Sidney's bridge at Athlone, 1566–7', in Thomas Herron and Michael Potterton (eds), *Ireland in the Renaissance c. 1540–1660* (Dublin: Four Courts Press), pp. 173–94.

Bradley, John, and Ben Murtagh (2003). 'Brady's Castle, Thomastown, County Kilkenny: A 14th-century fortified town house', in John R. Kenyon and Kieran O'Conor (eds), *The medieval castle in Ireland and Wales: Essays in honour of Jeremy Knight* (Dublin: Four Courts Press), pp. 194–216.

Bradshaw, Brendan (1974). *The dissolution of the religious orders in Ireland under Henry VIII* (Cambridge: Cambridge University Press).

Brady, Niall (2006). 'Mills in medieval Ireland: Looking beyond design', in Steven A. Walton (ed.), *Wind and water in the middle ages: Fluid technologies from antiquity to the Renaissance* (Tempe, AZ: Arizona Centre for Medieval and Renaissance Studies), pp. 39–68.

Breen, Colin (1997). 'A medieval landing place at Ringhaddy Castle, Strangford Lough', *Lecale Miscellany*, 15, 60–5.

Breen, Colin (2001). 'The maritime cultural landscape in Gaelic medieval Ireland', in P. J. Duffy, David Edwards and Elizabeth FitzPatrick (eds), *Gaelic Ireland c. 1250–c. 1650: Land, lordship and settlement* (Dublin: Four Courts Press), pp. 418–36.

Breen, Colin (2005). *The Gaelic lordship of the O'Sullivan Beare: A landscape cultural history* (Dublin: Four Courts Press).

Breen, Colin (2007a). *An archaeology of southwest Ireland 1570–1670* (Dublin: Four Courts Press).

Breen, Colin (2007b). 'The post-medieval coastal landscape of Bantry and Beara, 1580–1850', in Audrey Horning, Ruairí Ó Baoill, Colm Donnelly and Paul Logue (eds), *The post-medieval archaeology of Ireland, 1550–1850* (Dublin: Wordwell), pp. 205–19.

Breen, Colin (2016). 'Marine fisheries and society in medieval Ireland', in James H. Barrett and David C. Orton (eds), *Cod and herring: The archaeology and history of medieval sea fishing* (Oxford and Philadelphia: Oxbow Books), pp. 91–8.

Britnell, Richard H. (1996). *The commercialisation of English society 1000–1500*, 2nd ed. (Manchester: Manchester University Press).

Brooks, Nicholas (2000). 'Medieval European bridges: A window onto changing concepts of state power', in Nicholas Brooks (ed.), *Communities and warfare 700–1400* (London: Hambledon Press), pp. 1–31.

Buchanan, Katherine (2014). 'Drawing upon the line? The use of landscape along shire borders in Scottish noble architecture', in P. Ettel, A.-M. Flambart Héricher and K. O'Conor (eds), *Chateau Gaillard 26: Etudes de castellologie médiéval, château et frontière* (Caen: Presses Universitaires de Caen), pp. 81–4.

Budd, R. G. (2004). 'The origins and development of the tower house in Ireland in the light of recent research' (PhD thesis, Trinity College Dublin).

Butlin, R. A. (1976). 'Land and people, *c.* 1600', in T. W. Moody, F. X. Martin and F. J. Byrne (eds), *A new history of Ireland*, vol. 3, *Early modern Ireland 1534–1691* (Oxford: Clarendon Press), pp. 142–68.

Cairns, C. T. (1987). *Irish tower houses: A County Tipperary case study* (Belfast: Group for the Study of Irish Historic Settlement).

Cambridge University Collection of Aerial Photography (CUCAP), University of Cambridge, www.cambridgeairphotos.com, accessed 16 March 2018. Cited as CUCAP.

Carus-Wilson, E. M. (1967). *The overseas trade of Bristol in the later middle ages*, 2nd ed. (New York: Barnes and Noble).

Carville, Geraldine (1981). 'The Cistercians and the Irish Sea link: Aspects of medieval trade', *Cîteaux: Commentarii cistercienses*, 31, 37–73.

Centering Spenser: A digital resource for Kilcolman Castle, East Carolina University, http://core.ecu.edu/umc/Munster/, accessed 16 March 2018.

Chambers, R. A., and M. Gray (1988). 'The excavation of fishponds', in Michael Aston (ed.), *Medieval fish, fisheries, and fishponds in England* (Oxford: Archaeopress), vol. 1, pp. 113–35.

Childs, Wendy R. (1978). *Anglo-Castilian trade in the later middle ages* (Manchester: Manchester University Press).

Childs, Wendy R. (1982). 'Ireland's trade with England in the later middle ages', *Irish Economic and Social History*, 9, 5–33.

Childs, Wendy R. (2000). 'Irish merchants and seamen in late medieval England', *Irish Historical Studies*, 32/125, 22–43.

Childs, Wendy R., and Timothy O'Neill (1987). 'Overseas trade', in Art Cosgrove (ed.), *A new history of Ireland*, vol. II, *Medieval Ireland 1169–1534* (Oxford: Clarendon Press), pp. 492–524.

Claridge, Jordan, and John Langdon (2011). 'Storage in medieval England: The evidence from purveyance accounts, 1295–1349', *Economic History Review*, 64/4, 1242–65.

Clarke, Howard B. (1998). 'Urbs et suburbium: Beyond the walls of medieval Dublin', in Conleth Manning (ed.) *Dublin and beyond the Pale: Studies in honour of Patrick Healy* (Bray: Wordwell), pp. 45–58.

Clarke, Howard B. (2013). 'Quo vadis? Mapping the Irish "monastic town"', in Seán Duffy (ed.), *Princes, prelates and poets in medieval Ireland: Essays in honour of Katherine Simms* (Dublin: Four Courts Press), pp. 261–78.

Coleman, Edward (2014). 'The Crusader's tale', in Sparky Booker and Cherie N. Peters (eds), *Tales of medieval Dublin* (Dublin: Four Courts Press), pp. 92–101.

Colfer, Billy (2013). *Wexford castles: Landscape, context and settlement* (Cork: Cork University Press).

Cooper, Alan (2006). *Bridges, law and power in medieval England, 700–1400* (Woodbridge: Boydell Press).
Costello, Eugene (2016a). 'Seasonal management of cattle in the booleying system: New insights from Connemara, western Ireland', in Michael O'Connell, Fergus Kelly and James H. McAdam (eds), *Cattle in ancient and modern Ireland: Farming practices, environment and economy* (Newcastle-upon-Tyne: Cambridge Scholars Publishing), pp. 66–74.
Costello, Eugene (2016b). 'Seasonal settlement and the interpretation of upland archaeology in the Galtee Mountains, Ireland', *Landscape History*, 37/1, 87–98.
Costello, Eugene (2016–17). 'Recent advancements in the study of past transhumance practices in Ireland', *Group for the Study of Irish Historic Settlement Newsletter*, 21, 19–20.
Coulson, Charles L. H. (2003). *Castles in medieval society: Fortresses in England, France and Ireland in the central Middle Ages* (Oxford: Oxford University Press).
Coulson, Charles L. H. (2016a). 'Specimens of freedom to crenellate by licence', in Robert Liddiard (ed.), *Late medieval castles* (Woodbridge: Boydell Press), pp. 221–40.
Coulson, Charles L. H. (2016b). 'Structural symbolism in medieval castle architecture', in Robert Liddiard (ed.), *Late medieval castles* (Woodbridge: Boydell Press), pp. 199–220.
Creighton, Oliver H. (2002). *Castles and landscapes* (London: Continuum).
Creighton, Oliver H. (2007). 'Town defences and the making of urban landscapes', in Mark Gardiner and Stephen Rippon (eds), *Medieval landscapes: Landscape history after Hoskins*, vol. 2 (Macclesfield: Windgather Press), pp. 43–56.
Creighton, Oliver H. (2010). 'Room with a view: Framing castle landscapes', in P. Ettal, A-M Flambard Héricher and T. E. McNeill (eds), *Château Gaillard 24: Château et représentations* (Caen: Publications du CRAHM), pp. 37–49.
Creighton, Oliver H., and Terry Barry (2012). 'Seigneurial and elite sites in the medieval landscape', in Neil Christie and Paul Stamper (eds), *Medieval rural settlement: Britain and Ireland, AD 800–1600* (Oxford: Windgather Press), pp. 63–80.
Creighton, Oliver H., and Robert Higham (2005). *Medieval town walls: An archaeology and social history of urban defence* (Stroud: Tempus).
Cronin, John (n.d.). 'Irish Battlefields Project report 189: Siege of Duncannon Fort (1645)', unpublished report.
Crooks, Peter (ed.) (n.d.). 'Destruction of the Irish Chancery Rolls (1304–1922)', *CIRCLE: A calendar of Irish Chancery letters c. 1244–1509*, Trinity College Dublin, https://chancery.tcd.ie/content/destruction-irish-chancery-rolls-1304-1922, accessed 4 April 2015.
Curtis, Edmund (1935–37). 'Rental of the manor of Lisronagh, 1333, and notes on "betagh" tenure in medieval Ireland', *Proceedings of the Royal Irish Academy*, 43, 41–76.
Daly, Aoife (2014). 'Fine-tuned chronology of medieval fishweirs on the Fergus estuary, County Clare, Ireland', *Journal of Wetland Archaeology*, 14, 6–21.
Database of Irish excavation reports, www.excavations.ie, accessed 21 March 2018.
Davies, Oliver, and David B. Quinn (1941). 'The Irish pipe roll of 14 John, 1211–1212', *Ulster Journal of Archaeology*, 3rd ser., 4/suppl., 1–76.
Davin, A. K. (1983). 'The tower houses of the Pale' (MLitt thesis, Trinity College Dublin).

De Courcy Ireland, John (1987). 'County Wexford in maritime history', in Kevin Whelan (ed.), *Wexford: History and society – interdisciplinary essays on the history of an Irish county* (Dublin: Geography Publications), pp. 490–506.

Dillon, Mary, and Penny Johnston (2009). 'Plant remains', in Christine Baker, *The archaeology of Killeen Castle, County Meath* (Bray: Wordwell), pp. 101–11.

Ditchburn, David, and Benjamin T. Hudson (2015). 'Economy and trade in medieval Man', in Sean Duffy and Harold Mytum (eds), *A new history of the Isle of Man*, vol. 3, *The medieval period, 1000–1406* (Liverpool: Liverpool University Press), pp. 377–410.

Dixon, Philip (1979). 'Towerhouses, pelehouses and border society', *Archaeological Journal*, 136, 240–52.

Dixon, Philip (1992). 'From hall to tower: The change in seigneurial houses on the Anglo-Scottish border after *c.* 1250', in P. R. Coss and S. D. Lloyd (eds), *Thirteenth century England*, vol. IV (Woodbridge: Boydell Press), pp. 85–107.

Donnelly, Colm J. (1998). 'Sectionally constructed tower houses: A review of the evidence from Limerick', *Journal of the Royal Society of Antiquaries of Ireland*, 128, 26–34.

Donnelly, Colm J. (2001). 'Tower houses and late medieval secular settlement in County Limerick', in P. J. Duffy, David Edwards and Elizabeth FitzPatrick (eds), *Gaelic Ireland c. 1250–c. 1650: Land, lordship and settlement* (Dublin: Four Courts Press), pp. 315–28.

Down, Kevin (1987). 'Colonial society and economy in the high middle ages', in Art Cosgrove (ed.), *A new history of Ireland*, vol. II, *Medieval Ireland 1169–1534* (Oxford: Clarendon Press), pp. 439–91.

Driver, J. T. (1971). *Cheshire in the later Middle Ages 1399–1540* (Chester: Cheshire Community Council).

Dryburgh, Paul, and Brendan Smith (2004). *Handbook and select calendar of sources for medieval Ireland in the National Archives of the United Kingdom* (Dublin: Four Courts Press).

Du Noyer, George Victor (*c.* 1815?). *Dunmoe Castle on the Boyne near Navan*. Royal Society of Antiquaries of Ireland, http://rsai.locloudhosting.net/items/show/22387, accessed April 1, 2018.

Dyer, Christopher (1994). 'The consumption of freshwater fish in medieval England', in *Everyday life in medieval England* (London: Hambledon Press), pp. 101–11.

Dyer, Christopher (2000). *Everyday life in medieval England* (London: Bloomsbury).

Dyer, Christopher (2013a), 'The archaeology of medieval small towns', *Medieval Archaeology*, 47/1, 85–114.

Dyer, Christopher (2013b). 'Living in peasant houses in late medieval England', *Vernacular Architecture*, 44, 19–27.

Dyer, Christopher, and Paul Everson (2012). 'The development of the study of medieval settlements, 1880–2010', in Neil Christie and Paul Stamper (eds), *Medieval rural settlement: Britain and Ireland, AD 800–1600* (Oxford: Windgather Press), pp. 11–30.

Eadie, Gillian (2009). 'A new approach to identifying functions in castles: A study of tower houses in Ireland' (PhD thesis, Queen's University Belfast).

Eadie, Gillian (2015). 'The tower houses of County Down: Stylistic similarity, functional difference', in Victoria McAlister and Terry Barry (eds), *Space and settlement in medieval Ireland* (Dublin: Four Courts Press), pp. 110–29.

Edwards, David (2000). *The Ormond lordship in County Kilkenny, 1515–1642: The rise and fall of Butler feudal power* (Dublin: Four Courts Press).

Edwards, David, and Brian C. Donovan (1997). *British sources for Irish history 1485–1641* (Dublin: Irish Manuscripts Commission).

Edwards, K. T., F. W. Hamond and Anngret Simms (1983). 'The medieval settlement of Newcastle Lyons, County Dublin: An interdisciplinary approach', *Proceedings of the Royal Irish Academy*, 83C, 351–76.

Ellis, Steven G. (1986). *Reform and revival: English government in Ireland, 1470–1534* (Woodbridge: Boydell Press).

Ellis, Steven G. (2015). *Defending English ground: War and peace in Meath and Northumberland, 1460–1542* (Oxford: Oxford University Press).

Ellison, Cyril (1983). *The waters of the Boyne and Blackwater: A scenic and industrial miscellany* (Dublin: Blackwater Press).

Empey, C. A. (1981). 'Medieval Knocktopher: A study in manorial settlement', *Old Kilkenny Review*, 2/4, 329–42.

Empey, C. A. (1985). 'The Norman period: 1185–1500', in William Nolan (ed.), *Tipperary: History and society* (Dublin: Geography Publications), pp. 71–91.

Empey, C. A. (1988). 'The Anglo-Norman community in Tipperary and Kilkenny in the Middle Ages: Change and continuity', in Gearóid Mac Niocaill and Patrick F. Wallace (eds), *Keimelia: Studies in medieval archaeology and history in memory of Tom Delaney* (Galway: Galway University Press), pp. 449–67.

Estyn Evans, E. (1969). 'Sod and turf houses in Ireland', in Geraint Jenkins (ed.), *Studies in folk life: Essays in honour of Iorwerth C. Peate* (New York: Barnes and Noble), pp. 79–90.

Everett, Nigel (2014). *The woods of Ireland: A history, 700–1800* (Dublin: Four Courts Press).

First Edition maps 1834–46, *Ordnance Survey Ireland*, http://map.geohive.ie/mapviewer.html, accessed 27 November 2018.

FitzPatrick, Elizabeth (2009). 'Native enclosed settlement and the problem of the "Irish ring-fort"', *Medieval Archaeology*, 53, 271–307.

Flanagan, Laurence N. W. (1988). 'Irish annals as a source for maritime history, 1400–1600 A.D.' in Gearóid Mac Niocaill and Patrick F. Wallace (eds), *Keimelia: Studies in medieval archaeology and history in memory of Tom Delaney* (Galway: Galway University Press), pp. 500–3.

Flavin, Susan M. (2004). 'The development of Anglo-Irish trade in the sixteenth century' (MA thesis, Bristol University).

Flavin, Susan M. (2011). 'Consumption and material culture in sixteenth-century Ireland', *Economic History Review*, 64/4, 1144–74.

Foley, Claire (1989). 'Excavation at a medieval settlement site in Jerpointchurch townland, County Kilkenny', *Proceedings of the Royal Irish Academy*, 89C, 71–126.

Fox, H. S. A. (2001). *The evolution of the fishing village: Landscape and society along the south Devon coast, 1086–1550* (Oxford: Leopard's Head Press).

Frame, Robin (2012). *Colonial Ireland 1169–1369*, 2nd ed. (Dublin: Four Courts Press).

Gaimster, David R. M. (2000). 'Hanseatic trade and cultural exchange in the Baltic circa 1200–1600: Pottery from wrecks and harbours', in *Schutz des Kulturerbes unter Wasser: Veränderungen europäischer Lebenskultur durch Fluß- und Seehandel* (Lübstorf, Germany: Archäologisches Landesmuseum), pp. 237–47.

Gaimster, David R. M. (2005). 'A parallel history: An archaeology of Hanseatic urban culture in the Baltic c. 1200–1600', *World Archaeology*, 37/3, 408–23.

Gaimster, David R. M. (2007). 'The Baltic ceramic 1200–1600: Measuring Hanseatic cultural transfer and resistance', in Herman Roodenburg (ed.), *Cultural exchange in early modern Europe*, vol. iv, *Forging European identities, 1400–1700* (Cambridge: Cambridge University Press), pp. 30–58.

Gaimster, David R. M. (2014). 'The Hanseatic cultural signature: Exploring globalization on the micro-scale in late medieval northern Europe', *European Journal of Archaeology*, 17/1, 60–81.

Galloway, James A. (2011). 'Waterford and its hinterland in the post-medieval period c. 1540–1700', in James Eogan and Elizabeth Shee Twohig (eds), *Cois tSuire: Nine thousand years of human activity in the Lower Suir valley, archaeological excavations on the N25 Waterford City Bypass* (Dublin: National Roads Authority), pp. 234–44.

Galloway, James A. (2015). 'The economic hinterland of Drogheda in the later middle ages', in Victoria McAlister and Terry Barry (eds), *Space and settlement in medieval Ireland* (Dublin: Four Courts Press), pp. 167–85.

Ganesh, Janan (2017). 'Goodbye to the rural bolthole', *Financial Times* (28 July), www.ft.com/content/cfba65ee-7225-11e7-93ff-99f383b09ff9, accessed 30 July 2017.

Gardiner, Mark (2000). 'Vernacular buildings and the development of the later medieval domestic plan in England', *Medieval Archaeology*, 44, 159–79.

Gardiner, Mark (2005). 'Excavations at Jordan's Castle, Ardglass, County Down, 1998–2000: Data structure report' (unpublished excavation report, Queen's University Belfast).

Gardiner, Mark (2007). 'Hythes, small ports, and other landing places in later medieval England', in John Blair and Helena Hamerow (eds), *Waterways and canal-building in medieval England* (Oxford: Oxford University Press), pp. 85–109.

Gardiner, Mark (2012). 'Time regained: Booley huts and seasonal settlement in the Mourne Mountains, County Down, Ireland', in Sam Turner and Bob Silvester (eds), *Life in medieval landscapes: People and places in the Middle Ages – papers in memory of H. S. A. Fox* (Oxford: Windgather Press), pp. 106–24.

Gardiner, Mark (2014). 'An archaeological approach to the development of the late medieval peasant house', *Vernacular Architecture*, 45, 16–28.

Gardiner, Mark, and Kieran O'Conor (2017). 'The later medieval countryside lying beneath', in Michael Stanley, Rónán Swan and Aidan O'Sullivan (eds), *Stories of Ireland's past: Knowledge gained from NRA roads archaeology* (Dublin: Transport Infrastructure Ireland), pp. 133–201.

Giles, Kate, and Christopher Dyer (eds) (2005). *Town and country in the Middle Ages: Contrasts, contacts and interconnections, 1100–1500* (Leeds: Maney).

Gillespie, Raymond (1985). *Colonial Ulster: The settlement of east Ulster 1600–1641* (Cork: Cork University Press).

Gillespie, Raymond (1991). *The transformation of the Irish economy 1550–1700* (Dundalk: Dundalgan Press).

GLAS – proposed new agri-environment scheme: Structure and payment rates, Department of Agriculture, Food and the Marine, www.itba.info/wp-content/uploads/2013/07/GLAS-Structure-and-Pay-Rates.pdf, accessed 18 January 2018.

Glasscock, R. E. (1970). 'Moated sites, and deserted boroughs and villages: Two neglected aspects of Anglo-Norman settlement in Ireland', in Nicholas Stephens and Robin E. Glasscock (eds), *Irish geographical studies in honour of E. Estyn Evans* (Belfast: Queen's University Press), pp. 162–78.

Glasscock, R. E. (1971). 'The study of deserted medieval settlements in Ireland (to 1968)', in Maurice Beresford and John G. Hurst (eds), *Deserted medieval villages: Studies* (New York: St. Martin's Press), pp. 279–91, and gazetteer.

Glasscock, R. E. (1987). 'Land and people, *c.* 1300', in Art Cosgrove (ed.), *A new history of Ireland*, vol. II, *Medieval Ireland 1169–1534* (Oxford: Clarendon Press), pp. 205–39.

Gleeson, Dermot F., and H. G. Leask (1936). 'The castle and manor of Nenagh', *Journal of the Royal Society of Antiquaries of Ireland*, 6/2, 247–69.

Gosling, Paul (1992). *Carlingford town: An antiquarian's guide* (Carlingford: Carlingford Lough Heritage Trust).

Graham, Brian J. (1974). 'Medieval settlements in County Meath', *Ríocht na Midhe: Records of Meath Archaeological and Historical Society*, 5/3, 40–59.

Graham, Brian J. (1975). 'Anglo-Norman settlement in County Meath', *Proceedings of the Royal Irish Academy*, 75C, 223–49.

Graham, Brian J. (1988a). 'The definition and classification of Irish medieval towns', *Irish Geography*, 21, 20–32.

Graham, Brian J. (1988b). 'Economy and town in Anglo-Norman Ireland', in John Bradley (ed.), *Settlement and society in medieval Ireland* (Kilkenny: Boethius), pp. 241–60.

Graham, Brian J. (1993). 'The high middle ages: *c.* 1100 to *c.* 1350', in B. J. Graham and L. J. Proudfoot (eds), *An historical geography of Ireland* (London: Academic Press), pp. 58–98.

Green, Low-Carbon, Agri-Environment Scheme – GLAS, Department of Agriculture, Food and the Marine, www.agriculture.gov.ie/farmerschemespayments/glas/, accessed 11 January 2018.

Grenville, Jane (1997). *Medieval housing* (London: Leicester University Press).

Grenville, Jane (2008). 'Urban and rural houses and households in the late middle ages: A case study from Yorkshire', in Maryanne Kowaleski and P. J. P. Goldberg (eds), *Medieval domesticity: Home, housing and household in medieval England* (Cambridge: Cambridge University Press), pp. 92–123.

Gwynn, Aubrey (1935). 'The Black Death in Ireland', *Studies: An Irish quarterly review*, xxiv, 25–42.

Hall, D. N., Mark Hennessy and Tadhg O'Keeffe (1985). 'Medieval agriculture and settlement in Oughterard and Castlewarden, County Kildare', *Irish Geography*, 18, 16–25.

Hall, Valerie A. (2000). 'The documentary and pollen analytical records of the vegetational history of the Irish landscape AD 200–1650', *Peritia*, 14, 342–71.

Hall, Valerie A. (2003). 'Vegetation history of mid- to western Ireland in the 2nd millennium A.D.: Fresh evidence from tephra-dated archaeological investigations', *Vegetation History and Archaeobotany*, 12, 7–17.

Hall, Valerie A. (2005). 'The vegetation history of monastic and secular sites in the midlands of Ireland over the last two millennia', *Vegetation History and Archaeobotany*, 15, 1–12.

Hansson, Martin (2014). 'Later medieval aristocratic landscapes in Scandinavia', in P. Ettel, A.-M. Flambart Héricher and K. O'Conor (eds), *Château Gaillard*

26: Etudes de castellologie médiéval, château et frontière (Caen: Presses Universitaires de Caen), pp. 207–15.

Hardiman, James (1820). *The history of the town and country of the town of Galway: From the earliest period to the present time* (Dublin: W. Folds), https://archive.org/details/historyoftowncou00hard, accessed 9 March 2018.

Harrison, David (2004). *The bridges of medieval England: Transport and society 400–1800* (Oxford: Clarendon Press).

Hayden, Alan R. (2009). 'Excavation of a site at High Street, Trim' in Michael Potterton and Matthew Seaver (eds), *Uncovering medieval Trim: Archaeological excavations in and around Trim, County Meath* (Dublin: Four Courts Press), pp. 257–70.

Hayes-McCoy, G. A. (1964). *Ulster and other Irish maps c. 1600* (Dublin: Stationery Office for the Irish Manuscripts Commission).

Hennessy, Mark (1988). 'The priory and hospital of New Gate: The evolution and decline of a medieval monastic estate', in W. J. Smyth and Kevin Whelan (eds), *Common ground: Essays on the historical geography of Ireland, presented to T. Jones Hughes* (Cork: Cork University Press), pp. 41–54.

Hennessy, Mark (1996). 'Manorial organisation in early thirteenth century Tipperary', *Irish Geography*, 29/2, 116–25.

Hoffmann, Richard C. (1996). 'Economic development and aquatic ecosystems in medieval Europe', *American Historical Review*, 101/3, 631–69.

Hoffmann, Richard C. (2000). 'Medieval fishing', in Paolo Squatriti (ed.), *Working with water in medieval Europe: Technology and resource use* (Leiden: Brill), pp. 331–93.

Hoffmann, Richard C. (2010). 'Elemental resources and aquatic ecosystems: Medieval Europeans and their rivers', in Terje Tvedt and Richard Coopney (eds), *A history of water* (London: I. B. Tauris), pp. 165–202.

Holton, Karina (2001). 'From charters to carters: Aspects of fairs and markets in medieval Leinster', in Denis A. Cronin, Jim Gilligan and Karina Holton (eds), *Irish fairs and markets: Studies in local history* (Dublin: Four Courts Press), pp. 18–44.

Horning, Audrey (2001). '"Dwelling houses in the old Irish barbarous manner": Archaeological evidence for Gaelic architecture in an Ulster plantation village', in P. J. Duffy, David Edwards and Elizabeth FitzPatrick (eds), *Gaelic Ireland c. 1250–c. 1650: Land, lordship and settlement* (Dublin: Four Courts Press), pp. 375–96.

Horning, Audrey (2013). *Ireland in the Virginian Sea: Colonialism in the British Atlantic* (Raleigh, NC: University of North Carolina Press).

Hudson, Benjamin T. (1999). 'The changing economy of the Irish Sea province', in Brendan Smith (ed.), *Britain and Ireland 900–1300: Insular responses to medieval European change* (Cambridge: Cambridge University Press), pp. 39–66.

Hutchinson, Gillian (1997). *Medieval ships and shipping* (London: Leicester University Press).

Jäger, Helmut (1983). 'Land use in medieval Ireland: A review of the documentary evidence', *Irish Economic and Social History*, 10/1, 51–65.

Jarvis, R. C. (1959). 'The appointment of ports', *Economic History Review*, 11/3, 455–66.

Johnson, Matthew (2002). *Behind the castle gate: From medieval to Renaissance* (London: Routledge).

Jones, Evan T. (2000). 'River navigation in medieval England', *Journal of Historical Geography*, 26/1, 60–82.

Jope, E. M. (1951). 'Scottish influences in the north of Ireland: Castles with Scottish features 1580–1640', *Ulster Journal of Archaeology*, 14, 31–47.

Jope, E. M. (1966). *An archaeological survey of County Down* (Belfast: HMSO).

Jordan, A. J. (1991). 'The tower houses of County Wexford' (PhD thesis, Trinity College Dublin).

Kean, Norman (ed.) (1995). *Sailing directions for the east and north coasts of Ireland* (n.p.: Irish Cruising Club Publications).

Kearney, H. F. (1955). 'The Irish wine trade, 1614–15', *Irish Historical Studies*, 9/36, 400–42.

Keegan, Mark (2005). 'The archaeology of manorial settlement in west County Limerick in the thirteenth century', in James Lyttleton and Tadhg O'Keeffe (eds), *The manor in medieval and early modern Ireland* (Dublin: Four Courts Press), pp. 17–39.

Kelleher, Connie (2007a). 'The fort of the ships', in Conleth Manning and P. David Sweetman (eds), *From ringforts to fortified houses: Studies on castles and other monuments in honour of David Sweetman* (Bray: Wordwell), pp. 195–208.

Kelleher, Connie (2007b). 'The Gaelic O'Driscoll lords of Baltimore, County Cork: Settlement, economy and conflict in a maritime cultural landscape', in Linda Doran and James Lyttleton (eds), *Lordship in medieval Ireland: Image and reality* (Dublin: Four Courts Press), pp. 130–59.

Kelleher, Connie (2013). 'Pirate ports and harbours of west Cork in the early seventeenth century', *Journal of Maritime Archaeology*, 8, 347–66.

Kelly, David, and Tadhg O'Keeffe (eds) (2015). *Youghal: Irish historic towns atlas no. 27* (Dublin: Royal Irish Academy).

Klingelhofer, Eric (2010). *Castles and colonists: An archaeology of Elizabethan Ireland* (Manchester: Manchester University Press).

Kowaleski, Maryanne (1995). *Local markets and regional trade in medieval Exeter* (Cambridge: Cambridge University Press).

Kowaleski, Maryanne (2007). '"Alien" encounters in the maritime world of medieval England', *Medieval Encounters*, 13, 96–121.

Kowaleski, Maryanne (2010). 'The seasonality of fishing in medieval Britain', in Scott G. Bruce (ed.), *Ecologies and economies in medieval and early modern Europe: Studies in environmental history for Richard C. Hoffmann* (Leiden: Brill), pp. 117–47.

Kowaleski, Maryanne (2014). 'Medieval people in town and country: New perspectives from demography and bioarchaeology', *Speculum*, 83/9, 573–600.

Landers, John (2003). *The field and the forge: Population, production and power in the pre-industrial west* (Oxford: Oxford University Press).

Langdon, John (1993). 'Inland water transport in medieval England', *Journal of Historical Geography*, 19/1, 1–11.

Langdon, John (2004). *Mills in the medieval economy: England 1300–1540* (Oxford: Oxford University Press).

Langdon, John, and Jordan Claridge (2011). 'Transport in medieval England', *History Compass*, 9/11, 864–75.

Leask, Harold G. (1944). *Irish castles and castellated houses*, 2nd ed. (Dundalk: Dundalgan Press).

References

Lee, Gerard A. (1965). 'Medieval Kilmallock', *North Munster Antiquarian Journal*, 9, 145–53.

Lennon, Colm (2013). 'Trades and services', in H. B. Clarke and Sarah Gearty (eds), *Maps and texts: Exploring the Irish historic towns atlas* (Dublin: Royal Irish Academy), pp. 183–96.

Lewis, Helen, Colum Gallagher, Wesley van Breda, Gareth Mulrooney, Stephen Davis, Jonathan Turner, *et al.* (2008). *An integrated, comprehensive GIS model of landscape evolution and land use history in the River Boyne Valley*, http://oldsitehc.info/seandalaiocht/hci-irish-page/instar-web-archive/view/?L=3&ins=15&cHash=f70b756879fb754e9b50ed70ca3b537c, accessed 27 November 2018.

Lewis, Samuel (1837). *A topographical dictionary of Ireland*, Library Ireland, www.libraryireland.com/topog, accessed 2 April 2008.

Liddiard, Robert (2005). *Castles in context: Power, symbolism and landscape, 1066–1500* (Macclesfield: Windgather Press).

Loeber, Rolf (2001). 'An architectural history of Gaelic castles and settlements, 1370–1600', in P. J. Duffy, David Edwards and Elizabeth FitzPatrick (eds), *Gaelic Ireland c. 1250–c. 1650: Land, lordship and settlement* (Dublin: Four Courts Press), pp. 271–314.

Longfield, A. K. (1929). *Anglo-Irish trade in the sixteenth century* (London: Routledge).

Lowry, T. K. (ed.) (1867). *The Hamilton manuscripts: Containing some account of the settlement of the territories of the Upper Clandeboye, Great Ardes, and Dufferin, in the County of Down, by Sir James Hamilton, Knight* (Belfast: Archer and Sons).

Lucas, A. T. (1953). 'The horizontal mill in Ireland', *Journal of the Royal Society of Antiquaries of Ireland*, 83/1, 1–36.

Lucas, Adam (2014). *Ecclesiastical lordship, seigneurial power and the commercialization of milling in medieval England* (London: Routledge).

Lyons, Susan (2016). 'The environmental remains from Bective Abbey: Archaeobotanical and charcoal analysis', in Geraldine Stout and Matthew Stout (eds), *The Bective Abbey Project, County Meath: Excavations 2009–12* (Bray: Wordwell), pp. 179–99.

Lyttleton, James (2007). 'The MacCoghlans of Delvin Eathra: The transformation of a later medieval lordship in early modern Ireland', in Linda Doran and James Lyttleton (eds), *Lordship in medieval Ireland: Image and reality* (Dublin: Four Courts Press), pp. 236–65.

Mac Curtain, Margaret (1988). 'A lost landscape: The Geraldine castles and tower houses of the Shannon estuary', in John Bradley (ed.), *Settlement and society in medieval Ireland* (Kilkenny: Boethius), pp. 429–44.

Mac Niocaill, Gearóid (1992). Introduction to the *Crown surveys of lands*.

Malcolm, John (2007). 'Castles and landscapes in Uí Fhiachrach Muaidhe c. 1235–c. 1400', in Linda Doran and James Lyttleton (eds), *Lordship in medieval Ireland: Image and reality* (Dublin: Four Courts Press), pp. 193–216.

Mallory, J. P., and T. E. McNeill (1991). *The archaeology of Ulster from colonization to plantation* (Belfast: Institute of Irish Studies).

Martin, G. (1981). 'Plantation boroughs in medieval Ireland, with a handlist of boroughs to c. 1500', in David Harkness and Marion O'Dowd (eds), *The town in Ireland* (Belfast: Appletree Press), pp. 23–53.

Masschaele, James (1993). 'Transport costs in medieval England', *Economic History Review*, 46/2, 266–79.

McAlister, Victoria (2013). 'Tower houses and the maritime economy *c*. 1400–1641: A County Down case study' (PhD thesis, Trinity College Dublin).

McAlister, Victoria (2015). 'The death of the tower house? An examination of the decline of the Irish castle building tradition', in Victoria McAlister and Terry Barry (eds), *Space and settlement in medieval Ireland* (Dublin: Four Courts Press), pp. 130–50.

McAlister, Victoria (2016). 'Castles and connectivity: Exploring the economic networks between tower houses, settlement, and trade in late-medieval Ireland', *Speculum*, 91/3, 631–59.

McAuliffe, Mary (1991). 'The tower houses of County Kerry' (PhD thesis, Trinity College Dublin).

McCormack, Anthony M. (2005). *The earldom of Desmond 1463–1583: The decline and crisis of a feudal lordship* (Dublin: Four Courts Press).

McCracken, Eileen (1971). *The Irish woods since Tudor times: Distribution and exploitation* (Newton Abbot: David and Charles).

McDonald, Theresa (2016). 'The "ups and downs" of booleying in Achill, County Mayo, Ireland', in Michael O'Connell, Fergus Kelly and James H. McAdam (eds), *Cattle in ancient and modern Ireland: Farming practices, environment and economy* (Newcastle-upon-Tyne: Cambridge Scholars Publishing), pp. 56–65.

McErlean, Thomas, and Norman Crothers (2007). *Harnessing the tides: The early medieval tide mills at Nendrum monastery, Strangford Lough* (Norwich: HMSO).

McErlean, Thomas, Rosemary McConkey and Wes Forsythe (2002). *Strangford Lough: An archaeological survey of the maritime cultural landscape* (Belfast: Blackstaff Press).

McErlean, Thomas, and Aidan O'Sullivan (2002). 'Foreshore tidal fishtraps', in Thomas McErlean, Rosemary McConkey and Wes Forsythe, *Strangford Lough: An archaeological survey of the maritime cultural landscape* (Belfast: Blackstaff Press), pp. 144–80.

McManama-Kearin, Lisa Karen (2013). *The use of GIS in determining the role of visibility in the siting of early Anglo-Norman stone castles in Ireland*, BAR British Series 575 (Oxford: Archaeopress).

McNeill, Tom E. (1980). *Anglo-Norman Ulster: The history and archaeology of an Irish barony, 1177–1400* (Edinburgh: John Donald Publishers).

McNeill, Tom E. (1997). *Castles in Ireland: Feudal power in a Gaelic world* (London: Routledge).

McNeill, Tom E. (2005). 'Three medieval buildings in the port of Ardglass, County Down', *Proceedings of the Royal Irish Academy*, 105C, 1–21.

Mitchell, G. F. (1965). 'Littleton Bog, Tipperary: An Irish agricultural record', *Journal of the Royal Society of Antiquaries of Ireland*, 95/1–2, 121–32.

Molloy, Karen, and Michael O'Connell (2016). 'Farming impact in Ireland from the Neolithic to recent times with particular reference to a detailed pollen record from east Galway', in Michael O'Connell, Fergus Kelly and James H. McAdam (eds), *Cattle in ancient and modern Ireland: Farming practices, environment and economy* (Newcastle-upon-Tyne: Cambridge Scholars Publishing), pp. 27–43.

Morgan, Hiram (1985). 'The colonial venture of Sir Thomas Smith in Ulster, 1571–1575', *Historical Journal*, 28/2, 261–78.

Murphy, Margaret (2009). 'Rural settlement in Meath, 1170–1660: The documentary evidence', in Mary Deevy and Donald Murphy (eds), *Places along the way: First findings on the M3* (Bray: Wordwell), pp. 153–68.

Murphy, Margaret (2015). 'Manor centres, settlement and agricultural systems in medieval Ireland, 1250–1350', in Margaret Murphy and Matthew Stout (eds), *Agriculture and settlement in Ireland* (Dublin: Four Courts Press), pp. 69–100.

Murphy, Margaret, and Kieran O'Conor (2006). 'Castles and deer parks in Anglo-Norman Ireland', *Eolas*, 1, 53–70.

Murphy, Margaret, and Michael Potterton (2010). *The Dublin region in the middle ages: Settlement, land-use and economy* (Dublin: Four Courts Press).

Murtagh, Ben (1985–86). 'St. David's Castle: A fortified town house, Naas, County Kildare', *Journal of the County Kildare Archaeological Society*, 16/5, 468–78.

Murtagh, Ben (1988). 'The Bridge Castle, Thomastown, County Kilkenny', in Gearóid Mac Niocaill and Patrick F. Wallace (eds), *Keimelia: Studies in medieval archaeology and history in memory of Tom Delaney* (Galway: Galway University Press), pp. 536–56.

Murtagh, Ben (1989). 'Hatch's Castle, Ardee, County Louth: A fortified town house of the Pale', *County Louth Archaeological and Historical Journal*, 22/1, 36–48.

Murtagh, Ben (1994). 'Archaeological investigations at Dysart, County Kilkenny 1989–1994: An interim report', *Old Kilkenny Review*, 46, 78–94.

Murtagh, Ben (2011). 'The dating of the White Castle, Athy, County Kildare: An outlying bastion of the Pale', in Michael Potterton and Thomas Herron (eds), *Dublin and the Pale in the Renaissance c. 1540–1660* (Dublin: Four Courts Press), pp. 145–81.

Naessens, Paul (2007). 'Gaelic lords of the sea: The coastal tower houses of south Connemara', in Linda Doran and James Lyttleton (eds), *Lordship in medieval Ireland: Image and reality* (Dublin: Four Courts Press), pp. 217–35.

Naessens, Paul (2009). 'The Uí Fhlaithbheartaigh Gaelic lordship of Iarchonnacht: Medieval lordly settlement on the Atlantic seaboard' (PhD thesis, National University of Ireland, Galway).

Naessens, Paul (2015). 'Murchadh Ó Flaithbheartaigh and the aggrandisement of Aughnanure Castle', in Richard Oram (ed.), *A house that thieves might knock at: Proceedings of the 2010 Stirling and 2011 Dundee conferences on 'the tower as lordly residence' and 'the tower and the household'*, Tower Studies 1 and 2 (Donington: Shaun Tyas), pp. 214–30.

National Monuments Service (2012). 'Ireland's Tower Houses', *Farmer's Journal* (24 March).

Nedkvitne, Arnved (2016). 'The development of the Norwegian long-distance stockfish trade', in James H. Barrett and David C. Orton (eds), *Cod and herring: The archaeology and history of medieval sea fishing* (Oxford: Oxbow Books), pp. 50–9.

Newman Johnson, David (1998). 'Lynch's Castle, Galway City: A reassessment', in Conleth Manning (ed.), *Dublin and beyond the Pale: Studies in honour of Patrick Healy* (Bray: Wordwell), pp. 221–51.

Nicholas, David (1976). 'Economic reorientation and social change in fourteenth-century Flanders', *Past and Present*, 70, 1–29.

Nicholas, David (1996). 'Settlement patterns, urban functions, and capital formation in medieval Flanders', in David Nicholas, *Trade, urbanisation and the family:*

Studies in the history of medieval Flanders (Aldershot: Variorum, Ashgate), pp. 1–30.

Nicholls, Kenneth W. (1972). *Gaelic and gaelicised Ireland in the Middle Ages* (Dublin: Gill and MacMillan).

Nicholls, Kenneth W. (1985). 'Gaelic landownership in Tipperary from the surviving Irish deeds', in William Nolan (ed.), *Tipperary: History and society* (Dublin: Geography Publications), pp. 92–103.

Nicholls, Kenneth W. (1987). 'Gaelic society and economy in the High Middle Ages', in Art Cosgrove (ed.), *A new history of Ireland*, vol. II, *Medieval Ireland 1169–1534* (Oxford: Clarendon Press), pp. 397–438.

Nicholls, Kenneth W. (2001). 'Woodland cover in pre-modern Ireland', in P. J. Duffy, David Edwards and Elizabeth FitzPatrick (eds), *Gaelic Ireland c. 1250–c. 1650: Land, lordship and settlement* (Dublin: Four Courts Press), pp. 181–206.

Nicholls, Kenneth W. (2003). *Gaelic and gaelicised Ireland in the Middle Ages* (Dublin: Lilliput Press).

Ní Loingsigh, Máire (1994). 'An assessment of castles and landownership in late medieval north Donegal', *Ulster Journal of Archaeology*, 57, 145–58.

Northern Ireland Sites and Monuments Record, Department for Communities, https://apps.communities-ni.gov.uk/NISMR-PUBLIC/Disclaimer.aspx, accessed 20 March 2018.

O'Brien, A. F. (1988). 'The royal boroughs, the seaport towns and royal revenue in medieval Ireland', *Journal of the Royal Society of Antiquaries of Ireland*, 118, 13–26.

O'Conor, Kieran D. (1993). 'The earthwork castles of medieval Leinster' (PhD thesis, University of Wales).

O'Conor, Kieran D. (1998). *The archaeology of medieval rural settlement in Ireland* (Dublin: Royal Irish Academy).

O'Conor, Kieran D. (2001). 'Housing in later medieval Gaelic Ireland', in Jan Klápště (ed.), *Ruralia IV: The rural house, from the migration period to the oldest still standing buildings* (Turnhout: Brepols), pp. 201–10.

O'Conor, Kieran D. (2004). 'Medieval rural settlement in Munster', in J. Ludlow and N. Jameson (eds), *Medieval Ireland: The Barryscourt lectures 1–10* (Kinsale: Gandon), pp. 225–56.

Ó Danachair, Caoimhín O. (1969). 'Representations of houses on some Irish maps of *c.* 1600', in Geraint Jenkins (ed.), *Studies in folk life: Essays in honour of Iorwerth C. Peate* (New York: Barnes and Noble), pp. 91–103.

Ó Danachair, Caoimhín O. (1977–79). 'Irish tower houses and their regional distribution', *Béaloideas*, 45–7, 158–63.

O'Donovan, John (2001). *Ordnance Survey letters Meath: Letters containing information relative to the antiquities of the County of Meath collected during the progress of the Ordnance Survey in 1836* (Dublin: Four Masters Press).

O'Keeffe, Tadhg (1999). 'Townscape as text: The topography of social interaction in Fethard, county Tipperary, AD 1300–1700', *Irish Geography*, 32/1, 9–25.

O'Keeffe, Tadhg (2000a). *Medieval Ireland: An archaeology* (Stroud: Tempus).

O'Keeffe, Tadhg (2000b). 'Reflections on the 'dispersed-nucleated' paradigm in medieval settlement archaeology', in Jan Klápště (ed.), *Ruralia III* (Prague: Institute of Archaeology), pp. 103–5.

O'Keeffe, Tadhg (2003). *Fethard: Irish historic towns atlas no. 13* (Dublin: Royal Irish Academy).

O'Keeffe, Tadhg (2015). *Medieval Irish buildings, 1100–1600*, Maynooth Research Guides for Irish Local History 18 (Dublin: Four Courts Press).

O'Neill, James (2013–14). 'The cockpit of Ulster: War along the River Blackwater 1593–1603', *Ulster Journal of Archaeology*, 72, 184–99.

O'Neill, Timothy (1987). *Merchants and mariners in medieval Ireland* (Dublin: Irish Academic Press).

O'Neill, Timothy (1988). 'A fifteenth century entrepreneur Germyn Lynch fl. 1441–1483', in John Bradley (ed.), *Settlement and society in medieval Ireland* (Kilkenny: Boethius Press), pp. 421–8.

Oram, Richard (2010). 'Medieval Scottish castles: Some insights, images and perceptions from archaeological and historical investigation', in P. Ettal, A.-M. Flambard Héricher and T. E. McNeill (eds), *Château Gaillard 24: Château et représentations* (Caen: Publications du CRAHM), pp. 213–22.

Oram, Richard (2011). 'The greater house in late medieval Scotland: Courtyards and towers *c.* 1300–*c.* 1400', in Malcolm Airs and P. S. Barnwell (eds), *The medieval great house* (Donington: Shaun Tyas), pp. 43–60.

Oram, Richard (ed.) (2015). *A house that thieves might knock at: Proceedings of the 2010 Stirling and 2011 Dundee conferences on 'the tower as lordly residence' and 'the tower and the household'*, Tower Studies 1 and 2 (Donington: Shaun Tyas).

Orpen, Goddard Henry, and E. St. John Brooks (1934). 'Charters of Earl Richard Marshal of the forests of Ross and Taghmon', *Journal of the Royal Society of Antiquaries of Ireland*, 4/1, 54–63.

O'Sullivan, Aidan (1998). *The archaeology of lake settlement in Ireland*, Discovery Programme Monograph no. 4 (Dublin: Royal Irish Academy).

O'Sullivan, Aidan (2001). *Foragers, farmers and fishers in a coastal landscape: An intertidal archaeological survey of the Shannon estuary*, Discovery Programme Monograph no. 5 (Dublin: Royal Irish Academy).

O'Sullivan, Aidan (2003). 'Place, memory and identity among estuarine fishing communities: Interpreting the archaeology of early medieval fish weirs', *World Archaeology*, 35/3, 449–68.

O'Sullivan, Aidan (2005). 'Medieval fish traps on the Shannon estuary, Ireland: Interpreting people, place and identity', *Journal of Wetland Archaeology*, 5, 65–77.

O'Sullivan, Aidan, and Colin Breen (2007). *Maritime Ireland: An archaeology of coastal communities* (Stroud: Tempus).

O'Sullivan, Harold, and Raymond Gillespie (2011). *Carlingford: Irish historic towns atlas no. 23* (Dublin: Royal Irish Academy).

O'Sullivan, Muiris, and Liam Downey (2007). 'Ridges and furrows', *Archaeology Ireland*, 21, 34–7.

Otway-Ruthven, A. Jocelyn (1951). 'The organization of Anglo-Irish agriculture in the Middle Ages', *Journal of the Royal Society of Antiquaries of Ireland*, 81/1, 1–13.

Otway-Ruthven, A. Jocelyn (1965). 'The character of Norman settlement in Ireland', *Historical Studies*, 5, 75–84.

Otway-Ruthven, A. Jocelyn (1968). *A history of medieval Ireland* (London: Ernest Benn).

Pirenne, Henri (1925). *Medieval cities: Their origins and the revival of trade* (Princeton, NJ: Princeton University Press).

Pollock, Dave (2004). 'The bawn exposed: Recent excavations at Barryscourt', in J. Ludlow and N. Jameson (eds), *Medieval Ireland: The Barryscourt lectures 1–10* (Kinsale: Gandon), pp. 153–73.

Potterton, Michael (2005). *Medieval Trim: History and archaeology* (Dublin: Four Courts Press).

Prunty, Jacinta, and Paul Walsh (2016). *Galway/Gaillimh: Irish historic towns atlas no. 28* (Dublin: Royal Irish Academy).

Rawcliffe, Carole (2013). *Urban bodies: Communal health in late medieval English towns and cities* (Woodbridge: Boydell Press).

Rees Jones, Sarah (2008). 'Building domesticity in the city: English urban housing before the Black Death', in Maryanne Kowaleski and P. J. P. Goldberg (eds), *Medieval domesticity: Home, housing and household in medieval England* (Cambridge: Cambridge University Press), pp. 66–91.

Riddy, Felicity (2008). '"Burgeis" domesticity in late-medieval England', in Maryanne Kowaleski and P. J. P. Goldberg (eds), *Medieval domesticity: Home, housing and household in medieval England* (Cambridge: Cambridge University Press), pp. 14–36.

Riordan, Brendan (2015). 'Farming and settlement: Some dynamic relationships', in Margaret Murphy and Matthew Stout (eds), *Agriculture and settlement in Ireland* (Dublin: Four Courts Press), pp. 162–93.

Roberts, Brian K. (1988). 'The re-discovery of fishponds', in Michael Aston (ed.), *Medieval fish, fisheries, and fishponds in England*, BAR 182 (Oxford: Archaeopress), vol. 1, pp. 9–16.

Robinson, Philip (2000). *The Plantation of Ulster: British settlement in an Irish landscape: 1600–1670*, 2nd ed. (Belfast: Ulster Historical Foundation).

Rondelez, Paul (2018). 'The metallurgical enterprises of Richard Boyle, first earl of Cork', in David Edwards and Colin Rynne (eds), *The colonial world of Richard Boyle First Earl of Cork* (Dublin: Four Courts Press), pp. 112–20.

Ronnes, Hanneke (2007). 'Continental traces at Carrick-on-Suir and contemporary Irish castles: A preliminary study of date-and-initial stones', in Thomas Herron and Michael Potterton (eds), *Ireland in the Renaissance c. 1540–1660* (Dublin: Four Courts Press), pp. 255–73.

Rubicon Heritage, 2011. *Lost and found: The rediscovery of a deserted medieval village*, Rubicon Heritage, www.rubiconheritage.com/2011/01/05/lost-and-found-the-rediscovery-of-a-deserted-medieval-village/, accessed 23 August 2017.

Rynne, Colin (2000). 'Waterpower in medieval Ireland', in Paolo Squatriti (ed.), *Working with water in medieval Europe: Technology and resource-use* (Leiden: Brill), pp. 1–50.

Rynne, Colin (2003). 'The development of milling technology in Ireland, c. 600–1875', in Andrew Bielenberg (ed.), *Irish flour milling: A history 600–2000* (Dublin: Lilliput Press), pp. 11–38.

Rynne, Colin (2006). 'Energy sources pre-1880', in Ronald Cox (ed.), *Engineering Ireland* (Cork: Collins Press), pp. 249–54.

Rynne, Colin (2009). 'Water-power as a factor of industrial location in early medieval Ireland: The environment of the early Irish water mill', *Industrial Archaeology Review*, 31/2, 85–95.

Rynne, Colin (2011). 'Technological continuity, technological "survival": The use of horizontal mills in western Ireland, c. 1632–1940', *Industrial Archaeology Review*, 33/2, 96–105.

References

Rynne, Colin (2018). 'Colonial entrepreneur and urban developer: The economic and industrial infrastructure of Boyle's Munster estates', in David Edwards and Colin Rynne (eds), *The colonial world of Richard Boyle First Earl of Cork* (Dublin: Four Courts Press), pp. 89–111.

Samuel, M. W. (1998). 'The tower houses of west Cork' (PhD thesis, University College London).

Seaver, Matthew (2005). 'Practice, spaces and places: An archaeology of boroughs as manorial centres in the barony of Slane', in James Lyttleton and Tadhg O'Keeffe (eds), *The manor in medieval and early modern Ireland* (Dublin: Four Courts Press), pp. 70–104.

Shanahan, Brian (2005). 'The manor in east County Wicklow', in James Lyttleton and Tadhg O'Keeffe (eds), *The manor in medieval and early modern Ireland* (Dublin: Four Courts Press), pp. 132–59.

Sherborne, J. W. (1965). *The port of Bristol in the middle ages* (Bristol: Historical Association).

Sherlock, Rory (2006). 'Cross-cultural occurrences of mutations in tower house architecture: Evidence for cultural homogeneity in late medieval Ireland?', *Journal of Irish Archaeology*, xv, 73–91.

Sherlock, Rory (2010). 'The evolution of the Irish tower house as a domestic space', *Proceedings of the Royal Irish Academy*, 111C, 115–40.

Sherlock, Rory (2015). 'The spatial dynamic of the Irish tower house hall', in Victoria McAlister and Terry Barry (eds), *Space and settlement in medieval Ireland* (Dublin: Four Courts Press), pp. 86–109.

Shine, Linda (2005). 'The manor of Earlstown, County Kilkenny: An interdisciplinary approach', in James Lyttleton and Tadhg O'Keeffe (eds), *The manor in medieval and early modern Ireland* (Dublin: Four Courts Press), pp. 40–69.

Shine, Linda (2011a). 'Antiquities of Meath project'. Unpublished report for Meath Partnership.

Shine, Linda (2011b). 'Later medieval cross-cultural interactions: The settlement evidence in the baronies of Overk, County Kilkenny, and Clanmahon, County Cavan' (PhD thesis, Trinity College Dublin).

Shine, Linda (2015). 'On the edge of the colony: Overk and the Carlow Corridor', in Victoria McAlister and Terry Barry (eds), *Space and settlement in medieval Ireland* (Dublin: Four Courts Press), pp. 64–85.

Simms, Anngret (1983). 'Rural settlement in medieval Ireland: The example of the royal manors of Newcastle Lyons and Esker in south County Dublin', in B. K. Roberts and R. E. Glasscock (eds), *Villages, fields, and frontiers: Studies in European rural settlement in the medieval and early modern periods*, BAR 185 (Oxford: BAR), pp. 133–52.

Simms, Anngret (1988a). 'Core and periphery in medieval Europe: The Irish experience in a wider context', in William J. Smyth and Kevin Whelan (eds), *Common ground: Essays on the historical geography of Ireland* (Cork: Cork University Press), pp. 22–40.

Simms, Anngret (1988b). 'The geography of Irish manors: The example of the Llanthony cells of Duleek and Colp in County Meath', in John Bradley (ed.), *Settlement and society in medieval Ireland* (Kilkenny: Boethius), pp. 291–326.

Simms, Katharine (2015). 'The origins of the creaght: Farming system or social unit?', in Margaret Murphy and Matthew Stout (eds), *Agriculture and settlement in Ireland* (Dublin: Four Courts Press), pp. 101–18.

Slater, Terry R. (2015). 'Lordship, economy and society in English medieval marketplaces', in Anngret Simms and Howard B. Clarke (eds), *Lords and town in medieval Europe: The European Historic Towns Atlas Project* (Farnham: Ashgate), pp. 213–31.
Smith, Brendan (2013). *Crisis and survival in late medieval Ireland: The English of Louth and their neighbours, 1330–1450* (Oxford: Oxford University Press).
Smith, C. V. (1996). *Dalkey: Society and economy in a small medieval Irish town*, Maynooth Studies in Local History no. 9 (Blackrock: Irish Academic Press).
Smith, Charles (1744). *The antient and present state of the county of Down: Containing a chorographical description, with the natural and civil history of the same* (Dublin: Edward Exshaw).
Smyth, William J. (1985). 'Property, patronage and population: Reconstructing the human geography of mid-seventeenth century County Tipperary', in William Nolan (ed.), *Tipperary: History and society* (Dublin: Geography Publications), pp. 104–38.
Steane, J. M. (1988). 'The royal fishponds of medieval England', in Michael Aston (ed.), *Medieval fish, fisheries, and fishponds in England*, BAR 182 (Oxford: Archaeopress), vol. 1, pp. 39–68.
Stout, Geraldine, and Matthew Stout (eds) (2016). *The Bective Abbey Project, County Meath: Excavations 2009–12* (Dublin: Wordwell).
Sweetman, David (2000). *Medieval castles of Ireland* (Woodbridge: Boydell Press).
Sweetnam, Robin (1986). 'Early 17th century ships' masters and merchants', *Carrickfergus and District Historical Journal*, 2, 9–15.
Tabraham, Christopher J. (1997). *Scotland's castles* (London: Batsford).
Tabraham, Christopher J. (1998). 'The Scottish medieval tower house as lordly residence in the light of recent excavation', *Proceedings of the Society of Antiquaries of Scotland*, 118, 267–76.
Truxes, T. M. (1988). *Irish-American trade 1660–1783* (Cambridge: Cambridge University Press).
Voorbeijtel Cannenburg, W. (1935). 'An unknown "Pilot" by Hessel Gerritsz, dating from 1612', *Imago Mundi*, 1, 49–51.
Wall Forrestal, Rebecca (2015). 'Studying early medieval Irish urbanization: Problems and possibilities', in Victoria McAlister and Terry Barry (eds), *Space and settlement in medieval Ireland* (Dublin: Four Courts Press), pp. 34–47.
Watt, J. A. (1987). 'Gaelic polity and cultural identity', in Art Cosgrove (ed.), *A new history of Ireland*, vol. II, *Medieval Ireland 1169–1534* (Oxford: Clarendon Press), pp. 314–51.
Went, Arthur E. J. (1953). 'Material for a history of the fisheries of the River Boyne', *Journal of the County Louth Archaeological Society*, 13/1, 18–33.
Went, Arthur E. J. (1955). 'A short history of the fisheries of the River Nore', *Journal of the Royal Society of Antiquaries of Ireland*, 85/1, 22–33.
Went, Arthur E. J. (1956). 'Historical notes on the fisheries of the River Suir', *Journal of the Royal Society of Antiquaries of Ireland*, 86/2, 192–202.
Went, Arthur E. J. (1959). 'Historical notes on some of the fisheries of County Louth', *Journal of the County Louth Archaeological Society*, 14/3, 179–90.
Went, Arthur E. J. (1960). 'Fisheries of the Munster Blackwater', *Journal of the Royal Society of Antiquaries of Ireland*, 90/2, 97–131.
Went, Arthur E. J. (1961). 'Fisheries of the Munster Blackwater (continued)', *Journal of the Royal Society of Antiquaries of Ireland*, 91/1, 19–41.

Went, Arthur E. J. (1961–63). 'Historical notes on the oyster fisheries of Ireland', *Proceedings of the Royal Irish Academy*, 62C, 195–223.

Went, Arthur E. J. (1981). 'Historical notes on the fisheries of the estuary of the River Shannon', *Journal of the Royal Society of Antiquaries of Ireland*, 111, 107–18.

Westropp, Thomas Johnson (1912–13). 'Early Italian maps of Ireland from 1300 to 1600, with notes on foreign settlers and trade', *Proceedings of the Royal Irish Academy*, 30C, 361–428.

Wilde, William R. (1849). *The beauties of the Boyne, and its tributary the Blackwater* (Dublin: James McGlashan), https://play.google.com/books/reader?id=PDo9AAAAIAAJ&printsec=frontcover&output=reader&hl=en&pg=GBS.PP6, accessed 22 March 2018.

Wood, Herbert (1919). *A guide to the records deposited in the Public Record Office of Ireland* (Dublin: Public Records Office), www.nationalarchives.ie/wp-content/uploads/2014/06/Herbert-Woods-Guide-to-Public-Records.pdf, accessed 19 July 2015.

Index

Note: 'n.' after a page reference indicates the number of a note on that page.
Page references in *italic* refer to illustrations.

1641 Rebellion 22, 194

Anbally Castle 35
Anglo-Irish
  ethnic group 1, 14, 27, 80, 197–8,
    210, 229, 231, 244
  government 9, 13, 21, 67
  territory 4, 21, 23, 27, 43, 51, 63, 69,
    78, 91, 94, 103, 109, 111, 122,
    148, 150, 211, 217, 227, 232–3
  see also Pale, the
Anglo-Norman Invasion/colonisation
  20, 43, 67, 103, 121, 144, 160,
  164, 175, 197, 237
Annamult Castle 98, 243
Antrim, County 21, 77, 137
Ardee, County Louth 78, 101, 102,
  164, 166–7, 181, 183, 209, 214,
  233
Ardglass Castle/the Newark 140, 160,
  172, 185, 190
  see also Ardglass, County Down
Ardglass, County Down 73, 118–20,
  137, 140, 149, 163, 172–3, 175,
  180, 185, 186, 188, 206, 214, 227
Ardkeen Castle 56, 132
Ardmayle Castle 27, 29, *30*, 31, *32*,
  33, 35, 43, 50, 53, 71
Ardmulchan, County Meath 58, 127,
  153
Armagh, County 91, 224
Athboy, County Meath 94, 104,
  164–6, 181–2, 209, 214
Athlumney Castle 101, 240

Athy, County Kildare 130, 149, 150–2
Atlantic World 2, 119, 192, 209, 228,
  230, 234
Audley's Castle 36, 56, 132, 140, 150,
  188
Aughnanure Castle 36, *37*, 40
Augustinians 98, 166

Ballingarry Castle 86, 173
Ballinlaw Castle 6, 145, 239
Ballyduff Castle 240
Ballyhack, County Wexford 128, 201
  Castle 110, 119, *120*, 142–3, 201
Ballymaloe Castle 240
Ballynacarriga Castle 81, *82*, 107
Ballynahinch Castle 27, 29, 31, *33*, *34*,
  35, 50, 131, 151
Baltimore, County Cork 111, 113,
  114, 129, 134, 218
Bangor Castle 11, 176, 190
Barryscourt Castle 28
Bartlett, Richard 27, 28, 41, 42, 51,
  52, 91
bawn(s) 8, 22, 24, 28, 31, 33, 35–42,
  54, 55, 58, 59, 108, 134–5, 150,
  152, 215
Bective Abbey 70, 122, 130, 243
Belfast 137, 218
Belvelly Castle 186
betaghs 27, 47, 50, 63, 68
  see also peasant statuses
Black Death 4, 11, 21, 24, 47, 48, 49,
  62, 68, 71, 75, 77, 79, 87, 98,
  199, 203–4, 230, 235–7, 242

Index

booleying 52, 63, 65, 71, 75, 87
Bourchier's Castle 55–6, *57*, 59
  see also Lough Gur, County Limerick
Brady's Castle 176, 178–9
  see also Thomastown, County Kilkenny
bridge castles 91, 149–51, 162
bridges 24, 29, 85, 91, 124–5, 140–2, 144–54, 156, 158, 165, 166, 167, 168, 174, 180, 183, 187
Bristol 103, 110, 128, 130, 131, 149, 197
Brownsford Castle 101
Buttevant Castle 173

Camphire Castle 131, 165
Carlingford, County Louth 102, 118, 138, 171, 176, 184, 185, 186–7, 191n.1, 194, 196, 206, 210, 214, 219, 220, 233
Carlow, County 40, 216
Carrickdexter Castle/Slanecastle Demesne 58, 130, 152, 166, 240
  see also Slane, County Meath
Carrickfergus, County Antrim 138, 196, 208, 221
Carrick-on-Suir, County Tipperary 71, 85, 88, 100, 101–2, 120, 145, 171–2, 181
Carrigafoyle Castle 131, 136, 215
Carrowbrickeen Castle 136
Cashelboy Castle 61, 178, *179*, 243
Cashlaundarragh Castle 59
Castleboy Castle 60
Castle Island Castle 142, 222
Castlejordan Castle 152
Castlelake Castle 131, 151
Causestown Castle 164–5
  see also Athboy, County Meath
causeways 124–5, 140–2
Cavan, County 123, 154, 219
cellar settlement 61–2, 121
Chester 98, 110, 186
Cistercians 70, 80, 98, 119, 130, 142, 201, 203, 243
Clare, County 123
Claregalway Castle 243–4

Clonmel, County Tipperary 100, 101, 128, 133, 181, 216, 219
Clonmines, County Wexford 73
Confederate Wars 22, 143, 194
  see also Cromwellian Wars
Conna Castle 99, 151
Connacht 48, 49, 225
Connemara 23, 116
Conva Castle 151–2
Coolhill Castle 130, *133*, 134
Cork
  city 132, 147, 182, 196, 199, 218, 225
  county 66, 72, 110, 127, 151, 152, 171, 215–16
  earldom/earls of 18, 66, 72–3, 99–100, 136, 148–9, 168
Cowd Castle 140, *141*, 172
  see also Ardglass, County Down
Cratloekeel Castle 72
Cratloemoyle Castle 72
creaght(ing) 14, 52, 63, 65, 75–6, 112
Cromwellian Wars 49, 63
  see also Confederate Wars
Cross East Castle 61, 178, 243
cruck construction 8, 35, 40–1
  see also vernacular housing

Dalkey, County Dublin 118, 137, 167, 171, 179, 187, 219, 226
Dardistown Castle 83
deer parks 20, 26, 102, 158
Derrymaclaughna Castle 60
deserted medieval villages (DMV) 26, 31, 35, 43, 48, 59, 62, 86, 94
Desmond, earldom/earls of 21, 99–100, 114, 127, 131, 145, 168, 200, 215
Desmond Rebellion 22, 55, 99
Dingle, County Kerry 114, 127, 215
Dissolution of the Monasteries 5, 19, 66, 68, 70, 99, 115, 119, 120, 177, 242–3
Dominicans 168, 185–6, 206
Donegal, County 23, 117–8
Donore Castle 15, *16*, 92, 164
Doolin Castle 71
Doonnagore Castle 71, 136
dovecotes 10, 26, 29, 38, 40, 54, 102

Dowdall family 6, 177
Down, County 7, 21, 80, 86, 98, 125, 135–7, 138, 142, 155, 176, 180, 186, 188, 191, 203, 221–2, 227, 239
Downmacpatrick Castle 186
Dowth Castle 40, 69, 101, 130
Drogheda, County Louth/Meath 100–1, 126–7, 129–30, 137, 145, 147, 149, 155, 162, 163, 172, 175, 181, 188, 196, 200, 203, 206, 209, 211, 214, 217, 225
Dublin
  city 4, 17, 20, 91, 100, 118, 122, 127–8, 137, 144, 155–6, 162, 167, 176, 177, 181, 182, 187, 189, 194, 196, 197, 200–2, 205, 207–9, 211–12, 214, 217–19, 222, 225–6, 240
  county 21, 40, 47, 89n.1, 94, 118, 138, 196, 203, 209, 214, 227
Dundalk, County Louth 183
Dunmanus Castle 115, *116*
Dunmoe Castle 56, 58, 83, *106*, *107*, 153
Dunnaman Castle 58
Dún na Seád/Baltimore Castle 111
  see also Baltimore, County Cork
Dysart Castle 99, 101
Dysert O'Dea Castle 35

earth-and-timber castles 15, 20, 35, 87, 240
  see also motte castles; ringwork castles
Easky Castle 117
Exeter 111, 185

Fennor Castle 101, 130, 152, 165
  see also Slane, County Meath
Fermanagh, County 123
Fermoy, County Cork 125, 149
ferries 24, 124, 131, 140–7, 149, 154
Ferrycarrig Castle 142, *143*, 144–5
Fethard, County Tipperary 167–71, 179, 186, 188, 216, 219
Fiddaun Castle 134, *135*
field systems 47, 68–71, 75, 165, 204, 231

fish
  cod 109–10, 195, 213
  eels 81, *96*, 98, 99, 101, 102–4, 195, 205
  hake 109–11, 119, 195, 205
  herring 109–10, 112, 115, 118–19, 194, 195, 203, 205–7, 209
  ling 109
  mackerel 110
  oysters 115
  salmon 6, 97–101 *passim*, 103, 110, 112, 118, 201, 205, 206, 209
fishponds 24, 26, 89, 98, 102–9, 121, 232
fish traps 97–8, 113, 116, 121, 232
fish weirs 29, 61, 80–1, 83–4, 86, 95–106, 113, 121, 122, 142, 152, 157, 214, 232
Flanders 5, 112, 161, 180
fords 91, 118, 124, 140–1, 146, 151–4, 156, 158, 174
fortified houses 105, 149, 165, 233, 239
Fraine Castle 36, 164–5
  see also Athboy, County Meath
Franciscans 243–4

Gaelic-Irish
  ethnic group and culture 1, 6, 9, 14, 21, 27, 63, 67, 69–70, 76, 80, 103, 122, 165, 181, 197–8, 210, 224, 229, 231, 239, 244
  territory 12, 21, 23, 27, 43, 49, 51, 71, 73, 76, 78, 88, 94, 98, 103, 111, 114, 128–30, 132, 135, 148, 157, 163, 211, 217, 219, 223–4
  see also O'Neill lordship
Gaelicisation (Gaelic Resurgence) 21, 51, 68, 88, 122
Galway
  city 97, 102, 110, 116, 173, 176, 178, 184, 186, 194, 196, 198, 200, 210, 212–14, 217–18, 225, 226, 228
  county 51, 77–8, 88, 116, 123, 136, 163
gardens 26, 28, 29, 31, 40, 41, 45, 46, 66, 85, 86, 167, 181
gentry 1, 157–8, 191, 229, 232

Index 275

Geraldines *see* Kildare, lordship of
Gernon, Luke 28, 42
Glenogra Castle 54, 55, 86
Glin Castle 152
Golden Castle 131, 152

hall 3, 9, 28, 35–41, 43, 54, 103, 150, 165, 188
Hanseatic League 7, 174, 208, 218, 228, 230
hinterland 5, 6, 27, 64, 104, 111, 128–9, 137, 161, 163, 172, 173, 196, 197, 215, 218–19

Irish Sea 20, 109–10, 114, 118–20 *passim*, 123, 129, 130, 190, 193, 195, 197, 206–7, 211–12, 218, 216, 225, 230, 234

Jordan's Castle 86, 115, 132, 172–3, 175, 180, 188, 204–5
see also Ardglass, County Down

Kerry, County 78, 114, 135, 171, 196, 215
Kilclief Castle 122, 136, 138, *139*, 140, 238, 243
Kilcolman Castle 28, 40, 70
Kilcrea Castle 107, *108*, 134, 243–4
Kildare
  county 21, 40, 47, 68, 89n.1, 91, 94, 163, 240
  lordship/earls of 21, 68, 74–5, 98, 132, 137, 150, 175, 227
Kilkenny
  city 46, 63, 80, 85, 95, 102, 128, 130, 134, 137, 147, 149, 152, 157, 210, 216, 226
  county 6, 7, 12, 40, 64, 67, 84, 127, 142, 147, 149, 163, 177, 186, 216
Killeen Castle 39, 155
Killegland Castle 105, 156
Killyleagh Castle 176
Kilmallock, County Limerick 6, 73, 86, 127, 132, 168, *169*, 177, 216
Kilteel Castle 92, *93*, 94, 155
Kinsale, County Cork 115, 134, 145, 200, 212, 216–17
Kirkistown Castle 238

Knights Hospitaller 92–4
Knockainy, County Limerick 6, *53*, 54, 56, 71, 177

Laois, County 78
Leamaneh Castle 105, *239*
Leighlinbridge, County Carlow 73, 152, *153*
Leinster 181
Leitrim, County 123
Limerick
  city 109, 115, 131, 132, 177, 182, 196, 212, 215, 225
  county 12, 40, 45–6, 49, 68, 86, 152, 165, 239
Liscartan Castle 238
Lisfinny Castle 73, 74, 99, 151
Lisronagh, County Tipperary 31, 77
London 5, 6, 95–6, 185, 211–12, 220
Lough Gur, County Limerick 55–6, 59, 109
Louth, County 6, 89n.1, 92, 177, 196, 219
Lynch family 97, 176, 212–14
Lynch's Castle 164, 173, 176, 178, 184, 186, *213*

Mahee Castle 125, 136, 149, 186, *221*
Mallow, County Cork 132
  Castle 35, 100
manors 27, 29, 31, 40, 43–5, 47–51, 56, 58, 59, 61, 64, 65–7, 69–72, 79–80, 86–7, 89, 123, 147, 164, 175, 232
Margaret's Castle 172
  see also Ardglass, County Down
Meath, County 6, 21, 43, 51, 56, 68, 76, 79, 86, 89n.1, 91, 94, 100, 124, 154, 165, 177, 181, 189, 196, 219, 239–40
millpond 81, 85, 107–8
mills
  tide mills 79, 89n.1
  tuck/fulling mills 79, 85–6, 88
  water mills 20, 24, 29, 41, 43, 45–6, 49, 54, 55, 65, 66, 67, 78–89, 96, 98, 100–1, 105–7, 121, 145, 157, 204, 214, 226, 231
Minard's Castle 127, *128*

mining 66, 73
Mint, the 164, 171, 176
   see also Carlingford, County Louth
motte castles 15, 29, 31, 37, *38*, 50, 83, 129, 138, 240
Mountgarrett Castle 7, 85, 243
   see also New Ross, County Wexford
Muckinish East Castle 116, *117*
Muckinish West Castle 116
Munster 4, 21, 22, 76, 181
murage grants 94, 127, 147, 157, 165, 181–2

Nangle's Castle 166
   see also Trim, County Meath
Navan, County Meath 80, 155, 162
navigation aids 24, 100, 125, 138–40, 172
Newcastle Lyons, County Dublin 26, 50
Newhaggard Castle 83, *84*, 86, 94, 101, 154
   see also Trim, County Meath
New Ross, County Wexford 128, 130, 134, 137, 147, 150, 152, 196, 216, 220
Newstone Castle 58
Newtown Jerpoint, County Kilkenny 26, 35, 73, 142
Newtown Trim, County Meath 122, 152, 166, 181
Nine Years' War 22, 196, 211, 219, 221
   see also Tudor Conquest
Nook Castle 119, 201
   see also Ballyhack, County Wexford

Offaly, County 7
Oldcourt Castle 129
O'Neill lordship 12, 14, 21, 77, 91
Oranmore Castle 116
orchards 29, 33, 39, 40, 45, 56, 66, 86, 167, 181
Ormond, earldom/earls of 18, 21, 43, 69, 88, 101, 132, 145, 150, 171, 177, 200

Pale, the 4, 6, 9, *16*, 20, 21, 36, 43, 48, 50, 65, 67, 68, 69–70, 76, 83, 87, 91–4, 111, 122, 128, 129, 150, 155–6, 163, 164–6, 177, 180, 196, 204, 208, 216, 219, 227, 232
parish church(es) 3, 20, 27, 29, 31, 37, 40, 43, 44, 45, 49, 50, 52, 54, 59, 60–1, 86, 138, 144, 151, 215, 235
peasant statuses 46–9, 51, 63
   see also betaghs
pilgrimage 176, 212, 220
Piperstown, County Louth 26, 48–9
Plantation 19, 22, 66, 197, 224, 227
pontage grants 146–8, 167, 172
Portaferry, County Down 139, 140, 142, 238
Poulakerry Castle 8
purveyance 126, 129, 187

Quoile Castle 142, 238

rabbit warrens 26, 29, 31, 41, 54, 71, 158
Raleigh, Sir Walter 100, 168
Rathcannon Castle 58
Rathmore Castle 37, *38*, 240
ridge and furrow 69, 89, 204
   see also field systems
Rindoon, County Roscommon 26
Ringhaddy Castle 220–2
Ringrone Castle 145
   see also Kinsale, County Cork
ringwork castles 31, 143
rivers
   Bann 98, 153, 191
   Barrow 101, 128, 131, 132, 133–4, 142, 145, 150
   Blackwater (Leinster) 94
   Blackwater (Munster) 91, 99–100, 127, 131–2, 151, 152, 153, 165
   Blackwater (Ulster) 91, 95
   Boyne 16, 58, 83, 91–2, 94, 99–101, 106, 125, 126–7, 129–30, 145, 152, 153, 155, 162, 166, 232
   Ilen 128–9
   Liffey 94, 100, 127, 232
   Nore 101–2, 127, 128, 132, 142, 149, 157, 180
   Shannon 102, 110, 115, 121, 131, 138, 215

Index

Slaney 127, 131, *143*, 144
Suir 6, 29, 71, 83, 100–1, 128, 131, 132, 133, 150–1, 171, 177
Three Sisters 48, 70, 91, 101, 119, 130, 132, 149, 163, 204
rural borough 44–7, 58, 59, 66, 160, 165, 220

St. Leger's Castle 164, 167, 183
  see also Ardee, County Louth
Scotland, castles in 14, 28–9, 176, 241
Scurlockstown Castle 101, 155–6
Ship-pool Castle 134
Sketrick Castle 125, 136, 149, 186–7
Slane, County Meath 58, 101, 152, 155, 162, 165–6, 178, 190
Sligo, County 112, 117, 136, 211, 225
Strancally Castle 85, 99–100, 131, 165
Strangford, County Down
  Castle 149–50, 170, 186
  Lough 136, 140, 227
  town 137, 139, 142, 170–1, 175, 180, 227
Sweetman's/Bridge Castle 176, 180, 183, 186, 188
  see also Thomastown, County Kilkenny

Taaffe's Castle 36, 171, 176, 187–8, 191n.1
  see also Carlingford, County Louth
Temple Michaell Castle 99, 131, 165
Thomastown, County Kilkenny 85, 99, 101, 120, 149–51, 175, 176, 178–80, 183, 186–7
Threecastles Castle 94
Tipperary, County 12, 40, 45, 53, 63, 64, 67, 77, 90, 100, 130, 149, 186, 216
town walls 162, 167, 168, 175, 180–3, 190
trade
  with Bristol 130, 131, 172, 192, 196, 198–9, 201–5, 207, 209–12, 216–17, 229
  with Chester 172, 199–200, 202–3, 205–6, 208–11, 217
  with continental Europe 79, 127, 173, 192, 196, 197, 200–2, 212, 214–15, 217–18, 226, 228–9, 232
  with England 110, 112, 116, 118–19, 121, 193, 196, 197–8, 200–4, 210–11, 213–15, 218, 226, 228–9, 234
  with Flanders 201–2, 210, 214, 216–17, 234
  with France 195, 200–3, 210, 214, 217, 234
  with Iceland 110, 193, 212–13, 218
  with the Isle of Man 193, 216
  with Italy 201–2, 216–17, 228, 234
  with the Netherlands 201, 225
  with the New World 192, 202, 209, 218, 234
  with Portugal 200–2, 210, 212, 214, 217, 225
  with Scotland 138, 191, 197, 210–11, 214, 219
  with Spain 114–15, 116, 121, 176, 193, 195, 200–3, 210, 212, 214, 216–17, 228, 234
  with Wales 193, 197, 198, 202, 205, 207–9, 216
trade goods
  building materials 127, 208–9, 219
  coal 202, 208–9
  cloth 119, 194, 196, 201, 203, 205, 209, 217, 220
  dairy 205
  fish 191, 193, 194, 195, 198, 200–3, 205–7, 209, 215, 219, 223, 226, 229
  grain 126, 163, 191, 194, 196, 203–5, 210, 216, 219, 223, 225–6
  hawk 196
  hides 112, 120, 126, 129, 194–6, 198–201, 203, 205, 214–16, 224
  horse 196, 230
  iron 119, 196, 199, 202, 207–10, 217–18, 226, 228
  linen 194, 209, 218, 230
  luxury and manufactured 196, 205, 207, 209–10, 217–18, 223, 226, 228–9, 234
  meat 196
  military arms 119, 208, 220

salt 112, 196, 201–3, 207–8, 210, 215, 217–18, 226, 228–9
skins 195, 198, 201, 203
tallow 195, 196, 203
timber 126–7, 129–30, 137, 163, 195, 207, 211, 219, 223–4
wine 114, 116, 119, 126, 130, 131, 176, 196, 199–202, 205, 210, 214–15, 217–18, 220, 225–6, 229
wool 129, 130, 131, 181, 191, 194, 196, 198, 201, 203, 205, 207, 215, 217
Trim, County Meath
 Castle 35, 37, 166, 187
 town 100–1, 104, 126–9, 147, 154–5, 166, 174, 181, 216
Tudor Conquest 12, 21, 22, 91, 95, 148, 190, 194, 210–12, 222, 232
 see also Nine Years' War
Tyrone
 county 21, 77, 91, 123
 earl of 91
 see also O'Neill lordship

Ulster 22, 42, 49–50, 67, 98, 196, 214, 218–19

vernacular housing 3, 28, 41, 42, 50, 52, 60, 76, 149
 see also cruck construction

Walshestown Castle 238
Waterford
 city 6, 127, 130, 133, 137, 163, 177, 187, 194, 196, 198, 199, 200, 202, 211, 216, 219, 225–6
 county 7, 72, 115, 127, 131, 142, 151, 152
Westmeath, County 123, 164, 178, 219
Wexford
 county 7, 67, 110, 119, 127, 131, 136, 142, 201, 206, 208–9, 211, 216
 town 144, 196
White Castle 85, 150
 see also Athy, County Kildare
Wicklow, County 49, 91, 92, 94, 111, 149, 167, 201

Youghal, County Cork 131–2, 164–5, 168, 182–3, *184*, 190, 196, 197, 200, 210–11, 216, 219, 228, 233

EU authorised representative for GPSR:
Easy Access System Europe, Mustamäe tee 50,
10621 Tallinn, Estonia
gpsr.requests@easproject.com